OCR

THE MANCHESTER COLLEGE
00194298

D0571202

AS

PHYSICAL EDUCATION

Dave Carnell • John Ireland • Ken Mackreth • Claire Miller • Sarah van Wely

www.heinemann.co.uk

✓ Free online support
✓ Useful weblinks
✓ 24 hour online ordering

01865 888080

Heinemann

Heinemann is an imprint of Pearson Education Limited, a company incorporated in England and Wales, having its registered office at Edinburgh Gate, Harlow, Essex, CM20 2JE. Registered company number: 872828

http://www.heinemann.co.uk/

Text © Dave Carnell, John Ireland, Ken Mackreth, Claire Miller and Sarah van Wely 2008

First published 2008

13
10 9 8 7

RECEIVED

5 – NOV 2013

19·80

British Library Cataloguing in Publication Data
A catalogue record for this book is available from the British Library

ISBN 978 0 435 466770

Edited by Val Rice and Nigel Copeland
Designed by Artistix Design Services
Typeset by Tek-Art, Croydon, Surrey
Cover design by Wooden Ark Studios
Picture research by Maria Joannou
Cover photo/illustration © Pearson Education Ltd/Photodisc/Photolink
Printed in Malaysia, CTP-PJB

All rights reserved. No part of this publication may be reproduced in any form or by any means (including photocopying or storing it in any medium by electronic means and whether or not transiently or incidentally to some other use of this publication) without the written permission of the copyright owner, except in accordance with the provisions of the Copyright, Designs and Patents Act 1988 or under the terms of a licence issued by the Copyright Licensing Agency, Saffron House, 6–10 Kirby Street, London EC1N 8TS (www.cla.co.uk). Applications for the copyright owner's written permission should be addressed to the publisher.

Websites
There are links to relevant websites in this book. In order to ensure that the links are up to date, that the links work, and that the sites are not inadvertently linked to sites that could be considered offensive, we have made the links available on the Heinemann website at www.heinemann.co.uk/hotlinks. When you access the site, the express code is 6770P

Acknowledgements

The author and publisher would like to thank the following individuals and organisations for permission to reproduce photographs:

Unit 1 Pg 30 Corbis/ Leo Mason; pg 31 PA Photos/ David Davies/PA Wire; pg 33 Corbis/ Paul Kingston/ EPA; pg 34 PA Photos/ AP Photo/ Jason DeCrow; pg 35 Rex Features.Unit 2 Pg 48 Corbis/ Bernd Thissen/ EPA; Corbis/ Andreas Meier/ Reuters; pg 49 Corbis/ Stephane Reix/ For Picture; Corbis/ Moodboard; PA Photos/ Gero Breloer/ DPA; PA Photos/ Joe Giddens/ Empics; pg 51 Corbis/ Chris Williams; pg 53 Corbis/ Dietmar Stiplovsek/ EPA. Unit 4 Pg 125 PA Photos/ AP Photo/ Armando Franca; pg 126 Getty Images/ Cameron Spencer; Corbis/ Smiley N. Pool/ Dallas Morning News; pg 127 Getty Images/ Harry How; Reuters/ David Gray; Corbis/ Tim de Waele; pg 128 Getty Images/ Andy Lyons; Corbis/ Barbara Walton/ EPA pg 129 Corbis/ Darren Hauck; Pg 131 PA Photos/ AP Photo/ Mike Derer; pg 132 Istockphoto/Rafal Zdeb; Pg134 Getty Images/ Brian Bahr; Pg 136 Corbis/ Shannon Stapleton/ Reuters; PA Photos/ AP Photo/ Marcio Jose Sanchez; Getty Images/ Taxi/ Jim Cummins; Rex Features Photolibrary/ Cassio Cassio; Getty Images/ Brian Bahr. Unit 5 Pg 143 Corbis/ Lucy Nicholson/ Reuters; pg 144 PA Photos/ AP Photo/ Luis; pg 146 Alamy Images/ Digital Vision; pg 147 Rex Features/ Marja Airio; pg Getty Images/ The Image Bank/ Peter Cade; pg 148 PA Photos/ AP Photo/ Stephan Savoia; Corbis/ Paul J. Sutton/ Duomo; pg 149 Getty Images/ Stone/ Christopher Bissell; Corbis/ Kai Pfaffenbach/ Reuters; Pg 151 Getty Images/ Michael Steele. Unit 6 Pg 160 Corbis/ Randy Faris; Getty Images/ Phil Walter; Pg 161 Istockphoto/ Ana Abejon; pg 163 PA Photos/ Clint Hughes/ PA Wire; pg 164 PA Photos/ AP Photo/ Obed Zilwa; pg 166 Corbis/ Zainal Abd Halim/ Reuters. Unit 7 Pg 175 Getty Images/ AFP/ Carl De Souza; Getty Images/ AFP/ Odd Andersen. Unit 8 Pg 188 Rex Features/ Damon Higgins; pg 190 Corbis/ Carmen Jaspersen/ EPA; pg 195 PA Photos/ AP Photo/ David Adame; pg 191 & 196 Photofusion/ Stan Gamester; pg 197 PA Photos/ Martin Rickett/ PA Archive. Unit 9 Pg 217 Photofusion/ Maggie Murray; pg 221 Corbis/ Nice One Productions; Photofusion/ Christa Stadtler; Getty Images/ Image Bank/ Yellow Dog Productions; pg 223 Getty Images/ Stone/ Dick Clintsman; pg 224 Rex Features/ Image Source. Rex Features/ Image Source pg 225 PA Photos/ AP Photo/ Lionel Cironneau PA Photos/; AP Photo/ Lee Jin-man; Corbis/ Elizabeth Kreutz/ NewSport. Unit 10 Pg 234 Rex Features/ Andrew MacColl; Reuters/ Ian Hodgson; pg 235 Reuters/ Darren Staples; Getty Images/ AFP/ Carl De Souza; pg 237 Mary Evans Picture Library; pg 244 Mary Evans Picture Library; pg 250 PA Photos/ Empics Sport/ Tony Marshall. Unit 11 Pg 265 English Institute of Sport; pg 267 English Institute of Sport; pg 268 Sport England; Sports Council for Northern Ireland; pg 269 Logo reproduced with permission from the Sports Council for Wales; pg 287 PA Photos/ Gareth Copley/ PA Archive; pg 299 PA Photos/ Frank Franklin II/AP; pg 304 Corbis/ Schlegelmilch; pg 312 Corbis/ Hulton-Deutsch Collection; pg 317 Getty Images/ Andrew Wong; pg 323 Alamy Images/Peter Marshall; pg 325 Getty Images/Jonathan Ferrey. Unit 12 Pg 336 Corbis/ Rick Rickman/ NewSport; Getty Images/ Taxi/ Javier Pierini; pg 337 Corbis/ Gary Houlder; pg 338 Getty Images/ Robert Cianflone; pg 340 PA Photos/ Empics Sport/ Tony Marshall; pg 342 Getty Images/ Stone/ Blasius Erlinger; pg 345 PA Photos/Gero Breloer; pg 348 Rex Features/ Jussi Nukari; Alamy Images/ Adrian Sherratt; PA Photos/David Davies/PA Archive. Unit 13 Pg 354 Artproem / Dreamstime.com; pg 356 Alamy Images/ Neil McAllister; pg 357 Getty Images/ The Image Bank.

Every effort has been made to contact copyright holders of material reproduced in this book. Any omissions will be rectified in subsequent printings if notice is given to the publishers.

Table of Contents

Acknowledgements   iii

Introduction   v

(OCR unit G451)

Anatomy and Physiology (Section A) Claire Miller & Dave Carnell

1. The skeletal and muscular systems   1
2. Basic concepts of biomechanics   47
3. The cardiovascular and respiratory systems

    Part I: Response of the cardiovascular (heart) system to physical activity   59

    Part II: Response of the cardiovascular (vascular) system to physical activity   80

    Part III: Response of the cardiovascular (respiratory) system to physical activity   100

Acquiring movement Skills (Section B) Ken Mackreth & John Ireland

4. Classification of motor skills and abilities   124
5. The development of motor skills   142
6. Information processing   154
7. Motor control of skills in physical activity   171
8. Learning skills in physical activity

    Part I: Motivation and arousal   183

    Part II: Theories relating the learning of movement skills   194

    Part III: Transfer of learning   203

Socio-cultural Studies Relating to Participation in Physical Activity (Section C) Sarah van Wely

9. Physical activity   210
10. Sport and culture   232
11. Contemporary sporting issues

    Part I: Impact on young people's aspirations   254

    Part II: Drugs, the media and sponsorship in sport   295

    Part III: The Olympic Games   311

(OCR Unit G452)

Acquiring, Developing and Evaluating Practical Skills in Physical Education (Section D) Ken Mackreth

12. Performance   332
13. Evaluating and planning for the improvement of performance   351

Index   361

Introduction

This book is designed specifically for students following OCR's AS Physical Education (PE) course. It will support and reinforce the teaching you receive in your centre following the principle of applying theory to practical performance and relating practical performance to theory. The OCR course also embraces the principle that:

Practical performance is essential to the understanding of theory – students will be assessed in their practical activities with those marks contributing to the overall AS grade.

Students should develop their knowledge and understanding of factors that enable them to be physically active as part of a balanced, active and healthy lifestyle.

The content of the book is presented in a form that is identical to the OCR specification arranged under the same sections and sub-headings. This means that the content will be in the same order as you are taught in your centre. The information is presented in a practical context wherever possible as an aid to your understanding and to prepare you for your examination questions.

ORGANISATION OF THE BOOK

The book is divided into four sections that represent the areas in which you will be examined.

1 Anatomy and physiology.
2 Acquiring movement skills.
3 Socio-cultural studies relating to participation in physical activity.
4 Acquiring, developing and evaluating practical skills in Physical Education.

The sections are divided into chapters. Each chapter has an introduction which explains the content and how the theories relate to each other and to practical activities.

Wherever possible, theory will be applied to practical activities in order that you become accustomed to this approach. This is how you will be taught and examined.

FEATURES

Throughout each chapter you will find a series of tasks and features which are designed to help you understand, apply and remember the topics they relate to.

The book includes the following features:

Examiners's tips – as well as being included within the introduction, there will also be smaller box features called 'exam tips' that will appear throughout the book that will offer advice from the examiner. These are meant to give you guidance on how to improve your knowledge in order to get better grades in your AS exams.

Key terms – an explanation of key words & concepts

Tasks – motivating activities to help you practice whilst you learn

Remember – this is to help you to remember key concepts

Apply it! – this feature will give practical examples or activities to reinforce how the theory is used in real-life situations

Take it further - these features will contain stretch questions to help facilitate your existing knowledge and are designed to challenge you further.

EXAM CAFÉ

Exam Café is there to offer examiner advice and general study support. The Exam Café section will appear at the end of each chapter and will contain questions with model answers. These model answers will show what you will have to know and write to get an 'A' grade.

The section will also contain a unique set of ideas and tips to help you prepare for your exams including revision checklists and revise as you go questions.

FREE CD ROM

You'll also find a free CD ROM in the back of the book. On the CD you will find an electronic version of the Student Book powered by LiveText.

As well as the student book, you will also find an interactive Exam Café. This contains a wealth of interactive exam preparation material: Interactive multiple choice questions, audio tips, Byte-size concepts and much more!

HOW YOU WILL BE EXAMINED

You have two units to complete, one of which has an examination paper with the second being a coursework unit for which your teachers will assess you. Unit 1 is examined in both January and the summer, but Unit 2 can only be taken in the summer.

Unit 1 (OCR unit G451)

This unit is worth 60% of your AS marks. It consists of a 2 hour examination paper consisting of three compulsory questions.

There will be:

- An anatomy and physiology question
- An acquiring movement skills question
- A socio-cultural studies, relating to participation in physical activity question.

Each question is worth a total of 30 marks but is broken down into smaller sections. Each of the smaller questions has the number of marks it is worth clearly indicated.

For some questions, the quality of your written communication, including spelling, grammar, punctuation, sentence construction and use of paragraphs will be assessed.

Unit 2 (OCR unit G452)

This unit is worth 40% of your AS marks. This is the practical (coursework) unit and is split into two parts.

Practical activities (30%) – you are assessed in two practical activities. This assessment will be either:

- Two practical performances or:
- One practical performance and coaching or:
- One practical performance and officiating.

Evaluating and planning for the improvement of performance. (10%) – an oral evaluative response relating to one of the activities you have been assessed in.

Good luck with your studies.

Ken Mackreth.

ExamCafé
Relax and prepare

Command words

When examiners set questions, they tend to use command words to tell you what they want you to do. The command words used in OCR examinations include:

Describe: Give an account or description of something in words without any interpretation or explanation:
Use a practical example to describe how angular motion is produced.

Explain: Give reasons for and show your understanding of the subject:
Using an example from an invasion game, explain why fast reaction time is important.

Give reasons for: Show your understanding of and explain:
Give reasons for physical activity (physical education, physical recreation and sport) being of such high status in Australia.

Outline: Give a brief description of the main features/give a summary of the main points:
Outline contemporary initiatives that impact upon young people's participation in physical activity.

Identify: Give the names of / write what it is:
Identify ways in which a warm up can help improve the strength of contraction during exercise.

Define: Give a precise meaning of the term, explain the meaning of…
Define stroke volume and give a maximal value for an aerobic athlete

Illustrate: explain with examples – you do not have to draw!
What factors could affect response time in physical activities. Illustrate your answer with a practical example.

Analyse: Split into parts and examine the parts critically:
Analyse the factors which shaped the development of Australian Rules football.

Examine: Look at/inspect the parts critically:
Examine the types of guidance used to improve performance.

Compare and contrast: Say what is the same and what is different – use comparative adjectives in your answer e.g. larger, quicker, and brighter:
Compare and contrast drive theory, inverted U theory and catastrophe theory as explanations for the relationship between arousal and performance of motor skills.

Interpret: What is meant by something:
Interpret the graph shown in the figure.

Discuss: Examine in detail and argue a case for both sides:
Discuss both the positive and the negative impact of participating in different types of physical activity on the joints and muscles of the body.

Evaluate: Determine the value of, assess the value of and say why:
Evaluate the impact of the media on sport in the United Kingdom.

To what extent: You are being asked to make a judgment on how far you agree with something:
To what extent does altitude affect performances in physical activities?

Justify: Give your reasons for your opinion, show why you are right:
Place a named skill on the environmental influence continuum and justify your placement.

Comment on: Give a commentary on which includes explaining or giving a critical analysi making personal observations or illustrating a point of view:
Comment on the impact of different types of physical activity on the respiratory system.

Getting Started

examiner's tips

- Read the questions thoroughly so that you understand what they are asking you to do.
- Relate your answer to the number of marks available for that question. Remember that you usually have to make one point in your answer for each mark that is available.
- Wherever possible, apply the theory to a practical activity and make sure that you name that activity.
- Make sure that in your anatomy, physiology and skill answers you use the appropriate technical terms.
- Make sure that you plan your answers – particularly in the questions that have 5–10 marks available.
- Make sure that your spelling, grammar and punctuation are correct, and that you write in sentences and use paragraphs where appropriate.
- Make sure that you plan the use of your time properly.
- In the exam, you will write your answers on the question paper. The number of lines available gives you an indication of the length of answer required.
- Make sure that you revise all aspects of each area.
- Make sure that you understand the command words which will be used in the questions.

Anatomy and physiology

CHAPTER 1:

The skeletal and muscular systems

LEARNING OBJECTIVES

By the end of this chapter, you should be able to:

- Describe an overview of the skeletal system to include its functions, the axial and appendicular skeletons as well as types of bone and cartilage
- Understand, describe and give examples of the different types of joint found in the body
- Use a variety of anatomical terms to describe a moving body during physical activity
- Analyse a range of sporting techniques in terms of joint movements
- Identify the major muscles associated with the main joints of the human body and explain their role as an agonist or an antagonist with reference to specific movements in physical activity
- Carry out a full movement analysis of specific movements in physical activity
- Understand the difference between concentric, eccentric and isometric muscular contraction
- Distinguish between the three types of skeletal muscle fibre in the body and apply their characteristics to suggest reasons why certain individuals choose to take part in specific types of physical activity
- Recognise the considerable benefits of a warm up and cool down on skeletal muscle
- Discuss the advantages of lifelong involvement in an active lifestyle in relation to bone, joint and muscle health and evaluate certain disorders of bones, joints and muscles that can result from different types of physical activity.

INTRODUCTION

The skeletal and muscular systems are very closely linked and are often referred to as the musculo-skeletal system. All sporting techniques, from the powerful executions needed in a game of rugby to the smooth elegance displayed by a gymnast on the beam, require the skeletal and muscular systems of our bodies to work together effectively and efficiently.

Our skeleton provides the framework that allows movement to take place and our skeletal muscles provide the energy to pull our bones and joints into the correct positions needed for different types of physical activity. In this chapter, we will look at the structure and function of both of these body systems, which will help us understand how we move our bodies during physical activity. We will learn to describe anatomically the movements that occur at the joints and to explain how these movements take place in terms of the muscles in action and the type of contraction occurring. We can then use this knowledge to carry out a full movement analysis for specific sporting techniques.

Towards the end of the chapter, we will look at the role that muscle fibres play in their contribution to movement by studying the different types of muscle fibre and seeing how each is adapted to suit certain forms of physical activity. This activity could be very powerful such as that demonstrated by Kevin Pietersen hitting a six, or more endurance based such as that required by David Walliams when he swam the English Channel. Like all human structures, bones, joints and muscles can suffer from disorders from time to time. These can be due to an injury caused while taking part in exercise or a condition that has developed due to a lack of exercise. So, we will try to critically evaluate the impact that an active lifestyle has in maintaining a healthy musculo-skeletal system.

EXAM TIP

Movement analysis is a very popular topic about which examiners like to test your knowledge. Make sure you are confident at applying the knowledge you have gained in this chapter to different types of sporting movements. Remember that practice makes perfect!

The skeletal system: introduction to the skeleton

The skeleton is the structure that gives us our shape, provides protection for our internal organs and offers a supportive framework for the attachment of muscles therefore facilitating movement. Our bones also act as a site for the production of blood cells and a store of minerals, particularly calcium.

APPLY IT!

The skeleton has five main functions: Support, Protection, Movement, Blood cell production and Mineral store. Give examples of how the functions of the skeleton enable you to carry out your every-day needs and routine.

KEY TERMS

Skeleton

The bony framework upon which the rest of the body is built. It provides attachments for the muscular system and carries and protects the cardiovascular and respiratory systems.

Skeletal muscle

This attaches to and moves the skeleton. It is often termed striated muscle because it has obvious stripes on it caused by the long muscle fibres of which it is composed. It is also called voluntary muscle because it is the only type of muscle under our conscious control.

Joint

A place on the body where two or more bones meet.

The average human adult has 206 bones that are divided into two different parts, the axial and the appendicular skeleton:

206 bones

Axial skeleton	Appendicular skeleton
Skull	Shoulder girdle and upper limbs
Thoracic girdle	Pelvic girdle and lower limbs
Vertebral column	

Table 1

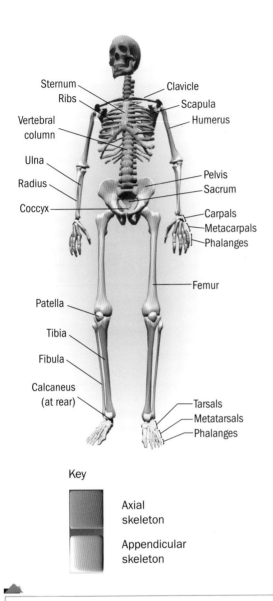

Sternum
Ribs
Clavicle
Scapula
Humerus
Vertebral
column
Ulna
Pelvis
Radius
Sacrum
Coccyx
Carpals
Metacarpals
Phalanges
Femur
Patella
Tibia
Fibula
Calcaneus
(at rear)
Tarsals
Metatarsals
Phalanges

Key

Axial
skeleton

Appendicular
skeleton

Fig 1.1 A labelled diagram of the axial and appendicular skeletons

You do not need to know the names of all these bones but you do need to be familiar with the main bones that make up the major joints that we use for movement. You will probably know many of them already, but it would be a good idea for you to use Fig. 1.1 to familiarise yourself with their names.

REMEMBER

The clavicle, scapula and pelvis belong to the appendicular skeleton. It is a common error to link them to the axial skeleton.

KEY TERMS

Appendicular skeleton

The bones of the upper and lower limbs and their girdles that join to the axial skeleton.

Axial skeleton

This forms the long axis of the body and includes the bones of the skull, spine and rib cage.

Ligament

A tough band of fibrous, slightly elastic connective tissue that attaches one bone to another. It binds the ends of bones together to prevent dislocation.

Tendon

A very strong connective tissue that attaches skeletal muscle to bone.

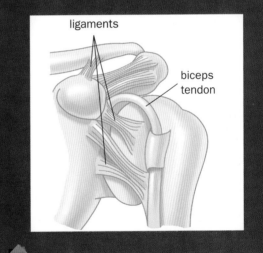

ligaments

biceps
tendon

Fig 1.2 Ligaments that stabilise the shoulder joint, and long tendon of biceps brachii

EXAM TIP

On your exam paper you will not be required to label a skeleton but it is recommended that you can identify the bones that articulate to form the following joints: wrist, radio-ulnar, elbow, shoulder, spine, hip, knee and ankle.

TASK 1

1. List the individual bones that make up
   the following regions of the skeleton:
   - thoracic girdle
   - shoulder girdle
   - upper limb
   - pelvic girdle
   - lower limb.

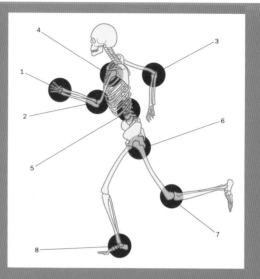

2. Classification of joints: Identify the joints numbered 1–8 in the diagram above and list
   the bones that articulate to form each of the joints you have identified. Record your
   answers in a table similar to the one below:

Joint number	Joint name	Bones that articulate	Helpful hints
1			List three bones
2			This is an easy one!
3			List three bones
4			List only two bones – find out the names of the *bony features* that articulate
5			Name the bones that make up the spine – find out the *five* areas of the spine and the names of the 2 bones at the top of the spine
6			List only two bones – find out the names of the *bony features* that articulate
7			Be careful here! List only two bones
8			Tricky! List three bones, but not the tarsals

TYPES OF BONE AND CARTILAGE

EXAM TIP

Your examiner is not going to directly test you on the detail of types of bone and cartilage. However, you will need to have a basic understanding of the structure and growth of a long bone to appreciate the condition of osteoporosis and to understand the occurrence of growth plate disorders. You will also need to understand the role that articular cartilage plays in the degenerative disease of osteoarthritis. All three of these disorders are discussed in greater detail on pages 36–39.

Bone is made of collagen fibres filled with minerals, mainly calcium salts. There are five types of bone in the skeleton that are classified according to their shape. One of these types is the long bone, which is longer than it is wide and consists of a shaft, called the *diaphysis* and two ends, each called the *epiphysis*. The epiphysis

is covered by *articular cartilage* that acts as a cushion to absorb shock and also prevents friction during joint movement. It is one of the three types of cartilage that we have in our bodies.

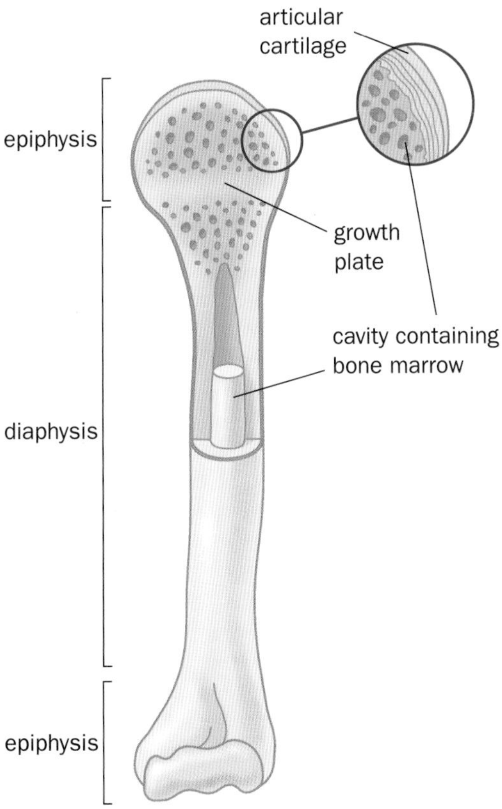

Children and young adults have a region between the diaphysis and each epiphysis called the *growth plate*, which is responsible for promoting longitudinal bone growth until physical maturity. Bones also contain cavities that are filled with *bone marrow*, which generates new blood cells. Long bones have a large cavity in the diaphysis and a network of small cavities in each epiphysis.

REMEMBER

All bones of the limbs, except the patella and the bones of the wrist and ankle are long bones. Even the bones of your hands and feet (metacarpals, metatarsals and phalanges) are long bones.

TASK 2

1. A long bone is one of the five types of bone found in the skeleton. Identify and give examples of the other four types of bone.
2. Articular cartilage is one of the three types of cartilage found in the human body. Identify, outline the function and give examples of the other two types of cartilage.

Fig 1.3 The structure of a long bone during adolescence

KEY TERMS

Collagen

A fibrous protein with great strength that is the main component of bone

Calcium

The mineral stored in bone that keeps it hard and strong. 99% of the body's calcium is stored in bone

Class of joint	Mobility	Stability	Examples from the skeleton	Diagram
Fibrous	No movement	Most stable	Joints between the bones of the skull and between the fused bones of the sacrum and coccyx	
Cartilaginous	Little movement	Stable	Joints between the bodies of adjacent vertebrae in the cervical, thoracic and part of the lumbar spine	
Synovial	Free movement	Least stable	Joints between the bones of the arms and legs	

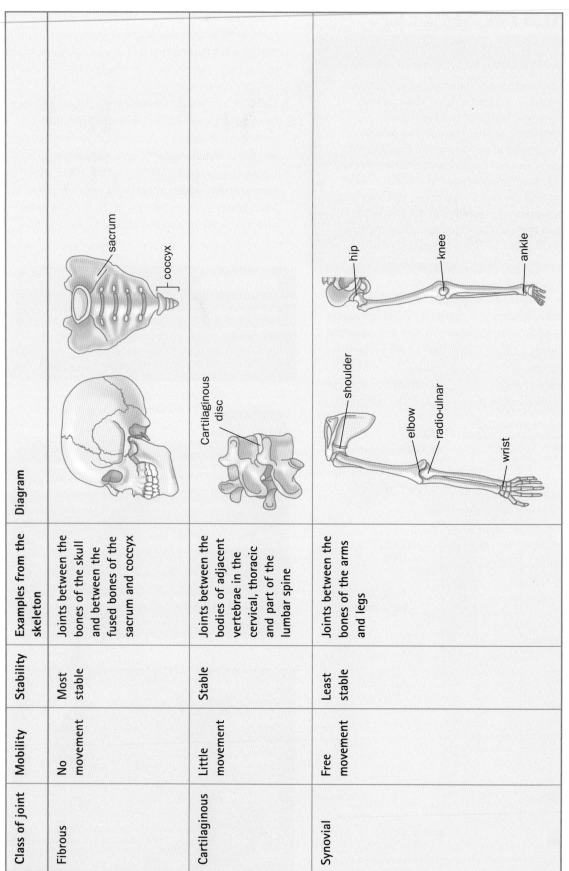

Table 2

Diaphysis

The shaft or middle part of a long bone.

Epiphysis

The end portion of a long bone.

Bone marrow

Connective tissue found in the spaces inside bone that is the site of blood cell production and fat storage.

Growth plate

The area of growing tissue near the end of long bones in children and adolescents, often referred to as the *epiphyseal plate*. When physical maturity is reached, the growth plate is replaced by solid bone.

Articular cartilage

A thin layer of glassy-smooth cartilage that is quite spongy and covers the end of bones at a joint.

JOINTS

Joints are links between the bones of the skeleton. They act to allow movement but also work to stabilise areas of the body. Consider the action of kicking a football. The knee of one leg is allowing the lower part of the limb to swing freely while the knee of the supporting limb is keeping the leg stable to maintain balance during the execution of the skill.

REMEMBER

Freely movable joints are located in the limbs of the appendicular skeleton, while immovable and slightly movable joints are more commonly found in the axial skeleton.

Joints are classified in three ways according to the balance that they allow between stability and mobility see table 2 on page 6.

EXAM TIP

As PE specialists, we are mainly interested in joints that allow free movement as they allow us to perform skills and techniques during physical activity. In preparation for your exam, be familiar with all classes of joint but focus your study on synovial joints.

Synovial joints

THE STRUCTURE OF SYNOVIAL JOINTS

Synovial joints have four main distinguishing features, shown and analysed in Table 3.

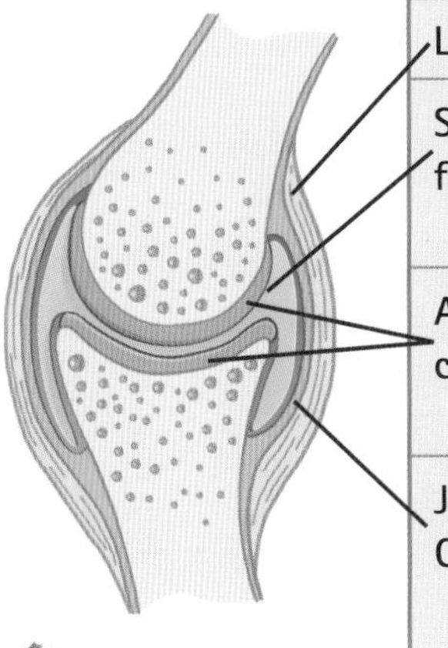

Fig 1.4

Feature	Structure	Function
Ligament	A band of strong fibrous tissue	To connect bone to bone
Synovial fluid	A slippery fluid the consistency of egg-whites that is contained within the joint cavity	To reduce friction between the articular cartilage in the joint
Articular cartilage	Glassy-smooth cartilage that is spongy and covers the ends of the bones in the joint	To absorb shock and to prevent friction between the ends of the bones in the joint
Joint Capsule	A tough fibrous tissue that has two layers, with the fibrous capsule lying outside the synovial membrane	The fibrous capsule helps to strengthen the joint, while the synovial membrane lines the joint and secretes synovial fluid

Table 3

KEY TERM

Joint cavity

A space within a synovial joint that contains synovial fluid.

REMEMBER

Synovial fluid is also found within the articular cartilage. When the joint is moved or compressed it seeps out to reduce friction between the cartilages. When movement stops, the synovial fluid is reabsorbed into the articular cartilage. This is called the *weeping lubrication theory*. It suggests that the articular cartilage acts a little like a sponge in water.

APPLY IT!

Discuss the importance of mobilising each of your synovial joints as part of a warm up routine before physical activity.

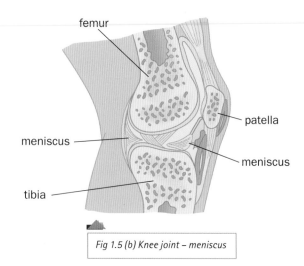

Fig 1.5 (b) Knee joint – meniscus

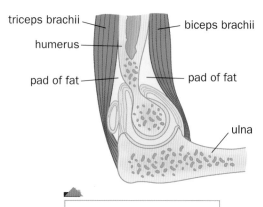

Fig 1.5 (c) Elbow joint – pad of fat

As well as the four features in Table 3, some synovial joints have additional features, the three most common of which are shown in Figures 1.5 a, b and c.

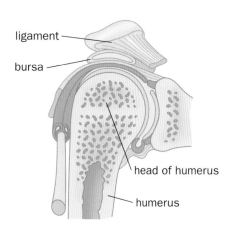

Fig 1.5 (a) Shoulder joint – bursa

KEY TERMS

Bursa (pl. bursae)

A flattened fibrous sac lines with synovial fluid that contains a thin film of synovial fluid. Its function is to prevent friction at sites in the body where ligaments, muscles, tendons or bones might rub together.

Meniscus (pl menisci)

A wedge of white fibrocartilage that improves the fit between adjacent bone ends, making the joint more stable and reducing wear and tear on joint surfaces.

Pad of fat

A fatty pad that provides cushioning between the fibrous capsule and a bone or muscle.

TYPES OF SYNOVIAL JOINT

As we have seen, synovial joints have many common structural characteristics. However, the shapes of the articulating surfaces within the joint capsules vary considerably and this determines how much movement is allowed at a particular joint.

For the purposes of your AS Anatomy and Physiology, synovial joints can be grouped into five types, which are summarised in Table 4 (see page 10).

KEY TERM

Planes of movement

A flat surface running through the body within which different types of movement can take place about different types of synovial joint. There are three main planes that describe the movement of the human body.

TASK 3

Synovial joints require a fine balance between stability and mobility. From your knowledge of the general structure of synovial joints:

1. List two features that increase joint stability, giving a specific function for each.
2. List two features that increase joint mobility, giving a specific function for each.

APPLY IT!

- See if you can find out the names and positions of the three planes of movement.
- Explain why the gliding joints and cartilaginous joints in the spine allow only restricted movement in these planes.
- Discuss the potential dangers of forces acting on these joints that would drive them beyond their normal range of movement and suggest the types of physical activity during which this might be more likely to happen.

EXAM TIP

As well as the two synovial joints found in the spine, pivot and gliding, there is also a cartilaginous joint found between the bodies of the adjacent vertebrae. You will need to remember all three types of joint found in the spine for your exam and be able to give examples.

MOVEMENTS OF SYNOVIAL JOINTS

The movements at any particular joint are possible because of its structure and the skeletal muscles that contract to pull the bone into a different position. This is explained in more detail on page 11, but for now we must understand that every skeletal muscle is attached to bone at a minimum of two points on opposite sides of a joint. When the muscle contracts across a joint, one point of attachment is pulled towards the other, causing joint movement.

TASK 4

Look at the shapes of the articulating surfaces of the types of joint explained in the table above. Comment on the degree of stability and mobility in each type, giving reasons for your answer. The information given in Table 4 on page 10 about joint stability might be a useful way to check your answers.

To allow us to describe the movements of synovial joints during physical activity, it is essential that we have a knowledge of the universally accepted initial reference position. This is the *anatomical position*, which is the upright standing position with the arms by the sides and palms facing forwards. Movements can occur away from or back towards the anatomical position. Therefore, most movements have an accompanying movement that moves the same joint in the opposite direction and are therefore best listed in pairs.

Type of Synovial Joint	Examples from the skeleton	Description	Mobility
Ball and socket	Shoulder (head of humerus with glenoid fossa of scapula) Hip (head of femur with acetabulum of pelvis)	A ball shaped head of one bone articulates with a cup like socket of an adjacent bone. Acetabulum of pelvis / Head of femur	Movement can occur in three planes. This joint allows the greatest range of movement.
Hinge	Elbow Knee Ankle	A cylindrical protusion of one bone articulates with a trough-shaped depression of an adjacent bone. Humerus / Ulna	Movement is restricted to one plane. This joint allows bending and straightening only.
Pivot	Radio–ular Spine (atlas/axis joint at the top)	A rounded or pointed structure of one bone articulates with a ring-shaped structure of an adjacent bone. Radius / Ulna	Movement is restricted to one plane. This joint allows rotation about its longitudinal axis only.
Condyloid	Wrist	Similar to a ball and socket joint but with much flatter articulating surfaces forming a much shallower joint. Radius / Ulna / Carpals	Movement can occur in two planes. This joint allows the second greatest range of movement.
Gliding	Spine (between the bony processes of the vertebrae in the cervical, thoracic and part of the lumbar regions)	Articulating surfaces are almost flat and of a similar size. body of vertebra / bony process / gliding joint / cartilaginous disc / bony process	Gliding allows movement in three planes, but it is severely limited.

Table 4

There are many types of movement in anatomy that apply to many joints, but the ones described below are the relevant ones for your AS Level PE. They have been divided into 'main movements', that can occur at more than one joint and 'other movements', that occur only at specific joints.

APPLY IT!

It is useful to be familiar with other anatomical terminology and try to use the correct terms in your exam paper. Read through the key terms below and do the following task.

With reference to the bones and joints of the skeleton, write one sentence that makes use of each of the anatomical terms listed below. The first one has been completed as an example.

- Anterior: example: The sternum is anterior to the scapula.
- Posterior
- Superior
- Inferior
- Medial
- Lateral

KEY TERMS

Anatomical position

An upright standing position with head, shoulders, chest, palms of hands, hips, knees and toes facing forwards.

Anterior

Ttowards the front of the body.

Posterior

Towards the back of the body.

Superior

Towards the head or upper part of the body.

Inferior

Towards the feet or the lower part of the body.

Medial

Towards the middle of the body.

Lateral

Towards the outside of the body.

EXAM TIP

Remember the starting point for these movements is the anatomical position. If you get confused with a joint movement, freeze your body in the position you want to describe and return to the anatomical position to work out what has happened at that joint. This might mean that you have to move in the exam – but that's OK!

Main movements

FLEXION AND EXTENSION

Flexion of a joint makes a body part move in a forwards direction from the anatomical position. *Extension* of a joint makes a body part move in a *backwards* direction. (The knee joint is the only exception to this rule where flexion moves the lower leg backwards and extension moves the lower leg forwards.)

EXAM TIP

For your exam you should focus on flexion and extension at the following joints: the wrist, the elbow, the shoulder, the spine, the hip and the knee.

REMEMBER

Consider the foetal position of a baby in the mother's womb: moving into the foetal position requires flexion of all the joints; straightening out of the foetal position requires extension of all the joints.

TASK 5

1. Working with a partner, identify both flexion and extension of the wrist, elbow, shoulder, spine, hip and knee joints.
2. For each of the twelve movements you have identified, give a sporting technique that demonstrates the movement. For example, flexion of the wrists occurs in the follow-through of a set shot in basketball.

HORIZONTAL FLEXION AND HORIZONTAL EXTENSION

Horizontal flexion and *horizontal extension* are movements of ball and socket joints, but tend to only be observable in the shoulder joint during sporting techniques. Horizontal flexion occurs when the shoulder is already flexed with the arm parallel to the ground and the shoulder joint moves towards the middle of the body. Horizontal extension occurs when the shoulder joint with the arm parallel to the ground moves away from the middle of the body.

REMEMBER

In horizontal flexion and horizontal extension – the fingers are already pointing at the horizon.

TASK 6

1. Working with a partner identify horizontal flexion and horizontal extension of the shoulder joint.
2. For each of the two movements you have identified, give a sporting technique that demonstrates the movement. For example, horizontal flexion of the shoulder occurs in the throwing arm during the execution phase of a discus throw.

EXAM TIP

For your exam you should focus on horizontal flexion and horizontal extension at the following joint: the shoulder.

ABDUCTION AND ADDUCTION

Abduction of a joint makes a body part move away from the midline of the body in the anatomical position. *Adduction* of a joint makes a body part move towards the midline of the body.

EXAM TIP

For your exam you should focus on abduction and adduction at the following joints: the shoulder and the hip.

REMEMBER

Think about the word 'abducted' when something or somebody is taken away or 'abducted by aliens'.

Think about the word 'add' in maths when you always add one number to another.

TASK 7

1. Working with a partner identify abduction and adduction of the shoulder and hip joints.
2. For each of the four movements you have identified, give a sporting technique that demonstrates the movement. For example, abduction of the hips occurs when performing the upward phase of a straddle jump.

ROTATION

Rotation of a joint is when a body part turns about its long axis from the anatomical position. For example, when using a screwdriver, rotation is occurring at the shoulder joint as the arm turns about an axis that travels straight through the arm from the shoulder to the wrist. Rotation does not have a separate opposite movement because it can be medial or lateral, which are opposite movements.

REMEMBER

To help recognise the difference between rotation and circumduction movements, identify the long axis of the moving body part and imagine there is a pen being held at the end. If the body part is *rotating*, the pen will draw a dot. If it is performing *circumduction*, the pen will draw a circle.

EXAM TIP

For your exam you should focus on rotation at the following joints: the shoulder and the hip.

CIRCUMDUCTION

Circumduction of a joint makes a body part move from the anatomical position, describing a cone shape. The joint performing circumduction stays still while the furthest end of the body part moves in a circle.

Other movements

PRONATION AND SUPINATION

Pronation and *supination* are anatomical terms unique to the radio-ulnar joint and are separate terms to describe rotation of the forearm. In the anatomical position the radio-ulnar joint is supinated. Pronation of the radio-ulnar joint makes the palm move to face backwards or downwards. Supination of the radio-ulnar joint is with the palm facing forwards or upwards.

REMEMBER

To help recognise the difference between pronation and supination by thinking how you would carry a bowl of soup ('sup'ination) in the palm of your hand!

EXAM TIP

For your exam you should focus on circumduction at the following joint: the shoulder.

LATERAL FLEXION

Lateral flexion is an anatomical term unique to the spine. It involves bending the spine sideways as you might do as part of a warm up to mobilise your spine.

TASK 8

1. Working with a partner, identify rotation of the shoulder and hip joints and circumduction of the shoulder joint.
2. For each of the three movements you have identified, give a sporting technique that demonstrates the movement. For example, circumduction of the shoulder occurs during the full arm action in front crawl.

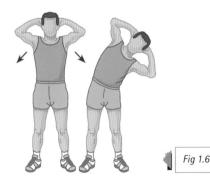

Fig 1.6

DORSIFLEXION AND PLANTAR FLEXION

Dorsiflexion and *plantar flexion* are anatomical terms unique to the ankle joint. Dorsiflexion of the ankle joint makes the foot move towards the shin as when you walk on your heels. Plantar flexion of the ankle joint makes the foot move away from the shin as when you walk on your tiptoes.

REMEMBER

Plantar flexion of the ankle occurs when you point your toes so remember 'p' for point and for plantar flexion.

(shoulder)	• Abduction and adduction • Rotation • Circumduction
Spine	• Flexion and extension • Lateral flexion
Hip	• Flexion and extension • Abduction and adduction • Rotation
Knee	• Flexion and extension
Ankle	• Dorsiflexion and plantar flexion

Table 5

TASK 9

1. Working with a partner, identify pronation and supination of the radio–ulnar joint, lateral flexion of the spine and dorsiflexion and plantar flexion of the ankle joint.
2. For each of the five movements you have identified, give a sporting technique that demonstrates the movement. For example, pronation of the radio–ulnar joint occurs in the execution and recovery phases of a top-spin forehand drive in tennis.

The table below summarises the movements of the major joints of the body that you need to know for your course:

Joint	Movements possible
Wrist	• Flexion and extension
Radio–ulnar	• Pronation and supination
Elbow	• Flexion and extension
Shoulder	• Flexion and extension • Horizontal flexion and horizontal extension

EXAM TIP

Make sure you know what each of the movements of each of the joints listed in the table looks like. Your examiner can ask you to identify the joint movements occurring at any of these joints in a large variety of sporting techniques. If you are good at identifying the joint movement you will find it easy to apply the muscles in action as discussed on page 16. Also, try to learn the movements in pairs so if one joint can carry out flexion, you automatically know that it can also extend.

TASK 10

For revision purposes, copy and complete the following table onto a sheet of A4 and insert it in your file. The stars indicate the number of points you need to make to ensure you do not miss out any important information!

EXAM TIP

In an examination question, provided you gave all the information required, each box would be worth one mark.

Joint	Joint type	Articulating bones	Movements possible at joint
Wrist	★★	★★★	★★
Radio-ulnar	★	★★	★★
Elbow	★	★★★	★★
Shoulder	★	★★	★★★★★★★★
Spine	★★★	★	★★★
Hip	★	★★	★★★★★
Knee	★	★★	★★
Ankle	★	★★★	★★

Table 6

The muscular system

There are over 600 skeletal muscles in the human body but, do not worry, you do not need to know them all! Most of the muscles you are required to know are shown in Fig. 1.7. You will be able to see that most of these muscles extend from one bone to another, are attached in at least two places and cross at least one joint. From our knowledge of the skeletal system, we know that muscles are attached to bones by tendons. These points of attachment at either end of the muscle form the *origin* and the *insertion*.

It is important to remember that muscles can only pull, they can never push. When a muscle contracts, the pulling of one bone towards another across a movable joint causes movement.

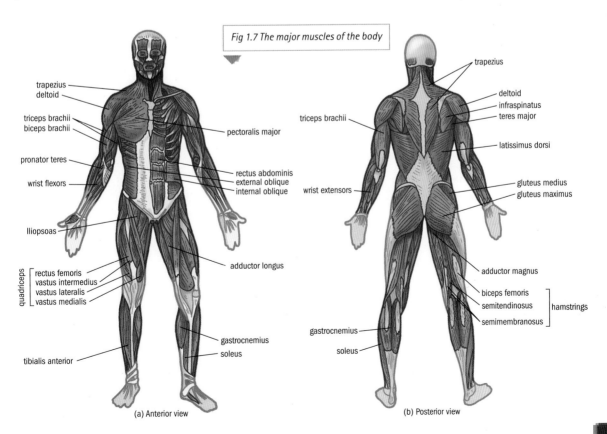

Fig 1.7 The major muscles of the body

trapezius
deltoid
triceps brachii
biceps brachii
pronator teres
wrist flexors
Iliopsoas
quadriceps
[rectus femoris
vastus intermedius
vastus lateralis
vastus medialis]
tibialis anterior

pectoralis major
rectus abdominis
external oblique
internal oblique
adductor longus
gastrocnemius
soleus

(a) Anterior view

trapezius
deltoid
infraspinatus
teres major
latissimus dorsi
gluteus medius
gluteus maximus
triceps brachii
wrist extensors

adductor magnus
biceps femoris
semitendinosus
semimembranosus
} hamstrings
gastrocnemius
soleus

(b) Posterior view

REMEMBER

When standing in the anatomical position, the origin of a muscle is the point of attachment closer to the head, while the insertion is the point of attachment closer to the feet.

We know that movements go together in pairs. As skeletal muscles are responsible for these movements, it makes sense that muscles are also arranged in pairs, for example the biceps brachii and triceps brachii. This is often termed *antagonistic muscle action*. This means that whatever one muscle can do, there is another muscle that can undo it to return the body to the original position.

As well as movement, muscles are also needed to provide support and stability to the body. For example, we have muscles such as the *transverse abdominis* and *multifidus* that are responsible for maintaining our posture and promoting our core stability and we also have muscles such as the *rotator cuff* group that work to enhance the stability of the shoulder joint. We will look in more detail at muscles that are used more for stability than movement on page 39.

TASK 11

Stand in the anatomical position and identify the position of the following muscles: biceps brachii   pectoralis major hamstrings   abdominals.

For each muscle, identify the approximate positions of:

- the origin
- the insertion
- the partner muscle that produces the opposite movement – can you name it?

MUSCLES IN ACTION

Muscles perform a specific role as members of a group to produce movement. For the purposes of your specification you will need to understand the role played by an *agonist* and an *antagonist* in producing a coordinated movement. You probably understand the concept of antagonistic muscle action already but to remind yourselves, consider the following example:

In the preparation of a shot in basketball or netball, the shooting arm flexes at the elbow. The biceps brachii, acting as the agonist, contracts to produce the movement, while the triceps brachii, acting as the antagonist, relaxes to allow the movement to take place. In the execution phase, there is extension at the elbow and the roles of these two muscles are reversed.

KEY TERMS

Origin

Point of attachment of a muscle that remains relatively fixed during muscular contraction.

Insertion

Point of attachment of a muscle that tends to move toward the origin during muscular contraction.

Antagonistic muscle action

As one muscle shortens to produce movement, another muscle lengthens to allow that movement to take place.

Agonist muscle

The muscle that is directly responsible for the movement at a joint.

Antagonist muscle

The muscle that has an action opposite to that of the agonist and helps in the production of a coordinated movement.

Core stability

The ability of your trunk to support the forces from your arms and legs during different types of physical activity. It enables joints and muscles to work in their safest and most efficient positions, therefore reducing the risk of injury.

LOCATION AND ACTION OF SPECIFIC MUSCLES

We will focus only on the muscles that you need to know for your specification. Learning these muscles is quite demanding, but the best way may be to take one joint at a time and for each movement that you know this joint can do learn the muscle responsible for producing this movement and its location in the body. It is worth noting here that many muscles are capable of producing more than one joint movement but in the tables below each muscle is associated with just one movement to help keep things relatively simple.

REMEMBER

Muscles are arranged in pairs, so whatever movement one muscle can do, it will have a partner muscle that can reverse that movement.

Joint	Joint movement	Muscle responsible	Location
WRIST	Flexion of the wrist joint	*Wrist flexors*	Anterior forearm wrist flexors
	Extension of the wrist joint	*Wrist extensors*	Posterior forearm wrist extensors wrist extensor

REMEMBER

The wrist joint is a condyloid joint with its articulating bones being the radius, ulna and carpals.

Table 7

Joint	Joint movement	Muscle responsible	Location
RADIO–ULNAR	Pronation of radio–ulnar joint	*Pronator teres*	Superior anterior forearm Pronator teres
	Supination of radio–ulnar joint	*Supinator*	Lateral anterior forearm Supinator

> **REMEMBER**
>
> The radio-ulnar joint is a pivot joint with its articulating bones being the radius and ulna.

Table 8

Joint	Joint movement	Muscle responsible	Location	
ELBOW	Flexion of elbow joint	*Biceps brachii*	Anterior upper arm 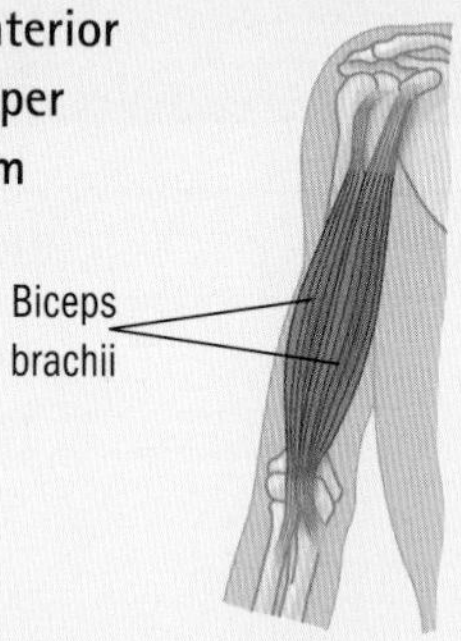	Biceps brachii
	Extension of elbow joint	*Triceps brachii*	Posterior upper arm 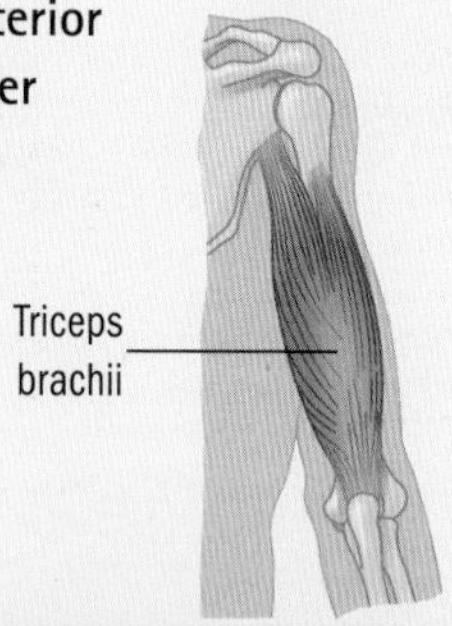	Triceps brachii

> **REMEMBER**
>
> The elbow joint is a hinge joint with its articulating bones being the humerus, radius and ulna.

Table 9

EXAM TIP

The deltoid is composed of three parts: anterior, middle and posterior. When revising for your exam it is advisable to learn the deltoid in these three sections as they each produce different movements of the shoulder joint as shown in Table 10. Therefore, by just learning the one muscle, you have the answer for the agonist of shoulder flexion, abduction and extension.

Joint	Joint movement	Muscle responsible	Location of muscle
SHOULDER (muscles associated with the main movements)	Anterior: Flexion Middle: Abduction Posterior: Extension	*Deltoid*	Covers shoulder joint Middle deltoid Anterior deltoid Posterior deltoid
	Adduction	*Latissimus dorsi*	Posterior trunk Latissimus dorsi
	Horizontal flexion	*Pectoralis major*	Top of chest Pectoralis major

Table 10 The shoulder joint: its movements and the muscles responsible for those movements

Joint	Joint movement	Muscle responsible	Location of muscle
SHOULDER (cont.)	Horizontal extension	*Trapezius*	Posterior trunk
	Lateral rotation	*Teres minor* and *Infraspinatus*	Attaches back of scapula to humerus
	Medial rotation	*Teres major* and *Subscapularis*	Attaches side and front of scapula to humerus

Table 10 (cont.)

REMEMBER

The shoulder joint is a ball and socket joint with its articulating bones being the scapula and the humerus.

Together with the supraspinatus muscle, the infraspinatus, teres minor and subscapularis form an important group of muscles called the *rotator cuff*. The shoulder joint has a large range of movement and is relatively shallow, so the surrounding ligaments alone can not keep the joint stable during physical activity. The rotator cuff muscles improve the stability of the shoulder joint by helping to hold the head of the humerus in contact with the glenoid cavity of the scapula. If you imagine gripping a shot put from the top to pick it up and compare the shot to the head of

KEY TERM

Rotator cuff

The *supraspinatus, infraspinatus, teres minor* and *subscapularis* muscles make up the rotator cuff. They work to stabilise the shoulder joint to prevent the larger muscles from displacing the head of the humerus during physical activity.

APPLY IT!

Injuries to the rotator cuff may result from a sudden force or from repetitive actions. Throwers are particularly at risk of injury to their rotator cuff through repetition, as the muscles work to control the acceleration of the arm after the point of release. They are therefore working eccentrically and this can produce a force of up to 80% of body weight to travel through the tendons of the rotator cuff muscles.

the humerus, you can gain some appreciation of the way the rotator cuff muscles work to prevent dislocation of the shallow shoulder joint.

Joint	Joint movement	Muscle responsible	Location of muscle
SPINE	Flexion	*Rectus abdominis*	Middle of abdomen Rectus abdominis
	Extension	*Erector spinae group*	Covers length of spine Erector spinae group

Table 11 The spine: its movements and the muscles responsible for those movements

Joint	Joint movement	Muscle responsible	Location of muscle
SPINE (cont.)	Lateral flexion & rotation	*External obliques*	Lateral abdomen external obliques
	Lateral flexion & rotation	*Internal obliques*	Lateral abdomen beneath external obliques internal obliques

Table 11 (cont.)

REMEMBER

The spine contains examples of cartilaginous, pivot and gliding joints with its articulating bones being the vertebrae.

REMEMBER

Contraction of one side of the obliques will cause lateral flexion to the same side but rotation to the opposite side.

Muscles associated with the spine and trunk are important because not only do they act as mobilisers to allow the joint movements above to take place, they also act as stabilisers to support the trunk while taking part in different types of physical activity such as running or playing tennis. The joints and muscles of the arms and legs can work more efficiently and safely if they have a solid foundation or core to pull from. This is the principle behind core stability and the reason why many performers now spend time training to specifically improve their core stability. The benefits gained include more efficient use of muscles and joints, decreased risk of injury and improved posture. Posture is closely related to core stability and is discussed in more detail on page 40.

Two muscles that make a significant impact on posture and core stability are the transverse abdominis and the multifidis. Good muscle tone in the transverse abdominis is also important in reducing lower back pain. The location of these two muscles are shown in Figure 1.8.

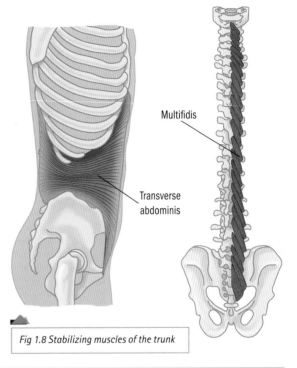

Multifidis

Transverse abdominis

Fig 1.8 Stabilizing muscles of the trunk

REMEMBER

The hip is a ball and socket joint with its articulating bones being the pelvis and femur.

Joint	Joint movement	Muscle responsible	Location of muscle
HIP	Flexion	*Iliopsoas*	Anterior pelvis Iliopsoas
	Extension	*Gluteus maximus*	Posterior pelvis gluteus maximus

Table 12 The hip joint: its movements and the muscles responsible for those movements

Joint	Joint movement	Muscle responsible	Location of muscle
HIP (cont.)	Abduction	*Gluteus medius & minimus*	Lateral hip (minimus is underneath medius)
	Adduction	*Adductor group (longus, brevis & magnus)*	Medial thigh

Table 12 (cont.)

REMEMBER

The gluteus maximus also produces lateral rotation of the hip, while the gluteus minimus produces medial rotation.

Joint	Joint movement	Muscle responsible	Location of muscle
KNEE	Flexion	*Biceps femoris* *Semitendinosus* *Semimembranosus* *(Hamstring group)*	Posterior thigh 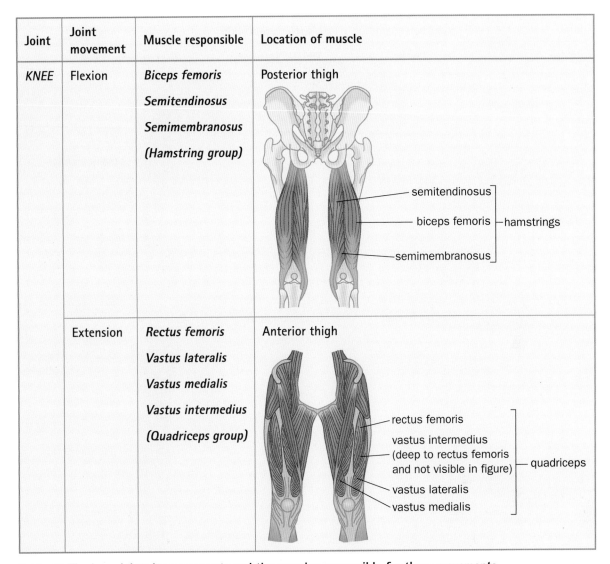
	Extension	*Rectus femoris* *Vastus lateralis* *Vastus medialis* *Vastus intermedius* *(Quadriceps group)*	Anterior thigh

Table 13 The knee joint: its movements and the muscles responsible for those movements

REMEMBER

The knee is a hinge joint with its articulating bones being the femur and tibia.

EXAM TIP

In an exam answer you must give the name of the individual muscles that make up the hamstring group or the quadriceps group. To simply state hamstrings or quadriceps will not gain you credit.

Joint	Joint movement	Muscle responsible	Location of muscle
ANKLE	Dorsiflexion	*Tibialis anterior*	Cover anterior tibia tibialis anterior
	Plantar flexion	*Gastrocnemius & Soleus*	Calf muscles gastrocnemius soleus

Table 14 The ankle joint: its movements and the muscles responsible for those movements

REMEMBER

The ankle is a *hinge joint* with its articulating bones being the tibia, fibula and talus.

TASK 12

1. Cut out some photographs of sports performers from magazines or newspapers and label as many of the muscles identified in this chapter as possible.
2. For each of the muscles identified above, give an example of a sport where the performer would need to heavily utilise this muscle. Try to think about the joint movement required.

TASK 13

For revision purposes, copy and complete the following table and insert it in your file.

Upper limb	Joint movement	Agonist muscle	Antagonist muscle
Wrist joint	Flexion		
	Extension		
Radio–ulnar joint	Pronation joint		
	Supination		
Elbow joint	Flexion		
	Extension		
Shoulder joint	Flexion		
	Extension		
	Horizontal flexion		
	Horizontal extension		
	Abduction		
	Adduction		
	Lateral rotation		
	Medial rotation		
Spine	**Joint movement**	**Agonist muscle**	**Antagonist muscle**
Spine	Flexion		
	Extension		
	Lateral flexion		
	Rotation		
Lower limb	**Joint movement**	**Agonist muscle**	**Antagonist muscle**
Hip joint	Flexion		
	Extension		
	Abduction		
	Adduction		
	Lateral rotation		
	Medial rotation		
Knee joint	Flexion		
	Extension		
Ankle joint	Dorsiflexion		
	Plantar flexion		

Table 15

THE ROLE OF MUSCULAR CONTRACTION

Muscular contractions occur as a result of a stimulus being sent to a muscle to produce tension. All muscular contraction can be classified as being either isotonic or isometric. Isotonic contraction can occur in two ways, concentric contraction and eccentric contraction.

Table 16 explains the three types of muscular contraction in relation to the biceps brachii muscle.

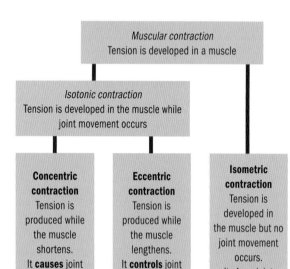

> **Muscular contraction**
> Tension is developed in a muscle

> *Isotonic contraction*
> Tension is developed in the muscle while joint movement occurs

> **Concentric contraction**
> Tension is produced while the muscle shortens.
> It **causes** joint movement

> **Eccentric contraction**
> Tension is produced while the muscle lengthens.
> It **controls** joint movement

> **Isometric contraction**
> Tension is developed in the muscle but no joint movement occurs.
> It **stops** joint movement

REMEMBER

The term *muscle contraction* can be confusing as it suggests the muscle is always shortening BUT in some types of contraction the muscle will stay the same length or even get longer, while producing tension. Try to remember that muscular contraction can be used to cause joint movement, control joint movement or stop joint movement.

Fig 1.9 Explains the three types of muscular contraction

Isotonic contraction		Isometric contraction
Concentric contraction	Eccentric contraction	
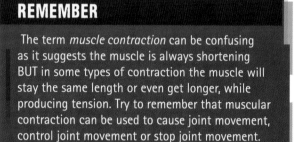 movement	movement	no movement
• concentric contraction in the biceps brachii during upward phase of exercise. • the biceps brachii produces tension and *shortens*. • it pulls the forearm upwards to *cause* flexion of the elbow.	• eccentric contraction occurs in the biceps brachii during the downward phase of the exercise. • the biceps brachii produces tension and *lengthens*. • it slows the lowering of the forearm and *controls* extension of the elbow.	• isometric contraction occurs in the biceps brachii when the muscle is holding the weight still. • the biceps brachii develops tension and *stays the same length*. • it *stops* flexion and extension of the elbow.

Table 16

KEY TERMS

Isotonic contraction

Tension is produced in the muscle while there is a change in muscle length. It is a dynamic contraction because the joint will move.

Isometric contraction

Tension is produced in the muscle but there is no change in muscle length. It is a static contraction because the joint will stay in the same position.

Concentric contraction

A type of isotonic contraction that involves the muscle shortening while producing tension.

Eccentric contraction

A type of isotonic contraction that involves the muscle lengthening while producing tension.

EXAM TIP

For any explosive sporting technique such as a penalty kick or conversion in rugby or a forehand in tennis, the type of contraction of the agonist is concentric.

If the examiner is asking about a sporting technique that involves working against gravity, for example, the lowering phase of a sit up or a press up, the type of contraction they are after is likely to be eccentric.

REMEMBER

Eccentric contraction *controls* a movement. If you can answer 'yes; to the following two questions, you have eccentric contraction:

- Is the muscle producing tension while lengthening?
- Is the muscle working to control the movement?

TASK 14

1. Complete another table similar to Table 16 on page 28 to show the three types of muscular contraction applied to the rectus abdominis muscle during the upward and downward phases of a sit up. Use diagrams to help illustrate your explanation.
2. Repeat the process for a muscle of your choice and an exercise of your choice.

TAKE IT FURTHER

1. The next time you are working out in the gym, for each resistance exercise you do, identify the muscle you are working and the type of muscular contraction occurring in (i) the lifting phase and (ii) the lowering phase. Make sure you can explain your answers.
2. Research a type of training called *plyometrics*, which involves movements that produce an eccentric contraction immediately followed by a concentric contraction, such as bounding, hopping and jumping. Identify the advantages and disadvantages of plyometric training.

Movement analysis of physical activity

A movement analysis of physical activity allows you to identify the joints, movement and muscles that are involved in carrying out a sporting technique. It requires knowledge on the following:

- the joint type
- the type of movement produced
- the muscles in action (the agonist and the antagonist)
- the type of muscle contraction taking place.

Tables 17 and 18 show a full movement analysis for the leg action of Jonny Wilkinson, arguably one of the most famous goal kickers in the history of rugby.

Preparation phase – Jonny Wilkinson preparing to kick for goal

EXAM TIP

In your exam it is likely that a question on 'Movement analysis of physical activity' will be in table format (similar to Table 17). Some of the detail will be given to you and some will be left out. You would need to be able to complete the missing information. If the question is not given in a table, it is advisable to draw one yourself.

EXAM TIP

The right and left sides refer to the performer in the diagram NOT your right and left.

Joint	Joint type	Joint movement	Agonist	Type of contraction of agonist	Antagonist
Right shoulder	Ball and socket	Abduction	Middle deltoid	Concentric	Latissimus dorsi
Left hip	Ball and socket	Extension	Gluteus maximus	Concentric	Iliopsoas
Left knee	Hinge	Flexion	Biceps femoris, semitendinosus, semimembranosus	Concentric	Recturs femoris, vastus lateralis, vastus medialis, vastus intermedius

Table 17 Preparation phase

Recovery phase: Jonny Wilkinson follow through after kick

TASK 15

Look through the sporting pictures in the daily or Sunday newspapers or on BBC Sport online. Select two action shots, one involving the upper limb and the other the lower limb and complete a full movement analysis for each.

Joint	Joint type	Joint movement	Agonist	Type of contraction of agonist	Antagonist
Right shoulder	Ball and socket	Horizontal flexion	Pectoralis major	Concentric	Trapezius
Spine	Cartilaginous Pivot Gliding	Rotation	External obliques	Concentric	Internal obliques
Left hip	Ball and socket	Flexion	Iliopsoas	Concentric	Gluteus maximus
Left knee	Hinge	Extension	Recturs femoris, vastus lateralis, vastus medialis, vastus intermedius	Concentric	Biceps femoris, semitendinosus, semimembranosus
Left ankle	Hinge	Dorsiflexion	Tibilais anterior	Concentric	Gastrocnemius

Table 18 Recovery phase

Muscle fibre types

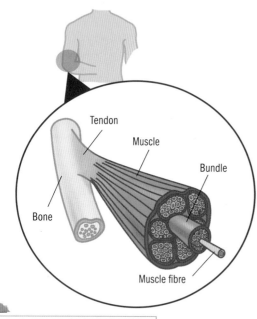

Tendon

Muscle

Bundle

Bone

Muscle fibre

Fig 1.10 Structure of skeletal muscle

KEY TERM

Muscle fibre

A long cylindrical muscle cell. Muscle fibres are held together in bundles to make up an individual skeletal muscle *see* Fig. 1.10.

KEY TERMS

Slow twitch muscle fibre

A type of muscle fibre associated with aerobic work. It produces a small force over a long period of time: high resistance to fatigue. It is suited to endurance based activities, e.g. marathon running.

Fast twitch muscle fibre

A type of muscle fibre associated with anaerobic work. It produces a large force over a short period of time : low resistance to fatigue. It is suited to power-based activities, e.g. sprinting, power lifting. There are two types: **fast oxidative glycolytic (Types 2a/FOG)** and **fast glycolytic (type 2b/FG)**. FOG fibres have a slightly greater resistance to fatigue than FG fibres.

Aerobic exercise

Is performed in the presence of oxygen at a submaximal intensity over a prolonged period of time, e.g. rowing.

Anaerobic exercise

Is performed in the absence of oxygen at a maximal intensity that can only be sustained for a short period of time due to the build up of lactic acid, e.g. sprinting.

Not all muscle fibres within a skeletal muscle are the same. There are two main types:

- Slow twitch fibres – type 1
  These are designed for aerobic exercise and use oxygen to produce a small amount of tension over a long period of time, as they are resistant to fatigue. Performers in endurance events tend to have a high percentage of slow twitch muscle fibres.

- Fast twitch fibres – type 2
  These are designed for anaerobic exercise and produce a large amount of force in a very short time, as they fatigue easily. Performers in power events tend to have a high percentage of fast twitch muscle fibres.

There are two types of fast twitch muscle fibre:

- Fast oxidative glycolytic fibres – type 2a or FOG fibres.
  These anaerobic fibres are more resistant to fatigue than type 2b, but generate slightly less force.
- Fast glycolytic fibres – type 2b or FG fibres
  These fibres have the greatest anaerobic capacity and therefore generate the largest amount of force.

The three types of muscle fibre mentioned above vary in structure and function as summarised in Table 19.

Structural differences			
Characteristic	Slow Twitch (Type 1)	Fast Oxidative Glycolytic (Type 2a / FOG)	Fast Glycolytic (Type 2b / FG)
Fibre size	small	large	large
Number of mitochondria	large	moderate	small
Number of capillaries	large	moderate	small
Myoglobin content	high	moderate	low
PC stores	low	high	high
Glycogen stores	low	high	high
Triglyceride stores	high	moderate	low
Functional differences			
Speed of contraction	slow	fast	fastest
Force of contraction	low	high	highest
Resistance to fatigue	high	low	lowest
Aerobic capacity	high	low	lowest
Anaerobic capacity	low	high	highest
Activity suited			
	Marathon	1500m	110m hurdler

Table 19

MUSCLE FIBRE TYPES IN RELATION TO CHOICE OF PHYSICAL ACTIVITY

Once you know a little about the characteristics of the different muscle fibre types, it is possible to predict the type of activity a performer might excel at. For example, we could say that performers who have a high percentage of slow twitch muscle fibres in their gastrocnemius would be well suited to endurance events, while performers who have a high percentage of FG fibres in their gastrocnemius, would be suited to speed and strength events.

So, if a performer can determine their relative percentages of the three types of muscle fibre, they could chose to take part in an activity that is highly suited to their physiological make up.

However, other factors will also affect their potential in endurance or strength and speed events such as training, muscle size and the efficiency of their cardiovascular and respiratory systems.

Asafa Powell has a high percentage of FG fibres in his gastrocnemius. This is because his legs can generate a large force in the absence of oxygen over a short period of time.

Paula Radcliffe has a high percentage of slow (twitch) fibres in her gastrocnemius. This is because her legs can produce force over a prolonged period of time without fatigue.

REMEMBER

An individual's mix of muscle fibre type is largely genetic. It is determined using *biopsy*, which involves a hollow needle being inserted into the muscle to extract a small sample of muscle tissue. This can then be analysed to determine the relative percentage of slow twitch to fast twitch fibres.

APPLY IT!

World Champion marathon runners have been reported to have up to 99% of slow twitch muscle fibres in their gastrocnemius muscle.

Table 20 shows the relative percentage of fibre type mix in male and female performers in different types of physical activity.

TASK 16

Cut out pictures of different types of performers from the sports pages of newspapers or BBC Sport online. Stick them on a sheet of paper and under each picture make a prediction on the relative percentages of the three types of muscle fibre in specific skeletal muscles. Justify your answers by using your knowledge of the structural and functional characteristics of muscle fibres shown in Table 19 on page 33.

EXAM TIPS

In a question on muscle fibre types, you will need to know the differences in structural and functional characteristics and explain why certain types of muscle fibre are suited to certain types of physical activity.

WARM UP AND COOL DOWN

Warm ups and cool downs are a crucial part to any sport. A warm up will increase the quality of performance on the day by preparing the body for exercise and reducing the risk of injury and a cool down will increase the quality of performance on subsequent days by limiting muscle soreness after exercise. For the purpose of this part of your specification, Table 21 on page 35 focuses on the effect of a warm up and cool down on skeletal

Athlete	Gender	Muscle	Slow twitch %	Fast twitch %
Sprinters	M	Gastrocnemius	24	76
	F	Gastrocnemius	27	73
Distance runners	M	Gastrocnemius	79	21
	F	Gastrocnemius	69	31
Shot putters	M	Gastrocnemius	38	62
Canoeists	M	Posterior deltoid	71	29

Table 20

muscle tissue as their effects on the cardiovascular system are discussed on page 71.

KEY TERMS

Warm up

Light aerobic exercise that takes place prior to physical activity, normally including some light exercise to elevate the heart rate, muscle and core body temperature, some mobilising exercises for the joints, some stretching exercises for the muscles and connective tissue and some easy rehearsal of the skills to follow.

Cool down

Low intensity aerobic exercise that takes place after physical activity and facilitates the recovery process.

TAKE IT FURTHER

There are always new ideas being tested to help with warm ups and cool downs such as weighted vests during a warm up and ice baths as part of a cool down. In pairs, research some of the latest thinking behind aids to warming up and cooling down and prepare a presentation to make to the rest of your class.

Sportsman in an ice bath

The impact of different types of physical activity on the skeletal and muscular systems

As you may be aware, the Government is keen to promote health-enhancing physical activity in young people, with the underlying objective being to maximise the opportunity for lifelong involvement in an active lifestyle. You can probably think of numerous benefits to increasing

Effect of a warm up on skeletal muscle tissue	Effect of a cool down on skeletal muscle tissue
An increase in core body temperature will produce the following physiological effects on skeletal muscle tissue: • a reduction in muscle viscosity, leading to an improvement in the efficiency of muscular contractions • a greater speed and force of contraction due to a higher speed of nerve transmission • an increased flexibility that reduces the risk of injury due to increased extensibility of tendons and ligaments	• an increase in the speed of removal of lactic acid and carbon dioxide that raise the acidity levels of the muscle and affect pain receptors due to oxygen rich blood being flushed through the muscle • a decrease in the risk of DOMS, which is the muscular pain experienced 24–48 hours after intense exercise due to microscopic tears in the muscle fibres

Table 21

the activity levels of the nation, but for the purpose of this section of your specification we will focus of the impact that an active lifestyle can have on bone, joint and muscle health. It is important to appreciate that while there are many benefits to being active, there are certain types of physical activity that can be a risk to the skeletal and muscular systems. The effect of exercise on the cardiovascular and respiratory systems is discussed in Chapter 3.

KEY TERMS

Osteoporosis

Weakening of bones caused by a reduction in bone density making them prone to fracture.

Sedentary

An inactive lifestyle with little or no exercise.

TASK 17

1. Consider the many different types of physical activity in which people enjoy to participate. Suggest the types of activity that provide the lowest risk to injury of the musculo–skeletal system and the types of activity that provide the highest risk. Give reasons for your answers.

2. All factors considered, it seems that the positive effects of exercise outweigh the negatives and lifelong involvement in physical activity is to be encouraged. Outline the effects of long term physical inactivity on the following:
the bones; the joints; the skeletal muscles.

BONE HEALTH AND BONE DISORDERS

Bone disorders or weakening can occur through an inactive lifestyle, general wear and tear and the natural ageing process or due to injury, either through an acute impact or overuse and repetition. Two disorders associated with the skeletal system that you are recommended to know about are *osteoporosis* and *growth plate injuries.*

OSTEOPOROSIS

Osteoporosis is a common bone disorder that is caused by a low bone density and a deterioration of bone tissue. This severely weakens the bone, making it prone to fractures. Bones in the hip, spine and wrist joints are most commonly affected, although the condition can occur in any bone. While osteoporosis is generally associated with the older generation and women are more at risk than men, people of any age or gender can be affected by it. For somebody with osteoporosis, any sudden bump or fall that might be experienced in contact or impact sports would cause a fracture. The following are some of the risk factors, relevant to your specification, that are associated with osteoporosis: inactivity in childhood, adolescence or adulthood; having a serious injury that leads to a sedentary lifestyle or immobility.

PHYSICAL ACTIVITY AND OSTEOPOROSIS

Physical activity is extremely important in maintaining healthy bones. Combined with a healthy diet, the best defence against osteoporosis is to build strong and healthy bones during childhood and adolescence.

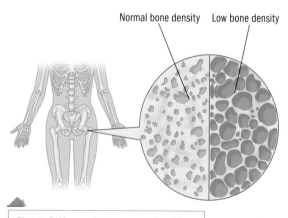

Normal bone density   Low bone density

Fig 1.11 Difference between normal and low bone density – leading to osteoporosis

TASK 18

1. Research the condition of osteoporosis to find out how bones become weaker and what other risk factors contribute to the disease.
2. It has been suggested that high impact sports have a greater effect on peak bone density in young people than non-impact sports. Discuss the relative benefits of the following sports and physical activities in minimising the risk of osteoporosis:

skipping	swimming	press-ups	biceps curls with dumbbells	basketball
bike riding	running	walking	tennis	netball

In early adulthood, bone growth is mostly complete and this represents a time when the bone is at its strongest or has *peak bone density*. A high peak bone density helps to minimise the risk of osteoporosis in later life, although other risk factors should be considered. High impact activity is thought to be more effective at achieving peak bone density than other types of physical activity. NICE (the National Institute for Health and Clinical Excellence) suggests that participation in resistance or strength training, weight-bearing activities and high impact activities has a positive effect on bone health and is associated with a long term reduced risk of osteoporosis

complete it closes and is replaced by solid bone. This usually occurs towards late adolescence.

GROWTH PLATE AND PHYSICAL ACTIVITY

During physical activity, injuries to the growth plate in young people are common because it is the weakest area of the growing skeleton, weaker even than ligaments and tendons. An impact injury that would cause a sprain in an adult can be associated with a growth plate injury in a child.

Growth plate injuries are fractures and are caused by a sudden force travelling through the bone in competitive, contact and impact activities such as football, rugby, hockey and basketball. However, injuries in young performers can also result from overuse caused by repetitive practice of specific skills such as a young tennis player who spends too much time continually trying to perfect their volley or their serve.

APPLY IT!

During space travel, astronauts who experience weightlessness due to the lack of gravity, can lose up to one third of their bone density within a few weeks of being in space.

GROWTH PLATE

Look back to page 7 to remind yourself that the growth plate is the delicate area found between the shaft and either end of a long bone in children and adolescents. When the growth plate is

APPLY IT!

Ask other students in your class if they have ever suffered a fracture. Discuss whether this could have been caused by damage to the growth plate in their bone and whether it was down to an impact or overuse injury.

TASK 19

If you have read through the impact of physical activity leading to osteoporosis and growth plates, it appears that there may be a slight disagreement in the value of high impact activities to young people. On the one hand, health professionals promote this type of activity to optimise bone density but, on the other hand, the risk of damage to the growth plate is high. How might you find a way to balance this? Suggest some guidelines that should be in place before young people take part in high impact activities.

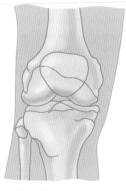
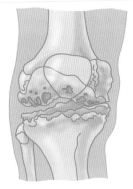

(a) healthy knee joint

(b) arthritic knee joint showing degeneration of articular cartilage and formation of bony spurs

Fig 1.12

JOINT HEALTH AND JOINT DISORDERS

Many of us take our joints for granted and carry out our daily activities and play our sport without giving them much thought. That is, until they are injured or painful and then we seem to notice them quite a lot! Most joint disorders result from impact injuries, such as sprains and dislocations but joint pain can also be due to inflammatory or degenerative conditions. Two disorders associated with joints that you are recommended to know about are *osteoarthritis* and *joint stability* issues.

OSTEOARTHRITIS

Osteoarthritis is caused by the breakdown and eventual loss of articular cartilage at one or more joints. From the work you did on the structure of synovial joints you will remember that articular cartilage covers the end of long bones to act to absorb shock, release synovial fluid and prevent friction between bones during movement. It has been said that articular cartilage offers less friction during movement than that of the blade of a skate on ice.

Osteoarthritis is a degenerative disease that commonly affects large weight-bearing joints, such as the hips and the knees. Repetitive use of these joints through sport and physical activity causes wear and tear on the articular cartilage, which gives rise to joint pain and swelling. The

articular cartilage begins to deteriorate and in advanced cases of osteoarthritis, there is total loss of the cartilaginous cushion. This causes friction between the bones and can lead to new bone spurs being formed around the joint giving considerable pain and severely limiting joint flexibility and movement.

KEY TERMS

Osteoarthritis

A degenerative joint disease caused by a loss of articular cartilage at the ends of long bones in a joint. It causes pain, swelling and reduced motion in your joints.

Bone spurs

Are small projections of bone that form around joints due to damage to the joint's surface, most commonly caused from the onset of osteoarthritis. They limit movement and cause pain in the joint.

REMEMBER

The symptoms of osteoarthritis include: pain, decreased range of movement, joint instability, joint deformity, reduced strength and endurance.

OSTEOARTHRITIS AND PHYSICAL ACTIVITY

For many people the cause of the onset of osteoarthritis is unknown although risk factors include a major injury to a joint or being overweight, both of which cause excessive mechanical strain on a joint and will contribute to the wear and tear of the articular cartilage.

There is also some evidence that suggests that injuries sustained when you are younger can lead to osteoarthritis in later life, depending on how the injury was managed in the first place.

It seems therefore that the risk factors associated with osteoarthritis are closely linked with physical activity, particularly those types where there is a risk of large or abrupt forces acting on the joints. However, the health of cartilage depends on it being used and the onset of osteoarthritis depends very much on the frequency, intensity and duration of physical activity that, if carefully managed, can have a positive effect on osteoarthritis. Exercise will increase aerobic capacity, manage weight and reduce body fat therefore reducing the mechanical strain on the joints. Regular activity will also improve joint stability by strengthening the surrounding muscles and joint mobility can also be maintained, or in some instances, improved.

APPLY IT!

Weightlifters are prone to early development of osteoarthritis of the knees due to their high body weight. Early development of osteoarthritis in the knees of some football players has been attributed to repeated trauma to ligaments, bones and cartilage. Interestingly, however, recent studies have not found an increased risk of osteoarthritis in long-distance runners. Can you suggest reasons for this?

JOINT STABILITY

Joint stability is a very important factor in lifelong involvement in physical activity because a stable joint is able to be constantly compressed and stretched without injury. On page 6, we looked at the how the shapes and depths of the articulating surfaces within a joint can contribute to its stability.

Deeper joints that have a larger surface area of connecting bone are the most stable types of joint. The ball and socket joint of the hip is particularly stable for this reason compounded by the fact that weight bearing pushes the head of the femur further into the deep socket of the acetabulum. Another factor that contributes to joint stability is ligaments. Usually, the more ligaments a joint has, the greater its stability. Consider the knee joint that has four ligaments, which work to limit mobility to flexion and extension.

Although the strength of ligaments is an advantage in increasing joint stability, it is a disadvantage in the fact that they are not very elastic, making them prone to stretching and even snapping.

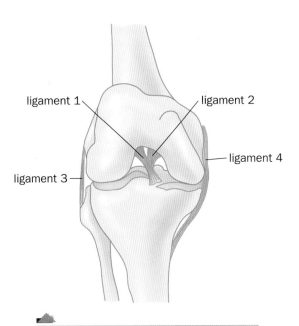

Fig 1.13 The four ligaments that give stability to the knee joint (anterior view with patella removed)

The third influence on joint stability is that caused by the location and tone of the surrounding muscles. Muscle tone is important because it helps to keep the tendons around a joint tight, adding stability to the joint. The use of muscles and tendons in joint stability is particularly important in the shoulder joint where the rotator cuff muscles add stability to the joint while the larger muscles such as the deltoid and pectoralis major provide the power for effective joint mobility. Refer to pages 19–20 to remind yourself of the muscles associated with the shoulder joint.

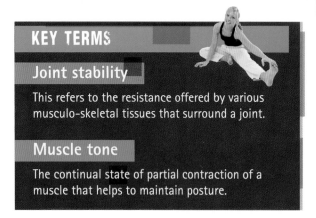

KEY TERMS

Joint stability

This refers to the resistance offered by various musculo-skeletal tissues that surround a joint.

Muscle tone

The continual state of partial contraction of a muscle that helps to maintain posture.

JOINT STABILITY AND PHYSICAL ACTIVITY

Physical activity is very important for the efficient functioning of the joint structures, especially the articular cartilage, ligaments and surrounding muscles. Exercise strengthens these structures and will lead to an increase in the stability of the joint. Without regular exercise, ligaments will shorten and become even less elastic, making them more prone to injury and muscle tone will be lost in the surrounding muscles decreasing their stabilising effect. The muscles will also shorten reducing the flexibility of the joint and increasing the chances of injury. Inactivity will also lead to a reduction in synovial fluid being released into the joint which can make the joint prone to other disorders.

However, the type of physical activity is again important as large forces exerted on a joint, such as those experienced in impact and contact sports can lead to ligament damage and dislocation of less stable joints. The knee and ankle joints are particularly at risk of ligament damage, while the shallow joint of the shoulder makes it susceptible to dislocation.

APPLY IT!

List some professional sports performers who have had to have time out of their sport due to joint damage. Analyse how their injury occurred and identify the structure within the joint that was damaged. How did this impact on the stability of the joint?

MUSCLE HEALTH:
POSTURE AND ALIGNMENT

You might remember being told by your parents to 'stand up straight' when you were young. This would have involved you using your skeletal muscles as stabilisers to maintain good posture. Posture can be thought of in terms of alignment and good posture, meaning that you can carry out physical activity with maximum efficiency and minimum risk of injury. The skeletal muscles responsible for posture tend to be centred around the trunk area and we mentioned two of them, the multifidis and the transverse abdominis on page 23. Even during rest, muscles are in a constant state of partial contraction, called *muscle tone*. The greater the muscle tone in the muscles that stabilise the trunk, the better your posture and core stability. This is important to lifelong involvement in physical activity because it prevents excess pressure being put on the lumbar spine, which causes lower back pain.

POSTURE AND PHYSICAL ACTIVITY

The right type of physical activity will improve your posture. Aerobic exercise will help to control body weight meaning less strain is put on the muscles and joints and it becomes easier to maintain the correct body alignment when standing, sitting and exercising.

Strength training or Swiss ball training will increase the muscle tone in the postural muscles of the trunk and develop core stability. This will improve the alignment of the spine and minimise the risk of lower back pain.

TASK 20

The above discussion focuses on the positive and negative factors that affect the musculo-skeletal system during different types of physical activity. For revision purposes, copy and complete the following table:

Factor affecting the musculo–skeletal system	Positive impact of physical activity and type of activity needed	Negative impact of physical activity and type of activity needed
Osteoporosis		
Growth Plate		
Osteoarthritis		
Joint Stability		
Posture and alignment		

EXAM TIP

Your examiner might ask you to critically examine or critically evaluate the impact of different types of physical activity on the skeletal or muscular system. In your answer make sure you:

- talk accurately and in detail about positive and negative factors using correct terminology
- relate these factors to different types of physical activity, e.g. contact & impact, repetitive, endurance work etc.
- mention the disorders given above as relevant examples where appropriate
- proofread your answer.

Refresh your memory

Revision checklist for the skeletal and muscular systems

You should be able to describe and explain:

The Skeleton

▷ an overview of the skeleton

Joints

▷ the different types of joint found in the body

Movements of synovial joints

▷ the anatomical position

▷ movements that relate to the following joints: wrist, elbow, radio-ulnar, shoulder, spine, hip, knee, ankle

Muscles

▷ the terms: origin, insertion, agonist, antagonist, antagonistic muscle action

▷ the major muscles associated with the main joints of the human body and explain their role as an agonist or an antagonist with reference to specific movements in physical activity

▷ full movement analysis of different types of sporting techniques

▷ the three types of muscular contraction: concentric, eccentric, isometric

▷ the three types of muscle fibre found in skeletal muscle: slow twitch, fast oxidative glycolytic and fast glycolytic

▷ the physiological benefits to skeletal muscle of a warm up and a cool down

Bone and Muscle Health

▷ factors affecting the efficiency of the musculo-skeletal system

▷ the positive and negative impact of different types of physical activity on the above conditions.

1. The shoulder, elbow, hip, knee and ankle joints, are all synovial joints:
   i.   identify the bones that articulate at each of these joints
   ii. identify the type of synovial joint located at each of these joints
2. The spine has a number of different types of joint located in its different regions. Explain this statement giving specific examples.
3. Identify the movement performed at each of the joints listed in brackets from the sporting techniques stated below:
   i.   upward phase of a sit up (spine and hip)
   ii. downward phase of a press up (shoulder and elbow)
   iii. preparation phase of a vertical jump(hip, knee, ankle)
   iv. execution phase of a top-spin forehand in tennis (shoulder, elbow, radio-ulnar)
4. Identify the agonist and antagonist muscles for each of the movements you have identified in your answer to question 3.
5. Identify, explain and give sporting examples of concentric, eccentric and isometric muscular contraction
6. What are the three types of muscle fibre found in skeletal muscle? Identify two structural and two functional differences in their characteristics.
7. Explain why elite marathon runners have a high percentage of slow twitch muscles in their gastrocnemius muscle.
8. Skeletal muscles work more efficiently if a performer caries out a warm up prior to the exercise session and a cool down afterwards. Explain this statement.
9. Describe the positive effects of exercise on preventing osteoporosis.
10. Describe the potential dangers of high impact and contact sports on the musculo-skeletal system.

Get the result!

Examination question

Taking part in physical activity is considered essential to maintaining a healthy lifestyle. However, taking part in some activities can result in injury and a reduction in activity levels.

Discuss **both** the positive and negative impact of participating in different types of physical activity on the joints and muscles of the body.   (10 marks)

- There is a lot being asked here, but you must expect this for the ten-mark question in 1e.
- The first thing to do is read the question, then read it again and pay attention to the command word – discuss.
- Now take some more time to organise your thoughts and plan your answer. Your examiner can only give you maximum marks if have covered all that is being asked
- A plan similar to one below seems sensible here:

Types of physical activity	Positive impact	Negative impact

- When you have finished your plan, check that you have enough information for all 10 marks.
- When it comes to writing your answer, make it concise (don't waffle!) and use accurate specialist vocabulary – check your spelling!
- At the end of your answer, give yourself sufficient time for proofreading.

Student answer

Types of Physical activity	Positive impact	Negative impact
low impact / endurance	builds strong, healthy bones – reduces risk of osteoporosis esp child, teens can increase health of joints: manage weight therefore less strain therefore reduced risk of osteoarthritis improve joint stability – strengthen surrounding muscles – ligaments – tendons – increased muscle tone e.g rotator cuff/knee improve posture/alignment = max eff/min injury: multifidis & transverse abdominis – increased muscle tone/core stability = reduced risk of lower back pain (Swiss ball training)	wear & tear on art cartilage = e.g. osteoarthritis
high impact	also good for osteoporosis – increases peak bone density	dangerous for osteoporosis sufferers = fracture stress fractures risk of sprains /dislocation esp less stable joints e.g. knee, ankle shoulder growth plate injuries strains / muscle tears = plyometrics
contact sports		growth plate injuries
repetitive movements		growth plate injuries wear & tear on art cartilage = osteoarthritis esp knee, hip & ankle

Examiner says:

Great plan!

Examiner says:

Concise introduction to set the scene on where the answer is heading and already shows me you know what is meant by different types of physical activity

There are many benefits to being active but certain types if physical activity can be a risk to the bones, joints and muscles. Low impact, endurance based activities seem to have the most positive effects on the skeletal and muscular systems, while high impact, contact sports cause the most potential risks.

Examiner says:

Good use of specialist vocabulary here – well done! Also like the way you have brought in high impact activity as it makes it a discussion.

Some more specialist vocabulary – good!

Regular aerobic exercise helps to build strong and healthy bones, which reduces the risk of osteoporosis in later life. This is especially the case if weight-bearing work is carried out during childhood and the early teens. However, high impact activities have a part to play here, as they can also increase the strength of bones. Endurance work also helps to manage weight, meaning that less strain is put on the joints during activity and this reduces the risk of contracting osteoarthritis. The fact that regular light exercise strengthens the skeletal muscles, ligaments and tendons, means that joint stability is increased as muscle tone has increased. This is particularly important in joints that rely on the surrounding muscles and ligaments to make them more stable, such as the shoulder joint relying on the rotator cuff muscles and the knee joint relying on the four ligaments that surround it. Performers who are at risk of injury to their shoulders and knees e.g. rugby and football players, would especially benefit from an increased joint stability in these areas. Another advantage of regular aerobic exercise is the positive effect it will have on posture and alignment. Performers with good posture can carry out sporting techniques with the maximum efficiency and the minimum risk of injury. This would be particularly important for weight lifters or performers who rely on good core stability such as gymnasts. Good posture also limits the risk of lower back pain and poor alignment of the lumbar vertebrae. Two muscles that play a major part in maintaining good core stability are the multifidis and transverse abdominis, which can be exercised using a Swiss ball.

Examiner says:

Good use of sporting example, which is just what you need to score in the top band.

Examiner says:

Great use of analysis – another important aspect of achieving max

On the other hand, performers who chose to take part regularly in high impact or contact sports are at greater risk of injury. Sudden impacts can cause fractures, sprains and dislocations. The less stable joints such as the shoulder, knee and the ankle are particularly at risk. The shoulder, being a shallow ball and socket joint, is relatively easy to dislocate while sprains at

Examiner says:

I like the way you have brought in types of muscular contraction – it's certainly relevant here

the knee and ankle joints are also common. High impact sports are especially risky in young players, whose bones are not fully matured, as there is a big risk of damage to the growth plate, which is very delicate while the bone is still growing. Performers who also carry out a lot of eccentric muscular contractions are at greater risk of muscle strains and tears, such as hurdlers and gymnasts. Another type of activity that can have a negative effect on joints is activity involving repetitive movements, which can also cause damage to the growth plate in children but will also cause wear and tear to the articular cartilage. When the articular cartilage is damaged, there is risk of contracting osteoarthritis. This is especially the case in the hip, knee and ankle joints that tend to take most of the force in all weight-bearing activities. Many old hockey and rugby players end up with osteoarthritis in one or more of their leg joints, while tennis players are more like to get this condition in their shoulder and elbow joints.

Examiner says:

Some more excellent examples!

Having weighed up the positive and negative effects of different types of physical activity on joints and muscles, it seems that the positives outweigh the negatives and an active lifestyle should be encouraged.

Examiner says:

A quick and simple way to finish

Overall this is a well structured answer. It has a brief introduction and conclusion (you need both for a discussion) and there is a paragraph related to the positive effects of exercise linked to low impact work and a paragraph related to the negative effects of exercise linked to high impact/contact and repetitive work. There is good quality of written communication throughout: an A grade answer.

CHAPTER 2

Basic concepts of biomechanics

LEARNING OBJECTIVES

At the end of this chapter you should be able to:

- understand the types of motion produced in different sporting techniques
- describe and give sporting examples of linear, angular and general motion
- apply all three of Newton's Laws of Motion to a variety sporting techniques
- understand the effect of size of force, direction of force and position of application of force on a body
- apply your knowledge of centre of mass to increasing or decreasing stability in sporting techniques
- carry out a practical analysis of typical sporting actions.

INTRODUCTION

The basic concepts of biomechanics are fundamental to all types of physical activity. You will have learned about mechanical principles that are used in our everyday lives from your GCSE science lessons, and in this chapter we will see these same principles being applied to sport.

Starting with motion and force, we will begin to understand that we need to be able to move the body in order to carry out all sporting techniques and that any movement is produced by force. We will see that all motion is governed by Newton's Laws of Motion, which give us an insight into the rules that affect movement in different types of physical activity. The effect of changes in position to a body's centre of mass will also help us to look at the mechanical principles behind stable and unstable positions in sport. A basic knowledge of these concepts of biomechanics is necessary for the analysis of movement. Once you can apply these principles with confidence to sporting techniques you will be able to suggest corrections to increase the likelihood of successful and efficient movement.

Motion

Motion is movement and is divided into three main categories:

- Linear motion
- Angular motion
- General motion.

KEY TERMS

Linear motion

When a body moves in a straight or curved line, with all its parts moving the same distance, in the same direction and at the same speed.

Angular motion

When a body or part of a body moves in a circle or part of a circle about a particular point called the axis of rotation.

General motion

A combination of linear and angular motion.

A sporting example of linear motion

LINEAR MOTION

Linear motion is motion along a line. This can be a straight line such as a performer sitting in a toboggan and travelling straight down the hill or a curved line followed by a performer lying in the skeleton bob event, as they slide around the corners of the downhill track. The flight path followed by the shot put after the point of release is another example of linear motion in a curved line.

ANGULAR MOTION

To produce angular motion, the movement must occur around a fixed point or axis, e.g. a bicycle wheel turning about its axle or a door opening on its hinges. When we apply this concept to the human body we often talk of athletes spinning, circling, turning and somersaulting, which implies that the athlete or part of the athlete is moving through a circle or part of a circle about a particular point. A good example of this is the circles produced by a female gymnast on the uneven bars or a male gymnast on the high bar.

However, more obvious examples of angular motion are the movements of our limbs because they move around our joints, which are fixed points and provide the axis of rotation. A good example of this can be seen in the arm action of front crawl. During one stroke cycle the arm moves a complete circle about the axis of rotation – the shoulder joint.

A sporting example of angular motion

REMEMBER

There are many actions in sport that occur as a result of the angular motion of our joints imparting linear motion to a ball, e.g. throwing a ball into the stumps when fielding in cricket or hitting a rounders ball.

Fig 2.1 Linear motion of a shot put – a curved line

EXAM TIP

When giving examples of pure linear or pure angular motion you must be very careful that the movement you have identified does not involve both these types of motion, because this is termed 'general motion'.

A sporting example of general motion

GENERAL MOTION

Most movements in sport are a combination of linear and angular motion. The approach run of a javelin thrower shows general motion. During the approach the javelin and the torso of the athlete are showing linear motion by moving in a straight line. However, the arms and legs of the athlete are showing angular motion as the non-throwing arm rotates around part of a circle about the shoulder joint, the upper legs about the hip joints, the lower legs about the knee joints and the feet about the ankle joints.

A second example of general motion is a wheelchair athlete. The body of the athlete and his chair are displaying linear motion as they move along the track, but the swinging action of the athlete's arms and the turning of the chair's wheels exhibit angular motion.

TASK 1

With a partner identify other sporting examples of:

a) pure linear motion
b) pure angular motion and
c) general motion.

Make sure you can explain why they are each type of motion.

A sporting example of general motion

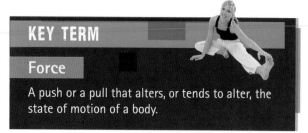

KEY TERM

Force

A push or a pull that alters, or tends to alter, the state of motion of a body.

TASK 2

Complete a table similar to the one above to show the five effects a force can have in a sport of your choice.

Force

A force can perform the following functions:

- Cause a body at rest to move
- Cause a moving body to change direction, accelerate or decelerate
- Change an object's shape.

Let's use a kick from the penalty spot in football to give a sporting example of the effects of a force described below.

The extent to which the forces have the effects mentioned above depends on where the force is applied and the size and direction of the applied force. The size and direction of the force will obviously affect the change of motion and this will be explained further when we look at Newton's Laws of Motion. The line of application of the force will also affect the subsequent motion and this is better looked at when we have an understanding of the centre of mass (pages 52–55).

Newton's laws of motion

You will now have noticed the direct link between motion and force, which can simply be stated

Effect of force	Example from a penalty kick in football
A force can cause a body at rest to move	The football will remain at rest on the penalty spot until the force of the footballer's boot on the ball causes it to move.
A force can cause a moving body to change direction	If the ball is travelling towards the goal and the goalkeeper makes a save, the force exerted by the hands of the goalkeeper will push the ball away in the opposite direction.
A force can cause a moving body to accelerate	Consider the penalty taker when they are approaching the ball. After initially starting to move, he can accelerate towards the ball by applying a larger force on the ground.
A force can cause a moving body to decelerate	If the kick is successful, the force of the net at the back of the goal on the ball will cause it to slow down. Likewise, is the goalkeeper catches the ball, the force of his hands on the ball will cause it to stop moving.
A force can cause a body to change its shape	At the point where the player's boot contacts the ball, the ball will be slightly deformed and no longer truly spherical. Likewise, the force of the ball on the net will cause the net to change shape.

Table 1

as 'Without force, there can be no motion.' This close relationship is explained by *Newton's Laws of Motion*, which govern the characteristics of all motion in sport.

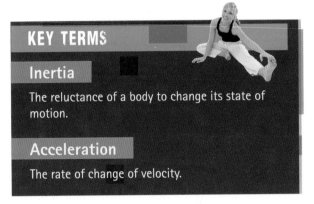

KEY TERMS

Inertia
The reluctance of a body to change its state of motion.

Acceleration
The rate of change of velocity.

EXAM TIP

At AS, your examiners will not require you to recount Newton's Laws perfectly, but they will want you to be able to apply each of them to various types of physical activity and sporting techniques. So, remember that practice makes perfect and start thinking about Newton's Laws every time you step onto the pitch, court or track.

NEWTON'S FIRST LAW OF MOTION
This is often termed the 'Law of Inertia' and states that:

'A body continues in a state of rest or uniform velocity unless acted upon by an external force.'

Let's consider the example of the penalty kick in football again. A body (the football) continues in a state of rest (on the penalty spot) unless acted upon by an external force (the force of the footballer's boot).

NEWTON'S SECOND LAW OF MOTION
This is often termed the 'Law of Acceleration' and states that:

'When a force acts on an object, the rate of change of momentum experienced by the object is proportional to the size of the force and takes place in the direction in which the force acts.'

Again, consider the football during a penalty kick. When a force acts on an object (the force of the footballer's boot on the ball) the rate of change of momentum experienced by the object (the acceleration of the football) is proportional to the size of the force (the ball will accelerate faster with a more powerful kick) and takes place in the direction in which the force acts (the ball accelerates towards the goal).

NEWTON'S THIRD LAW OF MOTION
This states that:

'For every action there is an equal and opposite reaction.'

In other words, whenever an object exerts a force on another, there will be an equal and opposite reaction exerted by the second on the first.

Once again, consider the football during the penalty kick as it hits the cross bar. For every action (the force of the ball hitting the cross bar) there is an equal and opposite reaction force (the cross bar exerts an equal force to the opposite direction to rebound the ball away from the goal).

APPLY IT!

Apply each of Newton's Laws to two other sporting activities.

The footballer is about to put all three of Newton's Laws of Motion into practice

Centre of mass

The mass of a body is the amount of material of which it is made, so it is quite easy to say that a shot put will have a greater mass than a football, as it is solid and therefore made from more as well as heavier material. The centre of mass of a body is the point where all of its mass could be considered to be concentrated.

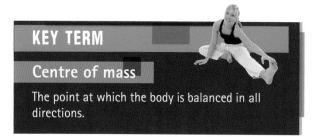

> ## KEY TERM
>
> ### Centre of mass
>
> The point at which the body is balanced in all directions.

In uniform symmetrical objects in which the mass is evenly distributed, the centre of mass is found at the geometrical centre of that object, e.g. a shot put or a discus. At this point, half of the mass is above and half is below, half the mass is in front and half is behind, half the mass is to the left and half is to the right of the centre of mass. However, centre of mass is not always as simple to locate, as it is an imaginary point that can lie outside the body. Consider a tennis ball – its centre of mass will be at its centre which is in the middle of its empty inside!

In the human body, the centre of mass is not a fixed point located in a specific part of the body. Its location will vary depending on body position and, as we will see, it can also be a point outside the actual body. This is because athletes' bodies are not uniform symmetrical shapes with mass evenly distributed from head to foot. They are made up of bone, muscle, fat and tissue, all of which vary in mass.

To complicate things further, athletes demonstrate a considerable range of body positions. In the simplest situation: an athlete standing upright with arms by his sides, the centre of mass for a male is about two to three centimetres above the navel and for a female it is slightly lower. This is because, in general, males tend to have more body mass concentrated in their shoulders and upper body whereas females tend to have more concentrated at their hips. As soon as the athlete moves from this symmetrical position, their centre of mass also shifts, meaning that an athlete's centre of mass rarely stays in the same position for very long. If the athlete raises his arms, the centre of mass will be higher to ensure that the body remains balanced in all directions from it. If the athlete raises his arms while holding a barbell the centre of mass will be raised even further as a majority of the mass is now concentrated at the top of the body.

In extreme body shapes such as a good pike jump in trampolining or a bridge in gymnastics, the centre of mass is a point that lies outside the body. In the case of a trampolinist, the athlete's arms and legs have moved so far forward that the centre of mass has also had to move forward so much that it has temporarily moved outside the body. Fig 2.2 on page 53 shows how the position of the centre of mass can change with body position.

> ## TASK 3
>
> Find some action pictures from the sports pages of newspapers or BBC sport online and identify the position of the athlete's centre of mass in each case.

> ## TAKE IT FURTHER
>
> The Fosbury flop technique in high jump is an extreme body shape involving considerable extension of the spine and hip joints. What do you think happens to the body's centre of mass in this position? Research the reasons why this technique was adopted by elite high jumpers after it was first seen by Dick Fosbury, who won an Olympic gold medal with it in 1968.

Fig 2.2 Locating an athlete's centre of mass

The Fosbury flop in high jumping

STABILITY

An athlete who is kneeling on all fours is more stable than an athlete who is standing on one foot because the first will require a greater force to tip them over.

Stability is important in sport as a stable body position will enable an athlete to resist motion, whereas an unstable one will enable an athlete to go into action. The stability of an athlete is determined by a number of mechanical principles that depend on the following:

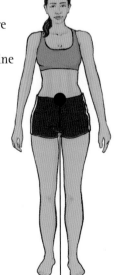

- position of athlete's centre of mass
- position of the athlete's line of gravity
- size of the athlete's area of support.

Fig 2.3 Athlete showing the position of their centre of mass and line of gravity

KEY TERMS

Stability

Relates to how difficult it is to disturb a body from a balanced position.

Line of gravity

A line extending from the centre of mass vertically down to the ground.

APPLY IT!

On a sheet of landscape A4 paper, draw a stability continuum similar to the one below:

←——————————————————————→

UNSTABLE   LESS STABLE   STABLE

Write on it as many sporting techniques you can think of from any sports of your choice but make sure you can justify your answers.

TASK 4

With a partner, complete the activities outlined below.

1. Ask a partner to take up the following stances:
   (a) standing with feet apart, one in front of the other
   (b) standing with feet together
   (c) kneeling on all fours, with knees and hands spread
   (d) standing with feet together on tip toe
   (e) standing in a stalk stand
   (f) standing with feet apart to the sides.
2. For each of the positions, push your partner with a consistent force:
   (a) from the side
   (b) from behind
   (c) from in front.
3. Stand with the backs of your shoulders, hips and heels against a flat wall. Bend forwards and try to touch your toes with your hands. Discuss your findings with a partner.
4. Discuss your findings with the rest of your class and try to write down the principles that influence stability under the following headings:
   - the position of the athlete's centre of mass
   - the athlete's base of support
   - the position of the athlete's line of gravity.

RELATIONSHIP BETWEEN CENTRE OF MASS AND APPLICATION OF FORCE

The direction of the application of a force in relation to the centre of mass will determine whether the subsequent motion of a body is linear or angular.

Linear motion: To generate linear motion, the line of action of the force passes through the body's centre of mass. For example, when an athlete performs a vertical jump they apply an action force on the ground with their legs, which applies a reaction force that passes directly through the athlete's centre of mass. This enables the athlete to jump straight up and straight down again with their centre of mass following a linear path. A force that passes through the centre of mass of a body is called a *direct force*.

Angular motion: To generate angular motion, the line of action of the force passes outside the body's centre of mass. For example, when an athlete performs a forward somersault on the trampoline, they pike slightly at the hips bringing their centre of mass forward. They then apply a force on the bed so the reaction force passes behind his centre of mass causing them to rotate forwards. A force that passes outside the centre of mass of a body is called an *eccentric force*.

KEY TERMS

Direct force

A force whose line of application passes through the centre of mass of a body causing the resulting motion to be linear.

Eccentric force

A force whose line of application passes outside the centre of mass of a body causing the resulting motion to be angular.

TAKE IT FURTHER

Some performers can change the speed of their angular motion. For example, a spinning skater can be seen to speed up the rate of spin or slow it down by altering body shape. Briefly research how they do this and suggest examples from other sports that use this mechanical principle.

TASK 5

1. Throw a tennis ball into the air without it spinning. Try to get the ball to travel straight up and down so that it demonstrates linear motion. Draw a diagram to show the ball's centre of mass, the point of application of the force and the direction in which the force acts. What is the scientific name given to the force resulting in linear motion?

2. Throw the same tennis ball into the air but this time try to get to spin so that it demonstrates angular motion. Draw a diagram to show the ball's centre of mass, the point of application of the force and the direction in which the force acts. What is the scientific name given to the force resulting in angular motion?

3. Throw the tennis ball into the air a few more times but try to vary the amount of spin the ball displays. Suggest what you must do in order to get the maximum amount of spin.

ExamCafé

Relax, refresh, result!

Refresh your memory

Revision checklist for basic concepts of biomechanics

You should be able to describe, explain and give sporting examples of:

▷ Linear, angular and general motion.

▷ The effect of size, direction and position of application of force on a body.

▷ Newton's Laws of Motion.

▷ The term centre of mass and its relationship to stability and type of motion produced.

▷ A practical analysis of physical actions using your knowledge of the above.

REVISE AS YOU GO!

1. Define linear, angular and general motion and give a sporting example for each type.
2. Define force and list four effects that a force can have on a body. Apply each of these four effects to a sporting example.
3. Apply each of Newton's Laws of Motion to a sporting example of your choice.
4. What do you understand by the terms centre of mass and line of gravity?
5. Why is the position of the centre of mass higher in males than females?
6. Explain how the position of the centre of mass can lie outside the mass of a body and give examples from sport of when this is the case.
7. List four factors that affect the stability of a body. Give sporting examples of a stable position and an unstable position.
8. Explain the relationship between centre of mass and force in producing (a) linear motion and (b) angular motion
9. Explain why a handstand is a more demanding balance than a headstand.
10. Describe the varying degrees of stability on a performer carrying out the three stages of a sprint start, 'on your marks', 'set', 'bang!'

Get the result!

Examination question

Centre of mass is an important basic concept of Biomechanics.

What do you understand by the term centre of mass? Using appropriate examples from sporting techniques, explain how changes in the position of a body's centre of mass can affect its stability.   (5)

examiner's tips

- There are two parts to this question so make sure you know what the command word is for both.
- In the first part, you are asked a simple 'what', meaning that a brief definition or description will do for the answer.
- In the second part you are asked to 'explain using examples', so make sure you do both!
- Now check what subject area you are being asked about – centre of mass and its link to stability.
- Then, before you begin, check the number of marks available – 5, and work out how many may be awarded for each part of the question. It seems sensible to assume that more marks will be awarded for an explanation, so think 1 and 4.

Student answer

Centre of mass is the point at which the body is balanced in all directions. In uniform objects, such as shot put it is found in the very middle.

Centre of mass is important in sport as its position can cause a performer to be very stable or very unstable. A low centre of mass makes a person more stable, while a high centre of mass makes them less stable. The more stable a person is, the harder they are to push over and the bigger the force required to make them unstable. An example of this is the position that rugby forwards take up in a scrum. They want to make themselves as stable as possible so that it requires a very large force from their opponents to move them backwards. To do this, they make their centre of mass as

Examiner says:

Simple, accurate and concise definition – well done!

Examiner says:

Good use of sporting examples, which is what the question is asking you to do.

Examiner says:

You have shown a good understanding of the theory being asked here and have got straight to the point without waffle – excellent!

Examiner says:

Great use of analysis and application of knowledge.

low as possible and their area of support as wide as possible. If their line of gravity is close to the centre of their base of support, they will also increase their stability. Other examples of stable positions in sport are the "on your marks' position in a sprint start and the stance taken up by sumo wrestlers!

Unstable positions come about by having a higher centre of mass, a smaller area of support and a line of gravity that is close to or falls outside the area of the base of support. There are lots of times in sport when a performer wants to adopt an unstable position as it allows them to move off quickly. For example, the "set" position in a sprint start, where the centre of mass is raised and the line of gravity has moved to the very front of the base of support. Swerving, side-stepping and dodging are other examples of when a performer would benefit from being unstable.

Examiner says:

Some more practical examples and good analysis here.

Examiner says:

This is a thorough, accurate and concise answer with plenty of sporting examples – an A grade answer.

The cardiovascular and respiratory systems

Response of the cardiovascular (heart) system to physical activity

INTRODUCTION

This is the first part of a three-part chapter entitled 'The Cardiovascular and Respiratory Systems in relation to the performance of physical activity and sustained involvement in an active and healthy lifestyle', which is subdivided into three distinct, but closely connected, parts:

- Part I: Cardiovascular (Heart) system
- Part II: Cardiovascular (Vascular) system
- Part III: Respiratory system.

LEARNING OBJECTIVES

Parts I, II and III

At the end of all three parts you should be able to describe and explain the:

- response of the cardiovascular (heart) system to physical activity
- response of the cardiovascular (vascular) system to physical activity
- response of the respiratory system to physical activity.

Part I

At the end of Part I you should be able to:

- describe the link between the cardiac cycle and the conduction system of the heart
- describe the relationship between stroke volume, heart rate and cardiac output, and resting values for each
- explain the changes that take place to stroke volume, heart rate and cardiac output during different intensities of physical activity
- explain the regulation of heart rate during physical activity.

The chapter assumes prior knowledge of the structure and function of the cardiovascular and respiratory systems. Assumed knowledge, indicated by (AK), is included for those who have not studied GCSE Physical Education, but it will not be directly examined.

Aerobic system – an overview

Exercise that relies predominantly on the supply and use of oxygen to supply the energy for prolonged performance is termed 'endurance' or 'aerobic' work. The aerobic system which provides the energy for this prolonged work consists of three distinct body systems: the heart, vascular and respiratory systems. These three systems closely interact to ensure a constant distribution of oxygen around the body, particularly to the muscles during exercise.

KEY TERMS

Aerobic

A process taking place in the presence of oxygen.

Anaerobic

A process taking place with insufficient oxygen.

APPLY IT!

The marathon, and long distance cycling are clear examples of aerobic exercise requiring a good supply of oxygen, but less obvious are sports with different positions/roles. Midfield players in sports like football, hockey, or the centre in netball to a lesser extent, can be termed aerobic as they require performers to run for prolonged periods, whereas forwards, and hockey or netball goalkeepers predominantly sprint or jump – activities which are dependent on energy supply with insufficient oxygen – and conversely termed anaerobic work.

So why do we need an understanding of the structure and function of the cardiovascular/respiratory systems?

REQUIREMENTS

An athlete's aerobic capacity – the ability to supply and use oxygen to provide the energy for prolonged periods – is limited by the efficiency of the three aerobic systems: heart, vascular and respiratory. Put simply, an athlete with a low aerobic capacity will be less able to supply sufficient oxygen/energy for their muscles to run, cycle or swim during predominantly aerobic sports or physical activity.

Fig. 3.1.1 shows the interaction between these three body systems. Remember, during exercise, the primary aim of the aerobic system is to ensure our working muscles have an adequate supply of oxygen to supply the energy for prolonged performance.

EXAM TIP

Examination questions about the close interaction between heart, vascular and respiratory systems very often require you to combine information from the three systems represented in Fig. 3.1.1, particularly the heart and vascular system.

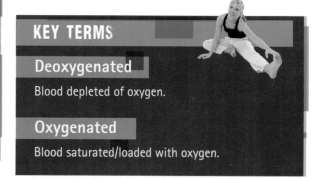

KEY TERMS

Deoxygenated

Blood depleted of oxygen.

Oxygenated

Blood saturated/loaded with oxygen.

TASK 1

1. Alone, select your two practical activities and decide if you think they are in general, predominantly aerobic or anaerobic or a close mixture of each.

2. Now think about your position, role or event and consider if this is any different from 1. Discuss/compare your responses with your peers.

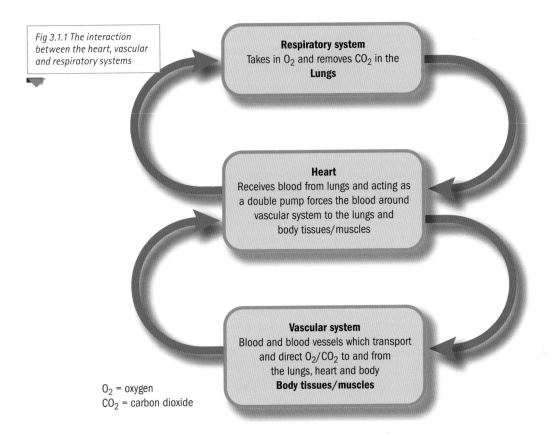

Fig 3.1.1 The interaction between the heart, vascular and respiratory systems

Respiratory system
Takes in O_2 and removes CO_2 in the **Lungs**

Heart
Receives blood from lungs and acting as a double pump forces the blood around vascular system to the lungs and body tissues/muscles

Vascular system
Blood and blood vessels which transport and direct O_2/CO_2 to and from the lungs, heart and body
Body tissues/muscles

O_2 = oxygen
CO_2 = carbon dioxide

Review of heart structure and function

(AK = assumed knowledge)

You will have learned about heart structure and function in your KS4 study. However, the following sections will help you review your knowledge so that you can describe and explain the events of the cardiac cycle, linked to the conduction system of the heart.

Skeletal muscles require a good supply of oxygen to supply the energy to perform physical activity. Fig. 3.1.1 shows that blood vessels of the vascular system transport the oxygen in the blood away from the heart, but where does the force or pressure to circulate the blood around the body come from? This is the primary function of the heart.

The heart acts as a 'dual action pump' – two separate pumps that work simultaneously to pump blood to two different destinations. The right side pumps deoxygenated blood (indicated below in blue) towards the lungs and the left side pumps oxygenated blood (indicated below in blue) towards the rest of the body – see Fig. 3.1.2.

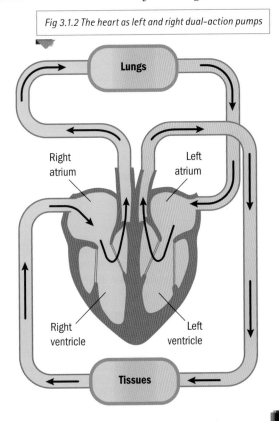

Fig 3.1.2 The heart as left and right dual-action pumps

Lungs

Right atrium

Left atrium

Right ventricle

Left ventricle

Tissues

EXAM TIP

You will not be required to draw a detailed diagram of the heart – a simple sketch of Fig. 3.1.2 will suffice.

Before we look further at how the heart works as a dual pump, it is essential to have a basic knowledge of its structure in order to describe, understand and explain how it functions.

The heart is located within the thoracic cavity, underneath the ribs of the chest, and is the approximate size of a clenched fist. Clench your right fist and place your extended thumb on top of your sternum. Your fist represents the approximate size and location of your heart just left of centre.

INTERNAL/EXTERNAL STRUCTURE OF THE HEART (AK)

CHAMBERS OF THE HEART

The heart consists of two pumps, separated by a muscular wall called the septum. The left and right pumps each consist of two chambers, an atrium and a ventricle, which make up the four chambers of the heart.

The left and right atria are the upper, low-pressure chambers that principally collect and store blood before pumping it below into the left and right ventricles. Having only to pump blood directly below, to the ventricles, the muscular walls of the atria are relatively thin compared with those of the ventricles.

The left and right ventricles are the lower, high-pressure chambers that generate the force/pressure required to pump blood around the whole body. The greater force generated requires a greater contraction, therefore the muscular walls of ventricles are thicker than the atria walls. Similarly, the right ventricle only pumps blood to the lungs, whereas the left ventricle pumps blood around the whole body and consequently the left ventricle has a thicker muscular wall than the right one.

HEART VALVES

Four one-way valves are situated within the heart and function to:

- control the forward direction of blood flow through the heart
- prevent the backflow of blood within the heart chambers.

Two atrioventricular (AV) valves separate the atria from the ventricles. The right AV valve is called the tricuspid valve and the left AV valve, the bicuspid valve. The two remaining valves are called the semilunar (SL) valves. The right SL valve is called the pulmonary valve, and exits the right ventricle into the pulmonary artery. The left SL valve, called the aortic valve, exits the left ventricle into the aorta – see Fig. 3.1.3.

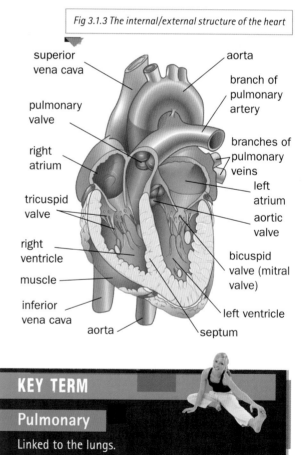

Fig 3.1.3 The internal/external structure of the heart

superior vena cava

aorta

branch of pulmonary artery

pulmonary valve

right atrium

branches of pulmonary veins

left atrium

aortic valve

tricuspid valve

right ventricle

bicuspid valve (mitral valve)

muscle

inferior vena cava

aorta

left ventricle

septum

KEY TERM

Pulmonary

Linked to the lungs.

BLOOD VESSELS OF THE HEART (AK)

The heart interacts with the blood vessels of the vascular system to transport blood to and from the heart. These blood vessels are more easily remembered by learning how they link with the internal structures of the heart. The points below show which blood vessels (in bold) transport blood to/from the internal structures of the heart.

1. **Superior/inferior vena cava** – deoxygenated blood from body to right atrium.
2. **Pulmonary artery** – deoxygenated blood from the right ventricle to the lungs.
3. **Pulmonary veins** (x 4) – oxygenated blood from lungs to the left atrium.
4. **Aorta** – oxygenated blood from left ventricle to whole body.

The heart wall is made of cardiac muscle and, like skeletal muscle, requires a good supply of blood oxygen to and from the heart for it to function as a pump. The blood vessels supplying oxygenated blood to the heart are called coronary arteries, and blood vessels removing deoxygenated blood are called coronary veins.

The coronary circulation follows on from the aorta in number 4 above:

5. **Coronary arteries** – left and right branches from the aorta encircle and supply the heart muscle with oxygen and glucose.
6. **Coronary veins** – alongside the coronary arteries, drain deoxygenated blood directly back into the right atrium via the coronary sinus.

TASK 2

1. Suggest reasons why the heart never fatigues.
2. Does the heart work aerobically or anaerobically?

TASK 3

Imagine you are a red blood cell returning to the aorta from the superior/inferior vena cava. Describe the structural features you pass through on route. Include where you are and what you are carrying.

HEART'S CONDUCTION SYSTEM LINKED TO THE CARDIAC CYCLE

Now that you have reviewed the structural features of the heart, it is time to look at how the heart functions as a dual action pump. You will have a basic understanding from KS4 that each individual pump of the heart represents one heartbeat, but the more technical term used is the cardiac cycle, i.e. the mechanical events of one heartbeat. However, because the heart generates its own electrical impulse to control these mechanical events, we need to consider the electrical conduction system first.

KEY TERM

Cardiac cycle

Events of one heart beat.

CONDUCTION SYSTEM

The electrical impulse responsible for stimulating the heart to contract is called the cardiac impulse. The heart is said to be myogenic – it generates its own electrical impulse. Figure 3.1.4 shows the location of the structures involved in the conduction system, and the path of the cardiac impulse through the heart. Follow this path with the numbers below that correspond to those in Fig. 3.1.4.

The cardiac impulse is initiated from the sino-atrial (SA) node (1) located in the posterior wall of the right atrium and is often termed the pacemaker. The impulse travels through the left and right atrial walls (2) causing both atria to contract. The ventricles are insulated from the atria and cannot be stimulated at this point. The cardiac impulse reaches and activates the AV node (3) in the right atrium which passes the impulse down into the Bundle of His (4) located within the septum of heart.

The AV node actually helps delay the impulse allowing the contraction of the atria to finish before the ventricles begin to contract. The Bundle of His splits into left and right branches

(5) and spreads the impulse down to the bottom of the heart and then up and around the walls of both the ventricles' walls via a network of Purkinje fibres (6), causing both ventricles to contract. The ventricles relax and the cycle is repeated with the next cardiac impulse initiated from the SA node.

EXAM TIP

You will be required to sketch a diagram to summarise the structures and route of the cardiac impulse.

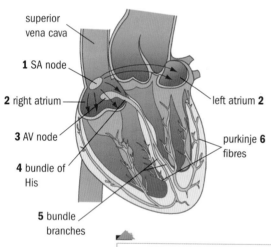

- superior vena cava
- **1** SA node
- **2** right atrium
- left atrium **2**
- **3** AV node
- purkinje **6** fibres
- **4** bundle of His
- **5** bundle branches

Fig 3.1.4 Structures involved in the conduction of the cardiac impulse

TASK 4

1. Sketch a diagram of the heart and label its four chambers.
2. Draw and number (in order) the structures involved in conducting the cardiac impulse through the heart – use arrows to represent the route.
3. Complete a bulleted flow table alongside your diagram relating the information in the above text to the corresponding numbers in your diagram.

CARDIAC CYCLE

The cardiac cycle represents the mechanical events of one heartbeat. At rest, one complete cycle lasts 0.8 seconds and is repeated approximately 72 times a minute. The cardiac cycle consists of two phases that represent the contraction and relaxation of the heart muscle.

1. **Diastole**: lasting 0.5 seconds, represents the relaxation phase.
2. **Systole**: lasting 0.3 seconds, represents the contraction phase.

Figure 3.1.5 summarises the phases and sequence of events occurring during the cardiac cycle.

REMEMBER

The events during the cardiac cycle occur simultaneously – what takes place on the right is occurring at the same time on the left side of the heart.

TASK 5

Complete a more detailed flow diagram to indicate and describe where the conduction system in Task 4 intersects the cardiac cycle flow diagram on page 65.

EXAM TIP

You will be required to link the conduction system to the events of the cardiac cycle as required in Task 5.

KEY TERMS

Bradycardia

A resting heart rate (HR) below 60.

Hypertrophy

Increase in size of heart muscle wall.

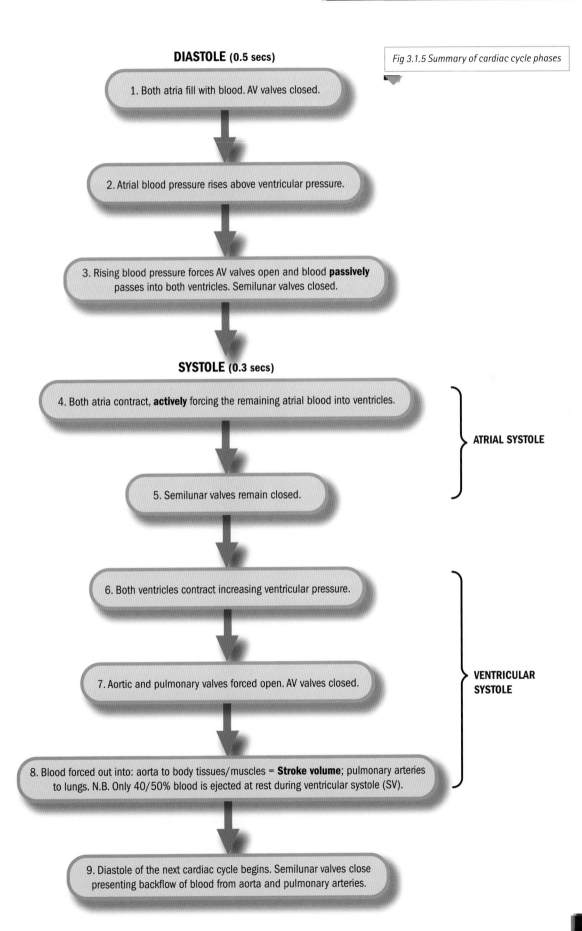

DIASTOLE (0.5 secs)

1. Both atria fill with blood. AV valves closed.

2. Atrial blood pressure rises above ventricular pressure.

3. Rising blood pressure forces AV valves open and blood **passively** passes into both ventricles. Semilunar valves closed.

SYSTOLE (0.3 secs)

4. Both atria contract, **actively** forcing the remaining atrial blood into ventricles.

5. Semilunar valves remain closed.

ATRIAL SYSTOLE

6. Both ventricles contract increasing ventricular pressure.

7. Aortic and pulmonary valves forced open. AV valves closed.

VENTRICULAR SYSTOLE

8. Blood forced out into: aorta to body tissues/muscles = **Stroke volume**; pulmonary arteries to lungs. N.B. Only 40/50% blood is ejected at rest during ventricular systole (SV).

9. Diastole of the next cardiac cycle begins. Semilunar valves close presenting backflow of blood from aorta and pulmonary arteries.

Fig 3.1.5 Summary of cardiac cycle phases

Relationship and resting values: heart rate, stroke volume and cardiac output

We have previously identified the primary function of the heart as a dual action pump. But how can we measure its performance and ability to pump and circulate blood around the body? Simple, measure its output – how much blood the heart pumps out per minute. The output of blood is calculated by measuring both the heart rate and volume of blood pumped with each heartbeat (stroke volume). Knowledge of how the heart rate and stroke volume interact is vital in measuring the performance of the heart and in identifying how its adaptations to sustained physical activity can lead to a more healthy lifestyle. Let us now look at them in more detail.

HEART RATE (HR)

HR represents the number of times the heart ventricles beat in one minute. The average resting HR is 70–72 beats per minute (bpm). Your approximate maximal HR is calculated by subtracting your age from 220.

$$220 - \text{Age} = \text{Max HR}$$

A low resting HR may indicate a high level of aerobic/endurance fitness and highly trained endurance athletes have been reported to have a HR as low as 28bpm. A resting HR below 60 is termed bradycardia, meaning slow HR; it is due to an increase in stroke volume due to its long term adaptation 'hypertrophy' – an increase in size of the heart muscle wall.

KEY TERM

Stroke volume

Blood ejected from heart ventricles every beat.

STROKE VOLUME

When we looked at the cardiac cycle, we observed that ventricular systole provides the force required to pump blood out of each ventricle. The volume of blood ejected each time a ventricle contracts is called the stroke volume (SV). In other words, SV is the difference in the volume of blood in the ventricle, before and after ventricle contraction.

TAKE IT FURTHER

The following terms are used to measure SV and will help to extend your knowledge:

End-diastolic volume (EDV) – before contraction, refers to the volume of blood in the ventricle at the end of the relaxation/filling phase.

End-systolic volume (ESV) – after contraction, refers to the volume of blood remaining in the ventricles at the end of contraction phase.

The average resting values for EDV and ESV show how we can calculate the average resting stroke volume as 70 millilitres (ml), about half a glass of wine – see Figure 3.1.6.

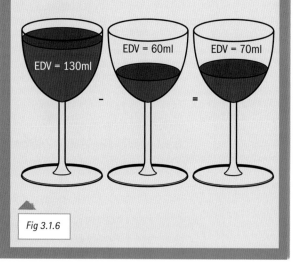

EDV = 130ml   EDV = 60ml   EDV = 70ml

Fig 3.1.6

TASK 6

If we know the average resting HR is 70–72bpm and SV is 70ml we can calculate a third volume by multiplying the above two figures. Calculate this figure and attempt to give a definition to describe this volume.

CARDIAC OUTPUT

If you have understood the relationship between SV and HR, your definition should read something like: the volume of blood ejected by the heart ventricles in one minute.

This is called your cardiac output (Q) and if you calculated the task above correctly you should already know the average resting value is around 5 litres per minute (L/min).

The relationship between Q, SV and HR is summarised as follows:

$$Q = SV \times HR$$
$$(L/min) = (ml\ per\ beat) \times (beats\ per\ min)$$

TASK 7

If an athlete has a resting Q of 5L/min, but a resting HR of 60, what is their resting SV? Suggest reasons to explain why SV has increased.

REMEMBER

1000ml = 1L. When calculating blood volumes, always present figures of 1000ml and above in L/min, especially when referring to Q.

SV, HR and Q response to different intensities of physical activity

In the last section we looked at SV, HR and Q at rest, but what happens to them during exercise? When an athlete begins to cycle or run, their breathing rate quickens, increasing their oxygen consumption in response to the increasing demand for oxygen by the working muscles. It is the role of the heart to increase its output in order to boost the rate at which oxygen is delivered to the working muscles.

Having identified that Q is a product of SV and HR, we now need to understand how they respond to meet the increasing demand for oxygen, during physical activity. Refer to the appropriate graph as you read through the following sections to help you understand the response of SV, HR and Q to exercise.

KEY TERM

Sub maximal

Exercise performed at an intensity below an athlete's maximal aerobic capacity or max VO_2 – hence it represents aerobic work.

TASK 8

1. Interpret the information in the table below.
2. Suggest reasons as to how and why HR decreases and SV increases in a trained athlete compared to a untrained athlete.

Definition	Number of ventricular contractions in one minute	Volume of blood ejected from heart in one ventricular contraction (beat)	Volume blood ejected from the heart ventricles in one minute
Untrained	70bpm	70/72ml	5000ml (5 litres)
Trained	50bpm	100ml	5000ml (5 litres)

Table 1

STROKE VOLUME RESPONSE TO EXERCISE

When an athlete starts running, their SV increases linearly as their running speed/intensity increases, but only up to 40–60% of their maximal running speed. After this point, SV values reach a plateau and this suggests that maximal SV values are reached during sub-maximal exercise (40–60%). SV increases from values around 70–80ml per beat at rest to maximal values of around 120–140ml per beat during exercise – see Figure 3.1.7.

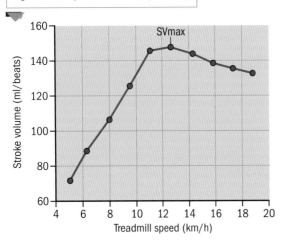

Fig 3.1.7 SV response to increasing intensity

The wine glass analogy will help you understand how SV increases – see Figure 3.1.8.

REMEMBER

Only 40–50% of the End Diastolic Volume is actually pumped out at rest – the remainder acts as a reserve volume which, during exercise, is utilised to increase SV and therefore Q.

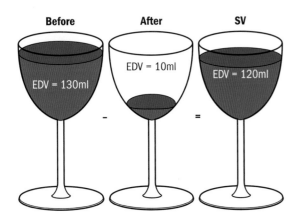

To understand why SV increases, we need to identify the factors that determine it. Put simply, SV is determined by the heart's ability to fill and empty at each beat.

1. The heart's ability to fill is dependent upon:
    *   venous return – SV primarily increases due to an increase in blood returning to the heart (venous return)
    *   the ventricles' ability to stretch further and enlarge.

    Together, these increase the filling capacity of the heart and hence the EDV.

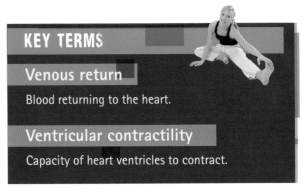

KEY TERMS

Venous return

Blood returning to the heart.

Ventricular contractility

Capacity of heart ventricles to contract.

2. The heart's capacity to empty is dependent upon:
    *   a greater EDV provides a greater stretch on the heart walls.
    *   a greater stretch increases the force of ventricular systole (contraction of ventricles).

Together this increases ventricular contractility which almost completely empties the blood from the ventricles, whereas, only 40–50% of the blood in the ventricles is pumped out at rest. At rest, venous return is lower and therefore less filling and emptying takes place.

Let us continue the example of the runner above. If the runner increases their running speed towards their maximal exercise intensity level, above 40–60%, they will need to increase their Q further. However, their SV has already reached its plateau (maximal value) during sub-maximal work, so what happens to allow Q to increase further?

Fig 3.1.8 SV average during exercise

REMEMBER

Q is made up of SV x HR. Hence, any further increase in Q must be due to a further increase in HR.

TASK 9

1. Suggest reasons to explain why:
   a) SV reaches maximal values during sub-maximal work, and
   b) SV may even decrease as heart rate increases towards maximal levels.
   Refer back to the timing of the cardiac cycle and see if this helps your reasoning.
2. Compare Fig. 3.1.6 with Fig. 3.1.8. Describe the changes in EDV, ESV and SV from rest to during exercise conditions. What are the benefits of an increased SV in regard to improving aerobic performance?

KEY TERM

Oxygen debt

Additional oxygen consumption during recovery, above that usually required when at rest.

HEART RATE RESPONSE TO EXERCISE

Before, during and after exercise HR is continually changing, but it may do any of the following depending upon the exercise undertaken (see Fig. 3.1.9, which shows HR response to both sub-maximal and maximal exercise):

A Increase well above resting values even before exercise is started. This is termed the anticipatory rise and is a result of the early release of adrenalin which stimulates the SA node to increase HR.
B Increase as exercise intensity increases.
C Increase with intensity but slow down just prior to maximal HR values.
D Decrease as exercise intensity decreases.
E Increase with intensity, but reach a plateau during sub-maximal work and represent the optimal steady state HR for meeting the demand for oxygen at that specific intensity of work.

If you are out running and you can happily chat away to your running partner, you are likely to be running at a sub-maximal steady state. However, any further increase or decrease in intensity, such as running up a hill, will require a new steady state HR.

F Decrease rapidly, immediately after exercise stops due to a decrease in the demand for oxygen by the working muscles.
G Gradually and more slowly decrease, but still remain elevated, towards resting values, to allow the body to recover – termed the oxygen debt.
H A much slower and longer recovery towards resting values due to a greater oxygen debt.

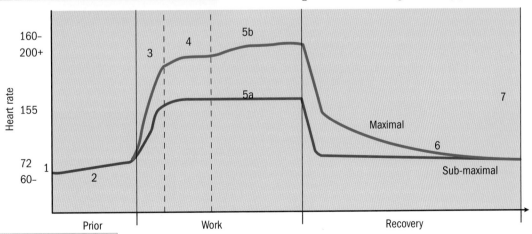

Fig 3.1.9 Heart rate response to sub-maximal and maximal exercise

TASK 10

Using your knowledge of HR, identify in Table 2 which responses, labelled A to H correspond with the numbers which reflect the changes in HR response at each stage in Fig. 3.1.9, for both sub-maximal and maximal exercise.

Sample	Sub-maximal exercise	Maximal exercise
A	E.g. 2	E.g. 2
B		
C		
D		
E		
F		
G		
H		

Table 2

We will look at HR response to sub-maximal and maximal exercise in more detail later in this chapter in regard to how HR is regulated.

CARDIAC OUTPUT RESPONSE TO EXERCISE

Cardiac output, being the product of SV and HR (Q = SV x HR), similarly increases directly in line with exercise intensity from resting values of 5L/min up to maximal values of 20–40L/min in highly trained endurance athletes such as marathon runners and cyclists – see Table 3. Cardiac output primarily increases, to supply the increased demand for oxygen from our working muscles.

	Exercise intensity		
	Resting	Sub-maximal (moderate)	Maximal
SV	60/80ml	80/100ml untrained 160/200ml trained	100/120ml untrained 160/200ml trained
HR	70/72bpm	Up to 100/130bpm	220–your age
Q	5L/min	Up to 10L/min	20–40L/min

Table 3

TASK 11

Investigate HR response to different body positions.

1. Use an HR monitor or take HR values manually at the radial (wrist) or carotid (neck) pulse.
2. Measure and record your HR whilst lying flat (prone), sitting, standing and during light exercise. Wait 2–3 minutes after changing posture, before measuring. If you measure manually, count for 10 seconds, starting from zero, and multiply by 6.
3. Complete the table here and plot your data onto a graph.

Activity	HR
Supine (lying flat)	
Sitting	
Standing	
Light exercise	

Table 4

4. Describe the changes in HR due to changes in body position from prone to exercising positions. Give reasons to account for these changes.
5. Compare HR values between members of your group. Why are there differences?

Table 3 gives a summary of HR, Q and SV related to exercise intensity. Note that the calculation of SV, HR and Q values at moderate exercise intensity are averaged between resting and maximal values.

STROKE VOLUME, HEART RATE AND CARDIAC OUTPUT IN SUMMARY

At the onset of exercise, Q is increased by an increase in both HR and SV. When the intensity of the exercise exceeds 40–60% of an athlete's maximal exercise intensity, SV begins to plateau and any further increase in Q is a result of an increase in HR – see Table 3.

TAKE IT FURTHER

The 'cardiovascular drift' is the gradual decrease in SV and increase in HR during prolonged exercise. Research and discuss what might cause the cardiovascular drift.

The heart's link to a healthy lifestyle

We have already identified that the heart's main adaptation to sustained involvement in physical activity – hypertrophy – decreases resting heart rate by increasing SV to maintain the same Q at rest, and increases its potential to increase the supply of O_2 during exercise.

Just as importantly, a more efficient and healthy heart – bradycardia – is under less effort/strain at rest, and over the period of one's lifetime arguably slows down the heart's deterioration in efficiency due to the natural ageing process. As a consequence, this may improve the length of an individual's quality of life (but not necessarily longevity) in relation to sustaining a more active and healthy lifestyle.

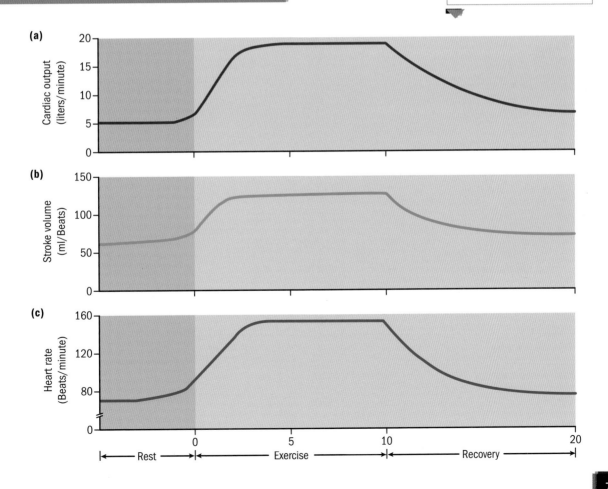

Fig 3.1.10 Response of heart rate (c) and SV (b) to control Q (a) from rest, exercise and recovery

TAKE IT FURTHER

There are however, some negative consequences of excessive endurance training and bradycardia. Heart rates lower than 40 bpm may fail to pump enough blood out causing fainting and develop longer ventricular pauses (periods of more than 2 secs between heart beats), increasing the risk of developing heart block (disease/damage to AV node interrupting natural ventricular rhythm), which sometimes requires pacemakers to be implanted.

TAKE IT FURTHER

In relation to Table 5:

1. Why does the swimmer have a higher SV?
2. Why has the cyclist the lowest SV of the three trained athletes?

Heart rate regulation during physical activity

Figure 3.1.10 (a) on page 71 shows that the heart is capable of increasing or decreasing cardiac output to meet the demand for oxygen made by the working muscles, but how is the heart regulated to control these changes? Heart control involves a series of very complex mechanisms that need simplifying to make them easier to understand.

CARDIAC CONTROL CENTRE

The medulla oblongata in the brain contains the cardiac control centre (CCC), which is primarily responsible for regulating the heart. The CCC is controlled by the autonomic nervous system (ANS), meaning it is under involuntary control and consists of sensory and motor nerves from

TASK 12

Test your knowledge and understanding of SV, HR and Q by applying them to body position both at rest and during the activities in the table below.

1. What happens to HR as exercise intensity increases?

2. What happens to SV from supine to standing and standing to increasing exercise intensity?

3. What happens to Q from supine to standing?

Summary of cardiac function:	HR	SV	Q	(bpm)	(ml)	(L/min)
Active untrained male						
From: laid flat/supine	50	95	5.2			
To: sitting	55	70/80	4.7			
standing/upright	60	60/70	4.2			
walking	90	80/90	9			
jogging	140	110	15			
Trained athletes						
Fast paced running	190	130	25			
Cycling	185	120	22			
Swimming	170	135	23			

Table 5

Source: Wilmore pp.229–30

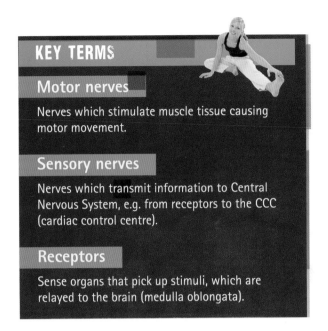

KEY TERMS

Motor nerves

Nerves which stimulate muscle tissue causing motor movement.

Sensory nerves

Nerves which transmit information to Central Nervous System, e.g. from receptors to the CCC (cardiac control centre).

Receptors

Sense organs that pick up stimuli, which are relayed to the brain (medulla oblongata).

either the sympathetic or parasympathetic nervous system.

Sympathetic nerves increase HR whilst parasympathetic nerves decrease HR. But how does the CCC actually regulate HR?

Each cardiac cycle is controlled by the conduction system, the SA node initiating the cardiac impulse causing the heart to contract. The CCC quite simply initiates the sympathetic or parasympathetic nervous systems to stimulate the SA node to either increase or decrease HR – see Fig. 3.1.12 on page 74.

FACTORS AFFECTING THE CARDIAC CONTROL CENTRE

Three main factors affect the activity of the CCC (see Fig. 3.1.11):

- Neural control – primary control factor
- Hormonal control
- Intrinsic control.

NEURAL CONTROL

During exercise the CCC is stimulated by the following sensory receptors.

- *Proprioreceptors* in muscles, tendons and joints inform the CCC that motor (movement) activity has increased.
- *Chemoreceptors* sensitive to chemical changes, in muscles, aorta and carotid arteries, inform the CCC that lactic acid and carbon dioxide (CO_2) levels have increased and oxygen (O_2) and pH levels have decreased.
- *Baroreceptors* sensitive to stretch within blood vessel walls, in aorta and carotid arteries inform the CCC that blood pressure has increased.

Fig 3.1.11 Factors affecting the CCC

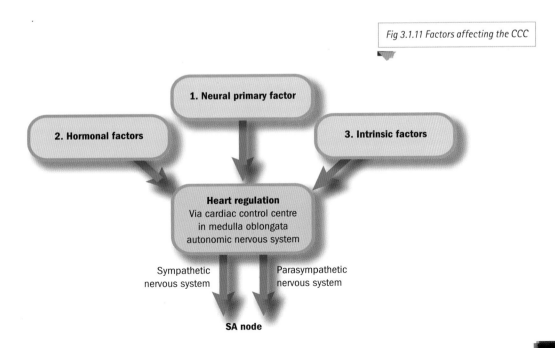

The CCC responds to the neural information above by stimulating the SA node, via the sympathetic cardiac accelerator nerve to increase HR and SV. After exercise stops, all the neural factors above are reversed gradually and the CCC increases stimulation via the parasympathetic vagus nerve, for the SA node to decrease heart rate – see Figure 3.1.12.

TAKE IT FURTHER

The CCC response during and after exercise looks at the effects of the sympathetic and parasympathetic nervous systems in isolation here, for simplicity and easier understanding. However it is worth noting that the CCC balances both the control of the inhibitory effects of the vagus nerve to decrease HR, *and* the stimulation of the accelerator nerve to increase HR. Hence, the stimulation of the vagus nerve is decreased simultaneously with the increased stimulation of the accelerator nerve. The net effect is a much more rapid increase in HR than if just one of the above occurred.

HORMONAL CONTROL

Before and during exercise, adrenalin is released from the adrenal glands into the bloodstream. Adrenalin directly stimulates the SA node to increase both HR and the strength of ventricular contraction which therefore in turn increases SV.

INTRINSIC CONTROL

During and after exercise there are a number of intrinsic (internal) factors that affect HR control:

1 **During exercise:**
   • temperature increases, which increases the speed of nerve impulses, which in turn increases HR
   • venous return increases which directly increases EDV and therefore SV (Starling's Law).
2 **After exercise:**
   • temperature decreases and HR decreases
   • venous return decreases, which in turn decreases SV (Starling's Law).

Fig 3.1.12 Sympathetic and parasympathetic control of HR via the ANS

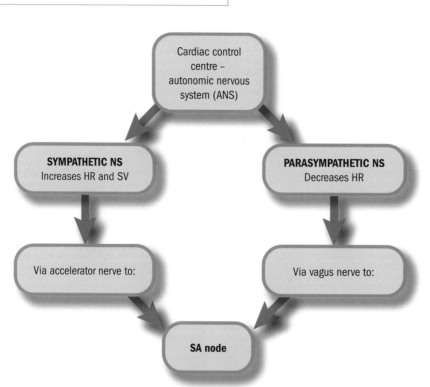

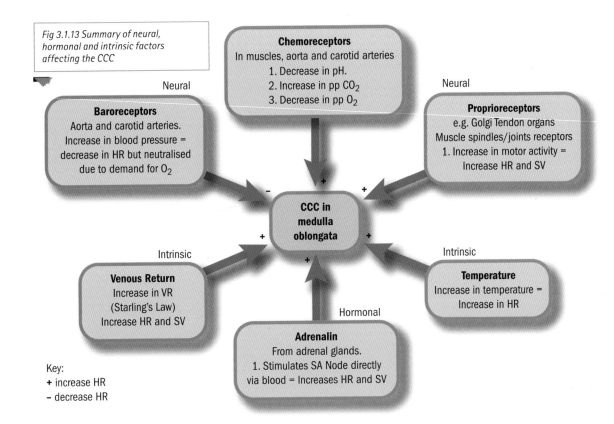

Fig 3.1.13 Summary of neural, hormonal and intrinsic factors affecting the CCC

Chemoreceptors
In muscles, aorta and carotid arteries
1. Decrease in pH.
2. Increase in pp CO_2
3. Decrease in pp O_2

Neural

Baroreceptors
Aorta and carotid arteries.
Increase in blood pressure = decrease in HR but neutralised due to demand for O_2

Neural

Proprioreceptors
e.g. Golgi Tendon organs
Muscle spindles/joints receptors
1. Increase in motor activity = Increase HR and SV

CCC in medulla oblongata

Intrinsic

Venous Return
Increase in VR (Starling's Law)
Increase HR and SV

Intrinsic

Temperature
Increase in temperature = Increase in HR

Hormonal

Adrenalin
From adrenal glands.
1. Stimulates SA Node directly via blood = Increases HR and SV

Key:
+ increase HR
− decrease HR

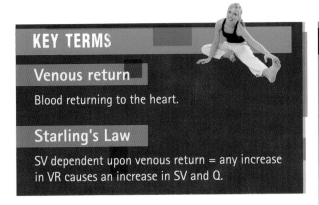

KEY TERMS

Venous return

Blood returning to the heart.

Starling's Law

SV dependent upon venous return = any increase in VR causes an increase in SV and Q.

HEART REGULATION DURING EXERCISE

We have already established that during exercise the HR increases to supply the increasing demand for oxygen from our working muscles and help remove by-products of respiration. Having identified the factors affecting the CCC (summarised in Fig. 3.1.13) and how it controls HR, you must now learn to apply this knowledge and be able to describe and explain how HR is regulated, at optimal levels, to supply the oxygen for both sub-maximal and maximal exercise.

TAKE IT FURTHER

Some useful guidelines:

- Use the table in Task 13 to help identify the area of HR response you are referring to.
- Compare your HR response with the typical HR response to sub-maximal and maximal exercise identified in Fig. 3.1.9.
- Use/link stages 1–7 in Fig. 3.1.19 to correspond with Table 6.
- Ensure you refer to all three work intensities, although it may be helpful to refer to two or more workloads if their responses are similar.
- Attempt to explain any differences between your own and the typical responses to sub-maximal and maximal exercise in Fig. 3.1.9. For example, how accurate were your testing procedures in terms of reliability and validity?

TASK 13

1. Using your knowledge of HR, the factors affecting CCC, and how HR is regulated, describe and explain the changes in HR response at each stage in Fig. 3.1.9 for both sub-maximal and maximal exercise.
2. Now complete the following exercise, using the table and graph in Fig. 3.1.14 to record your HR response to varying work intensities:
(a) Cycle, row or run for three minutes attempting to keep within each of the three HR intensities, as follows:
   • Low 5 120–30
   • Medium = 135–50
   • High 5 155–70.
   Use an HR monitor to obtain the HR values, or take them manually at the radial (wrist) or carotid pulse (neck).
(b) Complete the table below and plot your data on the graph.
(c) Using your knowledge and understanding of HR response to exercise, factors affecting the CCC and heart regulation, describe and explain your own/your partner's HR response to the three work intensities.
   Note: If the table is set up in MS Excel, the graph will automatically format as you input your HR values.

Graph area	Time/Period	Intensity		
		Low	Med	High
1	Resting HR			
2	Pre Exercise			
3	Exercise 1min			
4	2min			
5	3min			
6	Recovery 1min			
7	2min			
8	3min			
9	4min			
10	5min			
11	6min			
12	7min			
13	8min			
14	9min			

Table 6

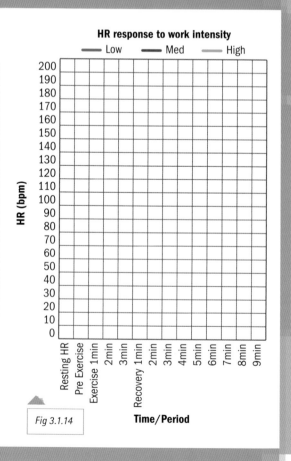

Fig 3.1.14

Refresh your memory

Revision checklist – Cardiovascular System Part I

You should now be able to describe and explain:

▷ The cardiac cycle (diastole and systole)

▷ The conduction system of the heart

▷ The link between the cardiac cycle and the conduction system of the heart

▷ The relationship between stroke volume, heart rate and cardiac output: definitions and resting values for each

▷ The changes that take place to stroke volume, heart rate and cardiac output during different intensities of physical activity

▷ The regulation of heart rate during physical activity – to include neural, hormonal and intrinsic factors

REVISE AS YOU GO!

HEART

1. Sketch a diagram to show the interaction between the heart, respiratory and vascular systems. Use arrows to indicate the direction in which they interact.
2. Describe the events and timing of the cardiac cycle.
3. Sketch a diagram of a heart to show the route and structures involved in the conduction system of the heart.
4. Explain the link between the cardiac cycle and the conduction system.
5. Define the terms HR, SV, Q and write an equation to show the link between them.
6. Compare resting and exercise values for HR, SV and Q.
7. Discuss the positive impacts of regular participation in aerobic activity on the heart. How does this help develop a lifelong involvement in an active lifestyle?
8. Describe the neural factors affecting the activity of the CCC. Why is this beneficial to performance?
9. Describe and explain the contribution of hormonal and intrinsic mechanisms in the control of HR.
10. Sketch graphs to show typical HR response prior to, during and recovery, after sub-maximal and maximal exercise.

Get the result!

Examination question

Explain how neural control of the heart helps to maintain the supply of oxygenated blood during exercise. [5]

examiner's tips

Check the command word ('explain').
Now check the key subject area + focus (heart + neural control)
Now check the marks available [5]

Student answer

Neural stimuli control the supply of oxygenated blood to the muscles during exercise. This stimulates the brain which in turn stimulates the SA node which increases heart rate.

Examiner says:

You have initially just repeated the question but the answer is too superficial and brief for a 5 mark question. You've identified the SA node structure that results in an increases heart rate for 2 marks, but missed the factors affecting the control centre involved. This lack of structure means the answer was directed immediately to the end of the explanation which discounted 8 of the available marks. This is a common error which you can avoid by either logically planning out your answer or by questioning your initial starting point in reverse, e.g. How does the brain stimulate the SA node? What stimulates the brain to initiate the stimulus of the SA Node? Why do neural factors stimulate the brain?

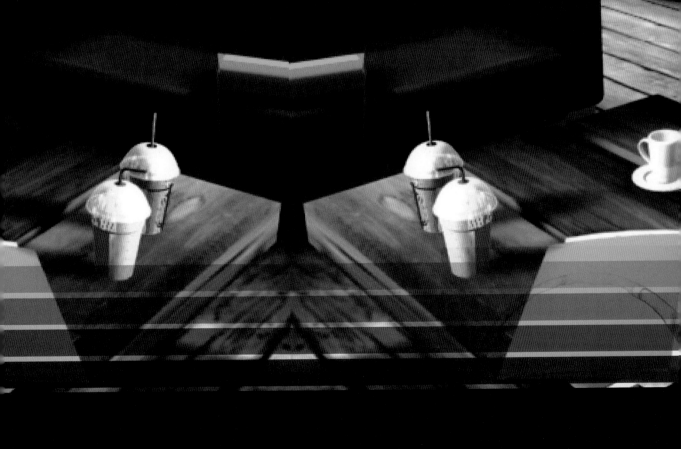

Student's improved answer

Neural factors controlling the heart are proprioreceptors which detect motor movement in the muscles, chempreceptors which pick up an increase in CO2/lactic acid and baroreceptors in blood vessels that blood pressure is increasing. These stimuli stimulate the cardiac control centre in the medulla oblongata which responds by increasing the activity of the sympathetic accelerator nerve to the SA node. At the same time the activity of the parasympathetic vagus nerve is decreased and in turn this increases heart rate which increases the supply of oxygenated blood during exercise.

Examiner says:

Logical start point

Control centre

Control mechanisms

Good conclusion & Link back to Q

Response of the cardiovascular (vascular) system to physical activity

LEARNING OBJECTIVES

At the end of Part II you will have learned about:

- The distribution of cardiac output at rest and during exercise (the vascular shunt mechanism)
- The role of the vasomotor centre and the involvement of arterioles and pre-capillary sphincters
- How carbon dioxide and oxygen are carried within the vascular system; how effective transportation of carbon dioxide and oxygen within the vascular system aids participation in physical activity; how smoking impacts on transportation of oxygen
- Blood pressure and identifying resting values
- The changes that occur during physical activity and hypertension
- How venous return is maintained
- The effects that a warm-up and cool-down period has on the cardiovascular system; how venous return impacts on the quality of performance
- Lifelong involvement in an active lifestyle, how to critically evaluate different physical activities, and the impact these have on the cardiovascular system: coronary heart disease (CHD); arteriosclerosis, atherosclerosis; angina, and heart attack.

INTRODUCTION

Fig. 3.1.1 on page 61 shows how the vascular system consists of blood and blood vessels which transport and direct oxygen (O_2) and carbon dioxide (CO_2) to and from the lungs, heart and body tissues. Cardiac output is distributed to the various organs/tissues of the body according to their need/demand for oxygen. In essence, blood represents the substance that actually carries the oxygen and carbon dioxide while the vast system of blood vessels represents a system of tubing that directs and delivers the flow of blood toward the body tissues.

Circulatory networks

(AK = assumed knowledge)

The heart consists of two separate pumps which pump blood to two different locations via two circulatory networks of blood vessels (see Fig. 3.2.1):

- **Pulmonary circulation** – deoxygenated blood from the right ventricle of the heart to the lungs, and oxygenated blood back to the left atrium.

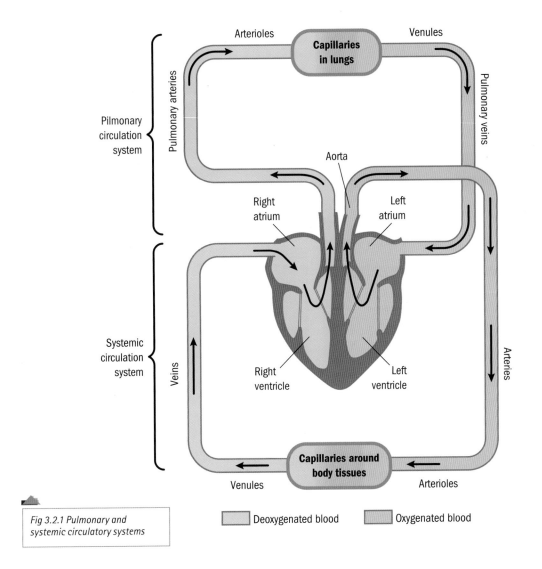

Fig 3.2.1 Pulmonary and
systemic circulatory systems

Deoxygenated blood   Oxygenated blood

- **Systemic circulation** – oxygenated blood from the left ventricle to the body tissues, and deoxygenated blood back to the right atrium.

BLOOD VESSELS OF THE SYSTEMIC CIRCULATION (AK)

The interaction and additional detail of blood vessels involved in the systemic circulation are more easily learned as a flow diagram – see Fig. 3.2.1.

Arteries are the largest blood vessels, and as they spread away from the heart, they reduce in size to become arterioles and finally capillaries, the narrowest blood vessels. Capillaries flow into larger venules and then even larger veins before entering the right atrium from either the inferior

vena cava from the lower body, or superior vena cava from the upper body.

BLOOD VESSELS OF THE PULMONARY CIRCULATION (AK)

We previously learned about the blood vessels of the pulmonary circulation when we looked at the blood vessels of the heart (see pages 62–63), namely the pulmonary arteries from the right ventricle to the lungs and the pulmonary veins from the lungs to the left atrium.

Considering that arteries normally carry oxygenated blood and veins carry deoxygenated blood, what is unusual about pulmonary circulation? The pulmonary artery is the only artery carrying deoxygenated blood and the pulmonary vein is the only vein to carry oxygenated blood.

REMEMBER

Pulmonary arteries/veins do not carry the blood normally associated with arteries and veins.

EXAM TIP

Exam questions often use the location of either the pulmonary artery or vein as a starting point to test your knowledge of heart/circulatory structure.

KEY TERMS

Smooth muscle

Involuntary muscle found in blood vessel walls.

Vasodilate

Widening of arterial blood vessels.

Vasoconstrict

Narrowing of arterial blood vessel walls.

Venodilate

Widening of venous blood vessels.

Venoconstrict

Narrowing of venous blood vessel walls.

BLOOD VESSEL STRUCTURE (AK)

There are three main groups of blood vessels (see Fig. 3.2.2.).

- **Arteries/arterioles** – which transport oxygenated blood away from the heart towards tissues/muscles.
- **Capillaries** – which bring the blood directly in contact with the tissues where oxygen and carbon dioxide are actually exchanged.
- **Veins/venules** – which transport deoxygenated blood back towards the heart.

Note that this is with the exception of the pulmonary arteries and veins.

You are not required to know the detail of the three layers of blood vessels. However it is helpful to understand structural differences to explain how blood vessels differ in their function – summarised as follows.

- **All blood vessels** have three layers except for single-walled capillaries.
- **Arteries and arterioles** have a large middle layer of smooth muscle to allow them to vasodilate and vasoconstrict to alter their shape/size to regulate blood flow.

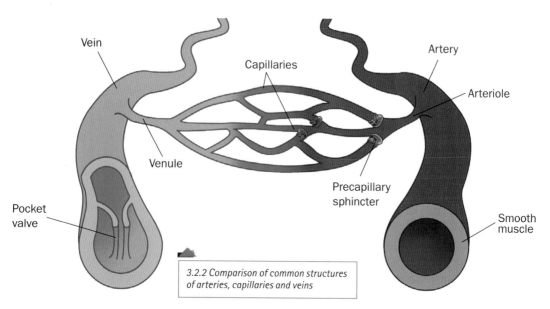

3.2.2 Comparison of common structures of arteries, capillaries and veins

Vein

Capillaries

Artery

Arteriole

Venule

Precapillary sphincter

Pocket valve

Smooth muscle

- **Arterioles** have a ring of smooth muscle surrounding the entry to the capillaries into which they control the blood flow. Called pre-capillary sphincters, they can vasodilate and vasoconstrict to alter their shape/size to regulate blood flow.
- **Capillaries** have a very thin, one-cell-thick layer, to allow gaseous exchange.
- **Larger veins** have pocket valves to prevent the backflow of blood and direct it in one direction back to the heart.
- **Venules and veins** have a much thinner muscular layer, allowing them to venodilate and venoconstrict to a lesser extent, and a thicker outer layer to help support the blood that sits within each pocket valve.

VENOUS RETURN

Venous Return (VR) is the transport of blood from the capillaries through venules, veins and then either the superior or inferior vena cava back to the right atrium of the heart. We know that the main function of the heart is to pump blood around the body, so why is it important to understand how and why blood returns to the heart? Let us look at the dynamics of venous return in more detail to find out why.

STARLING'S LAW OF THE HEART

Starling's Law of the Heart states that stroke volume is dependent upon venous return. Hence, if VR increases, stroke volume (SV) increases; if VR decreases, SV decreases.

REMEMBER

SV directly affects cardiac output (Q), so if SV increases then Q increases. So VR is important because it determines SV and Q.

At rest VR is sufficient to maintain SV and Q to supply the demand for oxygen. However, during exercise the pressure of blood in the veins is too low to maintain VR, and SV and Q therefore decrease. The body needs additional mechanisms to help push the blood against gravity through the veins back to the heart to increase VR and therefore SV.

MAINTENANCE OF VENOUS RETURN (VR MECHANISMS)

There are five venous return mechanisms that help maintain VR.

- **Pocket valves** – One-way valves in the veins prevent backflow of blood and direct it towards the heart – see Fig. 3.2.3 (a).

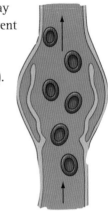
(a)

- **Muscle pump** – Veins are situated between skeletal muscles, which when contracting and relaxing, help to push or squeeze blood back towards the heart – see Fig. 3.2.3 (b).
- **Respiratory pump** – During exercise, breathing becomes deeper and/or faster, which causes pressure changes in the thorax and abdomen. This increases the pressure in the abdomen, squeezing the large veins in that area and helping force the blood back to the heart.

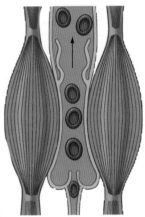
(b)

- **Smooth muscle** – Contraction and relaxation of smooth muscle in the middle layer of the vein walls also helps to push blood through the veins and towards the heart – see Fig. 3.2.3 (c).
- **Gravity** – Blood from the upper body is aided by gravity as it descends to the heart.

(c)

Fig 3.2.3

TASK 1

Use your knowledge to show how venous return may impact on the quality of performance. You may wish to consider before, during and after physical activity.

BLOOD POOLING

VR requires a force to push the blood back towards the heart. If there is insufficient pressure the blood will sit in the pocket valves of the veins. This blood pooling (see Fig. 3.2.4) is often described as a feeling of heavy legs. Increased cardiac output (Q) sent to the muscles in the legs actually pools or sits here with insufficient pressure to return it to the heart.

Pocket valves, gravity and smooth muscle are quite sufficient to maintain VR during rest but not during or immediately after exercise. The additional mechanisms of the skeletal and respiratory pump are needed to ensure VR is maintained. How can we maintain the muscle and respiratory mechanisms?

An active cool-down helps to maintain these two important mechanisms. An elevated respiration rate maintains the respiratory pump, and

continued skeletal muscle contractions maintain the effect of the skeletal muscle pump. All these mechanisms help maintain VR and redistribute Q to prevent blood pooling.

TAKE IT FURTHER

Consider the following scenario which is a problem faced by all athletes.

A cyclist completes an exhausting high intensity training programme and immediately stops, climbs off the bike and stands against the wall whilst recovering. Feeling light headed or dizzy they faint, falling to the floor. Use your knowledge of VR to explain this sequence of events and give your recommendations to avoid recurrence.

VENOUS RETURN'S IMPACT ON THE QUALITY OF PERFORMANCE

VR is important to performance because it determines SV and Q. Starling's Law, dictates that if VR decreases, stroke volume (SV) decreases; and this directly decreases cardiac output (Q). A reduction in SV/Q decreases blood/oxygen transport to the working muscles reducing their ability to contract/work aerobically. The net effect on performance is that exercise intensity has to be reduced or muscles will have to work anaerobically, and muscle fatigue will result.

Although more significant in prolonged aerobic-based exercise (which is dependent upon oxygen supply), it can also affect performance in anaerobic activities in that a good VR will speed up recovery and therefore allow performers to work anaerobically for longer.

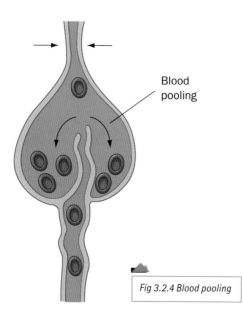

Blood pooling

Fig 3.2.4 Blood pooling

APPLY IT!

A centre in Netball, or midfielder in Hockey/football would benefit from a good VR by increasing oxygen supply, allowing them to cover more ground over the whole game and delaying fatigue. Similarly, during game stoppages a good VR ensuring oxygen supply will increase their recovery allowing them to repeatedly sprint more often during the whole game.

DISTRIBUTION OF CARDIAC OUTPUT AT REST AND DURING EXERCISE

We have already identified that cardiac output (Q) increases during exercise and the importance of VR in this role, but how does the cardiovascular system redistribute the blood to the working muscles which demand an increased supply of oxygen? The process of redistributing Q is called the vascular shunt mechanism. Let us first consider the distribution of Q, and then where and how it is redistributed during exercise. Consider Table 1.

We are primarily concerned with the distribution of Q to the working muscles and in this respect the following conclusions can be made from the table below.

At rest:

- only 15–20% resting Q is supplied to muscles
- the remaining Q (80–85%) supplies body organs.

During exercise:

- increased Q (80–85%) is supplied to the working muscles as exercise intensity increases
- decreasing percentage of Q is supplied to body organs
- blood supply to the brain is maintained

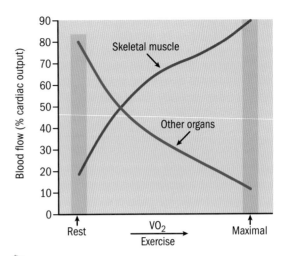

Fig 3.2.5 Redistribution of Q via vascular shunt mechanism

- increased blood supply to the skin surface during lighter work, but decreased as exercise intensity increases.

Fig. 3.2.5 simplifies the data in the table above to show the redistribution of Q from organs to muscle tissues during exercise.

EXAM TIP

Always link the Redistribution of Q with the vascular shunt mechanism and vice versa.

Tissue	Rest		Light		Moderate		Maximal	
	%	ml	%	ml	%	ml	%	ml
Liver	27	1350	12	1100	3	600	1	300
Kidneys	22	1100	10	900	3	600	1	250
Brain	14	700	8	750	4	750	3	750
Heart	4	200	4	350	4	750	4	1000
Muscle	20	1000	47	4500	71	12500	88	22000
Skin	6	300	15	1500	12	1900	2	600
Other	7	350	4	400	3	500	1	100
Total	100	5000	100	9500	100	17600	100	25000

Table 1 Distribution of Q during rest, light, moderate and maximal exercise

THE CYCLIST

Let us use the scenario of the cyclist who fainted after a bout of training, to exemplify the distribution of Q due to the changing demands for oxygen from the body tissues/organs.

At rest and prior to training, the cyclist's Q was spread around the body organs and tissues related to their resting needs for oxygen. When exercise began, skeletal muscle in the legs increased its demands for oxygen and blood flow was increased. In contrast, the tissues/organs not directly required during exercise (liver, kidneys, intestines etc.) had their blood flow reduced.

Initially blood flow to the skin surface increased to help decrease rising temperature, but as the intensity of exercise increased, the ever-increasing demand for more oxygen by the muscles overrode the need to decrease temperature, and blood flow to the skin decreased. Once exercise stopped, Q was gradually redistributed back towards resting levels as the body recovered.

FAINTING ANALYSED

Remember that our cyclist fainted. In immediately stopping and standing, blood pooling occurred in the pocket valves of the veins in the cyclist's legs due to insufficient pressure to maintain venous return against gravity. By immediately stopping, the cyclist switched off the muscle and respiratory pump mechanisms of venous return. As venous return decreased, SV, and therefore Q, decreased (Starling's Law) and reduced blood pressure thus threatening the blood supply to the brain which simply responded by making the cyclist dizzy/faint.

The cyclist fell which lowered the head, which aided venous return and therefore blood pressure, SV and Q, restoring blood flow to the brain. Recall that an active cool-down is essential to maintain venous return and prevent blood pooling.

Vasomotor control centre

CONTROL OF THE VASCULAR SHUNT MECHANISM

The vascular shunt mechanism redistributes Q during rest and exercise, but how is this controlled? The Vasomotor Control Centre (VCC) located in the medulla oblongata of the brain stimulates the sympathetic nervous system to either vasodilate or vasconstrict the pre-capillary sphincters and arterioles supplying muscles and organs. Vasomotor control works very much in the same manner as in the CCC. The VCC receives information from:

- **chemoreceptors** in muscles, aorta and carotid arteries. These inform the VCC that lactic acid and carbon dioxide levels have increased and oxygen and pH levels have decreased
- **baroreceptors** in aorta and carotid arteries. These inform the VCC that systolic blood pressure has increased/decreased.

SYMPATHETIC NERVOUS SYSTEM

When the VCC receives this information, it responds by sending messages only via the sympathetic nervous system. Importantly, arterioles are the blood vessels primarily responsible for the vascular shunt mechanism. In relation to their overall size, they have the thickest muscular layer; they are vast in number and have rings of smooth muscle called pre-capillary sphincters, which lie at the opening of capillaries. The arterial blood vessels are always in a state of slight contraction, known as vasomotor tone, but during exercise the VCC is able to control blood flow to organs and muscles in the following way.

KEY TERMS

Chemoreceptors

A sensory receptor that is selective for a chemical substance.

Baroreceptors

A sensory receptor that responds to pressure or stretch. Refers to the blood pressure receptors of the carotid artery and aorta.

pH level

A measure of acidity. A low pH = high acidity, and vice versa.

1. Organs (during exercise)

The VCC controls blood flow by increasing sympathetic stimulation which vasoconstricts the arterioles and pre-capillary sphincters which both decreases and distributes blood flow away from the non-essential capillaries of the organs.

2. Muscles (during exercise)

The VCC controls blood flow by decreasing sympathetic stimulation which vasodilates the arterioles and pre-capillary sphincters which both increases and distributes blood flow toward the capillaries of the working muscles.

REMEMBER

Recall that when we looked at the structure of the blood vessels we learned that they have a middle layer of smooth muscle which is able to vasoconstrict or vasodilate.

EXAM TIP

In explaining the vascular shunt mechanism during exercise, there are up to four marks available:

- two marks are for vasodilation (one for arterioles of muscles; one for pre-capillary sphincters of muscles)
- two marks are for vasoconstriction (one for arterioles of organs; one for pre-capillary sphincters of organs).

TASK 2

Sketch a summary flow diagram to describe and explain the control of the vascular shunt mechanism. Starting from rest, include the factors affecting the VCC and how it controls the redistribution of blood flow during exercise.

Oxygen and carbon dioxide transport

We have already identified that Q increases with exercise intensity and that blood carries the oxygen demanded by our working muscles. But how is oxygen and carbon dioxide carried in the blood, and does the supply of oxygen and removal of carbon dioxide limit performance? Blood consists of 45% blood cells and 55% plasma. It is within these substances that oxygen and carbon dioxide are transported.

OXYGEN TRANSPORT

Oxygen transport is achieved in two ways:

- (97%) transported within the protein haemoglobin, and packed with red blood cells, as oxyhaemoglobin (HbO_2)
- (3%) within blood plasma.

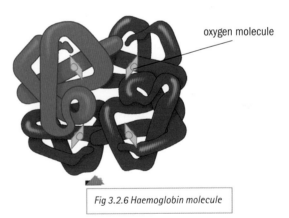

oxygen molecule

Fig 3.2.6 Haemoglobin molecule

Having a high affinity for oxygen, haemoglobin happily combines with oxygen when it is available and just as importantly, it readily gives up oxygen to tissues where oxygen concentrations are low. Each haemoglobin molecule can carry four molecules of oxygen – see Fig. 3.2.6.

CARBON DIOXIDE TRANSPORT

Carbon dioxide transport is achieved in three ways:

- (70%) combined with water within red blood cells as carbonic acid
- (23%) combined with haemoglobin as carbaminohaemoglobin ($HbCO_2$)
- (7%) dissolved in plasma.

EXAM TIP

Easy marks can be earned by simply remembering that Hb and plasma transport both O_2 and CO_2.

PERFORMANCE AND O_2/CO_2 TRANSPORT

Recall from the introduction to this chapter that the efficiency of the CV system to deliver oxygen affects performance. The actual transport of oxygen is therefore essential in that an efficient heart is very much wasted unless the blood it is pumping is carrying sufficient oxygen to meet the needs of the working muscles.

EFFICIENT TRANSPORT

Efficient O_2 and CO_2 transport aids participation (exercise), in that it:

- prolongs the duration of anaerobic and, especially, aerobic activity
- delays anaerobic threshold, which
- increases the possible intensity/work rate for the activity, and
- speeds up recovery during and after exercise.

With efficient O_2 and CO_2 transport providing such positive effects on performance, it is essential to understand how a common social habit, smoking, can reduces these benefits and reduce an active and healthy lifestyle.

SMOKING'S IMPACT ON O_2 TRANSPORTATION

Smoking has the obvious detrimental influence/s to breathing/lung disorders, but, among other gases, cigarette smoke contains carbon monoxide (CO). Haemoglobin has a higher affinity (240+ times) to carbon monoxide, so combines with CO in preference to O_2. This reduces HbO_2 association in the lungs and therefore the performer's maximal O_2 uptake. As a result blood O_2 transport is reduced with the net effect of reducing both the supply of O_2 to the working muscles, and the lactate threshold which decreases optimal performance – this is especially so in aerobic activities. Hence, all the positive effects of an efficient O_2 and CO_2 transport listed above are reversed.

TAKE IT FURTHER

AIR POLLUTION
Interestingly, vehicle emissions also contain CO, along with five other harmful contents that carry a health and/or performance impairment risk, and peaks around congested roads and polluted cities; concentrations are highest inside slow-moving cars.

1. What are the implications for athletes performing and travelling to competitions by car in such areas?
2. Can you suggest any preventative measures when such travel is unavoidable?

APPLY IT!

Ask a performer, who is a smoker you know, if they would like to prolong both aerobic and anaerobic activity, increase their intensity/work rate, delay their fatigue and speed up their recovery during and after exercise? When they respond yes, explain to them how smoking is preventing them achieving all the above and reinforce to them that their lungs will have a much greater rate of recovery if they stop smoking while they are younger.

Effects on vascular system of warm-up and cool-down

WARM-UP

It has always been a recommendation for athletes to complete a warm-up before they participate in exercise, but generally on grounds of reducing the risk of injury. Specifically in regard to the vascular system, you will be required to explain the benefits of a warm-up, which are as follows:

A gradual increase in blood flow/Q due to the vascular shunt mechanism via:

- Vasoconstriction of arterioles/pre-capillary sphincters to organs, decreasing blood flow to organs and thereby increasing blood flow to working muscles.

- Vasodilation of muscle arterioles/pre-capillary sphincters increasing blood flow delivery to working muscles.
- Increased body/muscle temperature causing a more rapid increase in transport of the enzymes required for energy systems and muscle contraction.
- Increase in body/muscle temperature, which
  - decreases blood viscosity, improving blood flow to working muscles.
  - increases the dissociation of oxygen from haemoglobin in muscle tissues.
- Decrease OBLA (onset of blood lactate accumulation) due to the early onset of anaerobic work when a warm-up is not carried out.

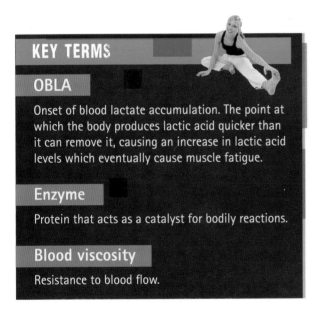

KEY TERMS

OBLA

Onset of blood lactate accumulation. The point at which the body produces lactic acid quicker than it can remove it, causing an increase in lactic acid levels which eventually cause muscle fatigue.

Enzyme

Protein that acts as a catalyst for bodily reactions.

Blood viscosity

Resistance to blood flow.

COOL-DOWN

It has also always been a recommendation for athletes to complete a cool-down after exercise, generally on grounds of reducing the risk of injury. We have already established that a cool-down should be active, but you will be required to explain, specifically in regard to the vascular system, the benefits of an active cool-down, which are as follows:

- keeps metabolic activity elevated which gradually decreases HR and respiration.

- maintains respiratory/muscle pumps which:
  - prevent blood-pooling in veins
  - maintain venous return.
- maintains blood flow (SV and Q) to supply oxygen, maintaining blood pressure.
- keeps capillaries dilated to flush muscles with oxygenated blood, which increases the removal of blood and muscle lactic acid and carbon dioxide.

Blood pressure (Bp)

Blood pressure is more often associated negatively in terms of an unhealthy lifestyle but before we look at this in more detail it is important to establish that Bp is essential to apply the force needed to circulate the blood around the body. So what actually provides this pressure?

MECHANISM

It is the contractive force of the heart ventricles that provides the pressure to force the blood through the arteries. Upon leaving the heart this force is then applied from the blood against the arterial blood vessel walls which defines blood pressure as the 'pressure exerted by blood against the (arterial) blood vessel walls'.

Bp is normally expressed as : $\dfrac{\text{Systolic}}{\text{Diastolic}}$

Systolic blood pressure represents the highest arterial pressure and reflects ventricular systole (contraction phase of the heart ventricles). Diastolic blood pressure represents the lowest arterial pressure and reflects ventricular diastole (relaxation phase of the heart).

The average resting Bp is $\dfrac{120\text{mmHg}}{80\text{mmHg}}$ (in the aorta)

(mmHg = millimetres of mercury)

Blood pressure is also expressed as: 'blood flow (Q) x resistance'. The contraction of the heart ventricles represents the high pressure force of 'blood flow' leaving the aorta. Hence, any increase in Q (blood flow) leaving the heart will cause Bp to increase.

RESISTANCE

The resistance is the friction of the blood cells as they travel against the vessel wall which is termed **viscosity** (fluid friction). If you recall that arterial blood vessels can vasodilate and vasoconstrict, due to their middle layer of smooth muscle, it helps explain how the body can decrease Bp by dilating (widening) and increase Bp by constricting (narrowing). This is how the body both regulates Bp and, as we have already looked at, controls the redistribution of Q via the vascular shunt mechanism.

Bp MEASUREMENT

Bp is measured using a sphygmomanometer – see Fig. 3.2.7.

1. Wrap the cuff around your bent upper arm and inflate it to about 180mmHg. At this pressure there is not sufficient pressure for blood to pass the pressure of the cuff. A stethoscope is placed over the brachial artery just below the cuff.

2. The air pressure is released and the pressure reading noted on the first audible noise. The 1st pressure represents the highest systolic pressure when pressure is sufficient to force blood past the pressure of the cuff.

3. Continue to release air pressure until the sound becomes muffled and then note when the sound disappears. This represents the lowest diastolic pressure.

There are now modern battery-operated Bp monitors available which do not require the stethoscope to listen for the sounds. The cuff is simply pumped up and self deflates displaying both your Bp and heart rate.

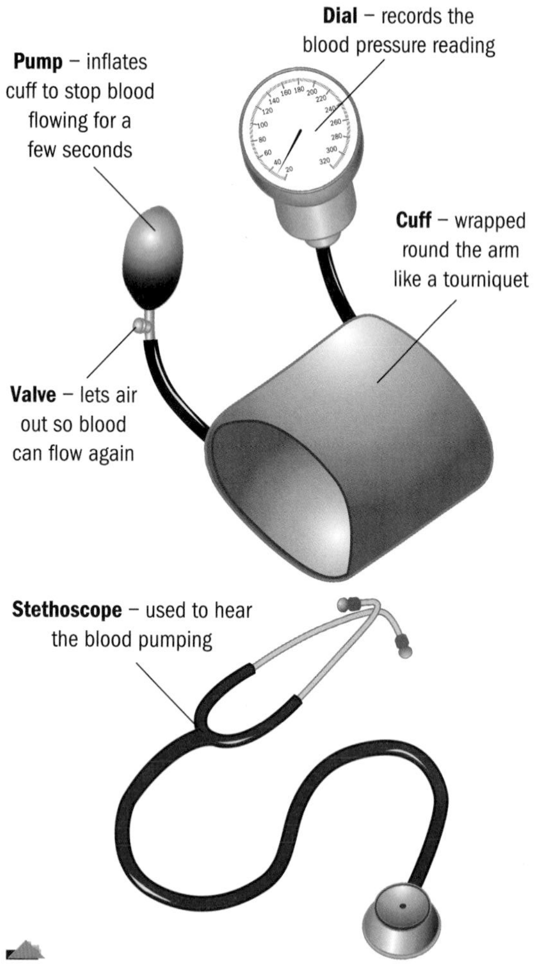

Dial – records the blood pressure reading

Pump – inflates cuff to stop blood flowing for a few seconds

Cuff – wrapped round the arm like a tourniquet

Valve – lets air out so blood can flow again

Stethoscope – used to hear the blood pumping

Fig 3.2.7 A sphygmomanometer and stethoscope

TASK 3

1. Measure and then share your group's Bp measurements.
2. Plot these results onto a scattergraph using the following coloured key: Red = female performer, Blue = male performer, X = aerobic, O = anaerobic, e.g. a red X = female aerobic performer
3. Evaluate and discuss any differences/similarities in your group's results.

TAKE IT FURTHER

Explain why the average Bp in the left ventricle is 120mmHg, and diastole in the aorta is 80mmHg, while it is only 25mmHg in the right ventricle and 10mmHg in the pulmonary artery?

Bp CHANGES DURING PHYSICAL ACTIVITY

Blood pressure fluctuates for many reasons. Generally it: fluctuates during the day; decreases when we sleep; increases temporarily during stress; increases as we age; increases in hot temperatures, decreases in cold temperatures and with body size; it even fluctuates across nationalities, but all you are required to know is how it changes during physical activity and during hypertension.

Bp DURING EXERCISE (ENDURANCE TRAINING)

- **Systolic** – Systolic Bp increases in line with exercise intensity and will plateau or steady-state during sub-maximal exercise (around 140–160), but may decrease gradually if this sub-maximal intensity is prolonged.

  As exercise intensity increases, systolic Bp continues to increase in line with intensity, from 120 mmHg to above 200mmHg during exhaustive exercise intensity. Systolic Bp of 240/250 have been reported in elite athletes at maximum exercise intensity.

- **Diastolic** – Diastolic Bp changes little during sub-maximal exercise, irrespective of intensity. However, during gross muscle activities like rowing and running, localised muscular diastolic Bp may fall to around 60–70mmHg. Diastolic Bp may increase a little (max 12%/>10mmHg) as exercise intensity reaches maximum levels.

Interestingly, in people with hypertension, systolic pressure rises to similar, high values of normal individuals without any undue pressure on the heart, and they therefore do not need to fear 'extreme' high Bp during exercise.

APPLY IT!

An athlete running may have a typical Bp of 200/60.

It is recommended that exercise should be stopped if diastolic Bp increases above 15mmHg at the resting Bp.

TAKE IT FURTHER

1. Can you account for the increase in systolic Bp in line with exercise intensity?
2. Why during sub-maximal exercise may systolic Bp decrease gradually if exercise is prolonged?
3. Can you explain why localised muscular diastolic Bp may fall?

ISOMETRIC/RESISTANCE TRAINING

Lifting heavy weights during strength/resistance training involves isometric work, and blood vessels are blocked by sustained static muscle contractions which restricts blood flow through arterial and venous blood vessels, and increases vascular resistance. This can cause a marked increase in both systolic and diastolic Bp as blood flow builds up behind this area of restriction, and Bp can exceed 480/350mmHg.

The Valsalva manoeuvre often occurs during such exercise when an athlete attempts to breath out while the mouth, nose and glottis are closed. This type of physical activity is NOT recommended for individuals already prescribed as hypertensive, and should be avoided.

However, resting blood pressure after resistance training tends not to change and may decrease.

POST-EXERCISE RECOVERY

Systolic blood pressure decreases temporarily below pre-exercise levels for up to 12 hours. Diastolic pressure also remains low, often, below normal resting levels and can remain low for hours afterwards. This may have an important application in promoting a healthy lifestyle in that it may help lower Bp, as exercising more

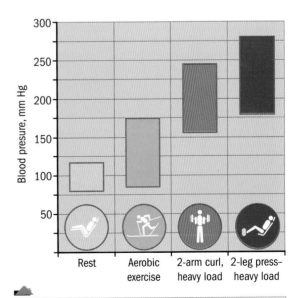

Fig 3.2.8 Blood pressure response: Rhythmic aerobic excercise and Heavy Resistance Training – small and large muscle mass

regularly can reduce Bp on a daily basis and this is more significant in individuals who are already hypertensive.

LONG TERM CHANGES

There is mixed evidence in regard to long term adaptations to Bp; any reasons behind such changes are still not fully understood, but are likely to be due to changes in: CV adaptations, diet, smoking, weight and stress, which are normally associated when undertaking a new training programme.

The following points are relevant:

- Mixed views that resting Bp may decrease with continued endurance training.
- Resting Bp is generally lowered in people already with mild or moderate hypertension.
- Endurance training can reduce the risk of developing high Bp.
- Bp changes little during sub-maximal or maximal work rates.
- Although resistance/isometric training significantly increases both systolic and diastolic Bp it does not increase resting Bp.

- Little or no changes to those who are already max hypertensive.

Bp CHANGES DURING HYPERTENSION

Before we look at Bp during hypertension you need some knowledge of Bp norms as outlined in Table 2, and an awareness that such 'norm' tables vary from one organisation/country to another. Table 2 is often misinterpreted in that high blood pressure is more often viewed negatively as hypertension and associated with a unhealthy lifestyle. Hypertension is only present if a high blood pressure is prolonged/long term. Hypertension is not short term temporary high blood pressure, like that induced by the stress during A Level examinations but long term, enduring high blood pressure.

Treatment is normally provided if Bp exceeds 140mmHg over 90mmHg, but 160 over 95 is more commonly regarded as real hypertension.

Hypertension interrupts the control system for maintaining a normal low blood pressure and if not treated makes hypertension worse and can lead to some harmful effects:

HIGH blood pressure symptoms: Stressed, sedentary, bloated, weak, fainting	
Systolic – Diastolic	Category
210–120	Stage 4 (very severe) High Blood Pressure
180–110	Stage 3 (severe) High Blood Pressure
160–100	Stage 2 (moderate) High Blood Pressure
140–90	Stage 1 (mild) High Blood Pressure
130/139	85/89 – High Normal
<130–<85	NORMAL Blood Pressure
110–75	Low Normal
90–60	BORDERLINE LOW
60–40	TOO LOW Blood Pressure
50–33	DANGER Blood Pressure
LOW blood pressure symptoms: Weak, tired, dizzy, fainting, coma	

Table 2 Blood pressure norms

- increased workload on heart (increased resistance to expel blood).
- increasing/accelerating atherosclerosis (hardening of arterial walls).
- increasing/accelerating arteriosclerosis (narrowing of arterial walls).
- arterial damage (above) increases the risk of a stroke & congestive (weakening) heart failure.

There is mixed evidence, but generally it is suggested exercise can reduce the risk of developing high blood pressure – and in some cases can bring down Bp in people that already have mild to moderate hypertension.

An active lifestyle can prevent high blood pressure indirectly by reducing the risk of obesity – which increases one's chances of hypertension. Exercise has also been strongly linked with reductions in stress, which may help to keep blood pressure at moderate levels.

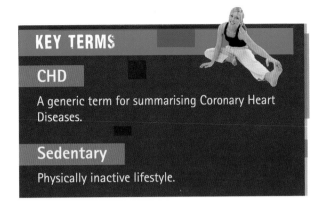

KEY TERMS

CHD

A generic term for summarising Coronary Heart Diseases.

Sedentary

Physically inactive lifestyle.

the single largest cause of death in the western world and is more likely to occur when a more sedentary lifestyle is followed.

The four cardiovascular (CHD) diseases you are required to know are shown below, and show a cause and effect relation where the two blood vessel diseases can lead to the two heart-related diseases.

BLOOD VESSELS: ARTERIOSCLEROSIS

Arteriosclerosis relates to a loss of elasticity, thickening/hardening of the arteries which reduces their efficiency to vasodilate/constrict and therefore regulates Bp and the vascular shunt mechanism.

Interestingly, smoking accelerates the hardening and narrowing process in your arteries, ahead of the natural ageing process, and if you start smoking younger the process will start earlier and blood clots are two to four times more likely.

ATHEROSCLEROSIS

Atherosclerosis is a form of arteriosclerosis that involves changes in the lining of arteries. High levels of cholesterol and fat deposits accumulate within arterial walls forming fatty plaque, leading to a progressive narrowing (diameter) of the lumen – space within the vessel – which increases the likelihood of blood clots forming. This can restrict blood flow and lead to high Bp (hypertension) see Fig 3.2.9 on page 94.

TAKE IT FURTHER

Why do you think a well trained athlete involved in an active lifestyle will have a lower exercising Bp compared with a more sedentary individual?

Note that Table 2 lists a Low Bp as dangerous. What are the implications of a low Bp?

Impact of different types of physical activity on the cardiovascular system

Before looking at the positive effects of a lifelong involvement in an active lifestyle on the cardiovascular system we need to investigate the common cardiovascular diseases (CHDs). CHD is

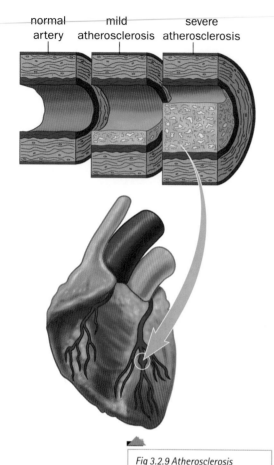

normal artery — mild atherosclerosis — severe atherosclerosis

Fig 3.2.9 Atherosclerosis developing in a coronary artery

HEART: ANGINA

Angina is a partial blockage of the coronary artery causing intense chest pain which occurs when there is an inadequate O_2/blood supply to the heart muscle wall, normally to a smaller area of the heart. Arteriosclerosis and atherosclerosis in the coronary arteries deprives areas of the heart of O_2/blood. This can occur during rest, anxiety, but more especially during physical effort/exercise, when the heart requires more O_2 than the partly blocked coronary arteries can supply.

HEART ATTACK

A heart attack is a more severe/sudden or total restriction in O_2/blood supply to a part of the heart muscle wall, usually causing permanent damage. More likely as a result of blood clots from larger coronary arteries that get stuck in smaller ones and plug them shut. Death can result if the damaged area is large enough to prevent the remaining heart muscle wall from supplying sufficient Q to the body.

IMPACT ON CHD OF LIFELONG INVOLVEMENT IN AN ACTIVE LIFESTYLE

Table 3 shows the five primary risk factors associated with developing CHD. You are required to evaluate critically the impact of physical activity on the CHD we have identified above.

TASK 4

Add up your scores for 1 to 5 in Table 3 to calculate a simplistic assessment of your level of risk of developing CHD. You will not know your blood lipids results but you may wish to estimate your diet in terms of its healthy lifestyle, from 1 to 5. You will also need to know your BMI. Look at the formula and example below Table 3, work out your own BMI, then find the range that your BMI fits into by looking in the table. Compare your own results with those of your group (min 5 to max 25).

The World Health Organization endorses the view that the risk of CHD is 2-3 times more likely in inactive sedentary individuals than that of those physically active. Inactivity is a major risk factor for CHD, almost doubling the risk of a fatal heart attack, and research suggests there is a 'cause-and-effect' relationship between physical inactivity and CHD. Hence, lifelong involvement in an active lifestyle will maintain significant protection from CHD.

CHD – LESSENING THE RISK

Let us now look more critically at how physical activity protects us from CHD both directly in terms of the CHD already identified, and to other CHD risk factors. Physical activity can:

- Improve heart-hypertrophy pumping capacity and circulation; vascularisation; increase capacity/size of coronary circulation.
- Decrease blood fibrinogen; decreases blood clotting and decreases blood viscosity improving blood flow to the coronary circulation.

	Level of risk				
	1	2	3	4	5
Risk factor	V low	Low	Mod	High	V high
1 – Physical/activity (mins/wk)					
Above 60%HR max	120	90	30	0	0
2 – Blood pressure (mmHg)					
Systolic	<110	120	130–140	156–160	> 170
Diastolic	<70	76	82–88	94–100	>106
3 – Smoking (cigarettes p/day)	0	5	10–20	30–40	>50
4 – Blood Lipids					
Cholesterol (mg/dl)	<180	<200	220–240	260–280	>300
Triglycerides (mg/dl)	<50	<100	<130	<200	<300
5 – Obesity (BMI)	>25–27	27–30	30–<35	35–<40	>40

Table 3 CHD primary risk factors

Adapted from Wilmore – CHD Primary Risk factors

Calculation of BMI

Example

1. Height squared: $1.88 \times 1.88 = 3.53$
2. Weight divided by height squared: $952 \div 3.53 = 26.9$
3. BMI =   27 (overweight)

- Decrease blood lipids (triglyceride/cholesterol) which can be deposited on arterial walls leading to athero- and arteriosclerosis.
- Decrease Low Density Lipoproteins (LDL – high in blood lipids/cholesterol which are deposited on vessel walls leading to arterio- and athero-sclerosis.
- Increase High Density Lipoproteins (HDL- low in blood lipids/cholesterol and act as scavengers removing cholesterol from arterial walls.
- Lower Bp and reduce the risk of developing hypertension.
- Reduce obesity controlling body weight which helps against hypertension and control of diabetes.
- Alleviate tension/stress helping reduce hypertension.

Net effect – reduce arterial damage/disease which in turn reduces risk of angina/heart attack.

Although there is an increased risk of angina/heart attack during exercise, in general, those who are physically active have a lower risk than those who are inactive, and far outweigh any potential risk.

OTHER FACTORS

It is not exercise alone that helps reduce CHD; additional factors also help protect us from CHD:

- Acts as a stimulus for a healthier lifestyle: to stop smoking and improve diet.
- Cessation of smoking reduces speeding up of arteriosclerosis.
- Proper nutrition/diet, thereby reducing: weight/obesity, blood lipids, glucose, body fat, and therefore most of the factors bulleted above.

To summarise: regular physical activity and weight control via good nutrition/diet offer the greatest protection against developing CHD.

It should be apparent that nearly all the risk factors interact to increase or decrease CHD. One primary risk factor may double the chance of CHD, whilst three risk factors may increase the

WHO Children & Young People	WHO Under 65 (Adults)	ACSM healthy adults under 65
All young people should participate in physical activity of at least moderate intensity for 60 minutes per day.	Every adult should accumulate 30 minutes or more of moderate-intensity physical activity on most, preferably all, days of week.	Do moderately intense cardio activity 30 minutes a day, five days a week
At least twice a week some of these activities should help to enhance and maintain muscular strength, flexibility, and bone health.	Those not engaging in regular physical activity to begin by incorporating a few minutes of increased activity a day, and build up gradually to 30 minutes per day.	Or, Do vigorously intense cardio 20 minutes a day, 3 days a week...
		And, Do 8 to 10 strength-training exercises, 8 to 12 repetitions of each exercise twice a week
Activity may be divided into shorter periods throughout the day, and should be as versatile and inspiring as possible.	The 30 minutes can be split up into shorter periods, ideally no less than 10 minutes, but even shorter bouts contribute to substantial health benefits.	The 30-minute goal can be split into short bouts of physical activity each with a minimum length of 10 mins.
Recent studies suggested physical activity levels in children should be about 30 minutes higher than the current guidelines of at least 60 minutes per day to prevent clustering of cardiovascular disease risk factors.	However, it is likely that for many people, 45–60 minutes of moderate-intensity physical activity per day is necessary to prevent weight gain or reduce overweight.	To lose weight or maintain weight loss, 60 to 90 minutes of physical activity may be necessary. The 30-minute recommendation is for the average healthy adult to maintain health and reduce the risk for chronic disease.
Moderate-intensity physical activity relates to quick or brisk walking. Cycling, swimming and gardening with moderate effort are other modes of moderate-intensity physical activity.	Moderate-intensity physical activity relates to quick or brisk walking. Cycling, swimming and gardening with moderate effort are other modes of moderate-intensity physical activity.	Moderate-intensity physical activity means working hard enough to raise your heart rate and break a sweat, yet still being able to carry on a conversation.

Table 4 WHO and ACSM recommendations for physical activity

Source: WHO/ACSM

chance of developing CHD by five times. This accentuates the value of physical activity in that it has an encompassing effect on nearly all the CHD risk factors that is not possible by modifying any other single risk factor in isolation.

RECOMMENDATIONS FOR PHYSICAL ACTIVITY

Having established the benefits of physical activity in reducing CHD we now need to consider what level of activity is recommended to help achieve protection against CHD. The answer is good news in that the health benefits against CHD do not require high intensity exercise, like that required to improve aerobic capacity. The level of activity required is generally low, hence, walking, low intensity jogging/cycling etc provides adequate protection against CHD, although higher intensity exercise will provides even greater protection.

WHO's (World Health Organization) Global Strategy on Diet, Physical Activity and Health and ACSM (American College of Sports Medicine) recommend that individuals engage in adequate levels of physical activity throughout their lives.

They recommend different types and amounts of activity for different health outcomes which are summarised in the table opposite.

APPLY IT!

'The take-home lesson is that dietary changes can help reduce/clear the coronary arteries, and that blockages are not irreversible. A healthier diet and a sustained programme of physical activity – can chip away at fatty deposits which block precious oxygen from getting to your heart and lead to a lifelong involvement in an active and healthy lifestyle.'

(Reversing Coronary Artery Disease, The Physician and Sports Medicine, vol. 22 (11), pp. 59–64,1994)

TASK 5

1. Evaluate the three recommendations for exercise prescription in Table 4.
2. Do you meet the recommended minimum guidelines for any of the three columns?
3. Look back at your assessment of your level of risk of developing CHD in Task 4. Discuss the implications of your 'risk factor' in respect of your response to Question 1 above.
4. What general conclusions can you draw, from comparing the three columns?
5. Use the table to establish your own generic set of recommendations for exercise.

Exam**Café**

Relax, refresh, result!

Refresh your memory

Revision checklist – Cardiovascular System Part II

You should now be able to describe and explain:

▷ The distribution of cardiac output at rest and during exercise (the vascular shunt mechanism).
▷ The role of the vasomotor centre and the involvement of arterioles and pre-capillary sphincters.
▷ How carbon dioxide and oxygen are carried within the vascular system; how effective transportation of carbon dioxide and oxygen within the vascular system aids participation in physical activity; how smoking impacts on transportation of oxygen.
▷ Blood pressure and identifying resting values.
▷ The changes that occur during physical activity and hypertension.
▷ How venous return is maintained.
▷ The effects that a warm-up and cool-down period has on the cardiovascular system; how venous return impacts on the quality of performance.
▷ Lifelong involvement in an active lifestyle, how to critically evaluate different physical activities, and the impact these have on the cardiovascular system: coronary heart disease (CHD); arteriosclerosis, atherosclerosis; angina, and heart attack.

REVISE AS YOU GO!

1. Define 'venous return' and describe the mechanisms that help maintain venous return during exercise.
2. How does maintaining venous return affect performance?
3. Sketch a diagram to summarise the redistribution of cardiac output from rest and during exercise. What is this process of blood redistribution called?
4. Explain how oxygen is transported in the blood and how this aids performance during physical activity.
5. What are the benefits of a warm–up to the vascular system of an athlete prior to them engaging in physical activity?
6. How does smoking affect oxygen transport?
7. Provide values to help explain the difference between blood pressure and Hypertension.
8. List the risk factors associated with developing coronary heart disease (CHD).
9. Outline the main coronary heart diseases (CHD), and explain how participation in physical activity protects us from CHD?
10. Describe how the vasomotor centre regulates the redistribution of cardiac output during exercise.

Get the result!

Exam question

The skeletal pump mechanism is one way of helping to maintain venous return.

Describe three other mechanisms involved in venous return.

Explain the importance of the skeletal pump mechanism during an active cool-down. (5)

Examiner says:

The candidate has initially just listed the VR mechanisms when the command word was 'describe'! The answer therefore lacks depth/detail required to merit the marks available. The candidate has gained a mark for describing the muscle-pump action but fell short of explaining why this is so important – hence they have not applied! The candidate's answer reflected that they had not read the question fully and rushed the answer; and a poor understanding of command words. Similarly, the candidate should have acknowledged that 3 marks were available for describing three other mechanisms and that listing four would not be sufficient to merit the marks available.

examiner's tips

- Check the command words: describe + explain.
- Now check the key subject area + focus (vascular + VR/cool-down)
- Now check the marks available (5) and decide if there is a logical split with this 2 part question.

Student answer

Respiratory pump, valves, smooth muscle and gravity help maintain venous return. An active cool-down keeps the muscles working helping pump blood back to the heart and this helps speed up recovery.

Student's improved answer

Three other VR mechanisms are; 1 – Pocket valves in veins prevent the back flow of blood directing it back to the heart, 2 – smooth muscle in veins veno-constricts to help squeeze blood back toward the heart. 3 – Gravity also helps VR for body parts above the heart.

The active cool-down is important because it keeps the skeletal muscle pump working so muscles help squeeze blood back towards the heart. This stops blood pooling in the pocket valves and also helps the removal of CO_2 and lactic acid from the muscles.

Examiner says:

Logical start point

Good link to Q ensuring answer specific to Q

Ordered answer

Good application to function

Response of the respiratory system to physical activity

LEARNING OBJECTIVES

At the end of Part III you will have learned about:

- The mechanics of breathing at rest and the respiratory muscles involved
- The changes in the mechanics of breathing during physical activity (to include reference to additional muscles involved & the active nature of expiration)
- How changes in the mechanics of breathing during physical activity are regulated by the respiratory centre
- The process of gaseous exchange that takes place between the alveoli & blood & between the blood & tissue cells
- The changes in gaseous exchange that takes place between the alveoli & blood & between the blood and the tissue cells as a direct result of participation in physical activity
- The effect of altitude on the respiratory system and how it influences the performance of different types of physical activity
- Evaluating critically the impact of different types of physical activity on the respiratory system with reference to lifelong involvement in an active lifestyle.

INTRODUCTION

Oxygen is essential to produce the energy to fuel all our body's activities. Endurance performance and an active healthy lifestyle depends on the supply of oxygen and removal of carbon dioxide from our working muscles. The primary aim of the respiratory system is to bring blood into contact with atmospheric air so that oxygen can be taken in and carbon dioxide removed.

The respiratory system performs three main processes which are linked via the heart and vascular system.

1. **Pulmonary ventilation** – the breathing of air into and out of the lungs.

2. **External respiration** – exchange of oxygen and carbon dioxide between the lungs and blood.

These two processes are linked to the third by the transport of oxygen and carbon dioxide in the blood to the heart, and around the systemic and pulmonary circulation.

3. **Internal respiration** – exchange of oxygen and carbon dioxide between the blood and the muscle tissues.

The respiratory processes are just as important as the heart and vascular system. It is no use having an efficient pump and transport network if the blood it carries has insufficient oxygen to produce the energy for the muscles to work.

First we will review the respiratory structures and then look at the resting mechanics of breathing, the processes of how oxygen and carbon dioxide are exchanged in the lungs and tissues, and respiratory volumes. Finally we will identify the changes in the mechanics of breathing, respiratory volumes, and gaseous exchange during exercise, identify how they are regulated and consider their impact on performance, including at altitude.

Review of respiratory structures (AK)

You will have learned about respiratory structures in your KS4 studies. However, the following section will help you review your knowledge so that you can describe and explain the efficiency of the respiratory system with reference to the mechanics of breathing and external respiration.

Pulmonary ventilation, i.e. breathing in and out, follows a common pathway through the respiratory structures before oxygen (O_2) and carbon dioxide (CO_2) are exchanged in the lungs – see Fig. 3.3.1. The action of breathing through the nose has the advantage of helping to moisten, filter and warm up air aided by the ciliated mucus lining and blood capillaries within the walls of the respiratory structure, before it enters the lungs; this improves the exchange of oxygen and carbon dioxide. From the nose the air passes through the pharynx, larynx and trachea before entering the lungs.

TASK 1

Put the following structures in order, to show the route of atmospheric air to the site where gaseous exchange takes place: nose/trachea, mouth, alveolus, larynx, pharynx, oral cavity, alveoli sacs, left and right bronchi, nasal cavity, lungs, bronchioles.

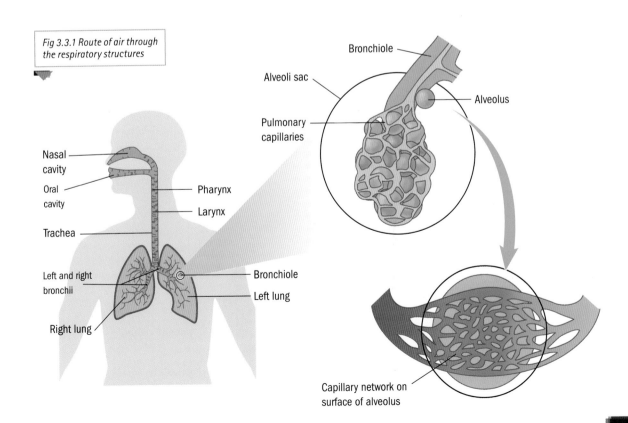

Fig 3.3.1 Route of air through the respiratory structures

Bronchiole

Alveoli sac

Pulmonary capillaries

Alveolus

Nasal cavity

Oral cavity

Pharynx

Larynx

Trachea

Left and right bronchii

Bronchiole

Left lung

Right lung

Capillary network on surface of alveolus

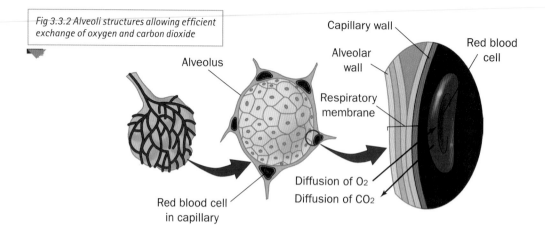

Fig 3.3.2 Alveoli structures allowing efficient exchange of oxygen and carbon dioxide

Capillary wall

Alveolar wall

Red blood cell

Alveolus

Respiratory membrane

Diffusion of O_2
Diffusion of CO_2

Red blood cell in capillary

LOBES OF THE LUNGS

Lobes are simply divisions of each lung, the right lung has three lobes and the left two – this is to accommodate the location of the heart.

The left and right bronchi branch further, forming bronchioles, which branch into each lobe of the lungs. Bronchioles terminate into alveoli ducts leading to alveoli sacs or grape-like clusters of tiny air sacs. Each individual air sac is called an alveolus and is the actual site of gas exchange. We need to look at their structure in more detail to understand how they function to allow the efficient exchange of oxygen and carbon dioxide.

Alveoli increase the efficiency of gas exchange by:

1. Forming a vast surface area (approximately half the size of a tennis court) for gaseous exchange to take place.

2. Having a single-cell layer of thin epithelial cells, reducing the distance for gas exchange with:
    *   a moist lining/film of water helping to dissolve and exchange oxygen
    *   an extensive network of narrow alveoli capillaries producing a short diffusion path
    *   alveoli capillaries have a single-cell layer reducing the distance for gas exchange.

PULMONARY PLEURA

Like the pericardium of the heart, the lungs have pulmonary pleura, double- walled sacs consisting of two membranes filled with pleural fluid, which help to reduce friction between the ribs and lungs during breathing. The outer layer attaches to the ribs and the inner layer to the lungs. This ensures the lungs move with the chest as it expands and relaxes during breathing – see Fig. 3.3.3.

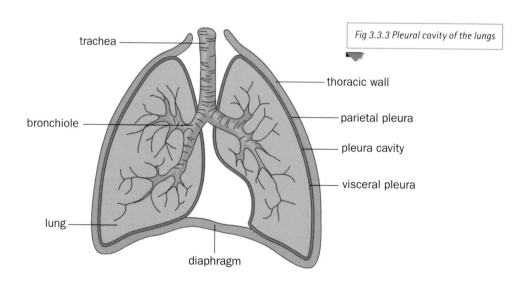

Fig 3.3.3 Pleural cavity of the lungs

trachea

thoracic wall

parietal pleura

bronchiole

pleura cavity

visceral pleura

lung

diaphragm

The inflation and deflation of the lungs, termed inspiration and expiration, result in pulmonary ventilation.

Respiration at rest

THE MECHANICS OF RESPIRATION

Recall that the pulmonary pleura attaches the lungs to the ribs so the lungs will inflate and deflate as the volume of the thoracic cavity increases and decreases. This describes the process of pulmonary respiration but what makes the ribs of the thoracic cavity expand and therefore initiate breathing? The term 'mechanics' suggests levers are involved but what applies the force for levers to move? Muscles produce the force to initiate respiration at both rest and during exercise. Figure 3.3.4 shows all the respiratory muscles involved in the mechanics of breathing.

The mechanics of respiration are easier to learn and understand by linking five steps.

1. **Muscles** – actively contract or passively relax, to cause
2. **Movement** – of the ribs and sternum and abdomen, which causes
3. **Thoracic cavity volume** – to either increase or decrease, which in turn causes
4. **Lung air pressure** – to either increase or decrease, which causes
5. **Inspiration or expiration** – air breathed in or out.

Let us now use these steps to describe the process of inspiration and expiration.

Follow these steps through inspiration and expiration in Table 1, and identify the active and passive muscles responsible in Figure 3.3.4.

Inspiration (active)	Expiration (passive)
1 Diaphragm contracts – active External intercostals contract – active	1 Diaphragm relaxes – passive External intercostals relax – passive
2 Diaphragm flattens/ pushed down Ribs/sternum move up and out	2 Diaphragm pushed upward Ribs/sternum move in and down
3 Thoracic cavity volume increases	3 Thoracic cavity volume decreases
4 Lung air pressure decreases below atmospheric air (outside)	4 Lung air pressure increases above atmospheric air (outside)
5 Air rushes into lungs	5 Air rushes out of lungs

Table 1 Mechanics of breathing, at rest

Fig 3.3.4 Active inspiration (a), and passive expiration (b) at rest

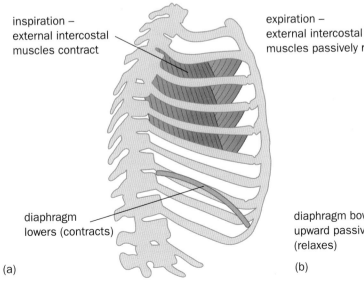

inspiration – external intercostal muscles contract

expiration – external intercostal muscles passively relax

diaphragm lowers (contracts)

diaphragm bows upward passively (relaxes)

(a)

(b)

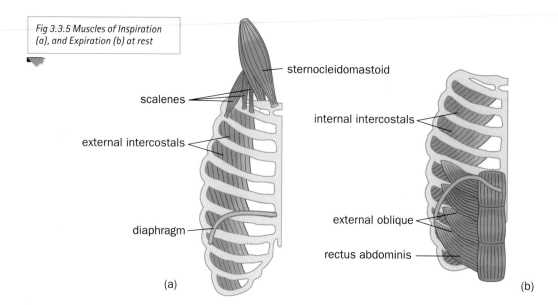

Fig 3.3.5 Muscles of Inspiration (a), and Expiration (b) at rest

sternocleidomastoid

scalenes

external intercostals

diaphragm

internal intercostals

external oblique

rectus abdominis

(a)

(b)

TASK 2

In pairs, one completes three minutes of aerobic exercise and one completes three minutes of anaerobic work. Record the frequency of breathing: at rest, one minute after completion, and the time it takes to return to resting values. Compare and discuss your results.

EXAM TIP

Respiratory muscles initiate breathing by increasing and decreasing the volume of the lung cavity and therefore lung pressures. Do not make the mistake of thinking the lungs or pressure differences themselves initiate breathing.

Mechanics of respiration during exercise

As you begin to exercise, the demand for oxygen by the working muscles increases, and respiration similarly needs to increase in both rate and depth of breathing. We have already identified that the respiratory muscles initiate breathing. It is therefore no surprise that to increase the rate/depth of

breathing during exercise, additional muscles to those of the diaphragm and external intercostals used at rest are required. The additional muscles for both inspiration and expiration are shown in Figure 3.3.5, and appear in italics in Table 2.

Inspiration (active)	Expiration (passive)
1 Diaphragm contracts External intercostals contract *Sternocleidomastoid* contracts *Scalenes* contract *Pectoralis minor* contracts	1 Diaphragm relaxes External intercostals relax *Internal intercostals* contract (active) *Rectus abdominus/ Obliques* contract (active)
2 Diaphragm flattens with more force Increased lifting of ribs and sternum	2 Diaphragm pushed up harder with more force Ribs/sternum pulled in and down
3 Increased thoracic cavity volume	3 Greater decrease in thoracic cavity volume
4 Lower air pressure in lungs	4 Higher air pressure in lungs
5 More air rushes into lungs	5 More air pushed out of the lungs

Table 2 Mechanics of breathing during exercise

The net effect of these additional respiratory muscles is to increase both the depth and rate of breathing so as to increase the supply of air containing oxygen to the site of gaseous exchange in the alveoli.

RESPIRATORY VOLUMES AT REST

Recall from Part I that to calculate the efficiency of the performance of the heart we used three definitions and their average values to compare resting with exercise levels. In exactly the same manner, the respiratory system has three definitions and values, which help calculate the efficiency of the respiratory system. Let us look at the link between these three definitions and values at rest.

LUNG VOLUMES

- **Tidal Volume** (TV) – the volume of air inspired or expired per breath – approximately 500ml during breathing at rest.
- **Frequency** (f) – the number of breaths taken in one minute – approximately 12–15 breaths during breathing at rest.
- **Minute Ventilation** (VE) – the volume of air inspired or expired in one minute. VE can be calculated by multiplying the tidal volume with the frequency of breaths in one minute.

The link between TV, f and VE is shown by the following equation:

$$VE = TV \times f$$
$$= 500ml \times 15$$
$$= 7500ml/min$$
$$= 7.5L/min$$

TASK 3

1. Recall and write down the corresponding equation for the heart alongside the respiratory equation above.
2. If an athlete has a resting TV of 500ml and respiratory frequency of 12 per minute what would their VE be?

EXAM TIP

Remember the close similarity between these two equations and don't confuse them when answering heart/respiratory volume questions. Remember respiratory refers to air and heart refers to blood.

LUNG VOLUME CHANGES DURING EXERCISE

Like the heart, respiration increases in line with exercise intensity in order to supply the increased oxygen demands of our working muscles. Table 3 summarises these changes. Both the rate (f) and depth (TV) of breathing increase, which in turn increase VE from resting values of 6 L/min up to maximal values of 160–180L/min in trained aerobic athletes.

TV and f increase at lower intensities of workload to increase VE but during maximal work it is an additional increase in the rate of breathing that increases VE further. It is not efficient to increase TV towards maximal values due to the time/effort it takes – try running while taking a maximal inspiration and expiration and see why this is not feasible.

TASK 4

A TV of 500ml and frequency of 12 produces a VE of 6L/min. Explain why increasing the frequency to 24 and a TV of 4000ml per breath during exercise would be beneficial to an aerobic athlete

Gaseous exchange

We now understand the way in which pulmonary ventilation ensures the supply of air in and out of the lungs through inspiration and expiration but we need to consider how the oxygen and carbon dioxide are actually exchanged.

Lung volume	Definition	Resting volume	Change due to exercise
Tidal volume X	Volume of air inhaled/exhaned per breath during rest	500ml per breath	Increases: up to around 3–4 litres
Frequency = VE Minute ventilation	Number of breaths in one minute Volume of air inspired/expired in one minute	12–15 6–7.5L/min	Increase: 40–60 Increase: values up to 120L/min in smaller individuals and up to 180+L/min in larger aerobic trained athletes

Table 3 Lung volume changes during exercise

REMEMBER

The exchange of oxygen and carbon dioxide takes place in the lungs and tissues and are called external and internal respiration respectively.

Hence, gaseous exchange refers to the exchange of gases, namely oxygen and carbon dioxide and relies on a process called **diffusion**. Diffusion is the movement of gases from an area of high pressure to an area of low pressure. The difference between the high and low pressure is called the **diffusion gradient** – the bigger the gradient, the greater the diffusion and gaseous exchange that takes place.

EXAM TIP

The simplest way to remember whether blood has a high or low partial pressure (PP) of O_2 or CO_2 is to think back to the terms oxygenated and deoxygenated blood. If the blood is oxygenated it has a high PP of O_2 and low PP of CO_2 and deoxygenated blood has the opposite. Similarly the tissues/muscles and alveoli PP of O_2 and CO_2 are the opposite to that of the PP of blood within the blood vessels of the vascular system.

PARTIAL PRESSURE

Central to the understanding of diffusion is an understanding of partial pressure (PP). The partial pressure of a gas is the pressure it exerts within a mixture of gases. The guiding principle of PP that you need to understand is that gases always move from areas of high partial pressure to areas of low partial pressure. While it is not necessary for you to know exact pressures, you do need to understand where and when these PP are higher or lower, in order for you to understand which direction gases are moving, during external and internal respiration. Let us consider external and internal respiration together to help you see where and when the PP is high or low.

Refer to Figure 3.3.6 as you follow Table 4.

EXTERNAL (ALVEOLI) RESPIRATION

The inspired air entering the alveoli in the lungs has a high PP of oxygen and low PP of carbon dioxide compared with the deoxygenated blood in the alveoli capillaries, which has a low PP of oxygen and high PP of carbon dioxide. These two pressure gradients cause diffusion of:

1. **Oxygen** from the alveoli into the blood of the capillaries to be transported back to the left atrium, and (diffusion of)
2. **Carbon** dioxide from the capillary blood into the alveoli of the lungs where it is expired.

REMEMBER

Recall from Part II (see page 87 and Fig 3.2.6) that oxygen is transported within the haemoglobin of the red blood cells (97%) and blood plasma (3%).

	External respiration	Internal respiration
Where?	Alveolar–capillary membrane, between alveoli air and blood in alveolar capillaries	Tissue capillary membrane, between the blood in the capillaries and the tissue (muscle) cells walls
Movement	O_2 in alveoli diffuses to blood; CO_2 in blood diffuses to alveoli	O_2 in blood diffuses to tissue; CO_2 in tissue diffuses to blood
Why? –O_2	PP of O_2 in alveoli higher than the PP of O_2 in the blood so O_2 diffuses into the blood	PP of O_2 in blood is higher than the PP of O_2 in the tissue so O_2 diffuses into the Myoglobin within tissues
Why? –CO_2	PP of CO_2 in the blood is higher than the PP of CO_2 in the alveoli so CO_2 diffuses into the alveoli	PP of CO_2 in the tissue is higher than the PP of CO_2 in the blood so CO_2 diffuses into the capillary blood

Table 4 Lung volume changes during exercise

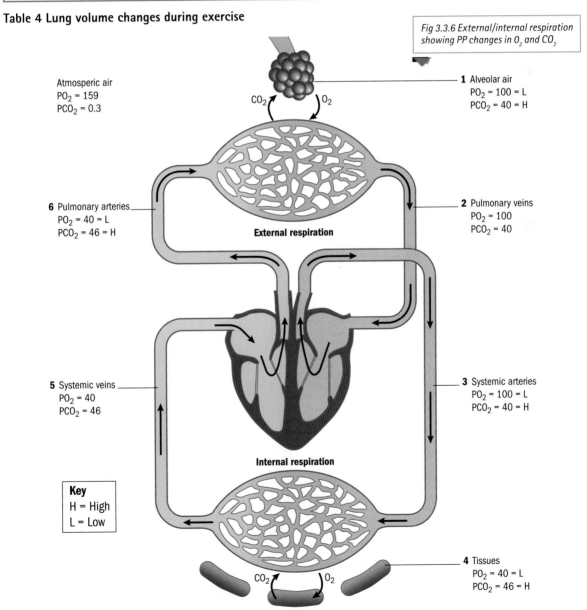

Fig 3.3.6 External/internal respiration
showing PP changes in O_2 and CO_2

Atmosperic air
$PO_2 = 159$
$PCO_2 = 0.3$

1 Alveolar air
$PO_2 = 100 = L$
$PCO_2 = 40 = H$

6 Pulmonary arteries
$PO_2 = 40 = L$
$PCO_2 = 46 = H$

External respiration

2 Pulmonary veins
$PO_2 = 100$
$PCO_2 = 40$

5 Systemic veins
$PO_2 = 40$
$PCO_2 = 46$

3 Systemic arteries
$PO_2 = 100 = L$
$PCO_2 = 40 = H$

Internal respiration

Key
H = High
L = Low

4 Tissues
$PO_2 = 40 = L$
$PCO_2 = 46 = H$

107

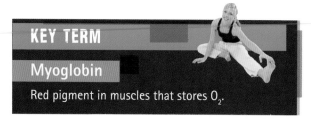

KEY TERM

Myoglobin

Red pigment in muscles that stores O_2.

INTERNAL (TISSUE) RESPIRATION

The oxygenated blood is pumped around the systemic circulation until it reaches the capillaries surrounding the body tissues/muscles. The capillary blood has a high PP of oxygen and low PP of carbon dioxide compared with the tissue/muscle cells, which have a low PP of oxygen and high PP of carbon dioxide, having used their oxygen for energy production and given off carbon dioxide as a by-product.

The oxygen passed into the muscle cells is transferred from the haemoglobin in the blood capillaries to myoglobin within the muscle tissue, which both stores and transports the oxygen to the mitochondria where it is used for energy production. Recall that carbon dioxide is transported in the blood as carbonic acid (70%), carbaminohaemoglobin (20%) and plasma (7%), back to the right atrium of the heart.

TASK 5

Outline the changes that take place in the PP of oxygen and carbon dioxide and the subsequent movement of these gases, as blood travels from the lungs to the tissues and back to the lungs.

Changes in gaseous exchange due to exercise

Having identified the process of gaseous exchange within both external and internal respiration we now need to understand the changes that occur in response to/during exercise. Both external and internal respiration increase during exercise in order to increase the supply of oxygen to the working muscles but to understand how, we need to have a basic understanding of an oxygen–haemoglobin dissociation curve.

OXYGEN-HAEMOGLOBIN DISSOCIATION CURVE

An oxygen–haemoglobin dissociation curve informs us of the amount of haemoglobin saturated with oxygen. Haemoglobin that is fully bound or loaded with oxygen is termed saturated or association, whereas oxygen unloading from haemoglobin is called dissociation. Figure 3.3.7 shows the dissociation curve at rest.

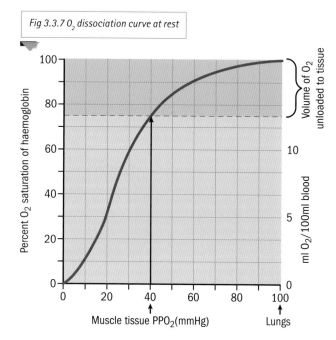

Fig 3.3.7 O_2 dissociation curve at rest

TASK 6

1. Look at the PP oxygen (mmHg) on the bottom 'x' axis in Figure 3.3.7 and familiarise yourself with what this curve is showing.
2. At rest, the PP of oxygen in the lungs is 100mmHg. Follow this line up from 100mmHg and see where it intersects the curve. Draw a line across to the side 'y' axis and record the value. If you have followed these steps

correctly you should have a figure around 98%. This represents the percentage of saturation/association of oxygen with haemoglobin in the alveoli capillary blood.

3. At rest the PP of oxygen in the tissues/muscles is around 40mmHg. Repeat the steps above and calculate the percentage saturation /association of oxygen and haemoglobin in the tissues/muscles' capillary blood.

4. What has happened to approximately 25% of the oxygen associated with haemoglobin?

PP COMPARISONS

If you have completed the task above correctly you should have a basic understanding of what the oxygen–haemoglobin dissociation curve is showing. Task 6 illustrates an important principle: the higher the PP oxygen, the higher the percentage of oxygen saturation/association to haemoglobin (Hb). Hence, a higher PP oxygen of 100mmHg in the lungs results in almost 100% saturation, compared with a lower PP oxygen of 40mmHg in the tissues which results in only 75% saturation/association.

Approximately 25% of the oxygen has dissociated from haemoglobin into the tissues/muscles. Where do you think we need the association and dissociation of oxygen and haemoglobin to take place in order to maintain an efficient supply of oxygen to the working muscles during exercise?

The answer is of course association in the lungs, so that the blood can carry the oxygen to the muscle capillaries where it can dissociate and unload the oxygen to the muscle tissue to provide energy for work.

Task 7 above demonstrates that a shift of the oxygen–haemoglobin dissociation curve to the right represents an accelerated dissociation of oxy-haemoglobin, hence, more oxygen unloading

TASK 7

Look at the oxygen–haemoglobin dissociation curves shown in Figure 3.3.8.

The red curve on the left represents the normal curve we have already looked at in Fig. 3.3.7. Read off the values for the percentage saturation/association of oxygen and haemoglobin in the tissues/muscles using the blue curve on the right.

What effect does moving the curve to the right have on the saturation of haemoglobin if we assume the PP of oxygen remains the same in the tissues?

What are the benefits for an athlete of the curve shifting to the right?

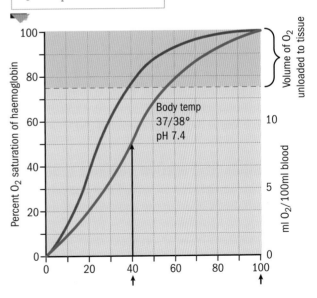

Fig 3.3.8 O_2/Hb dissociation curve

from the haemoglobin in the blood to the muscle tissue. Now that you have an understanding of the oxygen dissociation curve, let us look at the changes taking place within external and internal respiration during exercise.

Partial pressure	Alveolar air	Direction of diffusion (High to low PP)	Alveoli capillary blood	Diffusion gradient
O_2	100 (high)	→	40 (low)	60
CO_2	40 (low)	←	46 (high)	6

Table 5 O_2 and CO_2 PP during External respiration

EXTERNAL RESPIRATION DURING EXERCISE

During exercise, skeletal muscles are using a greater amount of oxygen to provide energy and consequently are producing greater amounts of carbon dioxide as a by-product. Hence, deoxygenated venous blood returning to the lungs from the right ventricle has a higher PP of carbon dioxide and lower PP of oxygen. In contrast alveolar air has a high PP of oxygen and low PP of carbon dioxide. This has the effect of increasing the diffusion gradient for both oxygen and carbon dioxide between the alveoli-capillary membrane resulting in both a quicker and greater amount of gaseous exchange. The high PP of oxygen in the alveoli and low PP of oxygen in the capillaries ensures haemoglobin is almost fully saturated with oxygen – see Table 5.

Although you are not required to provide actual partial pressures, they do help to explain how the diffusion gradient works. The oxygen and carbon dioxide will diffuse across until the partial pressures are equal, hence, the greater the diffusion gradient the greater the amount of oxygen and carbon dioxide exchanged.

INTERNAL RESPIRATION DURING EXERCISE

You should already understand that a greater oxygen dissociation in the muscle tissues during exercise is required in order to increase the supply of oxygen to the working muscles. Four factors, shown below, all have the effect of shifting the dissociation curve to the right or, more simply, increasing the dissociation of oxygen from Hb in the blood capillaries to the muscle tissue.

1. Increase in blood and muscle temperature.
2. Decrease in PP oxygen within muscle, increasing the oxygen diffusion gradient.
3. Increase in PP of carbon dioxide, increasing the carbon dioxide diffusion gradient.
4. Bohr effect – increase in acidity (lower pH).

Interestingly all of these factors increase during exercise. The effect is that the working muscles:

- generate more heat when working
- use more oxygen to provide energy, lowering the PP oxygen
- produce more carbon dioxide as a by-product
- increase lactic acid levels, which increase muscle/blood acidity (lowers the pH).

Collectively all four of these factors increase the dissociation of oxygen from haemoglobin, which increases the supply of oxygen to the working muscles and therefore delays fatigue and increases the possible intensity/duration of performance – see Fig. 3.3.9 and Table 6.

Partial pressure	Capillary blood	Direction of diffusion (High to low PP)	Muscle tissue	Diffusion gradient
O_2 resting	100	→	40	60
O_2 during exercise	100	→	<5	95
CO_2 resting	40	←	45	6
CO_2 during exercise	40	←	80	40

Table 6 O_2 and CO_2 PP during Internal respiration

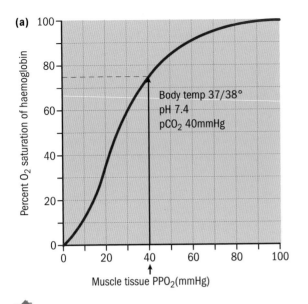

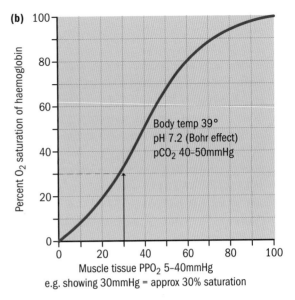

Fig 3.3.9 Comparison of Hb/dissociation curve at rest (a), and during exercise (b)

VENTILATORY RESPONSE TO LIGHT, MODERATE AND HEAVY EXERCISE

Recall that VE is the volume of air inspired or expired in one minute. Figure 3.3.10 shows the pulmonary ventilation (VE) response from resting to sub-maximal and maximal exercise intensities which you are required to describe and explain.

Ventilatory response to exercise mirrors that of the heart except that it is the Respiratory Control Centre (RCC), controlling the respiratory muscles, which increases or decreases breathing. Let us look at the VE response in steps which correspond to the stages on Figure 3.3.10, to make this process easier to understand.

1. **Anticipatory rise** – prior to exercise in all three work intensities, due to the release of hormones (adrenalin), which stimulate the RCC.

Fig 3.3.10 VE response to varying intensities of exercise

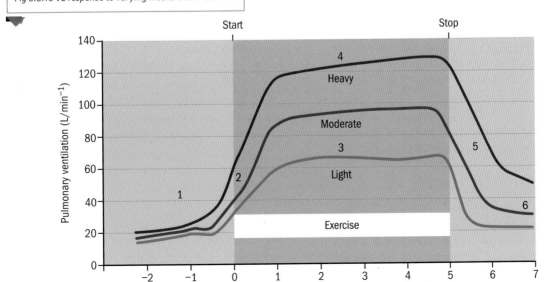

2. **Rapid rise in VE** – at the start of exercise due to neural stimulation of RCC by muscle and joint proprioreceptors.

3. **Slower increase/plateau** – in sub-maximal exercise, due to continued stimulation of RCC by proprioreceptors, but with additional stimulation from temperature and chemoreceptors due to an increase in temperature, CO2 and lactic acid levels and a decrease in oxygen in the blood. Plateau represents a steady state where the demands for oxygen by the muscles are being met by oxygen supply.

4. **Continued but slower increase** – in VE towards maximal values during maximal work due to continued stimulation from the receptors above and increasing chemoreceptor stimulation due to increasing CO2 and lactic acid accumulation.

5. **Rapid decrease in VE** – in all three intensities once exercise stops due to the cessation of proprioreceptor and decreasing chemoreceptor stimulation.

6. **Slower decrease** – towards resting VE values. The more intense the exercise period the longer the elevated level of respiration required to help remove the increased by-products of exercise, e.g. lactic acid.

Control of breathing – respiratory control centre

The respiratory control centre (RCC) regulates pulmonary respiration (breathing). As with all the cardiorespiratory systems, the RCC is located in the medulla oblongata of the brain and responds in conjunction with the CCC (Cardiac Control Centre) and the VCC (Vasomotor Control Centre). Recall from the mechanics of breathing that the respiratory muscles actually initiate breathing. Let us now consider how the RCC controls these respiratory muscles to regulate pulmonary ventilation.

NERVOUS/NEURAL CONTROL

The respiratory muscles are under involuntary neural control. Although we can voluntarily change our rate and depth of breathing with conscious thought, during exercise we may be more concerned with concentrating on where the ball or opponent is than on breathing!

The respiratory control centre has two areas, the inspiratory and expiratory centres, which are responsible for the stimulation of the respiratory muscles at rest and during exercise.

AT REST

1. **The inspiratory centre** – is responsible for the rhythmic cycle of inspiration and expiration to produce a respiratory rate of 12–15 breaths a minute:
   a) The inspiratory centre sends impulses to the respiratory muscles via:
      - phrenic nerves to the diaphragm
      - intercostal nerves to the external intercostals.
   b) When stimulated these muscles contract, increasing the volume of the thoracic cavity, causing inspiration (active).
   c) When their stimulation stops, the muscles relax, decreasing the volume of the thoracic cavity, causing expiration (passive).

2. **The expiratory centre** – is inactive during quiet/resting breathing. Expiration is passive as a result of the relaxation of the diaphragm and external intercostals.

DURING EXERCISE

Pulmonary ventilation increases during exercise, which increases both the depth and rate of breathing. This is regulated by:

1. **The inspiratory centre**, which:
   a) increases the stimulation of the diaphragm and external intercostals
   b) stimulates additional inspiratory muscles for inspiration – the sternocleidomastoid, scalenes and pectoralis minor – which increase the force of contraction and therefore the depth of inspiration.

2. **The expiratory centre**, which stimulates the expiratory muscles – internal intercostals, rectus abdominus and obliques – causing a forced expiration which reduces the duration of inspiration.

In response, the inspiratory centre immediately stimulates the inspiratory muscles to inspire. The net effect of the above is that as exercise intensity increases, the depth of breathing decreases and the rate of breathing increases.

FACTORS INFLUENCING THE NEURAL CONTROL OF BREATHING

Emotions, pain, respiratory irritants are all factors that affect breathing. However, we need to identify those factors more concerned with the primary purpose of respiration – to maintain appropriate levels of blood and tissue gases (oxygen and carbon dioxide) and pH levels in order for athletes to continue exercising.

SEVERAL FACTORS

Control of breathing during physical activity does not result from a single factor but the combined effects of chemical and neural stimuli which stimulate the RCC, and summarised in Figure 3.3.11. The main receptors and the information they send to the RCC during exercise that you need to know are:

1. **Chemoreceptors** from within the medulla and carotid arteries send information to the inspiratory centre on:
   (a) increase in PP carbon dioxide – thought to be the primary factor
   (b) decrease in PP oxygen
   (c) decrease in pH (increasing acidity).
2. **Proprioreceptors** located in the muscles and joints send information to the inspiratory

centre on motor movement of the active/working muscles.
3. **Thermoreceptors** send information to the inspiratory centre on increase in blood temperature.
4. **Baroreceptors** or stretch receptors located in the lungs, send information to the expiratory centre on the extent of lung inflation during inspiration.

Receptors 1–3 above all stimulate the inspiratory centre to increase the force/depth of breathing. Baroreceptors stimulate the expiratory centre to actively expire, reducing the duration of inspiration, and thereby increasing the rate of breathing.

TASK 8

1. Follow the numbered steps in Figure 3.3.12.
2. Which area of the RCC is responsible for increasing the depth of breathing?
3. Which area of the RCC is responsible for increasing the rate of breathing?

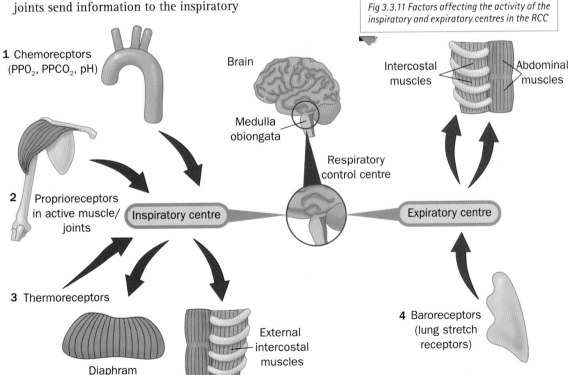

Fig 3.3.11 Factors affecting the activity of the inspiratory and expiratory centres in the RCC

1 Chemorecptors (PPO$_2$, PPCO$_2$, pH)

Brain

Intercostal muscles

Abdominal muscles

Medulla oblongata

Respiratory control centre

2 Proprioreceptors in active muscle/joints

Inspiratory centre

Expiratory centre

3 Thermoreceptors

External intercostal muscles

Diaphram

4 Baroreceptors (lung stretch receptors)

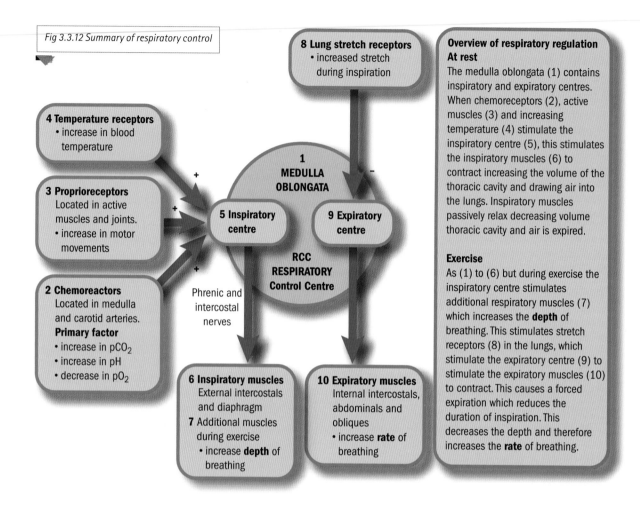

Fig 3.3.12 Summary of respiratory control

8 Lung stretch receptors
• increased stretch during inspiration

4 Temperature receptors
• increase in blood temperature

3 Proprioreceptors
Located in active muscles and joints.
• increase in motor movements

2 Chemoreactors
Located in medulla and carotid arteries.
Primary factor
• increase in pCO_2
• increase in pH
• decrease in pO_2

1 MEDULLA OBLONGATA

5 Inspiratory centre

9 Expiratory centre

RCC **RESPIRATORY Control Centre**

Phrenic and intercostal nerves

6 Inspiratory muscles
External intercostals and diaphragm
7 Additional muscles during exercise
• increase **depth** of breathing

10 Expiratory muscles
Internal intercostals, abdominals and obliques
• increase **rate** of breathing

Overview of respiratory regulation
At rest
The medulla oblongata (1) contains inspiratory and expiratory centres. When chemoreceptors (2), active muscles (3) and increasing temperature (4) stimulate the inspiratory centre (5), this stimulates the inspiratory muscles (6) to contract increasing the volume of the thoracic cavity and drawing air into the lungs. Inspiratory muscles passively relax decreasing volume thoracic cavity and air is expired.

Exercise
As (1) to (6) but during exercise the inspiratory centre stimulates additional respiratory muscles (7) which increases the **depth** of breathing. This stimulates stretch receptors (8) in the lungs, which stimulate the expiratory centre (9) to stimulate the expiratory muscles (10) to contract. This causes a forced expiration which reduces the duration of inspiration. This decreases the depth and therefore increases the **rate** of breathing.

Effects of altitude on the respiratory system

We have already identified that an adequate supply of oxygen to the working muscles is essential for performance. Exposure to high altitude has a significant effect upon performance by affecting the normal processes of respiration. At high altitude (+ 1500m) the PP of oxygen in the atmospheric air is significantly reduced (hypoxic) – see Fig. 3.3.13 – and it is primarily this reduction in PP that causes a sequence of knock-on effects, which decrease the efficiency of the respiratory processes and consequently negates performance. Figure 3.3.14 summarises the effects of exercising/training at altitude on the respiratory system.

The course specification requires you to explain the effect of altitude on the respiratory system and how it influences performance to different intensities of physical activity. You should also be able to discuss the benefits of the different methods of altitude training used as ergogenic training aids.

KEY TERM

Ergogenic

Anything that improves performance.

APPLY IT!

Performance at altitude leads to decreased power outputs, e.g. slower running and cycling speeds.

TASK 9

What are the proposed adaptations and benefits of the body's response to altitude when an athlete then runs at sea level?

ALTITUDE TRAINING

The main rationale behind altitude training is that due to the hypoxic conditions, the body adapts by increasing the release of erythropoietin (EPO) which stimulates an increase in red blood cell (rbc) production along with an increase in capillarisation, which are primarily vascular adaptations. The main benefit being that upon return to sea level this increases O_2 carrying capacity (VO_2 max) and this will increase aerobic-based performance.

FEEDBACK

Altitude training remains an expensive and logistical headache and research evidence is often

At 9000m
Barometric pressure = 231
PPO_2 = 59

Altitude (m)	Barometric P (mmHg)	PPO_2
9000	231	59
4000	462	97
3000	526	110
2000	596	125
1000	674	141
0 sea level	760	159

At sea level
Barometric pressure = 760
PPO_2 = 159

Fig 3.3.13 Changes to PPO_2 with change in altitude

Fig 3.3.14 Effects of altitude on respiratory system

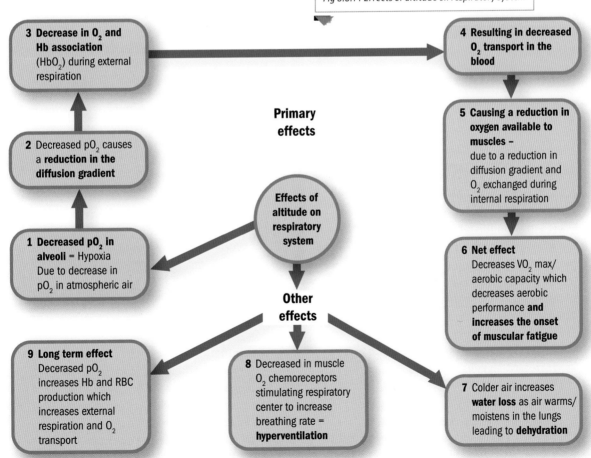

3 Decrease in O_2 and Hb association (HbO_2) during external respiration

4 Resulting in decreased O_2 transport in the blood

Primary effects

2 Decreased pO_2 causes a **reduction in the diffusion gradient**

5 Causing a reduction in oxygen available to muscles – due to a reduction in diffusion gradient and O_2 exchanged during internal respiration

Effects of altitude on respiratory system

1 **Decreased pO_2 in alveoli** = Hypoxia Due to decrease in pO_2 in atmospheric air

6 **Net effect** Decreases VO_2 max/ aerobic capacity which decreases aerobic performance **and increases the onset of muscular fatigue**

Other effects

9 **Long term effect** Decerased pO_2 increases Hb and RBC production which increases external respiration and O_2 transport

8 Decreased in muscle O_2 chemoreceptors stimulating respiratory center to increase breathing rate = **hyperventilation**

7 Colder air increases **water loss** as air warms/ moistens in the lungs leading to **dehydration**

mixed and conflicting, and requires further study. Most research indicates that training at altitude provides no significant additional benefit to that achieved at sea level. High altitudes prevent athletes training at the same volume and intensity as they can at sea level due to the hypoxic air, decreasing VO_2 max and having a detraining effect which can negate the positive adaptations that occur as a result of being at altitude. Also, any adaptations that do occur are not significant and short lived so only offer an advantage for a few days after returning to sea level.

Although the actual performance at altitude decreases it will help athletes to adapt and perform better than those having not acclimatised to altitude conditions at all. If an athlete is competing at altitude some acclimatisation is therefore essential, or alternatively a 4–6 week block of **Inspiratory Muscle Training** before acclimatisation will help overcome the huge increase in respiratory effort when competing at altitude (see page 119).

APPLY IT!

100/200m sprints, long/triple/high jump, javelin/ discus are all events that may improve as a result of performance at altitude.

Respiratory adaptations to physical activity

The net effect on the respiratory system of training is an increase in its efficiency to supply O_2 to the working muscles during higher intensities of physical activity. The specific respiratory adaptations that improve this efficiency are shown here:

1. **Respiratory structures:**
   - Increased alveoli, increasing surface area for diffusion.
   - Increased elasticity of respiratory structures (lungs, alveoli, pleura).
   - Increased longevity of respiratory structure efficiency.

TAKE IT FURTHER

LIVING HIGH AND TRAINING LOW (LHTL)
There is however growing evidence that LHTL does benefit performance at sea level, as this maintains both the training volume/intensity and gains the positive hypoxic adaptations. Portable altitude simulators in the form of house/tent/rooms are now available and help athletes replicate the LHTL conditions from home and alleviate the problems of expense and practicality. The use of altitude simulators pose an interesting question: Are they an ethical ergogenic aid in the same way as training at altitude?

Interestingly, anaerobic activity is less affected by altitude, as these activities do not rely on aerobic energy provision dependent upon O_2, and the thinner hypoxic air will also offer less air resistance, so that short duration explosive/sprint type activities may actually increase in terms of performance. There is also some supporting evidence that LHTL can increase anaerobic performance, primarily due to an increased lactate-buffering capacity of muscles.

TASK 10

There are three main methods of altitude training which have mixed and conflicting research. Research and discuss the three methods of altitude training below in relation to their benefits to improving performance.

1. Live High Train High – LHTH
2. Live Low Train High – LLTH
3. Live High Train Low – LHTL

2. **Breathing Mechanics:**
   - Increased efficiency/economy of respiratory muscles reduces the O_2 costs of the respiratory muscles, reducing respiratory fatigue.
   - Increase in strength, power and endurance of respiratory muscles.

3. **Respiratory Volumes:**
   - In general lung volumes and capacities change little with training, at rest and during sub-maximal activity (VC/TLC).
   - However, TV can increase during maximal exercise.
   - Respiratory frequency decreases at rest/sub-maximal activity but can increase during maximal work.
   - Maximal VE can significantly increase from around 120Lmin in an untrained athlete to 150Lmin following training.
   - 180–200+ in elite athletes, due to increase in TV and f (see also 2 on page 116) at maximal exercise.
4. **Diffusion:**
   - Diffusion unchanged at rest and sub-maximal exercise.
   - Increase in pulmonary diffusion during maximal activity.
   - Increased VO_2 diff (arterial–venous oxygen difference) at maximal activity (less O_2 in venous blood representing increased delivery and extraction of O_2 to active muscles).

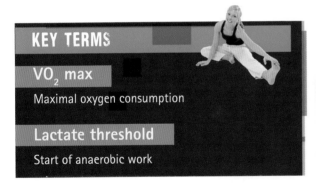

KEY TERMS

VO_2 max

Maximal oxygen consumption

Lactate threshold

Start of anaerobic work

OUTCOMES

The net effect of all the above efficiency improvements is that VO_2 max and the lactate threshold increase, both of which improve performance.

The main performance benefits are:

- aerobic performance during higher/maximal work rates is both increased and prolonged
- more effect with aerobic endurance activity that is dependent more upon O2, although it

will delay the anaerobic threshold and therefore delay fatigue during anaerobic activity
- reduces the effort of sub-max work therefore increasing duration of performance
- a more efficient and healthy respiratory system encourages and promotes a lifelong involvement in an active/healthy lifestyle.

APPLY IT!

If an athlete increases their lactate threshold they can run, swim or cycle faster aerobically, at an intensity that would have previously have been anaerobic and caused an accumulation of lactate levels, thus causing fatigue.

Respiratory system and an active lifestyle

Having identified the specific respiratory adaptations to training, we are now better able to critically evaluate these effects alongside those of asthma and smoking in reference to a lifelong involvement in an active/healthy lifestyle.

TAKE IT FURTHER

BACKGROUND
Sports scientists have long thought that there is no respiratory limit to pulmonary ventilation/VO_2 max and this therefore does not limit endurance performance, even during maximal work. This is further backed up in that athletes still breathe out O_2 within expired air during maximal exercise. It was therefore thought it was ability of the muscles to use O_2 that was a limiting factor to performance and not the respiratory system, so there was no need to train the respiratory system.

However, as already identified, all the major respiratory adaptations are more apparent during higher intensity/maximal activity when the respiratory system is most stressed, and this now suggests that pulmonary ventilation/VO_2 max can limit performance, especially in the 'highly trained', during exhaustive higher intensity activity.

IMT:

OVERVIEW

So how do we train the respiratory system? The above points highlight the link with a more recent/growing form of ergogenic training called *Inspiratory Muscle Training* (IMT). IMT is aimed directly at increasing the efficiency of the respiratory muscles to increase performance and also has an application for the treatment of asthma which we will look at later.

It is now accepted that during and after sustained higher intensity endurance activity the respiratory muscles do become fatigued and this can limit performance – this is termed *Inspiratory Muscle Fatigue* (IMF). We do of course train the respiratory muscles during normal training/ physical activity, but it is now thought we need to increase this resistance even further to increase their fatigue resistance on to new heights.

THEORY

Simply put, when the key muscles of respiration, the diaphragm and intercostals tire/fatigue, breathing capacity drops and the exercise feels harder and this decreases performance. It is also thought that fatigued respiratory muscles may require more O_2 and subsequently divert O_2 away from the working muscle which impairs lactate removal reducing their intensity of work, or leading to muscle fatigue.

TECHNIQUE

So what does IMT entail? IMT, like all other skeletal muscle training, provides a resistance to the respiratory muscles which adapt by increasing their strength, power and endurance. IMT uses a form of spirometer, which the athlete breathes into against a set resistance. Various brands, of which 'POWERbreathe' is one, are available, with the better models allowing the resistance to be

increased as the respiratory muscles adapt and become stronger. They have many benefits in relation to their applied use; they have no side effects, time efficient (4–15mins/day), and as they can be taken/used anywhere they are very practical.

BENEFITS

The benefits of IMT are summarised below.

- Effort of IMT is low so is suitable for even older/ill patients.
- Reduces both IMF during and after exercise.
- Reduces IMF within first few days of use & reduction in IMF in just 3 weeks.
- In short it reduces the perceived effort for any given workload/activity therefore reducing breathlessness.
- Improved respiratory efficiency saves O_2 use from respiratory muscles for skeletal muscle use.
- Used alongside a specific warm up it better prepares respiratory muscles for physical activity.
- IMT is important in pulmonary rehabilitation; NICE endorse its use in the management of COPD (Chronic Obstructive Pulmonary Disease).
- Increased exercise tolerance and quality of life.

A quote from a leading rowing coach in 'peak performance' best summarised IMT in that it was a 'no brainer' – *'there's nothing else you can add to training that takes so little time and provides such a large guaranteed benefit to performance'*, and in this respect IMT is now viewed as a credible training aid.

TASK 11

Research and discuss the use of the 'POWERbreathe' training aid.

ASTHMA AND AN ACTIVE LIFESTYLE

In respect of a lifelong involvement in an active/ healthy lifestyle you need to be able to evaluate critically the following factors in relation to asthma:

- awareness of symptoms to be able to detect its presence
- awareness of tests to measure its severity
- understand what conditions trigger its symptoms

- understand its effects on physical activity/
performance
- understand the treatments to help its
management.

SYMPTOMS

Asthma is characterised by a reversible narrowing
of airways with common symptoms of:
hyperirritability of airways, coughing, wheezing,
breathlessness or mucus production. Asthma
occurs in response to a trigger or allergen.

MEASUREMENT

Asthma is measured by inhaling into a spirometer
and measuring the exhaled volume of air. If an
individual improves their expiratory volumes
after inhaling bronchodilator treatments they are
considered to have asthma. The IOC now requires
medical evidence of asthma and accepts a 15%
improvement in forced expiration in 1 sec, within
10 min of using a bronchodilator treatment. There
are challenges to this rule due to variations in
triggers, e.g. exercising above 85% intensity for 6
mins to allow the airways to dry, hyperventilating
for 6 mins, and inhalation of triggers to induce
the asthmatic response.

TRIGGERS

The major trigger is the drying of the respiratory
airways, normally due to water loss from the
airway surfaces causing an inflammatory
response, and triggering the constriction/
narrowing of airways termed *bronchoconstriction*.

Bronchoconstriction is often brought on shortly
after exercise or some hours after. The link
between exercise and asthmatic symptoms is
termed '*exercise induced asthma*' (EIA). Other
common allergens inducing asthma are: exhaust
fumes, air pollutants, dust, hair and pollens.

EIA is particularly high in cold weather sports, as
cold air is dryer than warm air and therefore is
more likely in winter when the respiratory airways
are processing ice-cold air. Similarly, ice surface
sports like ice hockey and skating act as triggers
due to the ice resurfacing machine pollutants,
and chlorine in water triggers swimming-related
asthma.

PERFORMANCE EFFECTS

Asthma and related respiratory problems are
increasingly common in athletes, especially elite
aerobic athletes, hence the respiratory system can
limit performance in people with asthma.

MANAGEMENT OF ASTHMA: MEDICAL TREATMENTS

- Normally treated by inhaled medication
– bronchodilators – which are 'reliever' (coded
blue) medication which relax muscles around
airways, and are normally taken before exercise
or in response to symptoms.
- Corticosteroids are 'preventer' (non-blue)
medication which suppress the chronic
inflammation and improve the pre-exercise
lung function and reduce the sensitivity of the
airway structures. A daily dose for mild asthma
is the normal treatment.

NON-MEDICAL TREATMENTS

- A warm-up, at least 10–30min at 50/60% max
HR provides a 'refractory period' for up to
2hrs, after which exercise is possible without
triggering EIA.
- Dietary modification of reducing salt and
increasing fish oils and (antioxidant) vitamins
C + E have also shown to help reduce the
inflammatory response to EIA.

Caffeine is also a bronchodilator, but you must be
aware that the IOC limit is 12mg/ml.

INSPIRATORY MUSCLE TRAINING (IMT)

Increased respiratory effort is a major principle
symptom of breathlessness; hence, there is a strong
relationship between the strength of the respiratory
muscles and the sense of respiratory effort.

IMT cannot cure asthma but it has shown to increase
airflow and alleviate breathlessness, so the benefit
to asthmatic athletes may be greater, in terms of
performance as well as control of the symptoms.

For competitive athletes, when asthma is short of
the IOC criteria for pharmacological treatments,
non–pharmacological approaches may be only
means of minimising the negative impact of EIA
on an athlete's ability to fulfill their potential.

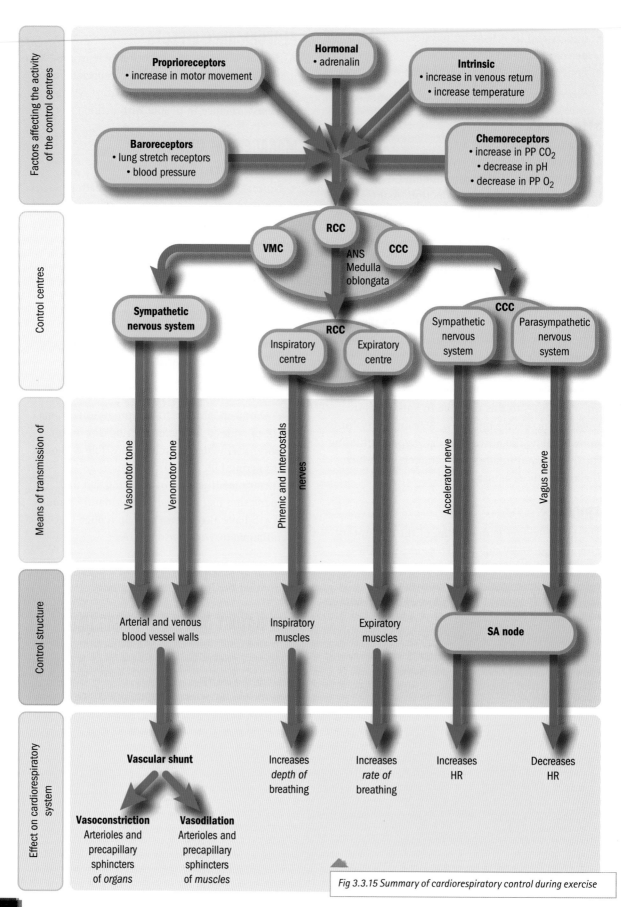

Fig 3.3.15 Summary of cardiorespiratory control during exercise

IMT therefore reduces the use of medication and improves quality of life.

'POWERbreathe' is now available on prescription and shows that IMT is now a well established drug-free method of managing asthma

The more obvious management strategies are simply to stop the conditions that act as triggers in the first place. Hence, refrain from endurance training when suffering respiratory infections, avoid exercise in cold (winter)/dry air conditions or if unavoidable, minimise the effects by wearing a mask to cover the nose/mouth to enable exhaled air to help raise the temperature of the air inhaled.

TAKE IT FURTHER

New evidence suggests a misdiagnosis of asthma with a condition termed 'Inspiratory Stridor' (IS). Research this condition and highlight its similarities in relation to the use of IMT.

SMOKING AND AN ACTIVE LIFESTYLE

In respect of smoking you need to be able to evaluate critically the effects of smoking on the respiratory system with reference to a lifelong involvement in an active/healthy lifestyle.

HEALTH EFFECTS

- Impairs natural development in teenagers.
- Impairs lung function and diffusion rates.
- Increased damage and likelihood of respiratory diseases, infections, and symptoms outlined below:

  – Asthma
  – Irritates/damages respiratory structures: cilia, alveoli, bronchioles, trachea and larynx.
  – Narrows/constricts respiratory airways.
  – emphysema (decreased elasticity of respiratory structures)
  – COPD (Chronic Obstructive Pulmonary Disease)
  – Cancers of respiratory structures
  – Shortness of breathe, coughing and wheezing, mucus/phelgm in the lungs.

PERFORMANCE EFFECTS

The bottom line is that smoking decreases the efficiency of the respiratory system to take in (VO_2 max) and supply O_2 to our working muscles, and works against the positive long term adaptations, already identified, from involvement in physical activity.

It is therefore no surprise that smoking impairs performance, even among highly trained athletes. Smoking mostly affects endurance-based exercise, especially high intensity maximal activity like the triathlon, but it reduces respiratory health in general so even walking the dog or walking a round of golf are impaired.

CARDIORESPIRATORY CONTROL

It is much easier to understand the control mechanisms of the heart, vascular and respiratory system as one. Many of the factors affecting the activity of the CCC, VCC and RCC are the same, and stimulate the control centres to respond at exactly the same time. Figure 3.3.15 (see page 120) shows the overlap between the heart, vascular and respiratory systems.

ExamCafé

Relax, refresh, result!

Refresh your memory

Revision checklist – Respiratory System Part III

You should now be able to describe, explain and evaluate the points below.

1. Describe the mechanics of breathing at rest and the respiratory muscles involved.
2. Explain the changes in the mechanics of breathing during physical activity (to include reference to additional muscles involved & the active nature of expiration).
3. Explain how changes in the mechanics of breathing during physical activity are regulated by the respiratory centre.
4. Describe the process of gaseous exchange that takes place between the alveoli and blood, and between the blood and tissue cells.
5. Explain the changes in gaseous exchange that takes place between the alveoli and blood and between the blood and the tissue cells, as a direct result of participation in physical activity.
6. Explain the effect of altitude on the respiratory system and how this influences the performance of different types of physical activity.
7. Evaluate critically the impact of different types of physical activity on the respiratory system with reference to lifelong involvement in an active lifestyle.

REVISE AS YOU GO!

1. Describe the mechanics of breathing at rest and during exercise.
2. Define the terms minute ventilation, tidal volume and respiratory frequency, and give average values for minute ventilation during rest and during maximal exercise.
3. Explain how gas is exchanged between the alveoli and the alveoli capillaries during exercise.
4. Explain how gas is exchanged between the capillaries and muscle cells during exercise.
5. Describe and explain the factors that affect the activity of the RCC.
6. Explain how the RCC controls respiration during exercise?
7. Explain the effects of exercise-induced asthma on the respiratory system and suggest how performers may treat/prevent these symptoms occurring.
8. How does smoking affect the efficiency of the respiratory system?
9. Describe the effects of altitude on the respiratory system and how altitude would affect the performance of a marathon runner?
10. Evaluate critically the impact of aerobic training on the respiratory system and how this affects performance/a lifelong involvement in an active lifestyle.

Get the result!

Exam question

Altitude (height in metres)	Atmospheric pressure (mmHg)	Partial pressure oxygen (mmHg)
Sea level	760	159.2
2000	596	124.9
4000	462	96.9

Table 7

Use the information in Table 7 to help explain the difficulties that an endurance performer might experience when performing at altitude, without a period of acclimatisation.

Examiner says:

A reasonable structured answer but which just lacked further depth/ detail. The candidate correctly identified that PPO$_2$ decreases as altitude increases (1 mark) and that this will decrease O$_2$ transport (1 mark) but did not identify why/how this occurs. The candidate identified performance decreased (1 mark) but linked this to adaptations to altitude training which was irrelevant to this question as it stated no acclimatisation had occurred. It is a common error in this area to jump to altitude adaptations and often to those which are vascular not respiratory adaptations. Good exam technique always starts with the PPO$_2$ at altitude and the knock-on effects to the normal respiratory exchange processes that they have already studied, before applying this to the net effect on performance.

examiner's tips

- Check the command word: 'explain'.
- Now check the key subject area + focus: respiratory + altitude.
- Now check the marks available (5)

Student answer

Table 7 shows that PPO$_2$ decreases as altitude increases and this results in less O$_2$ transport to the working muscles so the athlete will not be able to work as hard or as long as they could at sea level. This is because they have not had time to adapt and increased their red blood cell production which increases their O$_2$ transport and which would increase their aerobic performance.

Student's improved answer

The PP of O$_2$ at altitude decreases so when they inspire the PP of O$_2$ is lower in the air in the alveoli than that at sea level. This means the diffusion gradient is reduced so less O$_2$ is diffused into the alveoli capillaries. This reduces O$_2$ transport so the O$_2$ supplied to the working muscles is also reduced. The net effect is that aerobic performance is reduced. The athlete will have to increase their rate and depth of breathing to compensate but overall they will either have to slow down or are likely to fatigue earlier than they would at sea level.

Examiner says:

Logical start point

Knock-on effects in order

Good application to performance

Good application to performer / individual

Acquiring movement skills

CHAPTER 4:

Classification of motor skills and abilities (developing an awareness of factors affecting involvement in physical activity)

LEARNING OBJECTIVES

At the end of this chapter you should be able to:

- Classify movement skills by placing them on a variety of continua
- Describe methods of manipulating skills practice to facilitate learning and improve performance
- Evaluate critically these methods and their effectiveness in the learning of movement skills
- Define and identify the characteristics of gross motor abilities and psychomotor abilities.

INTRODUCTION

In our everyday lives we all utilise millions of skills which we have mastered and which enable us to take part in social, thinking and performing situations. Whilst all these skills are important, in PE we focus on motor skills which are essential in sport. It is essential that we learn and master these skills if we are to be able to take part in physical activities which are an essential part of a balanced, active and healthy lifestyle.

In this section we examine the classification of skills which enables us to embark on their analysis which is important to our understanding of how we should best learn and teach skills.

We also look at different ways in which skills can be learned and the types of practice that are best for particular types of skills.

Distinguishing between the terms 'skill' and 'ability' helps us to understand how individuals differ in the way they master skills and how some are able to perform at a higher level than others.

EXAM TIP

Make sure that you can apply all the theories that you learn to a practical example. Questions in the exam will usually ask you to do this.

KEY TERM

Continuum (pl. continua)

An imaginary scale between two extremes which shows a gradual increase/decrease in a number of characteristics.

Classification of motor skills

We can analyse movement skills by classifying them. Psychologists have identified a range of classifications or characteristics to use.

The classification of movement skills is not simple, nor is it an exact science. It is difficult to be specific about the characteristics of a skill because many of them can change depending on the situation in which the skill is performed.

Many skills also have elements of all characteristics. Because of this, skill classification uses *continua* that allow us to illustrate that skills have characteristics to a greater or lesser extent dependent on the situation that they are being performed in. This also means that whenever we use continua to classify skills we have to explain how we have arrived at our decision.

The most commonly used classification continua are:

- Muscular involvement (Gross–Fine)
- Environmental Influencer (Open–Closed)
- Continuity (Discrete–Serial–Continuous)
- Pacing (Self-paced–Externally paced)
- Difficulty (Simple–Complex)
- Organisational (Low–High)

These are detailed in Figures 4.1–4.6.

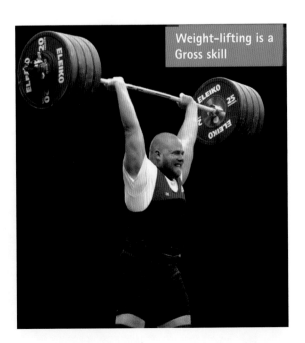

Weight-lifting is a Gross skill

MUSCULAR INVOLVEMENT (GROSS–FINE) CONTINUUM

GROSS	FINE
Running	Wrist/finger action of a spin bowler in cricket.
Swimming	
Hammer throwing	

Fig 4.1

In this classification we look at the precision of the movement.

Gross skills involve large muscle movements where there is little concern for precision. Examples are running, swimming and hammer throwing.

Fine skills involve more intricate movements using small muscle groups. They usually involve accuracy and emphasise hand-eye co-ordination. An example of a fine movement skill is the wrist/finger action of a spin bowler in cricket.

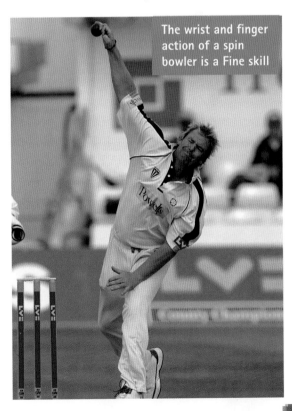

The wrist and finger action of a spin bowler is a Fine skill

ENVIRONMENTAL INFLUENCE (OPEN-CLOSED) CONTINUUM

OPEN	CLOSED
Pass in rugby/netball	Tennis serve
Sailing	Hammer throwing
	Gymnastics through vault

Fig 4.2

In this classification we are concerned with how environmental conditions affect the movement skill. In referring to the environment we take into account all the factors in the surroundings, where the activity takes place, that affect the performance, e.g. team mates, opponents, playing surface. Additionally, if performed outdoors, the weather may also be a factor.

Open skills involve movement skills that are affected by the environment. They are predominantly perceptual and involve decision making. Movements have to be adapted to suit the situation. They are generally externally placed in an environment that is unpredictable. Examples of open skills would be a pass in a rugby or netball game,

Closed skills are movement skills that are not affected by the environment. In these skills we aim to do the same set technical model at each performance and they are therefore habitual. They are usually self paced, with the performer knowing exactly what they have to do. Examples of closed skills are the tennis serve or gymnastics through vault.

EXAM TIP

Always explain/justify why you have placed a particular skill at that point on the continuum.

CONTINUITY (DISCRETE-SERIAL-CONTINUOUS) CONTINUUM

DISCRETE	SERIAL	CONTINUOUS
Catching a ball	Gymnastics/trampolining sequence	Running/cycling
Penalty in soccer/hockey	Triple jump	Swimming

Fig 4.3

In this classification we are concerned with how clearly defined the beginning and end of the movement skill are.

Discrete skills are movement skills that have a clear beginning and a clear end. If this single skill is to be repeated it must start again. Examples of discrete skills are catching a ball in cricket or rounders, a penalty in soccer or hockey, or a high serve in badminton.

Serial skills are movement skills that have a number of discrete elements that are put together in a definite order to make a movement or sequence. Examples of serial skills are a gymnastic or trampolining sequence and a triple jump.

Shooting in netball is an Open skill

A gymnastics vault is a Closed skill

Continuous skills are movement skills that have no definite beginning or end. The end of one cycle of the movement is the start of the next. The movement skill usually has to be repeated several times for the skill to be meaningful. Examples of continuous skills are running, cycling and swimming.

PACING (SELF-PACED-EXTERNALLY PACED) CONTINUUM

SELF-PACED	EXTERNALLY PACED
High jump	Receiving a pass
Tennis serve	Windsurfing

Fig 4.4

In this classification we are concerned with the level of control that the performer has over the timing of the movement skill. This control can relate to both when the movement is started as well as the rate at which it is performed.

Self (internally) paced – the performer determines when the movement skill starts together with the rate at which it proceeds. Self-paced skills are normally closed skills. Examples of self-paced skills are high jump and tennis serve.

A trampolining sequence is a Serial skill

Externally paced – the control of the movement skill is not determined by the performer but by the environment. In many cases this involves opponents to whom the performer has to react. They are normally open skills. Examples of externally-paced skills are receiving a pass in soccer or hockey, receiving a serve in tennis and windsurfing.

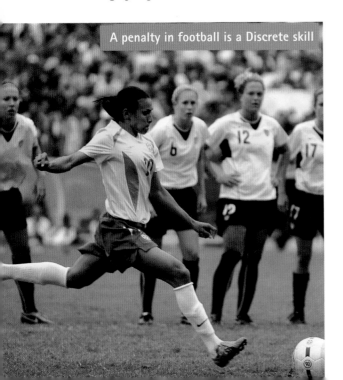

A penalty in football is a Discrete skill

Cycling is a Continuous skill

DIFFICULTY (SIMPLE–COMPLEX) CONTINUUM

SIMPLE	COMPLEX
Swimming	Tennis serve
Sprinting	Somersault

Fig 4.5

Sprinting is a Simple skill

B. Clay

In this classification we are concerned with how complex the movement skill is, which is determined by analysing the following six aspects:

- perceptual load together with the degree of decision making
- time available to carry out the perceptual and decision-making tasks
- quantity of sub-routines together with their speed and timing
- speed/power needed
- accuracy needed
- use of feedback.

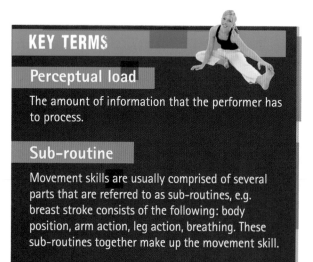

KEY TERMS

Perceptual load

The amount of information that the performer has to process.

Sub-routine

Movement skills are usually comprised of several parts that are referred to as sub-routines, e.g. breast stroke consists of the following: body position, arm action, leg action, breathing. These sub-routines together make up the movement skill.

Simple skills would have very low levels of some of the aspects identified above. Performers would have little information to process and few decisions to make, as well as a small number of sub-routines in which the speed and timing would not be critical. The use of feedback would not be significant. Whilst such movement skills are simple they may still be difficult to learn and perform. Examples of simple skills are swimming and sprinting.

Complex skills would have high levels of most of the aspects identified above. Performers will have a high perceptual load leading to many decisions which have to be made. The skill will have many sub-routines where speed and timing are critical, together with significant use of feedback. Examples of complex skills are a tennis serve and a somersault.

The tennis serve is a Complex skill

ORGANISATIONAL (LOW–HIGH) CONTINUUM

LOW	HIGH
Swimming strokes	Cartwheel
Trampolining sequence	Golf swing

Fig 4.4

In this classification we are concerned with how closely linked the sub-routines of the movement skill are.

Low organisation skills are made up of sub-routines that are easily separated and practised by themselves. Having been practised separately the sub-routines can be put back together into the whole skill quite easily. Examples of low organisation skills are swimming strokes, trampolining or gymnastics sequences.

High organisation skills are movement skills where sub-routines are very closely linked together and very difficult to separate without disrupting the skill. Consequently highly organised skills are usually practised as a whole. Examples of highly organised skills are cartwheels and the golf swing.

TASK ANALYSIS

It is important for us to be able to analyse movement skills in order to appreciate and

The golf swing is a highly Organised skill

understand the requirements of the skill and adopt the best approaches to teach, practise and improve it. Placing a skill on each of the continua and justifying this positioning will be very helpful in deciding how the skill can be practised and improved. This will be helpful to you when you focus on developing skills in your evaluation and planning for the improvement of performance response in your practical assessment.

Swimming is a skill which has low levels of organisation

TASK 1

- Select three skills from practical activities in which you have taken part and classify them on the six continua (page 128).
- Identify the situation in which each skill is being performed and explain your reasons for its position on the organisational continuum.

REMEMBER

Remember the features of each of the six classification continua you have studied when you look at the organisation of practices.

The application of classification to the organisation and determination of practice

EXAM TIP

You should ensure that you are able to critically evaluate each practice method by knowing the advantage and disadvantages of each method and the classes of skills they are best suited for. You should also be able to give practical examples of the application of each type of practice.

The method of practising a skill so that performers learn and improve is determined by the skill to be learned being classified. This classification of skills using the continua we have studied in the previous section enables teachers to decide how best to structure the skill practices. To decide on the best method of manipulating the skill they will place the skill on the organisational and difficulty continua. This is often referred to as task analysis. In deciding where it is placed on these continua they will consider the following:

Can the skill to be learned:

- Be broken down into separate parts? – Low in organisation
- Not be broken down into separate parts? – High in organisation

Does the skill to be learned:

- Involve many decisions, have lots of sub-routines, have to be carried out quickly and accurately? – Complex skill
- Involve few decisions to be made, doesn't involve great accuracy? – Simple skill

KEY TERM

Task analysis

Analysing a skill using the classification system to gain an understanding of how that skill needs to be taught.

Methods of manipulating skills practice

PART PRACTICE

If a skill is low in organisation it can be broken down into meaningful parts or sub-routines to reduce its complexity. These meaningful parts are

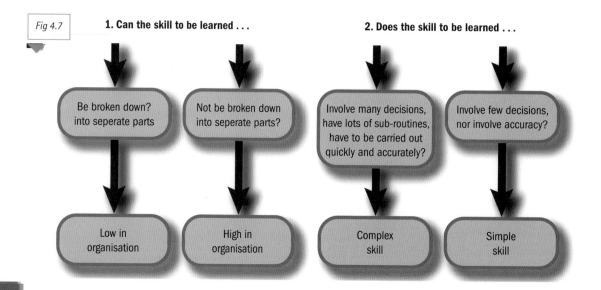

Fig 4.7

1. Can the skill to be learned . . .

Be broken down? into seperate parts → Low in organisation

Not be broken down into seperate parts? → High in organisation

2. Does the skill to be learned . . .

Involve many decisions, have lots of sub-routines, have to be carried out quickly and accurately? → Complex skill

Involve few decisions, nor involve accuracy? → Simple skill

This skill can be separated into sub-routines

KEY TERM

Serial skill

A movement skill that has a number of discrete elements which are put together in a definite order to make a movement or sequence, e.g. trampoline sequence, triple jump.

It is essential that the sub-routines of the skill are divided into meaningful units for practice to help the positive transfer into the whole skill. For example the gymnast may practise two movements of a sequence together rather than as two separate skills helping their positive transfer into the sequence, e.g. handstand and forward roll.

It is also essential that the learner sees the whole skill demonstrated prior to practice in order that they have a realistic image of the skill they are learning.

Disadvantages of the part method are that it can take longer than other methods and that

then practised and perfected in isolation before putting the whole skill back together. A good example is the *tennis serve* which can be broken down into the following sub-routines:

- grip
- stance
- back swing
- ball toss
- ball contact
- follow through.

The part method reduces the amount of information to be processed and is good if the task is complex or dangerous as it lessens fear and the risk. Many closed skills are taught in this way particularly in gymnastics, trampolining, swimming and diving where the danger element is high. Additionally the learner may be motivated by being successful in the parts of the skill whilst also gaining in confidence. It is also good for learning serial skills.

APPLY IT!

Part Practice
When learning to swim you learn the leg action, then the arm action and then join the two skills together.

Swimming is broken down into parts to lessen fear and the danger

transferring the parts back into the whole skill can sometimes be difficult. Learners also lose the overall kinaesthetic sense and flow of the skill.

APPLY IT!

Part Practice
The gymnast learns the individual movements in their sequence, e.g. handstand, forward roll, somersault, handspring and then joins them together in the sequence.

KEY TERMS

Positive transfer

The process of one skill helping the learning and performance of a separate but similar skill.

Kinaesthesis

The awareness of the relative position of the limbs and joints in space and the state of contraction of the muscles.

Whole practice

The whole method of practice is when the skill is learned in its complete form.

Cycling is taught as a whole

APPLY IT!

Whole Practice
Cycling is taught as a whole because it is difficult to break down. You may use stabilisers to help with balance at first but the skill itself is taught as a whole.

WHOLE PRACTICE

Ideally a skill should be taught as a whole. Skills that are high in organisation and low in complexity are usually taught by this method. Examples of such skills include sprinting, cycling and the golf swing.

Teaching by this method allows the learner to experience and develop a feel for the movement and its flow. This feel for the movement is termed *kinaesthesis*.

A feel for the movement allows the learner to appreciate the relationship between the parts of the movement and help the smooth and efficient flow of the skill. It is therefore good for learning skills which are *ballistic*. This method can also can help with the learner's understanding of the movement.

KEY TERM

Ballistic skills
Short and fast skills.

Disadvantages of this method are that it is not suitable for complex or dangerous skills but an advantage is that learning by the whole practice can be quicker than using the part method.

PROGRESSIVE PART PRACTICE

In this method parts of a complex skill are practised in isolation. They are then linked together to form larger parts before finally combining into the whole skill.

Examples of skills learned by this method would be gymnastic floor routines, triple jump and trampoline routines. The gymnast would learn and practise the skills of the routine in isolation, e.g. headstand, overswing, backward roll, handstand, forward roll. They would then link some of the skills together into larger skills, e.g. headstand, forward roll, overswing, backward roll. These would then be joined together forming large routines, before linking all elements of the sequence together to form the whole routine.

Some psychologists view the progressive part method as teaching the sub-routines in the order in which they occur in the whole skill. This means that after the first sub-routine has been practiced in isolation, the second part is practiced in isolation and then together with the first part. The third part will then be practised in isolation before being put together with parts 1 & 2. If we apply this to the learning of the triple jump (fig. 4.8) the learner would practise:

- the run up
- the hop
- the run up and hop
- the step
- the run up, the hop and the step
- the jump
- the run up, the hop, the step and the jump.
- the landing
- the run up, the hop, the step, the jump and the landing.

Fig 4.8

It is a good method to use for complex serial skills as it reduces the information load, helps the flow of the skill and can also help the transfer of skills into the whole (fig. 4.9). This method is sometimes referred to as 'chaining'.

THE WHOLE-PART-WHOLE METHOD

This method involves the learner trying the whole skill first. By doing this they get the feel for the skill and the teacher is able to identify the parts of the skill that the learner has difficulty with. The parts of the skill the learner has difficulty with would then be practised and perfected in isolation before being put together as the whole skill.

TASK 2

The model below is an illustration of progressive part practice and assumes that a movement has three clear and separate routines.

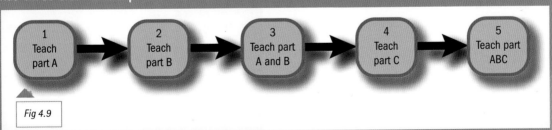

Fig 4.9

Think of a skill that could be taught using the progressive part method. Explain how you would structure the part practices.

Discuss the advantages and disadvantages of the progressive part practice method.

An example is the tennis serve. The learner tries the whole serve. The teacher identifies that the ball is not being tossed up high enough. The learner practises the toss up and when they have mastered it they then go back to the whole serve.

The advantages to this method are that the learner gets the feel for the skill and the flow and it can be quicker when compared to the part method as only the weak parts of the skill are practised in isolation. It is not suitable for highly organised skills which cannot be broken down or for skills which are dangerous.

TAKE IT FURTHER

1. Use practical examples to explain the classes of skills which each method of manipulating skills is most suitable for.
2. Explain the advantages and disadvantages of each of the methods of manipulating practices.
3. Choose a skill from one of your practical activities and create a plan to teach it to a fellow student. Explain how and why you decided to use the methods of manipulating the skills in your plan.

REMEMBER

Remember the classification types of skills that are best suited to each method of organising practice.

Classification of abilities relating to movement skills

We have studied classifying skills and methods of practising them. Often we use the term 'ability' instead of 'skill' but we will now examine the term 'ability' to show that the two are in fact different.

The characteristics of skill are that it is learned, goal-directed and follows a technical model. If we are to learn a particular skill we must have certain abilities that the skill relies on. For example, to be able to perform a handstand you must have the strength in your arms to support your body weight as well as the balance to keep your legs above your hands.

Below are the words that can be used to describe abilities:

- **Innate/genetically determined** – we are born with abilities determined by the genes we inherit from our parents.
- **Stable and enduring** – abilities tend to remain unchanged but can be affected by our experiences and are developed by maturation.

Performing a handstand needs strength and balance

- **Support, underlie or underpin skills** – each skill usually needs us to have several supporting, underlying or underpinning abilities if we are going to be able to learn the skill effectively.

APPLY IT!

Abilities underpin skills

Flexibility, strength and co-ordination are needed if you are to successfully perform a handspring whilst eye–hand co-ordination is needed for games involving catching and striking.

Abilities are thought to be the foundation blocks that we possess and build on, helping us to learn and perform skills. We inherit our abilities from our parents. Some psychologists believe that they cannot be modified or improved by practice, whilst others think that they are modified by maturation and experience.

However, all psychologists tend to agree that abilities determine your learning and performance of skills and activities. If you are born with a lot of slow twitch muscle fibres you could become a good endurance athlete but will never excel in sprinting.

Similarly, if you are born with low levels of flexibility it is unlikely that you will ever be a top class gymnast. The ability levels we are born with, therefore, determine to an extent the activities which we will participate in as part of our balanced, healthy and active lifestyle.

Having identified these characteristics of ability they can be the focus of a definition. A psychologist named Schmidt defined ability as:

> 'an inherited, relatively enduring trait that underlies or supports various kinds of motor and cognitive activities or skills. Abilities are thought of as being largely genetically determined.'

Whilst another psychologist, Bull stated:

> 'Abilities are usually thought of as stable and enduring traits that underpin skills and contribute to the speed with which individuals learn psychomotor skills and to the quality of their performance.'

REMEMBER

Remember the three characteristics of ability.

TYPES OF ABILITY

Research into types of ability is as yet inconclusive and different psychologists use different methods to identify them. A psychologist named Fleishman who carried out research into ability identified two types:

- Gross motor ability
- Psychomotor ability

Gross motor abilities, also referred to as *physical proficiency abilities*, usually involve movement and are related to physical fitness. Fleishman identified nine of them:

- **Dynamic strength** – exerting muscular force repeatedly over a period of time, e.g. press-ups
- **Static strength** – the maximum strength that can be exerted against an external object

A weightlifter uses static strength

Explosive strength

- **Explosive strength** – energy used effectively for a short burst of muscular effort, e.g. vertical jump
- **Stamina** – the capacity to sustain maximum effort involving the cardiovascular system, e.g. a marathon
- **Extent flexibility** – flexing or stretching the trunk and back muscles.
- **Dynamic flexibility** – being able to make several rapid flexing movements
- **Gross body co-ordination** – the organisation of the actions of several parts of the body whilst the body is moving.
- **Gross body equilibrium** – being able to maintain balance using the internal senses
- **Trunk strength** – the strength of the abdominal muscles.

There are also other gross motor abilities besides the nine that Fleishman identified, such as static balance, dynamic balance, eye–hand co-ordination and eye–foot co-ordination.

Gross body co-ordination

Gross body equilibrium

TASK 3

For each of the gross motor abilities above, identify a skill/activity that you do that it underpins/supports.

EXAM TIP

Be able to define both gross motor ability and psychomotor ability and give a practical example of each.

Fleishman identified eleven of Psychomotor abilities including:

- **Multi-limb co-ordination** – being able to organise the movement of several limbs at the same time
- **Response orientation** – choosing quickly the position in which an action should be made (as in choice reaction time)
- **Reaction time** – being able to respond quickly to a stimulus
- **Speed of movement** – being able to make gross rapid movements
- **Finger dexterity** – being able to work with tiny objects using the fingers
- **Manual dexterity** – being able to make accurate arm/hand movements involving objects at speed
- **Rate control** – being able to change the speed and direction of responses accurately
- **Aiming** – being able to aim accurately at a small object.

KEY TERM

Psychomotor abilities

Usually involves the processing of information, making decisions and putting these decisions into action. These actions are usually movements.

Psychologists have devised tests which aim to measure some of these abilities.

A skill will rely on several abilities to support, underlie or underpin it. That does not mean that the performer who has high levels of those abilities is automatically guaranteed success. The performer has to learn to apply and co-ordinate those abilities through practice if they are to be effective and successful in the skill.

Coaches and teachers often refer to performers being 'natural' athletes or games players in that they are successful in most sports. This implies that there is one ability that supports or underpins all these activities. Present research evidence does not support this idea, instead indicating

Aiming

Reaction time

that specific skills/activities require particular abilities. Some skills/activities require very similar combinations of abilities to support them. By developing and practising these abilities athletes or games players may well transfer these to other similar skills.

Research has also shown that skills are sometimes underpinned by different abilities at different stages of learning and mastering a skill. In the early stages of learning a complex skill, many perceptual abilities will be important, whereas when you are more proficient kinaesthesis is an essential ability.

TASK 5

Identify the abilities that underpin the activities you have chosen to be assessed in for your coursework. For each one, explain how they underpin your activity.

HOW ARE ABILITIES DEVELOPED?

Some psychologists believe that abilities can be developed and, this being the case, how does the teacher do this? It is generally thought that

TASK 4

1. Measure gross body equilibrium (static balance). You will need to use the gym or sports hall floor and wear your trainers. Work with a partner who will time you with a stopwatch. Stand on your preferred leg with your foot flat on the floor. Place the sole of your other foot flat against the inside of your straight knee. Place your hands on your hips. Your partner will commence timing when you close your eyes. They will stop the watch when you: open your eyes, take your hands off your hips, or move either of your feet.
2. Measure your performance against the figures in the table below.

Men		Women	
Best time(s)	Points	Best time(s)	Points
60	20	35	20
55	18	30	17
50	16	25	14
45	14	20	11
40	12	15	8
35	10	10	4
30	8	5	2
25	6		
20	4		
15	3		
10	2		

Table 1

abilities can be developed during early childhood and it is important that during this period children are exposed to a wide range of experiences and the opportunity to practise. Children should also receive expert teaching and coaching, as well as have access to the necessary facilities and equipment. Children who have the support of their family and friends, who may also be suitable role models, tend to enhance their abilities.

EXAM TIP

You should know how abilities are developed, particularly those which are applicable to your practical activities.

TAKE IT FURTHER

Explain why the people who believe that sports men and women who are expert at several sports and therefore possess a 'sporting ability' are not supported by current research.

Exam Café

Relax, refresh, result!

Refresh your memory

After studying this chapter you should be able to:

▷ Classify movement skills by placing them on a variety of continua.

▷ Describe methods of manipulating skills practice to facilitate learning and improve performance.

▷ Evaluate critically these methods and their effectiveness in the learning of movement skills.

▷ Define and identify the characteristics of gross motor abilities and psychomotor abilities.

REVISE AS YOU GO!

TEST YOUR KNOWLEDGE AND UNDERSTANDING

1. Describe what is meant by the term 'continuum'?
2. Why do we use continua?
3. Name the six continua used to classify skills. Classify a skill from your practical activities on all six continua and explain your classifications.
4. What factors concerning the skill should the teacher consider before deciding on the type of practice?
5. Describe what is meant by whole–part–whole practice and list the advantages and disadvantages of this practice type. Give an example of a movement skill which you would teach by this method.
6. Describe the term part practice and list the advantages and disadvantages of this practice type. Give an example of a movement skill which you would teach by this method.
7. Explain the term whole practice and list the advantages and disadvantages of this practice type. Give an example of a movement skill which you would teach by this method.
8. Explain the term progressive practice and give practical example of using it to teach a skill.
9. Identify the characteristics of abilities.
10. Identify the two different types of abilities and give examples of them both.
11. Identify the abilities which underpin your assessed activities.

Get the result !

Examination question

The continuity continuum contains three elements: discrete, serial and continuous. Use practical examples to explain each of these elements.

examiner's tips

- First check the command word 'explain'.
- Are you required to give practical examples? – yes
- How many marks are available? – 6

Examiner says:

The student has covered the correct continuum and has explained discrete skills but without giving a practical example. They have not really explained continuous skills or given a practical example and have not covered serial skills at all. A better approach might be to explain each type of skill and give a practical example of each without linking them together.

Student answer

Discrete skills are those which have a clear start and finish whilst continuous skills don't.

Student's improved answer

A discrete skill has a clear start and a clear end to it. An example of a discrete skill is a forward roll which starts as you bend down and finishes as you get to your feet and stand up.

A serial skill is a movement skill that has a number of discrete elements that are put together in a definite order to make a movement or sequence. An example of s serial skill is the triple jump in athletics when the athlete runs up, hops, steps, jumps and then lands.

A continuous skill is a movement skill which has no definite beginning or end. The end of one cycle of the skill is the start of the next. The movement skill has to be repeated several times for the skill to be meaningful. An example of a continuous skill is swimming where the performer has to keep repeating the arm, leg action and breathing to make progress.

Examiner says:

The candidate has structured his answer which has enabled them to ensure that they have covered all aspects of the question.

They have clearly defined each of the elements of the continuity continuum and explained the elements using good clear examples.

A grade A answer. Well done.

CHAPTER 5:

The development of motor skills and the use of practice methods

LEARNING OBJECTIVES

At the end of this chapter you should be able to:

- Identify Fitts and Posner's phases of learning
- Apply these phases to practical activities
- Describe different types of guidance used in difference phases of learning to improve performance
- Evaluate critically these different types of guidance
- Describe methods of practice
- Explain the role of mental practice and rehearsal as compared to physical practice rehearsal
- Explain the appropriate use of practice methods to maximise effectiveness
- Evaluate critically different types of practice methods and their application to the performance of movement skills.

INTRODUCTION

We have all experienced the learning of movement skills in the physical activities we participate in as part of our balanced, active and healthy lifestyle. In learning these skills we have gone through the stages of learning, i.e. forming a mental picture of the skill, practising it and perfecting it, then after lots of practice being able to do it without too much thought. These are the *three stages of learning* which we will study.

The teacher will have shown us what we were going to learn and then told us the important things we should to concentrate on. The teacher has, therefore, 'guided' us. We can all remember learning to swim and using arm bands and rings and these, along with being supported when learning gymnastic skills, are other forms of guidance which we will look at.

This chapter is not only about learning but also about how we practise the skills we learn. We will look at how we structure our practices so that we

gain the most benefit from the time we spend and the factors we should think about when deciding how to structure our practices.

Phases/stages of movement skill learning that affect participation and performance in physical activity

Fitts and Posner (1967) were amongst the first psychologists to examine how motor skills in sport were learned and to suggest that learning is sequential and that we move through specific phases or stages as we learn.

Learners do not suddenly move from one stage to the next but undergo a gradual change in learning characteristics from stage to stage. It is important that the teacher and coach have an understanding of each of the phases of learning to ensure that learning experiences are structured to ensure success.

The phases/stages of movement skill learning are:

- Cognitive
- Associative
- Autonomous.

COGNITIVE

This is the initial or first phase of learning. The learner is trying to create a mental picture of the skill. Demonstrations and verbal explanations of the skill are very important if the learner is to form an accurate picture of the skill and understand the linking of the movements and the flow of the skill. The more complex the skill is, the longer this will take. Teachers also need to be careful that they do not give too much information for learners to take in. Learners should be given guidance as to the important cues to focus on. This is known as *selective attention*.

They will start to practise the skill with trial and error. It is vital that their successes should be reinforced with positive feedback. Performances will be inconsistent, lack co-ordination, lack flow and be full of errors with learners needing specific feedback to enable them to correct these errors.

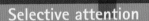

KEY TERMS

Selective attention

The process of picking out and focusing on the relevant parts of the display. This filtering out is also important because irrelevant information is ignored.

Kinaesthesis

The sense that tells the brain about the movement and the state of contraction of the muscles, tendons and joints. It allows the performer to know whether or not the movement has been performed correctly.

ASSOCIATIVE

This is the practice (second) phase of learning. It is usually a longer phase than the cognitive phase with some learners staying in it for a long time and some never progressing beyond it. In this phase the learner begins to eliminate mistakes and errors are fewer and less gross. The fundamentals of the skill are learned and mastered and become more consistent.

Motor programmes are developed and sub-routines become more co-ordinated resulting in the skill becoming smoother. This increase in the flow of the movement is also influenced by the learner attending to the relevant and specific cues. The learner concentrates on practising and refining the skill in a variety of conditions.

APPLY IT!

Cognitive phase

When being taught the overhead clear in badminton the teacher will demonstrate the stroke and explain the coaching points to the learner. This enables the learner to form a mental picture or visualise the skill.

Badminton overhead clear is demonstrated in the cognitive phase of learning

The learner develops an ability to use internal/kinaesthetic feedback in detecting some of their errors. More detailed verbal feedback is given to the learner who is able to utilise it.

The learner may have to return to the cognitive phase in order to review and refine their mental image.

APPLY IT!

The learner has formed a mental picture of the overhead clear and has practised performing it. The overhead clear goes high and over the net. The teacher gives feedback and the learner focuses on getting the shuttle into the back court tramlines. The learner starts to know what aspects of the stroke he is performing correctly and those which are wrong without being told by the teacher. He tries to correct the faulty aspects of the stroke.

AUTONOMOUS

This is the final (third) phase of learning. After a lot of practice the learner can execute the skill with a minimum of conscious thought and is therefore able to concentrate on other factors.

He is able to focus on the demands of the environment and focus on subtle cues. The tennis player is able to focus on where to place the ball to beat the opponent when serving rather than thinking about the grip, ball toss, backswing, ball contact and follow through. Similarly the golfer can focus on subtle changes to his normal swing to enable them to cut or fade the ball rather than the swing itself. Team game players are able to focus on tactics and strategies rather than on executing the skills.

This is an advanced stage of learning in which the motor programme is established and stored in the long term memory and put into action in response to an appropriate stimulus. Cognitive elements remain in skills where fine adjustments have to be made but closed skills can be practised so that a consistent, habitual performance is produced.

Self-confidence increases and the learner develops an ability to detect errors and correct them. There is less need for external feedback which, when given, can be specific and highlight errors in order to ensure improvement. Improvements in performance are slow as the learner is very capable however, if practice is not maintained, then the learner may regress to the associative stage.

A footballer in the antonomons phase can make subtle changes to their kick

APPLY IT!

Autonomous phase

The learner can now perform the overhead clear consistently and with confidence with little attention being paid to it. He is now able to focus on his opponent's position on the court and on placing the shuttle appropriately.

REMEMBER

Ensure that you know the three phases of learning and their characteristics.

TAKE IT FURTHER

Explain the types of feedback which are important to each phase of learning.

EXAM TIP

Make sure that you are able to identify the characteristics of each of the phases and give a practical example of each one.

Types of guidance and their impact upon effective performance and participation

There are four types of guidance that can be used by the teacher or coach to help the learning process:

- Visual
- Verbal
- Manual
- Mechanical.

VISUAL GUIDANCE

This is used at all stages of learning but is particularly useful and effective in the cognitive/ early stages of learning. Visual guidance is important because vision is usually the dominant sense and because we tend to learn through imitation. Visual guidance helps the learner form a mental image of the skill to be learned.

Demonstrations provide an excellent means of transmitting information about what needs to be done in all phases of learning the skill. It is essential that demonstrations are accurate and they should focus the learner's attention on the important aspects of the skill. The teacher may demonstrate a chest pass in basketball, directing the learner's attention to the position of the fingers on the ball, the extension of the elbows and the transfer of body weight. Demonstrations should be appropriate and not be too complicated or long.

Visual aids such as wall charts, pictures, diagrams and models are another form of visual guidance. They are useful for highlighting technical points, particularly in complex skills. However, these static displays quickly lose their impact and therefore have limited use.

Sometimes visual guidance is given by modifying the display in the learning environment. Examples of this would be the badminton coach marking a particular zone in the service area for the learner to serve the shuttle into or marking out the

Demonstration basketball chest pass

back tramlines to get their overhead clears into. Similarly the basketball court may be chalked as an indicator of the take off point for the lay-up shot. This visual guidance is being used to focus the learner's attention and to reduce the information overload. Some sports development schemes for young children use brightly coloured equipment to help focus the learners' attention.

In modern day sport video footage is often used not only to show beginners top class performers as demonstrators to help them form a mental picture of the skill but also to enable skilled performers analyse their performance and plan for improvement.

There are some drawbacks to visual guidance:

- The teacher/coach must ensure that visual guidance given in the form of demonstrations is accurate. This may necessitate them getting someone else to demonstrate or using a video it they are unable to give a good demonstration themselves.
- Some complex skills may have too much information in them for the learner to take in when demonstrated.
- Static visual aids may not give a lot of information about movement patterns and may not keep learner's attention.

Verbal guidance – talk by team coach

Verbal guidance is thought to be more effective with advanced learners in the autonomous phase when the information conveyed may be detailed and technical. An example of this would be the teacher or coach telling the performer about tactics and strategies.

When using verbal guidance the teacher needs to ensure that the learner has understood and can remember what has been said as well as being able to put it into the skill movement.

There are some drawbacks to verbal guidance:

- The teacher/coach has to be able to get the information across to the learners and the learners have relate the information they receive to the skill being learned.
- The amount of information given has to be limited.
- Some complex skills are difficult to describe concisely and learners become bored.

APPLY IT!

Visual guidance

The teacher gathers the learners together, ensures that they can all see and then demonstrates the skill they are teaching e.g. the chest pass. In badminton when introducing the short serve the teacher may place small hoops for the learner to aim their serves into.

APPLY IT!

Verbal guidance

The teacher tells the learner the coaching points they need to focus on in the basketball chest pass, i.e. fingers/hand position, flexed elbows, extend elbows aiming ball at partners chest, transfer body weight onto front foot, extend fingers.

VERBAL GUIDANCE

This is a frequently used method. It is often used in conjunction with visual guidance to direct the learner to the important cues. Verbal guidance should be clear and concise. This is essential if the learner is to understand and remember it.

MANUAL

Manual guidance involves the teacher or coach holding and physically manipulating the body of the learner through the correct pattern of movement. This could be guiding the arm through a forehand shot in tennis or holding the gymnast in a handstand.

MECHANICAL

Mechanical guidance involves the use of equipment to help support the learner and shape the skill. Examples of this form of guidance are the use of floats in swimming and a harness in trampolining or gymnastics. They allow the learner to experience the spatial and timing aspects of the movement.

Manual and mechanical guidance are very useful in the early stages of learning and particularly in allowing the learner to develop a kinaesthetic sense of the movement. They are also very useful in giving confidence to and ensuring safety for the learner particularly where there is an element of danger in the skill.

It is important that this form of guidance is removed as soon as possible so that the learner does not become dependent on it.

The disadvantages are that the feel of the movement the learner experiences with this guidance is different to the actual movement and therefore the learner should not become too accustomed to this 'adapted' feel. This also makes it of limited value for the experienced learner. Mechanical guidance is also designed to eliminate errors and does not, therefore, give the learner the opportunity to experience and correct mistakes. Manual guidance is difficult with groups.

An example of manual guidance

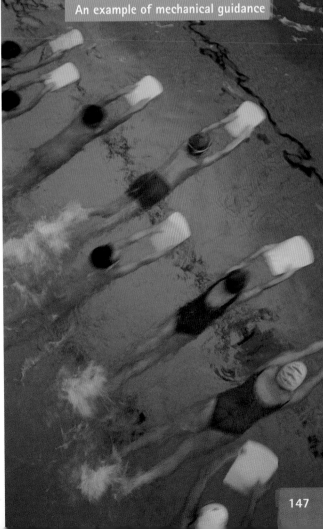

An example of mechanical guidance

APPLY IT!

Manual/mechanical guidance can help reduce fear in the learning of skills which have an element of danger in them. Arm bands and floats are used in swimming, safety ropes in climbing and harnesses in trampolining.

REMEMBER

The types of guidance and the types of learning they are most appropriate for.

TASK 1

1. Perfect a demonstration for a skill in one of your activities, video it and see if it would be suitable to use with learners.
2. Write down the verbal guidance you would use with this skill remembering that learners must be able to understand it and remember it.
3. What are the advantages and disadvantages of both manual and mechanical guidance.

EXAM TIP

You need to know the advantages and disadvantages of each method of guidance and which phase of learning they are most appropriate for. Make sure you can give practical examples of the use of each method of guidance.

TAKE IT FURTHER

Try to teach a skill to a fellow student using just one form of guidance. You should then realise that you need to use more than one form of guidance to teach a skill and find out the strengths and weaknesses of each form of guidance.

Practice methods and their impact upon effective and efficient performance of movement skills

We now look at the ways in which the teacher can organise physical practices when teaching movement skills.

MASSED PRACTICE

This is when the learners practise continuously at a skill without any breaks or rest intervals. The practice sessions are usually long. It is good for the grooving in of habitual skills. It is good for experienced, highly motivated learners who have good fitness levels.

When determining the length of these sessions the fitness and maturity levels of the learners should be taken into account as long sessions can lead to boredom and fatigue.

Basketball set shot can be grooved in and become habitual through massed practice

Massed practice is suitable for simple, discrete skills of short duration. It can save on time in that skills do not have to be re-introduced after breaks between sessions however, beginners can be affected by lack of concentration and attention.

Massed practice is also suitable when the coach wishes to simulate performance conditions where there is an element of fatigue. Disadvantages of massed practice are that it can cause fatigue and de-motivation which lead to poor performance and learning

Potentially dangerous skill best learned by distributed practice

APPLY IT!

Massed practice – basketball players practise their shooting by doing drills of ten shots at each of five points around the 'd'.

DISTRIBUTED PRACTICE

Practice sessions have rest intervals included. It is good for most skill learning, particularly for beginners and learners with low levels of motivation and low levels of fitness. It is also good for the learning of continuous skills.

The rest intervals allow time to recover both mentally and physically whilst also giving the learner the opportunity to receive extrinsic feedback. The rest intervals also permit mental practice to be undertaken by the learner.

Research has shown this method to be the most effective form of practice. It also helps to maintain motivation and is good for potentially dangerous or complex skills.

APPLY IT!

Distributive practice – the learner in swimming does a width of the pool and then rests whilst receiving feedback and coaching points from the teacher.

FIXED PRACTICE

Fixed practice is when a specific movement pattern is practised repeatedly in the same environment. This method is sometimes referred

Fixed practice is ideal for closed skills

TASK 2

1. Discuss what type of practice is best suited to learning a potentially dangerous skill.
2. What type of performer would benefit from having massed practice?

to as a *skill drill*. It is the most suitable method of practice for closed skills which require specific movement patterns to be overlearned and become habitual. Attention can then be directed elsewhere. The environment in which these skills are performed is always the same and the movement once learned and perfected never changes.

The discus thrower when learning and practising can use fixed, repetitive practices or skill drills because the skill and the environment it is performed in never changes. The diameter of the throwing circle, weight of the shot and throwing area are always the same.

KEY TERM

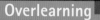

Overlearning

Is when the performer has already perfected the skill being learned but still carries on practising. This extra time can strengthen motor programmes and schema.

APPLY IT!

Fixed practice – the gymnast practises vaults over the same apparatus with the same run up etc.

VARIED PRACTICE

This is where the skill is practised in many different environments. It is the most suitable method of practice for open skills. Practising in a variety of situations allows *schema* to be developed. The performer is able to adapt the skill to suit the environment, and the information relating to these adaptations is stored, thereby expanding the schema. It is essential that the practice conditions should be as realistic as possible. Variable practice also develops the learner's perceptual and decision-making skills.

An example of variable practice is a 4 v 5 passing game in football in which passing skills, support and positional play will improve in an environment which is realistic.

If varied practice is used for closed skills it is essential that the essential stimuli are not varied but the irrelevant stimuli can be varied.

Before being introduced to varied practices the learner should establish the motor programme in a fixed practice environment. The repetitive action allows the learner to overlearn the skill which then becomes habitual enabling the learner to focus on the changing environment of the variable practice situation.

APPLY IT!

Varied practice

When learning a chest pass in basketball or netball the learner first perfects the actual skill of the chest pass and then practises it in a 2 v 3 passing practice which means that each passing situation differs from the others.

KEY TERM

Schema

A schema is a store of information in the long term memory that updates and modifies programmes, e.g. information about the environment and kinaesthetic feedback.

TASK 3

1. Discuss the most appropriate forms of practice for open skills.
2. Discuss the most appropriate form of practice for closed skills.

EXAM TIP

Make sure that you are able to explain the appropriate use of each of the practice methods in order to maximise effectiveness. You should relate this to different ability levels, different skill classifications and the formation of schema.

MENTAL PRACTICE OR MENTAL REHEARSAL

Mental practice or rehearsal is when the performer goes through the movement in their mind without any physical movement occurring. In the early/cognitive stage of learning mental rehearsal, sometimes referred to as *imagery*, consists of building up a mental picture. It can also be used to focus attention. More advanced performers use it to rehearse complex skills or to go over strategies and tactics. The gymnast, prior to performing, will go through the routine visualising the performance of each movement in the routine. It can also be used for reinforcing successful movements. The golfer who has just hit a successful shot mentally practices the successful swing as he walks down the fairway.

Experienced performers also use mental rehearsal for emotional control and to establish optimum levels of arousal. It is also used to reduce anxiety, increase confidence and to focus on winning or being successful.

It is thought that when mental practice takes place that the muscular neurones fire as if the muscle is actually active. Research has shown that mental rehearsal can improve performance. It is useful for experienced performers but can also improve learning.

It should not be used as an alternative to physical practice as on its own it is not as effective as physical practice. Used in conjunction with physical practice, e.g. in the rest intervals of distributive practice, it can increase the speed of learning. Mental practice used on its own is not as effective as physical practice. Skills that have a high cognitive element e.g. team game strategies, gymnastic routines gain more from mental rehearsal then simple skills e.g. those which rely on strength.

tal rehearsal
tes a picture
e mind of the
ete to help
earning and
ormance of
ement skills

APPLY IT!

Mental rehearsal

Before beginning his pole vault the athlete will go through the routine in his mind by creating a mental picture of each stage of the vault.

REMEMBER

Ensure that you are able to explain mental rehearsal and can give a practical example of it.

TAKE IT FURTHER

Discuss the strengths and weaknesses of each method of practice explaining both the type of learner and the type of skill most suitable to be used with them.

ExamCafé

Relax, refresh, result!

Refresh your memory

You should now be able to:

▷ Identify Fitts and Posner's phases of learning.

▷ Apply these phases to practical activities.

▷ Describe different types of guidance used in difference phases of learning to improve performance.

▷ Evaluate critically these different types of guidance.

▷ Describe methods of practice.

▷ Explain the role of mental practice and rehearsal as compared to physical practice rehearsal.

▷ Explain the appropriate use of practice methods to maximise effectiveness.

▷ Evaluate critically different types of practice methods and their application to the performance of movement skills.

REVISE AS YOU GO!

1. Name and use practical examples to explain Fitts and Posner's phases of learning.
2. Name four types of guidance used in the teaching of motor skills.
3. Give the advantages and disadvantages of each of these types of guidance.
4. Identify the phases of learning which each of these forms of guidance is most suitable for.
5. Describe four methods of practice used in the teaching of motor skills.
6. What are the advantages and disadvantages of each of these methods of practice?
7. Why is distributed practice usually better than massed practice?
8. Why is varied practice so important in developing schema?
9. Which is the best method of practice for closed skills?
10. Use a practical example to explain mental rehearsal.

Get the result!

Examination question

Identify the characteristics of the cognitive phase of learning and using practical examples describe two different types of guidance used in the cognitive phase of learning. (5)

examiner's tips

- Firstly check the command words in the question: identify, describe.
- Check the focus of the question – Cognitive phase of learning and guidance.
- Check number of marks available. In this case, it's 5.
- Do you need to use practical examples? Yes

Examiner says:

There are five marks available in this question so the first part is likely to be worth two or three marks. It would be wise to put at least three characteristics of the cognitive phase of learning in the answer. Whilst the question only asks you to identify these characteristic the candidate identifies that it is the first phase of learning but then doesn't identify a second because they fail to say that they watch a demonstration in order to form a mental picture. The candidate needs to have gone further on this their second characteristic and put a third characteristic in to ensure that they get all the marks available. The second part of the question requires the candidate to describe two different types of guidance and the candidate has simply identified them and not used practical examples to describe them.

Student answer

The cognitive phase of learning is the first phase of learning when the learner watches a demonstration. Visual and verbal guidance are used in this phase.

Student's improved answer

The cognitive phase is the first or beginner stage of learning. A lot of concentration is needed at this stage, the performer concentrates on the separate sub-routines which causes the skill to be jerky. A lot of mistakes are made in this stage as the performer doesn't have a feel for the movement. Mechanical guidance can be used during this stage of learning, for example armbands are used in swimming to support the performer in the water but also so they get the feel of the movement. Manual guidance can also be used: this is the physical manipulation of the performer, for example the swimming teacher may get in the water and support the learner's body while they are swimming which also allows the learner to get a feel of the movement.

Examiner says:

The candidate clearly identifies three characteristics of the cognitive phase of learning, these being:

- First or beginner stage
- Concentrates on separate sub-routines which cause the skill to be jerky
- A lot of mistakes are made because they don't have a feel for the movement.

The candidate missed the more obvious characteristic of the performer forming a mental picture of the skill, however three characteristics is sufficient.

The candidate clearly identifies two forms of guidance and used good, relevant practical examples to give good explanations of both forms of guidance.

A grade A answer. Well done!

CHAPTER 6:

Information processing during the performance of skills in physical activity

LEARNING OBJECTIVES

At the end of this chapter you should be able to:

- Understand the key components of information processing
- Describe and draw the information processing models of Welford and Whiting and apply them to the learning and performance of physical activities
- Describe the multi-store model of the memory process and the interaction of memory with the perceptual process
- Describe the components of memory and the roles they play in information processing
- Describe strategies to improve both short and long term memory storage
- Apply the memory process to the learning and performance of physical activities
- Define reaction time, movement time and response time
- Describe the impact of reaction time on performance
- Explain factors affecting response time in practical activities
- Demonstrate knowledge and understanding and the application of theories relating to reaction time.

INTRODUCTION

Information processing focuses on how we deal with the vast amount of information that is available to us when we are performing skills. Information processing theories compare our systems to those of a computer in order to help us understand the various procedures that we apply to the information, which is important to our performing our skills successfully. These procedures include the detection and interpretation of the information and the use of it to make decisions and put them into action.

We also need to have an understanding of the way in which we make decisions and the factors that influence the speed at which we make them.

Information processing theories also help us to understand the important part that our memories play as well as the role that feedback, both from ourselves and teachers/coaches, has in performing

skills. We have to understand the theories and ensure that we know how to apply them effectively to the learning and performing of our practical activities.

Models of information processing and effectiveness in the learning and performance of movement skills

WHAT IS INFORMATION PROCESSING?

The theories of information processing attempt to explain how we take in the vast amount of information from our surroundings, interpret it and make decisions about courses of action we should take. They compare us to computers but also take into account the more personalised nature of our interpretation and decision-making processes. If we were to identify three key processes in the working of a computer, we would say:

- inputting information
- processing information
- outputting information.

In humans this is the same as:

- sensory input
- central mechanisms (brain)
- effector mechanisms (muscles).

We are, therefore, looking at how information enters our system, how we interpret it and make decisions, how we put those decisions into action, together with what we do with the new information our actions generate. This can be explained as follows:

- **Stimulus identification** – we first have to decide if a stimulus has occurred and this is done by our sensory systems receiving information. Patterns of movement are also detected and interpreted, e.g. we would interpret the information to decide the direction

and speed that a ball was travelling. It can be seen that this stage involves the *perceptual processes.*

- **Response selection** – this stage acts on the information received from stimulus identification stage and is concerned with deciding which movement to make, e.g. the ball is high and to my left so I must move to my left and catch it.
- **Response programming** – this next stage receives the decision about which movement to make and is responsible for organising our motor system (nerves and muscles) to carry out the appropriate movement.

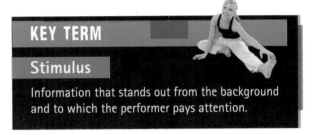

KEY TERM

Stimulus

Information that stands out from the background and to which the performer pays attention.

There are numerous information processing models but we will focus on two.

WELFORD'S MODEL

Welford's model is a little more complicated than Whiting's. Both have the same basic processes of information processing. Welford's model identifies the following components:

- Display
- Sensory information
- Sense organs
- Perceptual mechanism
- Effector mechanism
- Response
- Feedback.

WHITING'S MODEL

Whiting emphasised that we should realise that, although we show these models as static diagrams, not only is our environment constantly changing but the components of the models, whilst retaining the same basic structure, are constantly changing and becoming more sophisticated. The models, therefore, should be seen as being dynamic.

Fig 6.1 Stages in information processing

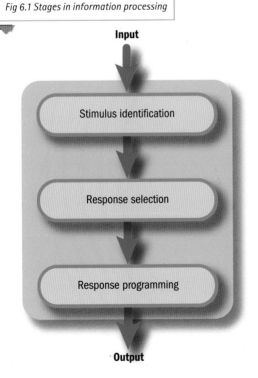

Input

Stimulus identification

Response selection

Response programming

Output

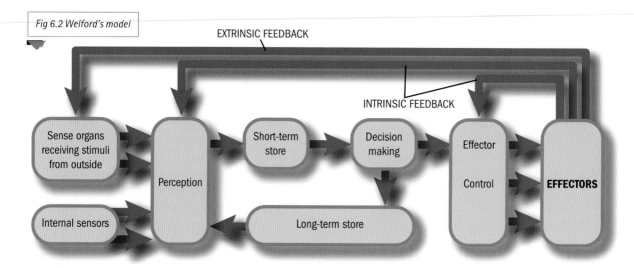

Fig 6.2 Welford's model

Whiting's model identifies the following components:

- Display
- Receptor systems
- Perceptual mechanism
- Translatory mechanism

- Output
- Feedback.

We need to look in a little more detail at the elements which make up these models if we are to have a better understanding of the process. These elements are:

Fig 6.3 Whiting's model

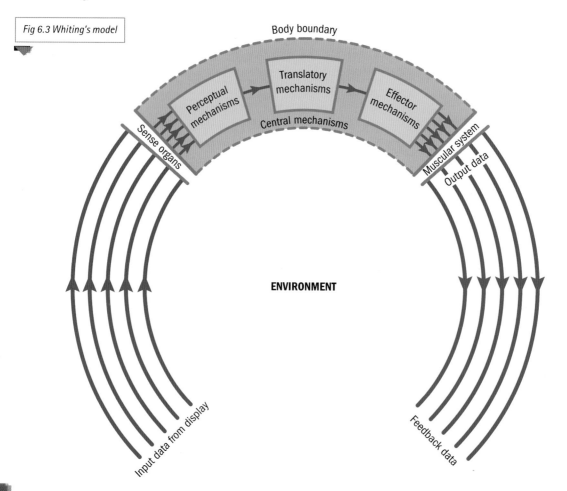

- **Display** – the surroundings or environment that the performer is in. For a netball player it would include the ball, teammates, opponents, spectators and the noise they make, the umpires and the coach/teacher. Some of the information generated by the display will be noticed by the performer and will stimulate the sensory systems.
- **Sensory information** – we use the senses of vision, hearing and *proprioception* to gather information in order that we are aware of what is happening around us. These senses detect information that stimulates their sensory receptors.

APPLY IT!

Sensory information

Hockey players use their eyes or vision to see the opponents' positions and the ball. They use their hearing to listen to their teammates calling for them to pass or dribble.

KEY TERMS

Proprioception

The sense that allows us to know what position our body is in, what our muscles and joints are doing and to feel things involved in our performance, e.g. the ball, hockey stick. Proprioception consists of: touch, kinaesthesis and equilibrium.

Perception

The process which involves the interpretation of information.

Motor programme

A series of movements stored in the long-term memory. They specify the movements the skill consists of and the order they occur. They can be retrieved by one decision.

Feedback

The information received by the performer during the course of the movement and as a result of it.

- **Touch** – allows us to feel pressure and pain so we know how hard we have kicked a ball or are gripping a racket. Awareness of pain helps us avoid serious injury.
- **Kinaesthesis** – gives us information relating to the contractions of muscles, joints and tendons. When you have mastered a skill you are able to 'feel' how it is to perform using kinaesthetic information. The golfer uses this sense to know if their swing is correct.
- **Equilibrium** – tells you whether you are balanced, and turning or falling. It also enables you to know your body position. Information is generated from the inner ear. Gymnasts and divers use this in their movements.
- **Perception** – the process which involves the interpretation of information. This is the process by which we make sense of the stimuli we receive. It consists of three elements:
  - detection – the brain identifies that a stimulus is present
  - comparison – having identified the stimulus it is now compared to similar stimuli that we have stored in our memory
  - recognition – when the stimulus is matched to one stored in the memory it is identified or recognised.
- **Memory** – this plays an important role in both the perceptual and decision-making processes. It consists of three parts:
  - short-term sensory stores
  - short-term memory
  - long-term memory.
- **Decision making** (translatory mechanism) – once the information has been interpreted the correct response has to be put into action. This correct action will be in the form of a motor programme which identifies the movements the action is made up of, the order they are in and where they take place.
- **Effector mechanism** – the motor programme is put into action by sending impulses via the nervous system to the appropriate muscles so that they can carry out the appropriate actions.
- **Effector** – the muscles which put the motor programme into action.
- **Feedback** – when the motor programme has been put into action by the effector mechanism the display changes and creates new information. This new information is known as feedback and can be internal as well as external. Feedback occurs as a result of the movements we make

and it is used to compare our performance with what we actually intended to do.

There are two major types of feedback:

- **Intrinsic** – feedback from internal proprioceptors about the feel of the movement. Kinaesthesis is also involved. For example, the feel of whether or not you have hit the ball in the middle of the bat in a cricket shot. It is important to experienced performers who may be able to use it during a movement in order to control it. Beginners should be made aware of this feedback in order that they pay attention to experiencing the movement's feel.
- **Extrinsic** – feedback from external sources such as the teacher/coach or team mates. It is received by the visual and auditory systems and is used to augment intrinsic feedback. It is important for beginners, as they are limited in their use of intrinsic feedback.

EXAM TIP

Make sure that you are able to draw and explain Welford's and Whiting's information processing models as well as being able to explain them using a practical activity.

EXAM TIP

Ensure that you know the appropriate uses of feedback particularly in relation different stages of learning that the performer goes through.

TASK 1

Describe the ways in which you get feedback about your performances in your chosen activity.

APPLY IT!

Feedback

A football player has the ball for a free kick. He sees all his teammates and opponents and decides where to play the ball. He decides where to kick the ball, how hard to kick it and how high etc. The ball goes over all his teammates and out of play. This feedback tells him that next time he doesn't need to kick it so hard or so high.

REMEMBER

Know the models of Welford and Whiting and be able to explain them.

Serial and parallel processing

Most information which we process is done sequentially or in stages. These stages are different and have an effect on each other and are known as serial processes. Serial processing would occur in a trampolining routine when the performer processes the information relating to each movement of the routine stage by stage.

Fig 6.4 Multi-store model of the memory process

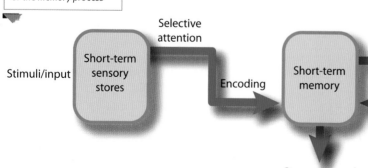

Stimuli/input — Short-term sensory stores — Selective attention — Encoding — Short-term memory — Encoding → Long-term memory — Retrieval — Perception and decision making

However, some processes occur simultaneously and are referred to as *parallel processes*. These do not have an effect on each other. An example would be in a team game when you will be processing information about the speed, height and direction of the ball coming towards you and also about the positions of teammates and opponents.

We have seen in the models of Welford and Whiting which we have examined that generally the same processes are involved but sometimes with different names.

TASK 2

Choose one of the two models identified (Whiting's or Welford's).

Use a skill or a number of skills in your chosen activities to explain and illustrate how each component of the model works in that activity.

Memory and its role in developing movement skills

Memory plays an important role in information processing, particularly in the interpretation of information when we rely on our previous experiences.

It is also important in determining the motor programme we are going to use to send the appropriate information to the muscles. This importance can be seen in the way memory links with other processes in Welford's information processing model.

THE MULTI-STORE MODEL OF THE MEMORY PROCESS

This model describes memory in terms of the information flow through a system. It identifies that the memory involves a sequence of three stages or stores:

- Sensory memory (SM)
- Short-term memory (STM)
- Long-term memory (LTM)

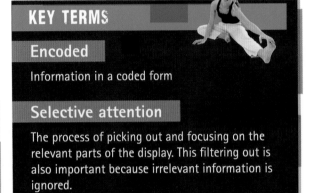

Fig 6.5

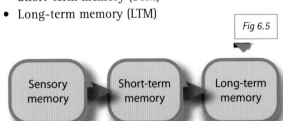

KEY TERMS

Encoded

Information in a coded form

Selective attention

The process of picking out and focusing on the relevant parts of the display. This filtering out is also important because irrelevant information is ignored.

- **Short-term sensory stores** – All stimuli entering the information processing system are held for a very short time (0.25–1 second). These stores have a very large capacity with a separate store for each sense. The perceptual mechanism determines which of the information is important to us and we direct our attention to this. This is the *recognition aspect of perception*.

Other irrelevant information is quickly lost from the sensory stores to be replaced by new information. This filtering process is known as *selective attention*. By focusing our attention on relevant information we filter this information through into the short-term memory. Selective attention enables the information important to our performance to be filtered and concentrated on. Information unimportant to the performance and therefore not attended to is filtered out. The importance of this process is highlighted by theories that suggest that there is a limited amount of information we can process. The process of focusing on the important and ignoring the irrelevant also helps us to react quickly. For example, sprinters will focus their attention on the track and the gun, ignoring fellow competitors and the crowd.

Sprinters focus their attention on the starter's gun

The short-term memory has a limited capacity, both in terms of the quantity of information it can store and the length of time it can be stored for. Generally, these limits are thought to be between 5 and 9 pieces of information for up to 30 seconds. The number can be increased by linking or *chunking* bits of information together and remembering them as one piece of information. The period of time can also be extended if you rehearse or repeat the information.

A good non-sporting example of this is when you look up a phone number before dialling it. You group the numbers together and repeat them to yourself until you dial the number. In rugby, line-out strategies are remembered by the players referring to them with a number or name.

Information in the short-term memory that is considered to be important is rehearsed or practised and by this process passes into the long-term memory for future use. This process is referred to as encoding.

Knowing what are the important aspects of the information in the display helps to avoid focusing on irrelevant cues. Focusing on irrelevant information is known as attentional wastage and will affect a beginner's learning and performance of skills.

KEY TERM

Chunking

Different pieces of information are put together and remembered as one piece of information.

TASK 3

What is the information you focus on and what do you ignore in your chosen activities?

REMEMBER

Be able to explain what selective attention is and how it is applied in the memory.

- **Short-term memory** – this aspect of memory is often referred to as the 'workplace'. It is here that the incoming information is compared to that previously learned and stored in the long-term memory. This is the *comparison aspect of perception*.

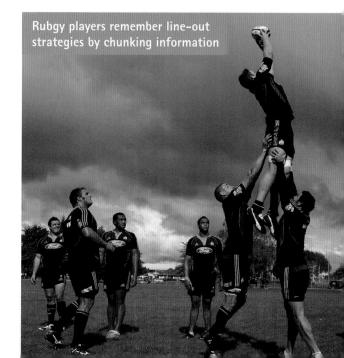

Rugby players remember line-out strategies by chunking information

APPLY IT!

Short-term memory

Teachers when they are giving coaching points to learners will only give two or three points so that the learners can remember them as they practise.

- **Long-term memory** – the long-term memory holds the information that has been well learned and practised. Its capacity is thought to be limitless and the information is held for a long period of time, perhaps permanently.

Motor programmes are stored in the long-term memory as a result of us practising them many times. You will no doubt realise that you never forget how to ride a bike or swim even when you have not done them for some time.

The long-term memory is the *recognition part of the perceptual process* when the stored information in the long-term memory is retrieved and compared to the new information which is then recognised.

Motor programmes are stored in the long-term memory and you never forget them

Strategies to improve retention and retrieval

Now we realise how important the memory is to our performance it would help us if we were able to improve our ability to store information and to be able to remember it. Psychologists think that we can do this by the following methods.

- **Rehearsal/Practice** – When learning we need to practise or rehearse the skill as much as possible. Expert performers do a lot of skill practice until they have *overlearned* the skill and it has become automatic. It is thought that practice carries the skill's image 'to and fro' between the short and long-term memories establishing a memory trace. This helps both retention and retrieval.
- **Association/Linking** – Coaches and teachers should always try to link new information to that which the performer already knows. Specific sports skills can be linked to fundamental motor skills, e.g. throwing the javelin can be linked to the overarm throw. This helps the learner mentally organise the skill. Linking parts of serial skills together both physically and mentally is also important. For example, parts of a basketball lay-up shot or parts of a gymnastics sequence.
- **Remember the limitation of the short-term memory.** Teachers and coaches should give learners three coaching points to remember when they go to practise. When they have mastered these three, more can be given.
- **Simplicity** – Learners should be given time to take in new information, which should be kept simple. More complex information can be added later. It is also important that similar information/skills should not be presented close together as they may interfere with each other. For example, beginners learning to swim should not be introduced to two different strokes in the same session.
- **Organisation** – Information is more easily remembered if it is organised in a meaningful

way. It is suggested that gymnastics and trampolining sequences will be remembered more easily if the individual movements are practised together in order that the performer links the end of one movement to the beginning of the next.

- **Imagery** – Information can be remembered better by having a mental image. Demonstrations are really important in order that learners are able to create an image of the skill in their mind. Some coaches link images to words. For example 'chin, knee, toe' gives the learner the picture of the correct body position in the shot putt.

- **Meaningful** – If the learner is made aware that the information being learned is relevant to them and their performance it becomes meaningful and is more likely to be remembered.

- **Chunking** – Information can be grouped together allowing more to be dealt with at one time. Experienced performers use chunking to look at the whole field of play, recognize developing patterns and anticipate what will happen. This chunking together of information is particularly important in the short term memory which has a limited capacity. In badminton if we have the grip, position of the racket, position of feet and body weight stored as one item, i.e. preparation it frees up the capacity in the short term memory to focus on other aspects.

- **Uniqueness** – If the teacher or coach presents information in an unusual or different way then it is more likely to be remembered.

- **Enjoyment** – If the teacher can ensure that the learner enjoys the experience this will increase the possibility of it being remembered.

- **Positive reinforcement** – Praise and encouragement when learning a skill will aid retention.

EXAM TIP

Make sure that you can describe strategies to improve storage and retrieval of information in both short and long term memory

Reaction time and developing effective performance in physical activity

Reaction time is the speed at which we are able to process information and make decisions. Being able to respond quickly is very important in many sports and often determines if we are successful. The speed at which we make decisions involves a complicated process which can be illustrated by the following information processing model.

Fig 6.6

Input → Decision making → Output

Put simply, there are four parts to reaction time, made up of the time it takes for:

1. The stimulus to activate the particular sensory system the stimulus to activate the particular sensory system
2. The stimulus to travel from the sensory system to the brain the stimulus to travel from the sensory system to the brain
3. The brain (central mechanisms) to process the stimulus the brain(central mechanisms) to process the stimulus
4. The relevant commands to be sent from the central mechanisms to the relevant muscle or group of muscles.

Reaction time is defined as the time between the onset of the stimulus and the start of the movement in response to it. In the sprint start, reaction time is the time from the gun going off to the sprinter putting pressure on his starting blocks. You will remember from Chapter 4 that reaction time is an ability.

There are two other components connected with performing movements quickly – movement time and response time.

KEY TERMS

Reaction time

The time between the onset of the stimulus and the start of the movement in response to it

Movement time

The time it takes from starting the movement to completing it

Response time

The time from the onset of the stimulus to the completion of the movement. Response time = Reaction time + Movement time.

- **Movement time** – Movement time is the time it takes from first starting the movement to completing it. In the sprint start it is represented by the time from the sprinter first pressing on their blocks to when they cross the finish line and hopefully finish first!
- **Response time** – This is the time from the onset of the stimulus to the completion of the movement. It is the total time, adding reaction time to movement time. For example, it is the time from the gun going off to the sprinter crossing the finishing line.

FACTORS WHICH AFFECT REACTION TIME

There are several factors that affect reaction time, which is an ability that varies between individuals, according to the following criteria.

Fig 6.7 Components of response time

Reaction time   Movement time

Response time

- **Age** – reaction time gets quicker until you are about 20 and then gets slower as you get older.
- **Gender** – males generally have quicker reaction times than females but as we get older the difference becomes less.
- **Limb used** – the further the information has to travel in the nervous system the slower the reaction will be. Normally the reaction of feet is slower than hands.
- **Personality** – extroverts tend to have quicker reaction than introverts.
- **Alertness/arousal/motivation** – levels of these will affect our reaction time. Optimum levels are needed to react quickly.
- **Body temperature** – if we are cold, our reactions are slower.
- **Sensory system receiving the stimulus** – reaction time will vary depending on the sense that is being used.

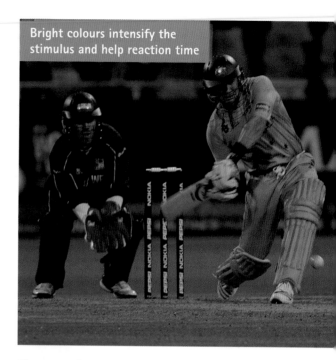
Bright colours intensify the stimulus and help reaction time

EXAM TIP

Make sure that you know the definitions of reaction, movement and response times as well as appreciating the differences between them. Be sure to be able to apply them to a practical activity.

TASK 4

Using a reaction time ruler, get each member in your group to have 10 trials with their preferred hand. Find the mean reaction time for the males and females.

There are also external factors which affect reaction time, which are:

- **If a warning is given** – if you are expecting the stimulus your reaction will be quicker. In the sprint start the starter says 'set' to warn the sprinter that the gun is about to go off.
- **Stimulus intensity** – loud sounds or bright colours stimulate quicker reactions. We use an orange football in the snow and a white cricket ball for night matches.
- **The likelihood of the stimulus occurring (stimulus–response compatibility)** – if the stimulus has a good chance of occurring you will react quicker than to one that occurs infrequently.

APPLY IT!

Stimulus–response compatibility – if your opponent in a game of badminton usually serves short you will react quicker to that serve than you will when they do a high long serve.

SINGLE CHANNEL HYPOTHESIS

This states that when receiving many stimuli from the environment the brain can only deal with one stimulus at a time. The way in which we process information is thought of as a single

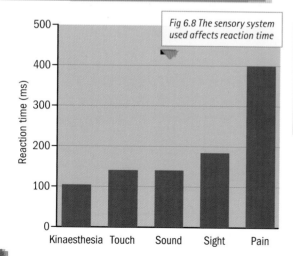

Fig 6.8 The sensory system used affects reaction time

Reaction time (ms) — Kinaesthesia, Touch, Sound, Sight, Pain

TASK 5

Work with a partner. You will need a stopwatch and a pack of playing cards. Your partner will time you for each of the tasks below.

1. Simply turn the cards, one at a time, onto one pile face up.
2. After shuffling the cards turn the cards over one at a time separating the cards into a red pile and a black pile.
3. After shuffling the cards turn them over one at a time now piling them into four suits.
4. After shuffling the cards turn them over one at a time now putting them into eight piles: the face cards and the number cards for hearts, clubs, diamonds and spades.

What do you notice about the times for each task?

channel which can only deal with one piece of information at a time. This one piece of information has to be processed before the next stimulus or piece of information can be dealt with. This is sometimes referred to as a *bottleneck*.

CHOICE REACTION TIME

In our previous examination of reaction time we have looked at the performer's reaction when there is just one stimulus, e.g. the sprinter reacting to the gun. This is simple reaction time. In many sporting situations performers are faced with more than one stimulus and more than one response. This is known as *choice reaction time*. For example, a badminton player having the stimuli of the different shots their opponent may play and the responses of which shot to select to return the shuttle.

You should see from Task 5 that the greater the number of piles, the more choices you have and the slower your time becomes. The greater the number of choices you have, the more information you have to process to make your decisions and this slows down your reaction time. A psychologist named Hick researched choice reaction time and found that a person's reaction time increased linearly as the number of choices increased.

KEY TERM

Hick's Law

Choice reaction time increases linearly as the number of stimulus/choice alternatives increases.

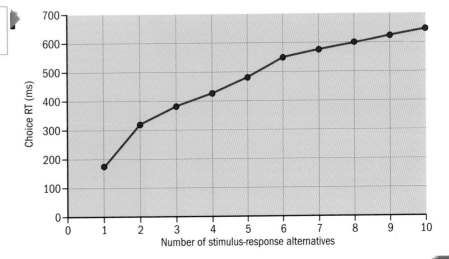

Fig 6.9 Reaction time increases as the number of stimulus/ response alternatives increase

Choice RT (ms)

Number of stimulus-response alternatives

165

When receiving a serve we should attempt to pick up clues as to which serve it is going to be, to reduce our reaction time

Hick's Law has important implications for us within sport. If we are trying to outwit our opponent we should aim to disguise our intentions. For example, our short and long serves in badminton should have exactly the same preparation. Our opponent then has to choose from a number of possibilities and therefore their reaction time is increased. If, however, we are receiving, we should attempt to pick up clues about which serve it is going to be thus reducing our choice of response and therefore our reaction time.

EXAM TIP

Make sure that you are able to sketch a graph to show Hick's Law.

HOW DO TEACHERS/COACHES ATTEMPT TO IMPROVE THE PERFORMER'S RESPONSE TIME?

- **Practice** – the more often a stimulus is responded to the shorter the reaction time becomes. If enough practice is done the response becomes automatic and requires little attention.
- **Mental rehearsal** – practice is done in the form of mental rehearsal. This enables the performer to ensure that they attend to the correct cues and expect and respond to the correct stimuli. It also activates the neuromuscular system acting like physical training. It is also thought to have an effect on the control of arousal levels. Mental rehearsal works better with complex tasks which require a lot of information processing.
- **Experience** – playing the activity enhances the performer's awareness of the probability of particular stimuli occurring.

KEY TERM

Mental rehearsal

This is the picturing of the performance in the mind and does not involve physical movement. It consists of mental imagery, viewing videos of the performance, reading or listening to instructions.

- **Stimulus–response compatibility** – if the response you are expected to make to the stimulus is the one you would normally make you will react quicker than with a different response.
- **Cue detection** – analysing an opponent's play to anticipate what they are going to do. For example, analysing a badminton player's shots so that you are able to detect the difference between their overhead clear and drop shot.
- **Improve the performer's physical fitness** – this will influence response time. The fitter you are, the quicker you will be.
- **Concentration/selective attention** – in simple reaction time situations you focus on the relevant stimulus and ignore everything else. This limits the information you process. For example, during a sprint start, focusing on the gun.
- **Level of arousal/motivation** – the teacher/ coach has to ensure that the performer is at the appropriate level of arousal/motivation for the activity.
- **Warm-up** – ensuring physical and mental preparation for the activity.
- **Anticipation** – we have left this to last because it is a very important strategy in reducing both types of reaction time. There are two main forms of anticipation:
  - Spatial – predicting what will happen. The cricket batsman who has detected the difference in the fast bowler's action is able to pick out the disguised slower ball.
  - Temporal – predicting when it will happen. The sprinter who has identified the period between the 'set' command and the gun will be able to move as the gun goes off.

Anticipation has very important implications for teachers and coaches. They should encourage their performers to look for relevant cues in their opponents' actions in order that they will then be able to predict what they will do and also to disguise their own actions to prevent opponents anticipating. They should also ensure that their performers do not become too predictable in what they do.

APPLY IT!

Anticipation

- The badminton player detects that his opponent takes his racket back further when he performs a long, high serve than when he performs a short serve. The player therefore uses *spatial anticipation* to attack the short serve and to move to the back of the court for the long, high serve.
- The sprinter knows that the starter always has a three second pause between the set command and the gun. The sprinter is able to use *temporal anticipation* to get a good start.

TASK 6

Look at the ways to improve response time and identify those which your teacher/ coach has used with you in your chosen activities.

EXAM TIP

Ensure that you able to explain the factors affecting response time and how they might be manipulated to improve response time in practical activities.

Psychological refractory period

Anticipation has many benefits but we should also be aware of the drawbacks. If we anticipate incorrectly what our opponents are about to do or when they will do it, our reaction time will be slowed down. If we have detected a stimulus and are processing that information when a second stimulus comes along, we are unable to attend to and process the second stimulus until we have finished processing the first one, making our reaction time longer. This extra reaction time is known as the *psychological refractory period* (PRP).

This is why it is so important that we both disguise our actions or deliberately try to make our opponents take a wrong decision, e.g. sell them a dummy, making them go one way when we are really going the other. The psychologists explain this by saying that we have a single channel for processing information and that it will only process one piece of information at any one time.

APPLY IT!

The PRP

The rugby player pretends to pass the ball to a team mate and the opponent goes towards that team mate but the player then keeps the ball and goes round the opponent on the other side.

TASK 7

Think of situations, deliberate and accidental, in your activities when the PRP operates, for example, the ball hitting the top of the net in tennis.

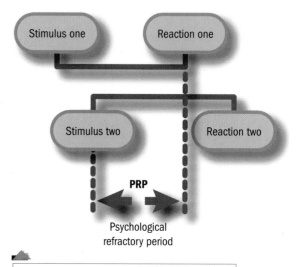

Fig 6.10 The PRP is the delay caused by being able to process only one piece of information at a time

ExamCafé

Relax, refresh, result!

Refresh your memory

You should now be able to:

▷ Understand the key components of information processing.

▷ Describe and draw the information processing models of Welford and Whiting and apply them to the learning and performance of physical activities.

▷ Describe the multi-store model of the memory process and the interaction of memory with the perceptual process.

▷ Describe the components of memory and the roles they play in information processing.

▷ Describe strategies to improve both short and long term memory storage.

▷ Apply the memory process to the learning and performance of physical activities.

▷ Define reaction time, movement time and response time.

▷ Describe the impact of reaction time on performance.

▷ Explain factors affecting response time in practical activities.

▷ Demonstrate knowledge and understanding and the application of theories relating to reaction time. These are:

- The psychological refractory period – PRP
- Choice reaction time – Hick's Law
- The single channel hypothesis
- Anticipation.

REVISE AS YOU GO!

Test your knowledge and understanding

1. Name the two information processing models you have studied. Draw and label both of them.
2. Identify the following information processing terms: display; sensory input; kinaesthesis; proprioception; effector mechanism.
3. Explain the difference between serial and parallel processing.
4. Identify the three components of memory.
5. Identify two characteristics of the short–term memory.
6. Explain what the term 'selective attention' means and give a practical example of its use.
7. Identify four strategies you could use to improve the retention and retrieval of information in your memory.
8. Name four factors which affect reaction time.
9. State Hick's Law and draw a diagram or graph to illustrate it.
10. What is the PRP?

Get the result!

Examination question

- Explain what is meant by simple reaction time and give a practical example of simple reaction time in sport.
- Choice reaction time (Hick's Law) can be explained through the use of a graph. Sketch a graph to illustrate the effect of choice reaction time on physical performance.   5 marks.

examiner's tips

- Firstly check the command words – explain and sketch.
- Check the key subject focus. Simple reaction time and choice reaction time.
- Check how many marks are available. 5 marks
- Check to see if practical examples are required. Yes

Examiner says:

The candidate has repeated the words used in the question and will not get any marks for doing this. Also they have not given a practical example. In sketching their graph the candidate has got the curve wrong and failed to label the axes and indicate the units of measurement on them. It indicates that they probably have the knowledge but haven't been able to put it in their answer.

Student answer

When you react simply to something.

Student's improved answer

Simple reaction time is the time between the presentation of a stimulus and the start of the movement in response to it. An example of this would be a sprinter reacting to the starter's gun in a 100 metre sprint race.

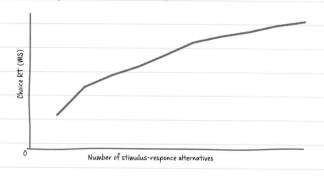

Examiner says:

This is a much better answer. Simple reaction time is clearly defined without using any terminology from the question and a good, clear practical example given. The sketch of the graph has the correct shape with the axes being clearly labelled together with the units of measurement being identified.

This is a grade A answer. Well done!

CHAPTER 7

Motor control of skills and its impact upon developing effectiveness in physical activity

LEARNING OBJECTIVES

At the end of this chapter you should be able to:

- Describe the nature and give examples of motor and executive programmes stored in long-term memory
- Explain how motor programmes link with open loop control and the autonomous phase of learning
- Describe open and closed loop control
- Explain the role of open and closed loop control in the performance of motor skills
- Evaluate critically different types of feedback to detect and correct errors
- Understand Schema Theory and its role in developing movement skills and strategies.

INTRODUCTION

In this chapter the focus will be on a description of motor and executive motor programmes and the control of motor skills during performance. This will lead to an understanding of how psycho-motor skills are learned and improved.

KEY TERM

Motor programme

A generalised series or pattern of movements stored in long-term memory.

Motor programmes

A motor programme (MP) or executive motor programme (EMP) is the plan of a whole skill or pattern of movement. For example, a plan of a forward roll in gymnastics. This plan is made up of generalised movements which are stored in the long-term memory. Every skill performed in sport is the product of a motor programme and so

there are countless examples. The example given in Fig. 7.1 is of a tennis serve. Although a serve is classified as a closed skill, adjustments to the motor programme are required each time a serve is performed.

APPLY IT!

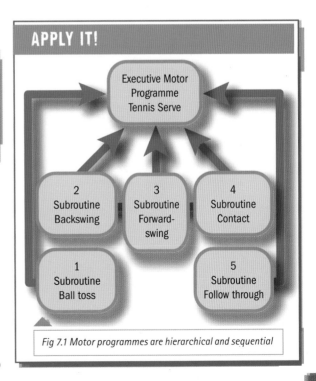

Fig 7.1 Motor programmes are hierarchical and sequential

EXAM TIP

Candidates are often asked the meaning of the term 'motor programme' – see Key Term page 171. When you give a definition remember to give a practical example, e.g. a smash shot in volleyball.

Motor programmes are hierarchical (they have an order of importance with the executive motor programme being of highest status). They are also *sequential*: this means they are performed in a particular order.

SUB-ROUTINES

Executive motor programmes are made up of sub-routines. These small components are often called mini skills or the 'building blocks' of the overall motor programme. Sub-routines are usually performed in sequence.

Novice performers experiencing a new skill begin at the cognitive stage of learning. As improvement is made they reach the associative stage. Some performers progress to become expert in a particular skill, and this is the autonomous stage. At the autonomous stage of learning the motor programme has been *overlearned* or *grooved* into long-term memory.

KEY TERMS

Hierarchical

Order of importance, e.g. the EMP is more important than the sub-routines.

Sequential

Sub-routines are often performed in a set order.

Grooved and overlearned

This means the motor programme has been well learned and is stored in long-term memory. A response can now be made automatically and the performer will be at the autonomous stage of learning.

TASK 1

After performing a motor programme in a practical lesson draw a model of a motor programme (it might be a discus throw). Your diagram should follow the pattern shown in the tennis example and will clearly indicate hierarchical structure and sequential organisation.

REMEMBER

Be able to identify the characteristics of the three stages of learning:

- Cognitive stage: the beginner's stage
- Associative stage: the practice stage
- Autonomous stage: the expert stage.

TAKE IT FURTHER

Why is it necessary for a teacher of Physical Education to know that psycho-motor skills in sport are made up of sub-routines?

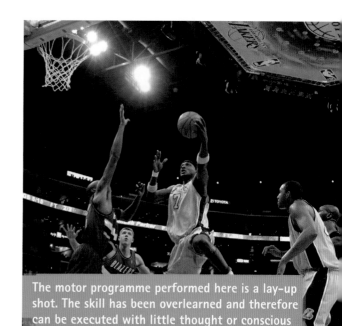

The motor programme performed here is a lay-up shot. The skill has been overlearned and therefore can be executed with little thought or conscious control. This is the link between the autonomous stage of learning and open loop control.

Once the motor programme has been well learned it can be performed with little conscious control. The performer does not have to think much about the required action. The movement appears to be automatic. As one decision will bring about the desired movement this is the basis of open loop control.

Open loop control

LEVEL ONE CONTROL

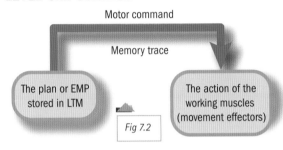

Fig 7.2

Open loop explains how rapid movements are performed in sport, e.g. a close catch in cricket is often thought to be instinctive or a reflex action. It is not. This rapid action occurs when a plan is triggered from long-term memory.

The plan of the action (EMP) is stored in long-term memory. When the situation demands the plan is quickly sent to the working muscles – known as the *movement effectors*. The transfer of information from the brain to the working muscle is done through the formation of a *memory trace*. The memory trace is formed when the skill has been well learned.

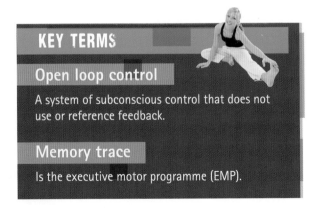

KEY TERMS

Open loop control

A system of subconscious control that does not use or reference feedback.

Memory trace

Is the executive motor programme (EMP).

The skills produced via open loop are performed without conscious control and are often associated with quick ballistic actions such as

those evident in closed skills, e.g. kicking and throwing.

REMEMBER

Be aware of the characteristics of open and closed skills. (See the Classification of motor skills pages 125–9.)

Open loop control does not produce feedback as there is no time to act upon any information about performance. The absence of feedback means that a movement cannot be changed during performance. Therefore open loop is only effective when the environment is predictable.

Open loop control is inflexible when unpredictable changes arise, e.g. once a golf swing has been initiated it is difficult to modify the action if a sudden environmental change takes place.

Open loop is regarded as level one control and is thought to start (initiate) motor skills. Motor skills are adjusted and concluded by other systems which are explained below.

Closed loop control

LEVEL TWO CONTROL

Fig 7.3

Closed loop involves feedback and this is termed the *perceptual trace*.

At level two the feedback loop is short. After the memory trace has triggered the response, internal feedback is gathered through *kinaesthesis* and *proprioception* during the execution of the skill. This allows quick subconscious corrections to take place, e.g. the slalom skier will make quick adjustments to retain balance.

Although these changes are produced subconsciously, the adjustment is stored in long-term memory for future reference.

KEY TERMS

Kinaesthesis

Is internal feedback, often referred to as the 'feeling tone'. The correct feel of the skill is fully in place at the autonomous stage of learning.

Proprioception

Implies information from within the body such as positions of joints and the forces within the muscles.

Closed loop control

LEVEL THREE CONTROL

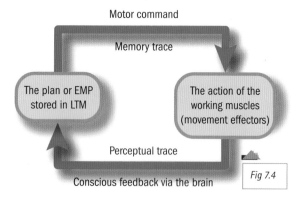

Fig 7.4

REMEMBER

The feedback loop is called the *perceptual trace* and is responsible for adjusting or correcting movement during execution and for completing the skill.

(See Information Processing, on page 154.)

At Level Three, the feedback loop is longer because information on performance is relayed to the brain. The brain in turn controls and modifies the movement by passing corrective messages back to the working muscles. Therefore, the loop involves conscious thought and attention to external feedback. For example, changing direction to avoid an opponent whilst controlling the ball in hockey requires conscious thought.

KEY TERM

External feedback

Is information taken from the environment concerning performance.

Furthermore at the associative stage of learning, novices tend to operate by referring to this level three loop. A reliance on external feedback is necessary at this stage because the learner has not yet acquired the correct feel of the skill.

The perceptual trace operates by comparing the performance as it is taking place with the plan released by the memory trace. If performance matches the plan, the skill is reinforced and allowed to continue. If however, performance does

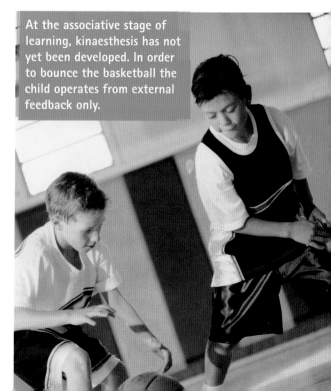

At the associative stage of learning, kinaesthesis has not yet been developed. In order to bounce the basketball the child operates from external feedback only.

KEY TERM

Reinforcement

Is the process that causes behaviour or an action to reoccur.

not match the plan, the skill is adjusted and this change is stored as a new motor programme.

Whilst the theory of open and closed loop attempts to explain how psycho-motor skills are controlled, an explanation as to how skills are learned is also evident. Learning takes place because the perceptual trace is developed and becomes stronger as the movement is practised. See also Knowledge of Results (KR) on page 176.

TAKE IT FURTHER

Explain why closed loop theory can explain both how skills are learned and how skills are controlled

APPLY IT!

Use the example of a gymnast performing a handstand to explain closed loop control.

TASK 2

By using live models or video performances, observe at least five skills in sport. Ensure that there is a mixture of open and closed skills. Discuss how the performance of each skill is influenced by open and closed loop theory

Although the work of Adams on open and closed systems has helped the understanding of how skills are controlled and learned, there are several drawbacks to the theory:

- If a separate plan or memory trace is required for each skill or movement it would not be possible to store such an infinite number of motor programmes. Therefore, retention is a problem.
- If it were possible to store all motor programmes, it would be difficult for the memory trace to recall the required plan in time to execute the skill.
- Often responses in sport are creative, unusual and apparently spontaneous. These adapted movements arise in open skills and are called 'novel responses'. If however, the relevant motor programme does not exist in memory the novel response can not be explained by this theory.

APPLY IT!

Open loop (memory trace) stores the plan and initiates the response. Closed loop (perceptual trace) provides feedback and makes adjustment if required. The perceptual trace completes the skills.

APPLY IT!

A novel response is often spontaneous and creative but never instinctive. They usually emerge as open skills and are difficult to pre-programme. Schema theory explains why such skills are possible.

Whilst explaining how the novel response is made possible, Schema Theory answers the problems relating to storage and retrieval of information.

Before giving focus to Schema Theory it is necessary to define explain and critically analyse *feedback*.

FEEDBACK

Feedback is the information received by the athlete both during and after the skill has been performed. In order to learn and develop skills, feedback is essential. It must be accurate, comprehensible and constructive.

There are several types of feedback:

- Positive
- Negative
- Extrinsic
- Intrinsic
- Terminal
- Concurrent
- Knowledge of performance
- Knowledge of results (KR).

Explanation of Feedback	Critical evaluation of different types of Feedback
1. *Positive feedback* can be given externally by the teacher or coach when the player is praised following success.	• Positive feedback should clearly indicate the parts of the skill that were performed correctly, e.g. the teacher would say the drive shot in cricket is good because the foot was to the pitch of the ball and there was a good follow-through. • Positive feedback reinforces learning and strengthens the stimulus-response (S–R) bond. • Learners at the cognitive and associative stages of learning are motivated by positive feedback but discouraged by negative feedback.
2. *Negative feedback* is received when the movement is incorrect. It can be intrinsic or extrinsic.	• Negative feedback should not be criticism but must address how the skill can be improved, e.g. the serve at tennis will improve with higher reach to strike the ball. • Negative feedback is beneficial to expert performers as it helps them to perfect their skills.
3. *Extrinsic feedback* comes from external sources such as the teacher, coach and team-mates. This type of feedback is also called augmented feedback. Augmented feedback is the general term give to all types of feedback that supplement sensory feedback.	• The learner can become dependent on external feedback and this does not help to develop kinaesthesis. • It is received by the performer through visual and auditory systems.
4. *Intrinsic feedback* is a form of sensory feedback about the physical feel of the movement as it is being performed. It is received via the internal proprioceptors and kinaesthesis is also involved. For example, the feeling of high knee lifts in sprinting.	• Performers at the autonomous stage of learning can access this type of feedback therefore performance will be fluent and well timed. • Performers at the associative stage are still learning what the skill should feel like. They require extrinsic (augmented) feedback.

Table 1 (cont. foll. page)

Table 1 (cont.)

5. *Terminal feedback* is received after the movement has been completed and is extrinsic feedback.	• It is can be given immediately by the teacher or some time after the movement has been completed. • Feedback given immediately is beneficial because it addresses the situation when it is fresh in the learner's mind. • A delay in feedback, for example until the next training session, can also be advantageous as it allows the athlete to think about the performance.
6. *Concurrent feedback* is received during the performance of the skill.	• It can be intrinsic thereby providing information as to how the skill feels, e.g. downward pressure on the ball when dribbling in basketball. • It can also be extrinsic in the form of verbal guidance from the coach or teacher. • This type of feedback is good for continuous skills. • It allows quick correction to take place.
7. *Knowledge of performance* (KP) is feedback that concerns the quality of the movement. KP can be internal as it arises from kinaesthetic awareness.	• KP is used to good effect only by the expert performer. • KP can also come from an external source, e.g. the teacher will provide information as to why the performance was successful or otherwise. • KP motivates the performer but only if used correctly.
8. *Knowledge of results* (KR) is feedback about the result or outcome of the movement and is extrinsic. It will be given by teachers or coaches actually seeing the result, e.g. did the ball go into the goal or by watching a visual recording of the movement.	• KR is essential in skill learning and in particularly during the early stages. • KR helps the development of Knowledge of performance. • KR can be both positive and negative. It is seen as being important in improving a particular phase in performance, e.g. if the hip position in javelin throwing is front on the throwing action can now be improved. • KR can motivate the performer but only if used correctly.

Table 1

Feedback is important to the sports performer because:

- confidence will improve
- motivation may increase
- drive reduction could be prevented
- feedback is vital to learning as it detects and corrects errors
- good actions can be reinforced through feedback so that stimulus–response bonds are strengthened.

KEY TERM

Drive Reduction

Is a loss of motivation.

EXAM TIP

Be aware of the type of feedback that is required at each of the three phases of learning. Candidates should be able to explain intrinsic and extrinsic feedback and give practical examples of each to support the explanation.

KEY TERMS

Schema

A store of information and experience.

Generalised movement

Adaptations of movement that will transfer to influence the performance and learning of other skills.

Transfer

Transfer of learning is the influence of one skill on the learning and performance of another skill.

KEY TERM

Goal setting

Refers to a target set by a teacher or coach. The effects of feedback are enhanced by goal setting.

In general terms feedback must be specific to the skill that is being performed and specific to the individual. The responses of individuals vary greatly to different types of feedback. Furthermore, it is proven that feedback is more effective when given following the completion of a set goal.

EXAM TIP

Candidates should be able to describe the function of feedback and to explain its value when learning and performing skills in sport.

APPLY IT!

For example, an experienced badminton player will have developed a motor programme for a smash in badminton but will not have a programme for playing this shot from all positions on court. However, the player will have many different experiences on which to draw. These experiences are schemas which are stored in long-term memory which can be transferred a new situation. Schemas are used to modify the programme of the smash shot so that the shot can be played from a variety of positions.

Schema theory

Schema Theory is based on the idea that motor programmes are not stored as separate items as presented by open loop theory. Instead they are retained in long-term memory as relationships with motor programmes. These relationships are termed *generalised movements* and they allow the performer to adapt quickly in response to a situation.

Schema is a build-up of experiences which, the theory states, can be adapted in order to meet the demands of new situations.

Schema theory states that experience is gathered from four areas. These areas are termed *memory items*. They are explained in the model below by using the example of two attackers approaching one defender in rugby. The example focuses on the attacker who is carrying the ball.

EXAM TIP

Candidates find the explanation and application of schema theory difficult. It is a topic that frequently appears on examination papers. Learn the memory items thoroughly. Be able to explain recall and recognition schema by using practical examples to support the explanation.

MEMORY ITEM 1
Knowledge of Initial
Conditions:
Relates to whether the
player in possession has
previously experienced a
similar situation in a
similar environment, e.g.
attacker approaching a
defender.

MEMORY ITEM 2
Knowledge of Response
Specifications:
Involves having
knowledge of what to do
in this situation, e.g. to
pass, dummy, dodge
or kick.

The collective term given to
memory items 1 and 2 is
Recall Schema

RECALL SCHEMA
Has two functions:

• to store information
about the production of
the generalised movement
• to start or initiate the
movement.

MEMORY ITEM 3
Knowledge of Sensory
Consequences:
Applies to kinaesthesis
(how the skill should feel),
e.g. attacker would need
to know how hard to
pass the ball in order
to reach the target.

MEMORY ITEM 4
Knowledge of Movement
Outcome:
Involves knowing what
the result of the skill is
likely to be, e.g. a dummy
would send the defender
in the wrong direction.

The collective term given to
memory items 3 and 4 is
Recognition Schema

RECOGNITION SCHEMA
Has two functions. It can:

• control the movement
throughout its execution
• evaluate the effectiveness
of performance.

Recognition schema enables the performer to store additional movement
relationships which will help to adapt the motor programme in novel situations.

Fig 7.5 *Development of schema allows the rugby player to adapt responses to meet the demands of new situations*

TAKE IT FURTHER

Discuss the links between the development of
schema, variability of practice and the effects of
transfer of learning.

Refresh your memory

You should now know and understand about:

▷ The nature of motor and executive programmes stored in Long-term Memory.

▷ How motor programmes link with open loop control and the autonomous phase of learning.

▷ Open and closed loop control.

▷ The role of open and closed loop control in the performance of motor skills.

▷ Different types of feedback and how feedback can detect and correct errors.

▷ Schema Theory and its role in developing movement skills and strategies.

REVISE AS YOU GO!

1. What is meaning of the term 'motor programme'?
2. Identify three sub-routines in a motor programme of your choice.
3. Explain the meaning of hierarchical and sequential structure of a motor programme.
4. What is open loop control?
5. Explain the function of the memory trace.
6. Explain the functions of the perceptual trace.
7. List eight forms of feedback.
8. Use practical examples to explain both intrinsic and extrinsic feedback.
9. Identify five functions of feedback.
10. Use a practical example to explain each of the four parameters of schema theory.

Get the result!

Examination question

Describe how a teacher or coach would encourage schema to be formed in training.
(6 marks)

examiner's tips

1. First check the command word. In this case it is 'describe'.
2. Check the key subject focus which is the formation of schema.
3. Finally check the number of marks available. (6)
4. Remember the examiner is looking for six facts relating to schema formation.

Student answer

A varied practice is good for the formation of schema. Experience can be gained from different situations. Experiences are then transferred to help a response to a new situation. The teacher can also help by providing positive reinforcement.

Examiner says:

This is a very superficial answer and only three marks have been scored. There are no practical examples. It is however, obvious that this candidate knows what is required of them.

Student improved answer

Schema is a build up of experiences that can be adapted in order to meet the demands of new situations. The teacher can form and expand schema in training by using the methods described below.

Varied practices would encourage schema to be formed. Variability of practice refers to replicating the changing environmental situations that would arise in an invasion game situation e.g. 4 attackers play against 3 defenders in hockey. The experiences acquired in this practice situation would transfer positively to the game. If training is enjoyable learning is facilitated and motivation is sustained thus preventing drive reduction from taking place.

Examiner says:

A useful introduction sets up the answer and informs the examiner that the candidate is familiar with the term 'schema'

Examiner says:

It is good to register a mark early. This demonstrates that you are getting to the point. Good use of a practical example.

Good use of technical language. The term transfer is important and scores a mark

Examiner says:

Feedback does help to form schema. It is good to add a little extra when relevant e.g. feedback and discrete skills. This is a critical evaluation of feedback

You demonstrate a broad knowledge of the syllabus and have scored 6 by the end of this paragraph.

Use of technical language e.g. kinaesthesis is commendable

Memorable or novel experiences serve to expand schema and are readily stored in long-term memory. Furthermore, all forms of feedback endorse learning, e.g. terminal feedback helps the acquisition of discrete skills like drop kicking in rugby. Actions that are positively reinforced are remembered and learning bonds help the formation of schema. Demonstration can help both the cognitive learner and autonomous expert to increase experience whilst both manual and mechanical guidance can develop kinaesthesis which is an important memory item in schema theory

A skill which has been grooved or overlearned through fixed drill repetition aids the expansion of schema because it is more easily adapted than a skill if it should remain at the associative phase.

Finally, the use of intervening variables such as mental and symbolic rehearsal are influential in schematic formation and are used to good effect in the cognitive theory of learning. This Gestaltian view puts forward the view that learning is most efficiently achieved if the whole problem is presented to the learner.

Examiner says:

The reminder is highly relevant but 6 marks have already been scored. Watch the time.

Examiner says:

Cognitive learning theory is not easily understood by candidates. Well done.

This response is outstanding!

Learning skills in physical activity

LEARNING OBJECTIVES

This chapter is divided into three parts. By the end of this chapter you will have learned about:

- Motivation and arousal and their impact upon young people's participation, performance and aspirations in physical activity
- Theories relating to the learning of movement skills and the development of positive behaviours associated with a balanced, active and healthy lifestyle
- Reinforcement of movement skill learning and behaviours associated with a balanced, active and healthy lifestyle
- Transfer of learning to develop effectiveness in physical activity.

Motivation and arousal and their impact upon young people's participation, performance and aspirations in physical activity

At the end of Part I you should be able to:

- Demonstrate knowledge and understanding of arousal as a drive affecting levels of motivation.
- Explain the major motivation and arousal theories: Drive Theory, Inverted U Theory and Catastrophe Theory.
- Explain Drive Reduction Theory and its impact on a lifelong, balanced, active and healthy lifestyle.
- Demonstrate knowledge and understanding of ways of motivating people (motivational strategies) and their application to encourage them to lead a balanced, active and healthy lifestyle.

- Evaluate critically motivation and arousal theories and the application of motivational strategies.

INTRODUCTION

Part I outlines how motivation and arousal impact upon young people's participation, performance and aspirations in physical activity

The term *motivation* implies the drive and energy an individual is prepared to expend to achieve a goal. It is a factor that determines the amount of effort applied in sports performance. Motivation is closely linked to ambition. It can strongly influence a young person's decision to take part in sport and to continue this throughout his/her life. Positive attitudes that are displayed through determination and perseverance during practice are invariably the product of a high level of motivation without which skill learning would not be possible.

REMEMBER

Feedback strongly influences motivation.

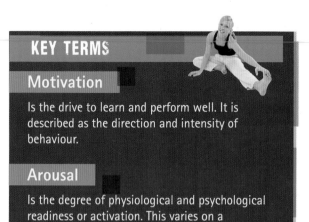

KEY TERMS

Motivation

Is the drive to learn and perform well. It is described as the direction and intensity of behaviour.

Arousal

Is the degree of physiological and psychological readiness or activation. This varies on a continuum from deep sleep to intense excitement.

The meaning of the terms motivation and arousal is often thought to be the same. Although the terms are closely related there are differences between the two. The relationships and differences are highlighted below.

Motivation has two branches:

1. **Intensity of behaviour.** This refers to the degree of emotional energy that is felt in different situations by a person. The degree of emotional energy determines and drives the direction of behaviour of that person.
2. **Direction of behaviour.** This is the course of action, or the response chosen by the individual as a result of emotional drive.

Intensity of behaviour is what is termed 'arousal'. Like motivation, arousal has two branches:

1. **Somatic or physiological arousal.** This relates to the changing state of the body, e.g. changes in heart rate, blood pressure and respiration.

2. **Cognitive or psychological arousal.** This relates to the mind, e.g. moment to moment changes in worry or negative thought.

Increases in both types of arousal may be experienced when performing ,and even when learning sports-related skills.

The interaction between arousal types will be outlined later when the Catastrophe Model of arousal is explained (see page 187).

EXAM TIP

It is important to understand arousal as a drive affecting levels of motivation.

Teachers, coaches and performers must be aware that motivation has two sources.

1. **Intrinsic motivation.** This arises when an individual participates in an activity for its own sake. For example, a skier may learn to snowboard because success will bring personal satisfaction.
2. **Extrinsic motivation.** This occurs when people perform and learn in order to receive a tangible reward. Perfecting fundamental gymnastic movements to achieve a certificate or playing to achieve a trophy or medal are examples of tangible rewards which generate extrinsic motivation.

Extrinsic reward given to a novice performer or to one who is considering participation for the first time can be very effective. However,

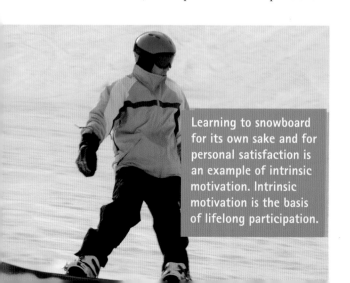

Learning to snowboard for its own sake and for personal satisfaction is an example of intrinsic motivation. Intrinsic motivation is the basis of lifelong participation.

Performing for certificates and medals is an example of extrinsic motivation. If tangible reward is withdrawn there may well be a reduction in performance motivation.

tangible reward may eventually be a drawback to the learning process as effort may only be applied if reward is given. Those who are intrinsically motivated are more likely to continue participation and be consistent in their efforts than those who seek reward. Intrinsic satisfaction can be developed and sustained by the performer if appropriate motivational strategies are applied by the teacher during the early learning stages. Motivation strategies as they apply to particular ability levels and disaffected young people will be considered later.

EXAM TIP

Theories of arousal are popular examination topics. It is advisable to learn them thoroughly as they are also part of the Sport Psychology study in A2.

It is essential to understand three theories of arousal.

DRIVE THEORY OF AROUSAL

Drive Theory was presented by two psychologists named Hull and Spence and is shown in Fig. 8.1.1.

Drive Theory indicates a relationship between arousal and performance. An increase in arousal is proportional to an increase in the quality of physical performance. The quality of performance depends on how well the skill has been learned.

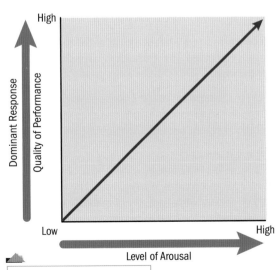

Fig 8.1.1 Drive theory of arousal

Motor programmes that have already been learned are said to be *learned behaviours* and are therefore **dominant responses**. A dominant response is a response or behaviour that is most likely to emerge when a performer experiences an increase in arousal. Hull predicted that as arousal increases, in a competitive situation or when a learner feels the pressure of assessment, there is a greater likelihood of his dominant responses occurring.

REMEMBER

There are three phases or stages in movement skill learning (see page 142).

KEY TERM

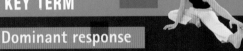

Dominant response

The behaviour or response that is most likely to be given by the performer.

TAKE IT FURTHER

- Behaviour = Habit x Drive (B = H x D) is the equation that supports the prediction made by Drive Theory. What is meant by behaviour, habit and drive?
- By using knowledge of Drive Theory explain why a performer would be at an advantage when a skill has been over-learned.
- Explain why the prediction made in Drive Theory is important at each of the three phases of learning.

THE APPLICATION OF DRIVE THEORY TO THE LEARNING AND PERFORMANCE OF MOVEMENT SKILLS

APPLY IT!

High arousal would be beneficial to the expert performer, i.e. one at the autonomous or independent stage of learning, because their dominant behaviour would tend to produce a response which is fluent and technically correct. The novice performer, i.e. one in the cognitive and associative stages of learning, should not be subjected to conditions that would evoke high arousal because at this level the dominant behaviour is likely to produce an ill-timed and mistake-ridden performance.

Drive Theory indicates that arousal level has a serious influence on learning. The novice would learn and perform more effectively in conditions of low arousal. A calm emotional state would enable full concentration to be given to feedback from the teacher and the correct sequence in which sub-routines are performed. Sub-routines cannot be 'run off' automatically in the early stages of learning; they initially require intense thought and concentration.

TASK 1

Look once again at the photos of the snowboarders on page 184. Apply your knowledge of Drive Theory to say why the novice (associative stage of learning) would learn more effectively in conditions of low arousal whilst the expert (autonomous stage of learning) would perform best when experiencing high arousal.

REMEMBER

See open and closed loop theory of control in Chapter 7 and review how this theory relates to cognitive, associative and autonomous phases of learning.

INVERTED U THEORY OF AROUSAL

The Inverted U Theory indicates or predicts that as arousal increases so does the quality of performance. Quality improves up to a point midway along the arousal axis. This point is called the *optimum point* or the *threshold of arousal* and predicts that best performance occurs at moderate levels of arousal. If arousal should

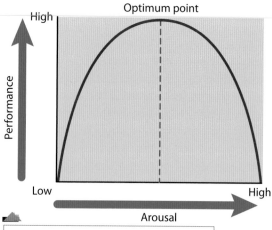

Fig 8.1.2 Inverted U hypothesis theory of arousal

increase beyond the optimum point, the performer becomes over-aroused and the capacity both to learn and to perform a motor skill will deteriorate.

The conditions both of under-arousal and over-arousal severely limit the capacity to learn skills and perform them up to potential. A person at the optimum arousal level however, will not only perform to their greatest potential but will also maximise their learning efficiency. The reasons for this are outlined below.

APPLY IT!

Under-arousal
In these conditions it is difficult for the performer to direct and focus attention or concentration onto the relevant environmental cues. Concentration is lost because the attention field of the performer is too wide. This means that attention spreads to many, and often unwanted, cues in the environment.

If concentration is limited the potential to learn is restricted. The learner may appear to be 'daydreaming'.

In these circumstances the process of selective attention cannot operate. Information overload will then prevent accurate decision making.

Optimum arousal
This is the perfect state in which the potential to learn and perform well is maximised. The attention field of the individual adjusts to the ideal width and as a result the learner or performer is able to concentrate fully.

An increased capacity to concentrate means the most important information can be absorbed from the environment. There is therefore greater accuracy in decision making.

The name of the theory that predicts detection of the most important information at the optimum point of arousal is called *Cue Utilisation Hypothesis*. It is a product of selective attention.

Over-arousal

If over-arousal occurs, the performer will experience an excessive degree of activation.

This condition may coincide with high anxiety levels and as with under-arousal the effectiveness of learning and performance is severely limited.

Over-arousal causes the field of attention to narrow excessively. As a result the relevant environmental cues are missed. The performer is often in a state of panic. The technical name for this advanced condition of nervousness is *hypervigilance*. The performer's selective attention cannot operate and the capacity for concentration is seriously impeded.

KEY TERMS

Attention field

The area in the environment of which the performer is aware.

Concentration

Focusing attention onto the relevant environmental cues.

Hypervigilance

A condition of nervousness and panic. Often accompanied by extreme anxiety.

Selective attention

The process of directing the focus of attention.

Cue utilisation

The process of focusing on the most important information or cues from the environmental display.

TASK 2

Work with a partner and list five benefits that an athlete would experience when the optimal level of arousal is achieved during a sporting event.

Inverted U Theory also predicts that the optimum point of arousal varies for each individual. This variation has a significant impact on learning and the performance of movement skills.

Variations in the optimum point of arousal are caused by one or any combination of the following factors:

- **Personality:** The person who is an extrovert performs and learns best under conditions of higher arousal. Conversely, introverted personalities function most effectively at a lower threshold of arousal.
- **Type of task:** Gross and simple skills which are often ballistic and classified as closed are performed better when arousal is high. On the other hand fine and complex tasks requiring precision and decision making as with open skills are performed better when arousal is low.
- **Stage of learning:** Learners at the cognitive and associative stages of learning operate more effectively in conditions of lower arousal whereas at the autonomous stage higher thresholds are beneficial.
- **Level of experience:** An experienced athlete would reach his/her maximum performance level when arousal is high. The novice would perform best when the optimum point is lower.

REMEMBER

The optimum point of arousal facilitates maximum focus and concentration.

CATASTROPHE THEORY OF AROUSAL

The Catastrophe Theory presented by a sports psychologist named Hardy is based on a three-dimensional model which examines how performance is influenced by the relationship between *somatic arousal* (physiological arousal) and *cognitive arousal* (worry and anxiety).

REMEMBER

Review the definition of somatic and cognitive arousal on page 184.

Catastrophe Theory like the Inverted U Hypothesis claims that as somatic arousal increases then the quality of performance improves. However, Catastrophe Theory adds a third dimension to this prediction by stating that performance will reach maximum potential at the optimum level only if cognitive arousal is kept low.

If high cognitive arousal coincides with high somatic arousal the athlete will go beyond the optimum level of arousal and is thought to have 'gone over the edge'. Under these conditions performance drops, not on a smooth curve as predicted in Inverted U Theory but drastically. In other words the athlete experiences a disaster or catastrophe.

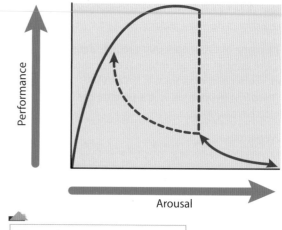

Fig 8.1.3 Catastrophe theory of arousal

TASK 3

Describe a situation in which you may have suffered a catastrophe in a sports situation. Was the effect short term or has it had a lasting influence on your sports performance? What strategies could be used to help a performer to recover from a catastrophe during a sporting event?

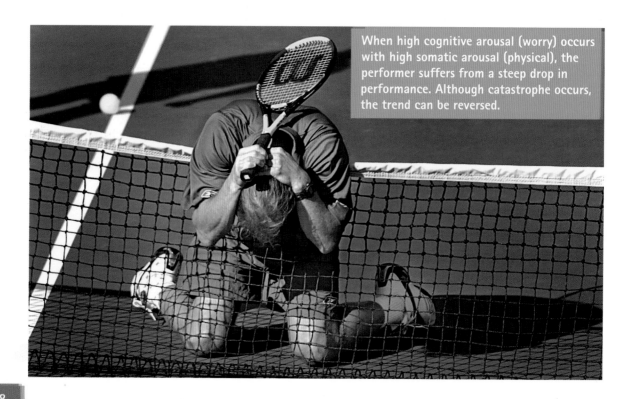

When high cognitive arousal (worry) occurs with high somatic arousal (physical), the performer suffers from a steep drop in performance. Although catastrophe occurs, the trend can be reversed.

THE APPLICATION OF CATASTROPHE THEORY TO THE LEARNING AND PERFORMANCE OF MOVEMENT SKILLS

APPLY IT!

If a catastrophe is experienced, the teacher should help the performer or learner to reduce cognitive arousal or worry. This can be done by implementing stress management techniques or by simply giving reassurance and applying positive feedback to the performer.

However, once performance has dropped sharply the athlete cannot return immediately to the optimum point. They must go back to lower anxiety levels to get on track and then gradually build up to the optimum threshold once again.

Significantly, Hardy predicted that when somatic arousal was low skill learning and performance can be enhanced if cognitive arousal is increased. Furthermore, serious deterioration in performance would occur when low levels of physiological and psychological arousal converge.

CRITICAL EVALUATION OF 'INVERTED U' AND 'CATASTROPHE' THEORIES

Although Inverted U Theory indicates clearly that increased arousal improves performance up to an optimal point it is unlikely that performance decreases in a smooth declining arc when over-arousal is experienced. It is more likely that the interaction between somatic and cognitive arousal when the optimal threshold of arousal has been passed causes a catastrophic drop in performance.

Drive reduction is the term given to a loss of motivation that an athlete may experience during performance if a skill has been previously well learned or the task has become tedious.

Initially, there is a great drive or motivation to solve a new problem or to learn a new skill. The performer will take action to satisfy the drive and this will show itself in the willingness to practise. When the skill has been well learned and the autonomous stage has been reached, a habit is formed and the S-R learning bond has become strong. It is at this point that the drive or motivation to continue performing the skill is reduced.

Decreased motivation occurs if too much practice has taken place and the skill has become over-learned. Over-learning may lead to inhibition which reduces drive. At this point new goals or targets need to be put into place to re-motivate the athlete.

KEY TERM

Inhibition

Inhibition is mental fatigue or boredom that will cause performance to deteriorate.

S-R Learning Bond

An S-R learning bond is the connection or link that is made between a *stimulus* and the *response* made to this stimulus.

REMEMBER

Over-learning is a positive term – it means that the skill is well learned, and grooved into long-term memory (page 172).

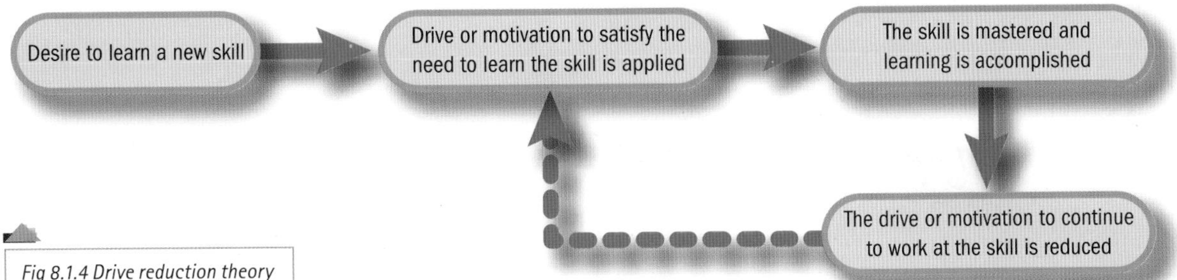

Desire to learn a new skill → Drive or motivation to satisfy the need to learn the skill is applied → The skill is mastered and learning is accomplished → The drive or motivation to continue to work at the skill is reduced

Fig 8.1.4 Drive reduction theory

EXAM TIP

This topic has given candidates problems as students tend to confuse Drive Theory with Drive Reduction Theory. They are different theories and should be considered carefully.

The prediction made by Drive Reduction Theory can impact significantly on a lifelong, balanced, active and healthy lifestyle. Therefore teachers and coaches must implement motivational strategies to prevent a loss in drive.

TASK 4

Design a repetitive fixed practice for your class or a partner. It might be shooting thirty lay-up shots in basketball or allowing the participant a high number of attempts at throwing a ball to hit a target. Observe and record performance. Does performance deteriorate as the practice progresses? Interview the participants and ask them for their views on the practice. Is Drive Reduction a possible reason for poor performance? Implement a strategy to eliminate Drive Reduction.

The promotion of a healthy lifestyle through sport is a major priority in Australia. This issue is first addressed in Australian primary schools through an initiative called *The Fundamental Skills Programme*. This programme highlights the basic motor skills which transfer into complex motor programmes in teenage years. The aim of the programme is not to produce 'superstars' but to give children the skills that will help them enjoy participating in sports at all levels throughout their lives.

Society in the UK must be reminded that sport:

- Improves both physical fitness and mental well-being
- Develops social skills and helps people to make friends

- Prepares people for active leisure and can be an influence on a future career
- Enriches the quality of life.

A CRITICAL EVALUATION OF MOTIVATION STRATEGIES

As Physical Education specialists we need therefore to consider motivational strategies that will encourage children of different ability levels and will also encourage young people who have become disaffected to participate in sport.

- External motivation can come in the form of tangible rewards such as medals certificates or intangible rewards such as praise from the teacher.
- Both are thought to be of greatest importance in attracting young people into sport and during early learning.
- Extrinsic rewards provide concrete proof of success and formulate status in the peer group.

However, the impact of external motivation must be considered a short term strategy compared with internal motivation.

- Internal motivation is the key to lifelong participation.
- It involves giving learners positive feelings about their performance.
- This can be established through positive reinforcement and the setting of achievable personal goals.

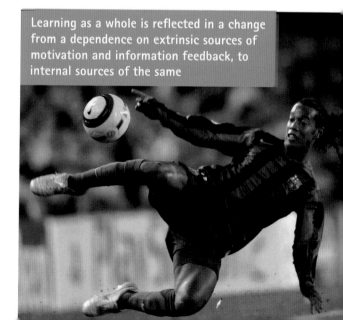

Learning as a whole is reflected in a change from a dependence on extrinsic sources of motivation and information feedback, to internal sources of the same

- Once interest has been stimulated, the teacher can endorse the value of participation by indicating that sport promotes confidence, personal satisfaction and self-realisation.

These are factors that encourage participation throughout life.

TAKE IT FURTHER

By way of a critical evaluation of motivation strategies, discuss how the message given in the caption may influence the possibility of an individual enjoying a lifelong balanced, active and healthy lifestyle.

KEY TERMS

Tangible rewards

Can be badges, medals and certificates.

Intangible rewards

Can be praise from the coach, peers or parents. Both are sources of external motivation.

TASK 5

PARTNER DISCUSSION

Discuss with a partner the factors that first motivated you to participate in your major sport. Do the same motivational factors drive you to continue with this participation? Can these factors be classified as internal or external motives?

EXAM TIP

Motivational strategies are central to effective learning and performance.

Fig 8.1.5 Motivational strategies for an active lifestyle

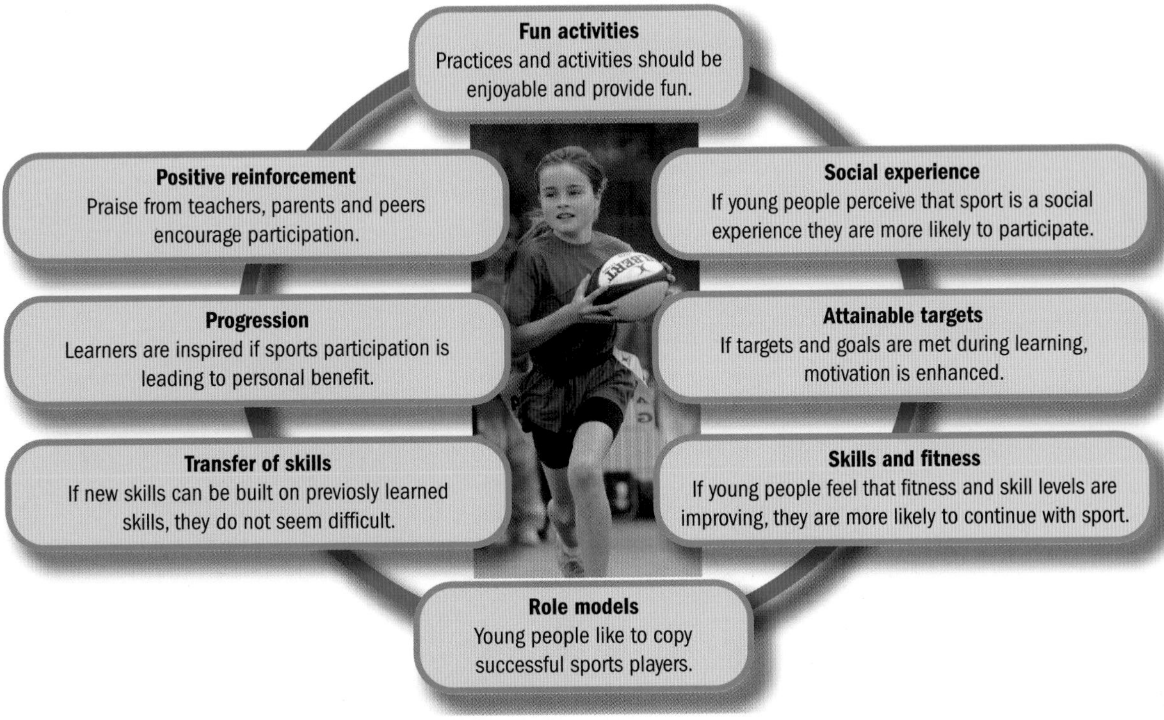

Other motivational strategies include:

Fun activities
Practices and activities should be enjoyable and provide fun.

Positive reinforcement
Praise from teachers, parents and peers encourage participation.

Social experience
If young people perceive that sport is a social experience they are more likely to participate.

Progression
Learners are inspired if sports participation is leading to personal benefit.

Attainable targets
If targets and goals are met during learning, motivation is enhanced.

Transfer of skills
If new skills can be built on previously learned skills, they do not seem difficult.

Skills and fitness
If young people feel that fitness and skill levels are improving, they are more likely to continue with sport.

Role models
Young people like to copy successful sports players.

ExamCafé
Relax, refresh, result!

Refresh your memory

You should now know and understand about:

▷ Arousal as a drive affecting levels of motivation.

▷ The major motivation and arousal theories: Drive Theory, Inverted U Theory and Catastrophe Theory.

▷ Drive reduction theory and its impact on a lifelong balanced, active and healthy lifestyle.

▷ Motivational strategies and their application in order to encourage participation in a balanced, active and healthy lifestyle.

REVISE AS YOU GO!

1. Define motivation.
2. Define arousal.
3. Identify two types of arousal.
4. Explain intrinsic and extrinsic motivation.
5. Explain the prediction made by Drive Theory.
6. What is the dominant response?
7. Why might the dominant response be of a good quality at the autonomous stage of learning?
8. Describe the Inverted U Theory of arousal.
9. Why is learning and performance most effective at the optimal point of arousal?
10. Describe the process of Cue Utilisation.

Examination question

Drive reduction is one method that can be used to motivate a performer in physical education & sport. Use a practical example to explain Drive Reduction Theory. (4 marks)

examiner's tips

- First check the command word. In this case it is 'explain'.
- Check the key subject focus which is 'Drive Reduction Theory'.
- Finally check the number of marks available. (4)
- Remember the examiner is looking for four facts relating to Drive Reduction.

Get the result !

Student answer

Drive Reduction Theory states that when you learn a new skill the drive to carry on is reduced and performance goes down. For example if you are practising basketball shots you will get bored after ten and your motivation goes. The coach must then set a new target.

Examiner says:

In essence this candidate is correct. On the first line, however, the words of the question are given as an explanation e.g. 'the drive to carry on is reduced' this tells the examiner nothing except 'performance goes down'. It would be better to use the word 'deteriorates'. The example is correct and boredom is a factor if the practice is repetitive. Avoid using the word 'you' in the answer. It is not a word that will give clear meaning and reflects a poor writing style.

Improved student answer

Drive reduction is the term given to a loss of motivation that an athlete may experience during performance if a skill has been previously well learned or the task has become tedious.

Initially, there is a great drive or motivation to solve a new problem or to learn a new skill. An example of a new skill may be learning how to perform a lay up shot in basketball. The performer will take action to satisfy the drive and this will show itself in the willingness to practice. When the skill has been well learned a habit is formed and the S-R learning bond has become strong. It is at this point that the drive to continue performing the skill is reduced and performance will deteriorate.

Decreased motivation occurs if too much practice has taken place and the skill has become over-learned, e.g. if a target of twenty lay-up shots is given, the performer may find this tedious and become bored with a task that has now become easy. Over-learning may lead to inhibition which reduces drive. At this point new goals or targets need to be put into place to re-motivate the athlete.

Examiner says:

A useful introduction that sets up the answer and informs the examiner that the candidate is familiar with Drive Reduction Theory.

Examiner says:

A good example. This example is followed through in third paragraph.

An explanation of drive reduction has been put in place very concisely. The technical term of S–R bond is highly relevant.

The key point about performance deterioration has been inserted.

Examiner says:

Paragraph three contains the final part of the explanation.

Technical terms such as 'over-learning' and 'inhibition' identify this student as a knowledgeable candidate.

Theories relating to the learning of movement skills and the reinforcement of movement skill learning and behaviours associated with a balanced, active and healthy lifestyle

LEARNING OBJECTIVES

At the end of Part II you should be able to demonstrate knowledge and understanding of:

- The associationist/connectionist theory of Operant Conditioning (Skinner)
- The Cognitive Theory related to the work of Gestaltist principles
- Social/observational learning theory; the importance of significant others in the adoption of a balanced, active and healthy lifestyle
- Bandura's model and the factors that affect modelling
- Reinforcement of movement skill learning and behaviours associated with a balanced, active and healthy lifestyle
- Positive reinforcement, negative reinforcement and punishment
- Thorndike's Laws as they apply to the formation and strengthening of the Stimulus–Response learning bond
- Appropriate use of reinforcement in skill learning and in promoting positive, healthy lifestyle behaviour.

OPERANT CONDITIONING

Operant Conditioning theory of learning was presented by a psychologist named Skinner. He believed that behaviour could be modified or conditioned if it was directed towards a stimulus. Skinner's experiments involved a rat which eventually learned through trial and error that if a lever was pressed a food pellet would be released. This principle can be applied to learning sports skills.

Operant conditioning involves the learner forming and strengthening a stimulus-response (S-R) bond. The link between the stimulus and the response is often called a *connection* or *association*.

Hence operant conditioning is referred to as a *connectionist* or *associationalist theory*.

The application of the theory to the learning of psycho-motor skills requires the teacher to present a stimulus to the performer in an environment that replicates the relevant sports situation.

The learner will, through trial and error, react or respond to the stimulus. In so doing, the response or behaviour of the learner will be shaped or modified. When the learner performs the correct response, the teacher will give a reward in the form of positive reinforcement.

PRACTICAL APPLICATION OF OPERANT CONDITIONING

APPLY IT!

1. In order to teach a smash shot in badminton the teacher could mark a target at the back of the court and then serve high to the learner.

2. The learner would attempt to smash the shuttle into the target. The stimulus has therefore been presented in a structured environment that is closely aligned to the game situation.

3. Through trial and error, the learner would attempt a number of responses to repeated serves. The learner's behaviour is now being shaped or modified during this process.

4. When the correct response is made into the target area positive reinforcement will be given by the teacher. Poor attempts are not rewarded and in time the correct technique becomes dominant. The actions would also be reinforced by the player's success.

5. At this point a desired S-R bond has been formed and strengthened. Any incorrect bonds are weakened due to the lack of reinforcement.

6. It is important that reinforcement is applied immediately and before the learner has another chance to act.

7. The target will eventually be removed and more advanced practices that transfer to the game situation can be administered.

Operant conditioning involves trial and error learning. Beaviour is shaped in a structured environment. It is then reinforced.

This process of behaviour shaping enables difficult skills to be learned in small steps. It is therefore related to the idea of part learning. A drawback to this theory, however, is that it does not allow the learner to gain a full understanding of the skill as it is performed in the real situation, e.g. the smash shot needs to be applied in the game situation.

TASK 1

Design and administer a practice session using Operant Conditioning to develop the skills involved in passing and receiving a ball

COGNITIVE THEORY OF LEARNING

The Cognitive Theory of Learning, in contrast to the Connectionist Theory, supports the view that learning is best achieved by presenting the whole skill to the learner in the context of a realistic situation.

In order to arrive at a solution, the learner must understand and think about the problem as a whole. This cognitive thought process is dependent on perception. Perception is the driving force in cognitive learning. Many factors influence the process of perception but most importantly the learner will use intelligence, current knowledge and previous experience to plan or predict a solution. A solution in the form of a response is an indication that psycho-motor learning has been achieved.

REMEMBER

Schema Theory relies on previous experience being transferred to help form a skilled response to an arising situation.

To help understanding the learner would focus on the problem by engaging mental rehearsal and reminiscence. These are mental processes and are termed *intervening variables*.

The process of solving the whole problem by using the process of thought is called *insight* or *intuitive learning*.

Kohler, Koffka and Wertheimer were the psychologists first involved in this theory and they became known as Gestalt theorists. *Gestalt* is a scientific term and not the name of a person. Gestalt means 'whole pattern'.

The contrast between connectionist and cognitive learning theories is endorsed by Gestalt philosophy which states: 'The whole is greater than the sum of its parts'.

For Gestalt theorists, part learning by way of connectionist theory is inefficient because it does not present to the learner all of the information necessary for complete understanding.

TASK 2

Design and administer a practice session using the Cognitive Learning Theory to develop the skills involved in passing and receiving a ball.

TAKE IT FURTHER

Discuss the differences between the Connectionist and Gestaltist views on learning.

APPLY IT!

If the skill is too complex or unsafe for a beginner to learn as a whole, problem solving can be facilitated by creating, adapting or conditioning a game, e.g. flag rugby.

KEY TERMS

Perception

Is the cognitive process of interpreting (making sense of) incoming environmental cues.

Transfer

Is when one skill or experience influences the learning and performance of another skill.

Mental rehearsal

Involves forming a mental image of the skill that is about to be performed.

Reminiscence

Is the conscious act of remembering a skill or movement experience.

Gestalt

Means whole patterning or wholeness of form.

Intervening variables

Are mental processes that help with problem solving.

Insight learning

Refers to problem solving that incorporates the use of perception, intelligence and previous experience.

Adapted games like Flag Rugby allow children to gain fundamental skills and basic understanding, that will later transfer to the fun version of the game

EXAM TIP

Candidates frequently confuse Cognitive
Learning Theory with the Cognitive Stage of
learning. They are two separate theories:

OBSERVATIONAL LEARNING

Observational or social learning involves copying
the behaviour of others and it is the way that most
of our learning takes place. Behaviour is most likely
to be copied if demonstrated and reinforced by a
role model who is significant and of high status.

In order to encourage young people to adopt a
balanced, active and healthy lifestyle it is essential
that the model is a positive one with behavioural
characteristics that are both inspirational and
exemplars for others to follow. It is thought that
a role model is more readily copied if they are
of the same gender as the learner. For example,
Kelly Holmes who won two gold medals in the
2004 Olympic Games remains an inspirational
role model for young women athletes. Similarly,
the dedication and perseverance of five times gold
medallist Sir Steve Redgrave are characteristics to
which young men could readily aspire.

A successful, significant role model
who is the same gender as the
learner can inspire a young person
to adopt a balanced, active and
healthy lifestyle.

Observational learning as it relates to skill
learning is a form of visual guidance that is
associated with the replication of a demonstration.

The aim of a demonstration is to present the
learner with a visual image which can be copied
and matched.

Learning by imitation is a very powerful principle
being both time saving and more interesting than
a lengthy verbal explanation.

Demonstrations are important at all stages of
learning. During the Cognitive phase it is easier
for the novice to understand a visual model rather
than to follow verbal instructions. A learner is
more likely to be motivated by the exhibition. At
the Autonomous stage, a demonstration is useful
in highlighting detailed and specific points in the
performance.

BANDURA'S MODEL OF OBSERVATIONAL LEARNING

Learning by demonstration is not a fail-safe
method. A psychologist named Bandura indicates
that observational learning takes place only if the
learner can put into place four elements:

1. Attention to the demonstration
2. Retention of the demonstration
3. Motor Reproduction of the demonstration
4. Motivation to match the performance of the
   demonstration.

Attention: The learner must focus directly onto
the model that is being demonstrated.

APPLY IT!

The teacher can help the process of attention by
telling the learner to watch for or attend toward
specific items in the demonstration. For example,
the hip turn before the discus is released. This
spoken instruction is called verbal guidance.
To hold the attention of the learner, the model
of performance must be brief, attractive and
meaningful.

Retention: The image of the demonstration must be stored or retained by the learner if it is to be copied successfully. Verbal guidance will prevent information overload and help to hold the image in the short-term memory.

APPLY IT!

Retention is more likely if the demonstration is repeated several times. The observer should be encouraged to picture the image in the 'mind's eye'. This process is called *mental rehearsal*. A good teaching technique to aid retention is to connect a second image to the demonstration. For example, to be told to 'put the ball onto the shelf' helps to achieve the correct trajectory of a set shot in basketball. This technique is called *symbolic rehearsal*.

Motor reproduction: The learner must have the physical ability and schematic development to copy or replicate the skill that is being demonstrated.

Motivation: A key element in learning and performance is motivation. In order to reproduce the demonstration, the observer must have the drive or motivation to match the performance of the skill being modelled. External reinforcement of the demonstration will increase the motivation to replicate it.

TASK 3

Design and administer a practice session using Observational learning to develop the skills involved in passing and receiving a ball.

Discuss the advantages and disadvantages as they arise in the three theories of learning

When dealing with Operant Conditioning, it was strongly emphasised that Connectionist or Association Theories rely on the learner linking or connecting a stimulus from the environment with a movement response.

For example, in football a goalkeeper may have to jump to catch a high cross. If successful, this response becomes connected or associated with the stimulus and is stored in long term memory. As we have seen connections are called 'S-R learning bonds'. When the demands of the environment allow, learning bonds can be recalled and repeated.

REMEMBER

S-R Learning Bond

An S-R learning bond is the connection or link that is made between a *stimulus* and the *response* made to this stimulus.

A learning bond can be formed and strengthened by a number of different strategies. In this section, however, focus will be given to the process of reinforcement as a way of establishing an S-R bond.

Reinforcement

Reinforcement has been defined as:

'the process that causes a response or behaviour to reoccur by forming and strengthening the S-R learning bond.'

There are two types of reinforcement:

POSITIVE REINFORCEMENT

- After a successful response or after the desired behaviour has been demonstrated by the learner the teacher would present a show of approval.
- Approval may be in the form of praise and is an intangible reward, e.g. 'well done'.
- Positive reinforcement could be presented by some other form of 'satisfier', e.g. a certificate is a tangible reward.

NEGATIVE REINFORCEMENT

- Negative reinforcement involves withdrawing or taking away a *negative* or *aversive stimulus*. For example the teacher may show disapproval when a poor response is given by the learner.
- When the learner eventually responds correctly the aversive stimulus of disapproval is withdrawn.
- Negative reinforcement is not punishment.
- Negative reinforcement is an operation that weakens the incorrect learning bond but most importantly it also strengthens the correct learning bond. For example when learning to dive in water most beginners experience pain on contact.
- When the correct technique is acquired pain is removed. Negative reinforcement has reinforced the correct diving technique.

PUNISHMENT

- Punishment involves giving an unpleasant stimulus to a performer to prevent a response from occurring.
- The unpleasant stimulus is called a *noxious stimulus*.
- A noxious stimulus is designed to break an undesired learning bond.
- For example, a player may be sent from the field after making a deliberately high tackle in rugby.

THORNDIKE'S LAWS

A psychologist named Thorndike strongly believed that connecting S-R bonds was the most effective way to learn. Thorndike applied three rules to the connectionist theory.

1. **The Law of Effect** states that if behaviour is reinforced, the learning bond is strengthened.

Positive reinforcement or the presentation of a 'satisfier' is the most effective way to strengthen the learning bond, e.g. positive feedback or approval given by the teacher following a good performance.

2. **The Law of Exercise** states that the S-R bond will be strengthened by practice and repeated reinforcement, e.g. the netball shooter will practise repetitively. A lack of practice will cause the S-R bond to weaken.

3. **The Law of Readiness** states that if reinforcement is to strengthen the learning bond the performer must be both physically and mentally capable of performing the skill, e.g. a young child would find shooting into a basket at full height impossible therefore behaviour could not be positively reinforced.

TASK 4

Choose a practical activity that your group will offer for practical assessment. Design a skill drill that focuses on a particular skill and administer that skill drill in a practice session. Discuss how Thorndike's Laws can be applied to your drill.

TASK 5

Discuss how appropriate use of reinforcement in skill learning can promote a positive, healthy lifestyle.

ExamCafé
Relax, refresh, result!

Refresh your memory

You should now know and understand about:

▷ The associationist/connectionist theory of Operant Conditioning (Skinner).

▷ The Cognitive Theory related to the work of Gestaltist principles.

▷ Social/observational learning theory.

▷ Bandura's model and the factors that affect modelling.

▷ Reinforcement of movement skill learning.

▷ Positive reinforcement, negative reinforcement and punishment.

▷ Thorndike's Laws as they apply to the formation and strengthening of the Stimulus-Response learning bond.

▷ Appropriate use of reinforcement in skill learning.

REVISE AS YOU GO!

1. What is a stimulus – response (S–R) bond?
2. Use an example from Physical Education or sport to explain how a performer learns by operant conditioning
3. Explain the cognitive theory of learning as proposed by Gestaltists and apply this to a practical situation
4. Describe the following terms as they relate to the Cognitive theory of Learning:
   a) Insight learning
   b) Whole learning
   c) Gestalt patterning
   d) Perception
   e) Past experiences
   f) Intervening variables.
5. Give examples of conditioned or adapted games as they apply to the Cognitive Theory of Learning
6. How is an S–R learning bond formed and strengthened?
7. Outline the purpose of positive reinforcement.
8. Explain what is meant by punishment.
9. Identify the three laws of Thorndike.

Get the result!

Examination question

Operant Conditioning is one way of learning movement skills. Use a practical example to explain Operant Conditioning. (4 marks)

examiner's tips

- First check the command word. In this case it is 'explain'.
- Check the key subject focus which is 'Operant Conditioning'.
- Finally check the number of marks available. (4)
- Remember the examiner is looking for four facts relating to Operant Conditioning.

Examiner says:

This candidate has not used an obvious basic knowledge of Operant Conditioning to best effect. Operant Conditioning is a way to teach sports skill and a practical example is given and followed through. The rat in the maze is not relevant to this question. Does the word 'it' at the beginning of the fourth sentence refer to the rat or Operant Conditioning? Two marks would have been gained with this answer.

Student answer

Operant conditioning is a way to teach skills in sport, e.g. a cross-court shot in tennis. It started when Skinner put a rat in maze and the rat had to find a food pellet. In order to do this the rat had to learn the route through the maze. It involves trial and error learning and the teacher gives reinforcement when a good response is given, e.g. a winning forehand shot in tennis.

Improved student answer

The application of Operant Conditioning is a connectionist theory and is an effective way of learning motor skills

The teacher would first structure or manipulate the environment to bring about the desired response. For example, when learning to play a cross court fore hand in tennis a target may be drawn at the back of the opponent's court during practice.

Examiner says:

A useful introduction that sets up the answer.

Examiner says:

The key points of Operant Conditioning are included and a practical example has been added and followed through in paragraph four.

Examiner says:

Reference has been made to Operant Conditioning being a connectionist theory and an explanation of positive and negative reinforcement is highly relevant.

A period of trial and error learning will occur as the learner attempts to perform the desired action e.g. to land the ball in the target. During this period the learner's response or behaviour is being shaped or modified. A good response is positively reinforced by the teacher in order to strengthen the S-R learning bond. Similarly negative reinforcement can serve to strengthen a correct learning bond. Any response receiving no reinforcement will disappear.

Complete reinforcement after every attempt increases the speed of learning but the drawback with this method is that behaviour tends to be forgotten more easily than if partial reinforcement is applied. When the desired behaviour has been over-learned e.g. the fore hand shot has become consistently successful, the target is taken away.

Examiner says:

There is no need to mention the origin of the experiment of the rat in the maze.

Transfer of learning to develop effectiveness in physical activity

LEARNING OBJECTIVES

By the end of Part III you should be able to:

- Describe types of transfer that occur in practical performance
- Demonstrate knowledge and understanding of ways of optimising the effect of positive transfer
- Demonstrate knowledge and understanding of ways of limiting the effect of negative transfer
- Critically evaluate different types of transfer and their impact on the development of movement skills
- Explain the effects of transfer of learning on schema development and the importance of variable practice.

TRANSFER OF LEARNING

Transfer means the influence that one skill has on the learning and performance of another. The process is extremely important to the acquisition of movement skills because practically all learning is based on some form of transfer.

The term 'transfer' has been mentioned previously during the explanation of Schema Theory and Cognitive Theory of Learning.

EXAM TIP

Understanding the link between variable practice, transfer and Schema theory is a key issue.

Indeed, the process of transfer is so central to learning and performance that it could be mentioned in every topic visited on the syllabus. A psychologist named Schmidt said: 'No learning takes place without transfer'.

It is thought that, after the early years of childhood, we rarely learn a new skill entirely from scratch as new patterns of movement are transferred or arise out of previous experiences. This idea aligns with the Gestalt view of cognitive learning and also endorses the need for the performer to have a broad and expanded schema.

As early as Key Stage One in infant school, emphasis must be on the teaching of very basic skills called *Fundamental Movement Skills* (FMS). FMS form the basis of more complex motor programmes that are acquired later, e.g. hopping is the basis of sidestepping in rugby. Without FMS more specific motor skills cannot be developed. Other FMS are running, throwing, balancing and catching which transfer positively to countless other skills. Children develop a *pool of experience* or a *movement schema*, which will transfer later into more difficult motor programmes.

It is important to learn five types of transfer:

1. **Positive transfer** occurs when one skill helps or enhances the learning and performance of another skill. For example, the skill of throwing transfers positively to the racquet arm action of a tennis serve.

The overarm throw must be taught in the early years as it transfers positively to many skills – some of which are shown in the pictures.

2. **Negative transfer** arises when one skill hinders or impedes the learning and performance of another skill. For example, a loose wrist required to play a badminton shot transfers negatively to the firm wrist needed to play a tennis shot.

3. **Proactive transfer** occurs when a previously learned skill influences a skill that is currently being learned. Similarly, a skill being learned at present will eventually influence a skill to be learned in the future. For example, a throwing motor programme learned as a child will later transfer positively and proactively to an overarm volleyball serve.

4. **Retroactive transfer** occurs when a newly learned skill influences a previous learned skill. For example, the acquisition of a successful tennis serve may influence the previously learned overarm throw used in cricket.

5. **Bi-lateral transfer** refers to the capacity of the performer who may be dominantly right sided to perform a skill with the left side of the body. For example a footballer who can shoot with the right and left foot with matching power and accuracy is a considerable asset to the team.

During the course of a Physical Education lesson the teacher must ensure that positive transfer is taking place and that its effects are optimised. Furthermore, care must be exercised to limit the possibility of negative transfer. Each of these issues is addressed in the following points:

Key point on transfer	Explanation and/or example
1. Learning situations need to allow for positive transfer.	Variability of practice, such as two–touch football, would recreate the conditions experienced in a real game and help to improve passing skills.
2. The learner must be made aware of the transferable elements of a previously learned skill.	The elbow position at the point at which the ball is released in a football throw–in transfers positively to the elbow position during the throwing phase in javelin.
3. Clear and concise demonstrations must be used.	The learner will be able to transfer elements of the demonstration to aid performance, e.g. the demonstration of bowling in cricket.
4. The environmental conditions need to be similar to the real situation.	Passing skills in hockey should for the most part be practised in a changing environment, e.g. a varied practice.
5. The elements of information processing may be similar.	'Cutting' in basketball has the same perceptual requirements as 'getting free' in netball.
6. The closer the practice is to the replication of the game situation, the greater is the chance of positive transfer.	This condition is stated in the Identical Elements theory (Thorndike).
7. Transfer will only operate successfully if previous skills have been well learned.	Development of a good throwing schema will enhance the learning and performance of a clear in badminton.
8. Diverse experiences enhance the probability of transfer.	A child must therefore learn a wide range of fundamental motor skills. It is from this 'pool of experience' that sophisticated executive programmes are learned at high school.
9. Reinforcement ensures that positive transfer can take place.	The teacher will know that strong S–R learning bonds from related skills are good foundations on which new skills can be established.
10. Simplify the task during initial learning and transfer it later into the real situation.	Feeding the ball underarm to the learner practising a drive shot in cricket.

Table 1 Optimising the effects of positive transfer

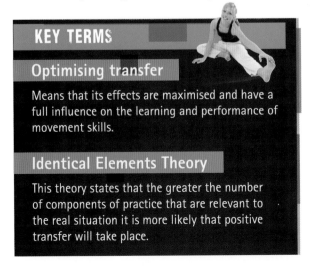

KEY TERMS

Optimising transfer

Means that its effects are maximised and have a full influence on the learning and performance of movement skills.

Identical Elements Theory

This theory states that the greater the number of components of practice that are relevant to the real situation it is more likely that positive transfer will take place.

LIMITING THE EFFECT OF NEGATIVE TRANSFER

To limit the effect of negative transfer the performer must be helped to understand the requirements of the task before beginning practice. The teacher must ensure that the environment in which the skill is learned and practised matches that experienced in the applied situation. Similarly, the learner's attention must be attracted to motor programmes that transfer positively to the skill being currently performed whilst being distracted from movements causing negative transfer. Negative transfer can be avoided if conflicting skills, e.g. badminton and tennis strokes, are not taught close together in time. Finally, it is essential that if a part presentation method of delivery is used by the teacher that the first subroutine is thoroughly learned before progressing to the second.

EXAM TIP

Be aware of the strong relationship between the topics of Transfer of Learning, Schema development and Variability of Practice.

VARIED PRACTICE

Open skills are best practised in a varying environment in which the situation is constantly changing.

The nature of a varied practice allows the learner to perform the same task in a number of different ways. For example, in order to improve the skill of slip catching in cricket the ball should be delivered to the fielder at varying heights and speeds.

Variability of practice is also essential to invasion games. For example, in a three on two attack on defence drill in rugby the varying environmental conditions will help to improve positional play

and passing technique in a situation which directly reflects a game. Most importantly, this mode of practice will develop decision making and perceptual skills. The player will also learn to adapt motor programmes in order to respond effectively to the situational demands.

Adaptations are stored in long-term memory and this is how the experience or the schema of the performer is expanded. When a new situation is encountered the appropriate schema is transferred to produce a modified pattern of movement.

TASK 1

Set up a three versus two attack on defence practice. It could be in basketball. One student must administer the practice and offer feedback and reinforcement as the practice progresses.

Move into a full game situation. Discuss the extent to which the skill demonstrated in practice transferred to the full game situation. Discuss the benefits of a varied practice.

Increasing the variability of the performer's experience leads to the development of a broad and strong schema. Schema is transferred when motor programmes need to be modified in response to a changing environment

ExamCafé

Relax, refresh, result!

Refresh your memory

You should now know and understand about:

▷ The types of transfer that occur in practical performance.

▷ The ways of optimising the effect of positive transfer.

▷ The ways of limiting the effect of negative transfer.

▷ Different types of transfer and their impact on the development of movement skills.

▷ The effects of transfer of learning on schema development and the importance of variable practice.

REVISE AS YOU GO!

1. What is meant by the term transfer?
2. Identify five types of transfer.
3. Explain each of the five types of transfer and give examples to support your answer.
4. How can the teacher optimise the effect of transfer?
5. Outline how the effect of negative transfer can be prevented.
6. What is a varied practice?
7. List the benefits of a varied practice.
8. Explain the links between varied practice, transfer of learning and Schema development.

Get the result!

Examination question

How can the teacher or coach ensure that positive transfer takes place? (5 marks)

examiner's tips

- First check the wording of the question. In this case there are no command words it is a straightforward question.
- Check the key subject focus which is the use of the word 'transfer'.
- Finally check the number of marks available. (5)
- Remember the examiner is looking for five facts relating to Transfer.

Examiner says:

This student has knowledge about transfer but appears to have rushed this response. The first sentence is in essence correct but it is poorly expressed. Who is he at the beginning of sentence two? It is essential to use the word 'teacher'. It is a valid point to say that positive reinforcement ensures that transfer takes place and a benefit of doubt mark (BOD) will probably be given. Once again expression is not good and the word 'thing' is meaningless and must be avoided at all times. Finally, Identical Elements Theory is relevant to this answer but it is obvious that the candidate cannot provide an explanation relating to it.

Student answer

The teacher must make sure the students know about transfer and that the skills being taught relate to each. He could make sure that previous skills that will transfer have been well learned and that everything is positively reinforced. Identical elements theory has a lot to do with this.

Improved student answer

Transfer of training can be described as the influence of one skill on the learning and performance of another skill.

The teacher must make the learner aware and strongly emphasise the transferable elements of a previously learned skill in relation to the new skill.

The environmental conditions need to be similar. For example, the elbow position at the point at which the ball is released in a football throw-in transfers positively to the elbow position during the throwing phase in javelin. Elements of information processing may be similar, e.g. 'cutting' in basketball has the same perceptual requirements as 'moving free' in netball and may be practised by implementing a varied practice.

Examiner says:

A useful introduction that sets up the answer and informs the examiner that the candidate is familiar with Transfer.

Examiner says:

This is an easy mark concisely expressed. Candidates must remember that uncomplicated answers can score high marks.

Examiner says:

Good use of a practical example. This example is very technical.

Examiner says:

Good technical language is shown the word perceptual and this has been linked to varied practice.

Examiner says:

Identical Elements theory has been included in support of the term 'replicates'. Replication of reality would earn the mark.

In the Identical Elements theory Thorndyke stated that the closer the practice replicates reality or the game situation then the chances of positive transfer are increased. Transfer will only operate successfully if previous skills have been well learned, e.g. the child who develops a good throwing schema will be advantaged when learning to serve in tennis.

Furthermore, a wide range of experiences and variability of practice enhances the probability of transfer therefore a child must learn fundamental motor skills thoroughly as it is from this 'pool of experience' or schema that sophisticated executive programmes are learned from eleven years.

Finally, the use of reinforcement ensures that positive transfer can take place and the teacher will be mindful that strong S-R learning bonds from related skills are good foundations onto which new skills can be established.

Examiner says:

Remember the link between varied practice, transfer and schema. This candidate has successfully made this link.

Examiner says:

This candidate has been very thorough and has eventually mentioned reinforcement. This is a valid point.

This is a top class response.

Socio-cultural studies relating to participation in physical activity

Physical activity

LEARNING OBJECTIVES

At the end of this chapter you should be able to demonstrate knowledge and understanding of:

- Physical activity as an umbrella term
- The meaning of the terms: exercise, healthy balanced lifestyles, lifetime sport/ lifelong physical activity, lifelong participation, physical prowess, physical endeavour, sportsmanship, gamesmanship, deviance
- The benefits of regular participation in physical activity
- Factors contributing to increasingly sedentary lifestyles
- Recommendations in terms of frequency, intensity and type of physical activity
- Possible barriers to regular participation in physical activity by young people
- Definitions, characteristics and benefits of: physical recreation, outdoor recreation, Physical Education, Outdoor Education and sport.

INTRODUCTION

Physical activity is widely accepted as being beneficial to health. However only 37% of men and 25% of women in the UK currently achieve the levels of physical activity recommended by the Department of Health (DH) and levels have declined in recent years as people's lives have become more sedentary or deskbound. This chapter describes the health benefits of physical activity and the factors which contribute to increased levels of inactivity. We will look at possible barriers to regular participation by young people and at the recommended amounts of activity needed for health. Finally, we need to examine various aspects of physical activity that can exist under the physical activity 'umbrella.'

Participation in physical activity

Let's start by sorting out the meaning of some terms. To some degree, **physical activity** is part of every able-bodied person's life and might involve walking up stairs or doing housework. It will include anything that gets the body moving and the heart pumping harder than at rest – but it doesn't have to be really vigorous. We also need to consider physical activity as an umbrella term, encompassing physical and outdoor recreation, physical and outdoor education and sport (each of which will be examined later in this chapter).

Fig 9.1 Physical activity as an umbrella term

What about **Exercise**? A straightforward dictionary definition of exercise is '*activity requiring physical effort*,' or a bit more formally '*bodily movement produced by skeletal muscles that results in energy expenditure.*' Unlike more gentle physical activity such as walking to your next lesson, strolling around the shops or tidying your room, the term *physical exercise* implies vigour, dynamism, drive or energy. Some tasks in the home and garden, such as carrying heavy items or digging are vigorous and energetic and, as such, could be classed as physical exercise. An individual's physical exercise might be their regular jogging, walking, swimming, aerobics, cycling or gym sessions all of which involve aerobic work using large muscle groups. Importantly, for our 'definition' exercise is done to improve health and fitness.

REMEMBER

For our study, physical activity is (a) anything that gets the body moving and the heart pumping (not necessarily vigorously) and also (b) an umbrella term.

A *healthy balanced lifestyle* is one of equilibrium, quality and wellness. It is a package deal or jigsaw and the different pieces include: a nutritious diet, sufficient rest, good levels of personal hygiene and having medical needs met. In addition, a healthy balanced lifestyle usually includes one or two hobbies or interests and of course physical exercise. It could be argued that the lives of many in contemporary Britain are out of balance with:

- high levels of stress
- little time to prepare healthy nutritious food
- difficulty in committing to or sticking to an exercise programme.

Not only that, but a heavy emphasis on consumerism and material possessions can all be detrimental to achieving a healthy balanced lifestyle.

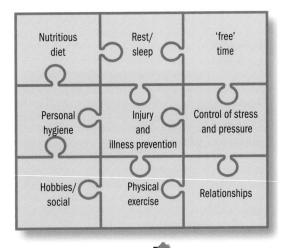

Fig 9.2 Components of a balanced healthy lifestyle

TASK 1

Choices to do with your: personal life, leisure, food, training, TV, video and computer use can all affect health and well–being.

Before everything you do today ask yourself: *Is this healthy?* Which activities promote a balanced healthy lifestyle? Which could lead to lack of balance and/or health?

Lifelong physical activity is enjoyable, health-enhancing movement that is part of daily life and is continued throughout life, resulting in life-long participation, for example going to the gym or a regular walking programme.

Lifetime sports are sports that can be enjoyed over the course of a lifetime, well into middle and even older age, e.g. badminton and tennis. The emphasis of lifetime sports is on participation and the promotion of well-being as part of a balanced healthy lifestyle. So (unlike at the Olympic Games or at Wimbledon), when played as a lifetime sport a game of badminton or tennis does not necessarily need high levels of competition, a serious attitude, commitment or high impact movement. Table tennis is one of the most popular lifetime sports in the UK having adopted the slogan *Table Tennis: Anybody, Anytime, Anywhere.*

APPLY IT!

The National Healthy Schools Programme believes that there is a strong link between health, behaviour and achievement. Research the Healthy Schools website (www.healthyschools.gov.uk) which states *'The Programme isn't just about physical health, it's about good health and happiness inside and out. And it's not just about pupils either; a Healthy School involves the whole school community – from parents to governors to school staff – in improving their health and their happiness and getting the most out of life.'*

Write a report (500 words max) on the Healthy Schools Programme including: its four themes of (1) personal, social and health education, (2) healthy eating, (3) physical activity and (4) emotional health and well-being. Add information on methods; funding and evaluation of success so far.

TASK 2

In twos make a list of possible life-long physical activity and 'lifetime sports' that can be enjoyed over the course of a lifetime.

TAKE IT FURTHER

Search the Department of Health website (www.dh.gov.uk) under the following key terms: balanced healthy lifestyles; lifetime participation; recommendations for health. Scan some government White Papers that have been published in recent years. What was the message for the health and wellbeing of the nation? How does/did the Government intend to achieve its aims? Evaluate the success rate by finding current statistics re health and well-being.

EXAM TIP

- Remember that using coloured pens and highlighters (selectively and sparingly) in your notes and files is likely to help with revision and learning.
- It's a good idea to build a glossary of key words for each of your theory units of work; keep it at the front of your file and add to it as you come across new terms.
- Be able to explain the meaning of all key words from the specification with an example from sport.

Millions of people are trying to lose weight. Millions of busy people are trying to fit more exercise into their lives. 70% of England's 10 million smokers want to stop smoking. Millions of parents are looking for cheap and convenient ways to provide good food for their children. That strong desire by millions of individuals in England to change to a healthier way of life is an opportunity.

(Government White Paper; Choosing Health-making healthy choices easier – 2005)

KEY TERMS

Physical activity

Anything that gets the body moving and the heart pumping harder than at rest. Also an umbrella term encompassing physical and outdoor recreation, physical and outdoor education, and sport.

Exercise /Physical exercise

Planned or structured physical activity requiring physical effort, aimed at improving health and fitness.

Healthy balanced lifestyles

Day-to-day life that has equilibrium, quality and wellness and which includes physical exercise, nutritious diet, injury and illness prevention, rest/sleep, hobbies/social, personal hygiene, 'free' time, control of stress and pressure, relationships.

Life-long physical activity

Enjoyable, health-enhancing movement that is sustained throughout life, e.g. yoga.

Lifetime sport

Activities that can be enjoyed over the course of a lifetime, e.g. table tennis, tennis or badminton.

POSSIBLE BENEFITS OF REGULAR PARTICIPATION IN PHYSICAL ACTIVITY

Obesity levels, especially among young people are at an all time high with the number of obese people in England having nearly doubled between 1980 and 2000. Nearly 7 out of 10 men and 6 out of 10 women in the UK are overweight or obese according to the National Audit Office (NAO).

Participation in regular physical activity (whether physical or outdoor recreation, physical or outdoor education or sport) can impact positively upon our body, mind and spirit, thus improving our quality of life.

Let's look at body, mind and spirit as bringing about **physical, mental and social benefits**.

TASK 3

Discussion – in groups discuss why obesity levels may have increased in recent years.

APPLY IT!

Is yours a 'healthy' school or college? What is served in the dining hall or canteen or restaurant? Are there:

- Vending machines for or rules against sweets crisps or fizzy drinks?
- Five minute activity breaks during double or longer lessons?
- Water fountains, or encouragement to drink water during lessons!

Consider: What connection is there between hydration and concentration? Can you find any statistics?

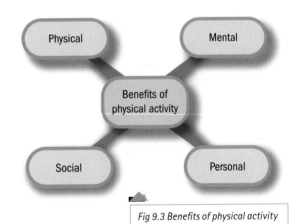

Fig 9.3 Benefits of physical activity

KEY TERMS

Physical benefits

To do with the body, e.g. potential to reduce the risk of disease or improved cardio-vascular fitness.

Mental benefits

To do with the mind, e.g. stress relief.

Personal benefits

To do with self, e.g. improved self-esteem.

Social benefits

To do with others, e.g. having positive relationships.

APPLY IT!

Some GP surgeries prescribe physical activity to treat various complaints and subsidise gym membership. Does this happen in your area?

You will study the numerous physical and physiological benefits of participation in physical activity in more detail in your Anatomy and Physiology work. Briefly though:

- People who are physically active have about a 50% reduced risk of coronary heart disease compared with those who are inactive.
- Some experts believe that lifestyle factors such as physical activity and a healthy balanced diet may prevent certain types of cancer.
- It can preserve bone density thus reducing the risk of osteoporosis.
- Physical activity improves co-ordination, strength, flexibility and balance and hence reduces the likelihood of falls and fractures which is especially important for older people.
- Blood pressure is likely to be lower in a physically active person than in someone who doesn't exercise regularly.
- Physical activity reduces the risk of stroke, mainly through beneficial effects on hypertension and blood clotting.
- The odds of suffering from insomnia, diabetes and stress are lessened for the physically active person, and body weight is likely to be maintained at a healthy level – which has to be good news.
- Exercise can contribute to a longer life and can increases energy levels
- Exercise can even help contribute to a healthier national economy by way of reduced health costs.

So all in all – some pretty good reasons to get moving and keep moving! We will leave it to your studies in Anatomy and Physiology to look at potential adverse effects of physical activity, such as overuse or other injury.

REMEMBER

Regular vigorous physical activity has the potential to:

- *Reduce risk of* coronary heart disease, some forms of cancer, osteoporosis, high blood pressure, stroke, diabetes, insomnia, stress.
- *Increase* co-ordination, strength, flexibility, balance, life expectancy, energy levels.

Regular vigorous physical activity can also impact on our mental health as it has the capacity to relieve anxiety, depression and sensitivity to stress. You may have experienced the feeling of being bit fed up, too worn out to exercise or that 'can't be bothered to go to training' feeling after an exhausting day, yet afterwards (and as a direct result of strenuous exercise) your mood has improved. There's even some evidence that academic performance might improve due to regular participation in physical activity.

The personal benefits are those to do with self. Self control, self discipline and self esteem due to achievement can all be heightened through

TAKE IT FURTHER

In the USA in the 1980s and 1990s Midnight Basketball Leagues were developed for young people. In parts of the UK the idea has been copied with similar 'Street Football' initiatives now operating in some communities.

Conduct some internet mini research into Midnight Basketball Leagues in the US and UK.

What are their aims? (Consider: relapse into undesirable behaviour, education, role modelling, employment, social inclusion and identity.) Can you find any evidence of their success?

regular participation in physical activity. We can also really get to know ourselves – our strengths, weaknesses, likes and dislikes – in a process referred to as self-realisation.

Finally, social benefits involve meeting new people and gaining a feeling of belonging and integration perhaps at clubs or classes. Wider social benefits can include decreased anti-social behaviour as a result of community recreation schemes.

APPLY IT!

According to the British United Provident Association (BUPA), a leading health care company in the UK, the risks of heart attack or stroke are about the same for adults with a sedentary lifestyle as for those who smoke.

FACTORS CONTRIBUTING TO INCREASINGLY SEDENTARY LIFESTYLES

- Seven out of 10 adults in the UK are sufficiently inactive to be classed as 'sedentary,' meaning that they are moderately active for less than one 30-minute period per week.
- As patterns of inactivity begin in early life, the promotion of physical activity among young people is essential.
- In the last 150 years Britain has changed from a rural to an urban society; from manual labourers to those who are desk-bound.
- Our day-to-day lives bear little resemblance to those of our forbears with modern technology enabling us to take the absolute minimum of physical exercise.

- For most people in the UK, exercise is now a lifestyle choice rather than a daily necessity.
- Cars are the most obvious example of new technology reducing exercise but lifts, escalators, washing machines, sit-on mowers and TV channel zappers have also had an impact.
- Both adults and young people stay seated in front of computer screens for hours the former possibly even ordering their groceries and doing other shopping on–line while the latter play computer games instead of playing physical games in the streets as their parents did.
- In America, some golf clubs do not allow members to walk the course, requiring them instead to use electric buggies.
- The trouble is that while societal 'progress' ensures that our bodies have less and less to do, our bodies are in fact crying out for more movement.
- The negative consequences of increasingly sedentary lifestyles are physical, mental, personal and social damage.

RECOMMENDATIONS – FREQUENCY, INTENSITY AND TYPE OF PHYSICAL ACTIVITY – TO DEVELOP AND SUSTAIN A BALANCED, ACTIVE AND HEALTHY LIFESTYLE

For adults, current advice from the Department of Health (DH) is to take part in at least 30 minutes of moderate physical activity at least five days a week. Moderate intensity is when you are able to hold a conversation during exercise, feel a bit breathless but are back to normal within 10 minutes of stopping.

Fig 9.4

DO YOU HAVE A HEALTHY, BALANCED LIFE STYLE?

TASK 4

Survey both staff and students to find out the percentage of people who take the recommended amount of exercise for health. Among those who do not – what are the barriers to participation?

Fig 9.5 Barriers to participation.

It is recommended that children and young people should do 60 minutes of moderate physical each day, ideally but at least twice a week. This should include higher impact activities to develop bone health, muscle strength and flexibility, e.g. jumping or climbing.

The news isn't good. Among young people (12-15 year olds), 16% of boys and 18% of girls spend less than one hour per day being moderately physically active. Among young adults (those aged 16-24), nearly half of men and more than half of women do not achieve recommended levels of activity. This increases to 93% of men and 96% of women aged 65 and over.

POSSIBLE BARRIERS TO REGULAR PARTICIPATION IN PHYSICAL ACTIVITY BY YOUNG PEOPLE

Young people do not automatically develop the skills, knowledge, attitudes and behaviours that lead to regular participation – they need to be taught them at home and at school. But no matter how good the role modelling and teaching, there are still barriers to participation.

Among secondary school children barriers include a general feeling of inertia, a preference for other activities and self-consciousness, especially among girls. There is also the 'I hate sports – I'm no good at them' barrier. Evidence is actually inconclusive as to whether children with low skill levels do not participate in sports and therefore have low levels of fitness, or whether those with better fitness are more likely to participate and hence develop their fundamental motor skills. Certainly the development of fundamental motor skills in primary age children is crucial. Most reasons for lack of participation stem from lack or inequality of one or more of the following key factors: **opportunity, provision and esteem.** That is, the chance to take part, the facilities to take part and the confidence to take part.

Further analysis of possible barriers to regular participation in physical activity by various groups in society including young people will be covered in Chapter 11, Part 1, pages 282–93.

REMEMBER

For a balanced, active and healthy lifestyle we need 30 minutes of moderate-intensity physical activity each day if possible – but at least three times per week. Children should do 60 minutes each day. (See Table 4 in Chapter 3, Part II – page 96)

TASK 5

Record a typical week. Are you achieving a balanced, active and healthy lifestyle? If not, what changes could you make?

KEY TERMS

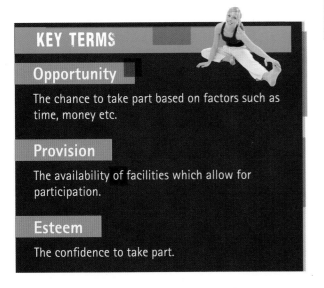

Opportunity

The chance to take part based on factors such as time, money etc.

Provision

The availability of facilities which allow for participation.

Esteem

The confidence to take part.

Physical recreation

Physical recreation is physical activity with a playful attitude in a recreational environment. To physically recreate is to take part in a game or activity for its own sake – not usually for any extrinsic reward. It may be the same sport or activity that occurs at the Olympic Games but when done as physical recreation the emphasis is on:

- participation, not standard of performance
- taking part, not winning

TASK 6

What features in the photographs below suggest that the activities are being pursued for recreation?

- enjoyment and satisfaction, not record breaking.

So, a game of badminton played for recreation is more 'playful' than competitive. It will probably also be played at a relatively unrefined level where skills may be quite low or inconsistent and where National Governing Body rules and scoring systems need not be strictly adhered to. There will be few if any requirements about type of kit and equipment. Interestingly, with the booming leisure and recreation industry now also a fashion industry, people dress in the most stylish gear irrespective of commitment, level of ability or even intention to be active at all!

And what about media coverage and sponsorship? Again, not likely to be evident when an activity is pursued as physical recreation. Physical recreation encompasses lifetime sports (see page 212) and could be defined as '**physical activities that are pursued for a variety of reasons and benefits at a relatively unsophisticated level**'.

TASK 7

Survey up to ten people to find out what motivates them to take part in their chosen physical recreation activities. Illustrate your finding in a pie chart or tally chart.

Fig. 9.6 shows that the activity being pursued may have the positive outcome of promoting health and developing physical skills in a friendly and enjoyable atmosphere, but also that physical recreation goes far beyond the physical. It also provides the opportunity to learn about ourselves and others. So, physical recreation is more than just an activity – it is also a potentially valuable experience.

EXAM TIP

Be able to compare characteristics of physical recreation with characteristics of sport.

Fig 9.7 Physical recreation: characteristics and benefits

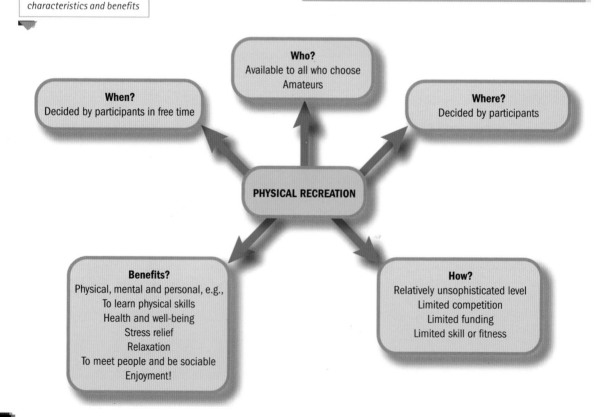

EXAM TIP

When asked to identify the characteristics of physical recreation in an exam it is important to be specific and clear in your answers. If simple, bland terms such as *'Anyone, anywhere, any time'* are offered as characteristics they will not gain marks. Be specific.

KEY TERMS

Physical recreation

Physical activities that are pursued for a variety of reasons and benefits at a relatively unsophisticated level.

Outdoor recreation

Physical activities which take place in the natural environment which are pursued for a variety of reasons and benefits.

REMEMBER

Physical activity is more than an activity – it is a valuable experience.

Outdoor recreation

Outdoor recreation is part of physical recreation so these two aspects of physical activity share many characteristics and benefits. The key difference is location with outdoor recreation taking place in the natural environment. The natural environment might be: 'Up a mountain or down a river, across an ocean or along a coastline, across the wilderness or along the outdoor way, through the air or under the surface of the earth.' (Colin Mortlock in *The Adventure Alternative.*)

Mortlock explains the potential of outdoor recreation as follows: 'The following journeys, providing you take any of them to the outer limits of your capabilities in a self-reliant manner, can take you along the road to truth and beauty, freedom and happiness.'

TASK 8

Discuss as a class any outdoor recreation experiences you have had. Where did you go? What did you do? How did you benefit from the experience? Did it help you along the road to 'truth and beauty, freedom and happiness?'

Outdoor recreation has benefits arising from its setting in the natural environment. Benefits include:

- appreciation of the natural environment
- respect for the natural environment
- gaining a sense of adventure.

Let's look at each of these in turn.

APPRECIATION OF THE NATURAL ENVIRONMENT

The natural landscape of the UK is beautiful – ideal surroundings for recreation, and beauty is there for all of us to enjoy. Some people live in stunning rural areas, whilst others need to travel to enjoy them. Whether climbing, walking, canoeing or orienteering, the scenery of the countryside rewards our senses with beauty and variety. We get to see, feel, smell and hear things that are way outside our normal day-to-day existence. We are able to leave behind the clutter of urban life and get in touch with the natural world. We get 'back to nature'. Life can seem simple again.

Importantly, we can also get in touch with ourselves. It is easy to be in awe of the surrounding splendour – poets, artists and writers certainly seem to. Outdoor recreation can be a spiritual experience – a time when we tune in to our inner selves, thoughts and feelings.

RESPECT FOR THE NATURAL ENVIRONMENT

Having been moved by the remarkable beauty of the natural environment, we are likely to value it and want to preserve its uniqueness for others to enjoy. We may feel concerned about issues such as conservation and pollution or even the fact that as more people escape to national parks and green-belt areas for refreshment and renewal they, in fact, create new problems. Some areas of the UK, for example, are already suffering from land erosion and disturbances to the natural world caused by increased numbers of visitors rambling or mountain biking.

GAINING A SENSE OF ADVENTURE AND PERHAPS RISK

As well as being beautiful, the natural environment is also unpredictable. The weather can change suddenly; tides can be erratic with invisible hazards lurking below water level; rock fall can make paths uneven and unpredictable. Each of these situations is potentially worrying, risky or even dangerous and can lead to some fear. The key to a positive experience of outdoor recreation is to avoid all danger by using common sense and by abiding strictly to safety codes. Any remaining worries can then be embraced with a feeling of excitement and adventure. Benefits can then be found – including a feeling of exhilaration, a great feel-good factor and a real sense of personal achievement.

EXAM TIP

Remember that outdoor recreation means using the natural environment, (e.g. hills, lakes or rivers) to gain physical, mental and personal benefits. Outdoor recreation is not just playing a game of hockey or golf which happen to be outside.

Physical education

Physical Education is a compulsory subject on the National Curriculum. Also, you may have chosen PE as a GCSE subject and are now developing your knowledge and understanding of both theory and practical PE at AS level.

What we need to do is:

- define Physical Education
- identify its characteristics
- establish its benefits to young people.

TASK 9

In pairs consider the following:

1. What activities did you experience at school in PE?
2. Did you enjoy them? Why or why not?
3. What skill level did you achieve?
4. Other than physical skills, what else, if anything did you learn that was valuable?
5. How did that come about?

Pool the information in small groups, then as a class. Chart your findings.

DEFINING PE

While PE is fundamentally physical, it is also concerned with personal, social, lifestyle and emotional development. It can be described as 'learning about and through physical activity'; a more formal definition is: 'Physical Education is the learning of physical, personal, preparatory and qualitative values through formal physical activity in schools'.

WHAT ARE THE CHARACTERISTICS OF PE?

Fig 9.7 Characteristics of Physical Recreation

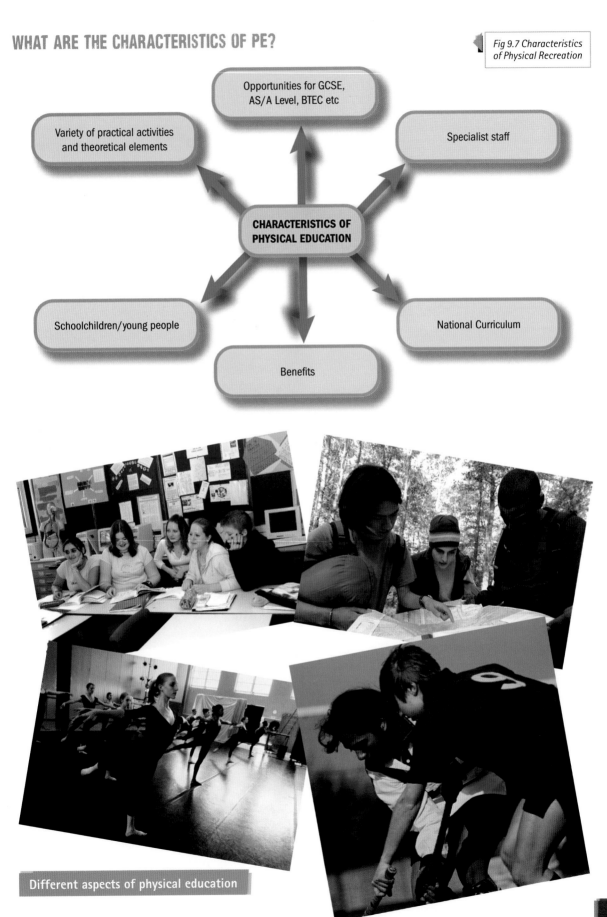

Opportunities for GCSE, AS/A Level, BTEC etc

Variety of practical activities and theoretical elements

Specialist staff

CHARACTERISTICS OF PHYSICAL EDUCATION

Schoolchildren/young people

National Curriculum

Benefits

Different aspects of physical education

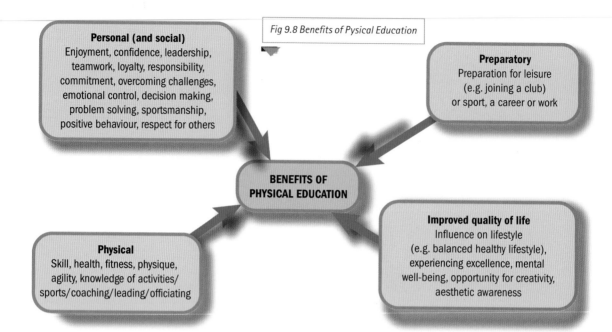

Fig 9.8 Benefits of Pysical Education

Personal (and social)
Enjoyment, confidence, leadership, teamwork, loyalty, responsibility, commitment, overcoming challenges, emotional control, decision making, problem solving, sportsmanship, positive behaviour, respect for others

Preparatory
Preparation for leisure (e.g. joining a club) or sport, a career or work

BENEFITS OF PHYSICAL EDUCATION

Physical
Skill, health, fitness, physique, agility, knowledge of activities/sports/coaching/leading/officiating

Improved quality of life
Influence on lifestyle (e.g. balanced healthy lifestyle), experiencing excellence, mental well-being, opportunity for creativity, aesthetic awareness

WHAT ARE THE BENEFITS OF PE?

According to the National Curriculum, PE is under-pinned by:

- Competence – body and mind skilfulness.
- Performance – applying competence.
- Creativity – problem solving, techniques and tactics.
- Healthy active lifestyles – physical activity for health.

So, a high-quality school PE experience enables young people to:

- Enjoy, succeed and become confident in a variety of physical activities as part of a healthy balanced lifestyle leading to lifelong involvement in physical activity.
- Develop a range of skills, tactics and strategies as well as creativity and decision-making skills. Observational and communication skills linked with improving pupils' own and others' performance can also be learned.
- Help pupils develop personally and socially due to working alone, in groups and in teams, thereby developing qualities such as fair play and responsibility.
- Get the chance to lead, coach and officiate as part of their PE programme, and they can learn to be effective in competitive, creative and challenging situations.

All of this can usefully be considered under the following headings:

- **Physical benefits** – that improve health and motor skills
- **Personal benefits** – that develop personal and social skills
- **Preparatory (or preparation) benefits** – that prepare for healthy balanced lifestyles, lifetime sport and/or a career.
- **Qualitative benefits** – that improve the quality of life.

TASK 10

In small groups, prepare and present a short role play of a Year 8 PE lesson which clearly shows the different benefits of PE (physical, personal, preparation, qualitative).

EXAM TIP

Be sure that you understand and can give examples of the four sets of values or benefits of PE (physical, preparation, personal, qualitative).

Fig 9.9 Outdoor Education: characteristics and benefits

When?
- As part of structured school or college programme
- Special trips or visits

Who?
- Young people
- Qualified/specialist leaders/staff

Where?
- In the natural environment (hills, lakes, rivers, mountains, coastlines, caves)
- Sometimes using semi-natural or artificial facilities, e.g., climbing walls

OUTDOOR EDUCATION

Benefits?
- Physical health and skill learning, e.g., physical fitness and knowledge of sailing or climbing
- Personal and social development, e.g., leadership, co-operation, mental strength, decision making
- Preparation for active leisure, e.g., a lifelong love of the outdoors
- Enhancement of quality of life, e.g., appreciation of environment, awareness of conservation issues

How?
According to strict health and safety regulations. Sometimes by overcoming potential constraints, e.g.,
- Distance from natural environment
- Expense of specialist activities or transport
- Lack of staff expertise or qualifications
- Expense in terms of time
- Reluctance of staff/health and safety concerns
- Lack of specialist facilities or equipment

Outdoor Education in the semi-natural environment using artificial facilities

Outdoor education

Outdoor Education can be defined as 'learning in and about the outdoors' and is part of structured school Physical Education in which positive, useful benefits are formally sought and taught. What distinguishes Outdoor Education from the rest

of PE is the element of risk and unpredictability which results from its setting in the natural or semi-natural environment. The semi-natural environment consists of artificial facilities which are used to simulate the real thing e.g. climbing walls, artificial ski slopes, man made water sports centres or swimming baths for canoeing.

As part of PE, Outdoor Education has the same potential benefits:

- physical health and skill learning
- personal and social development
- preparation for life-long physical activity and health balanced lifestyles
- enhancement of quality of life.

The thrill of outdoor adventurous education is uniquely valuable to young people. But how can we provide a sense of adventure and maximise learning and development opportunities while at the same time keeping the young people completely safe? This is the key concern of every provider of Outdoor Education and here we need to understand the difference between real and perceived risk.

Beginners ← → **Committed experts**

Perceived risk
(completely safe)

This imagined risk is sought by teachers and leaders to give learners a sense of adventure and opportunities for personal challenge and development.

Real risk
(can be dangerous or even fatal)

This is avoided at all costs by careful preparation and use of appropriate kit and equipment. Real risk is sometimes embraced by committed experts seeking great challenges (but not as part of Outdoor Education).

Fig 9.10 Real and perceived risk

Real risk might be a natural disaster such as a flash flood or a freak accident resulting from the natural environment. Real risk is avoided at all costs. Thorough planning, attention to weather reports and the use of appropriate kit and equipment by qualified and experienced group leaders all go towards avoiding real risk. A leader will never be afraid to abandon an expedition for safety reasons – the alternative could be injury or even death caused by hypothermia, avalanche, blizzard or flood. Even then, disaster still occasionally happens and lives are tragically lost.

The young people are kept in predictable, safe situations, but those that offer challenge and a sense of adventure. The activity or location may appear dangerous to the young person, but in reality, the risk is imagined and students are kept completely safe within staff leader risk assessment guidelines. For example, abseiling for a beginner feels risky, but correct procedures and safety equipment ensure complete safety.

'It's a buzz because your body senses a risk. It feels great to overcome a fear, to feel that you've done it!'

'It might look and feel risky – but is completely safe!'

REMEMBER

Perceived risk is imagined. Real risk is really real!

CONSTRAINTS ON WIDESPREAD PARTICIPATION IN OUTDOOR EDUCATION BY YOUNG PEOPLE

Unfortunately, most schools find it difficult to provide a broad and regular outdoor education experience for their young people with various factors limiting widespread, regular participation.

- Firstly, there is the problem of funding. Coach transport is expensive and voluntary contributions from pupils may be insufficient to cover these and other costs.
- Secondly, teachers need specialist, time-consuming and expensive training for outdoor education and staff ratios need to be generous.

TASK 11

Writing in the role of a school Head of PE department, prepare a short presentation for parents to advertise a proposed Year 10 outdoor activity week. Include:

- activities on offer
- qualifications of staff
- valuable experiences that their children are likely to gain
- likely costs
- health and safety systems and procedures.

- And, PE staff may be unwilling or unable to give the required time while their colleagues may be reluctant to sanction release of pupils from their classes due to pressure on the curriculum and examination work.
- There is also the very real concern of health and safety, with some staff being increasingly reluctant to take on the responsibility of organising and managing trips.
- Also, of course, suitable facilities may simply be too far away.

Sport

> 'Serious sport has nothing to do with fair play. It is bound up with hatred, jealousy, boastfulness, disregard for all rules and sadistic pleasure in witnessing violence. In other words, it is war minus the shooting.'
> George Orwell (author of '1984' – published in 1949)

Some would argue that the view of George Orwell over half a century ago is rather depressing. Is it really that bad? Is sport really a global opportunity for violence, deviance and hatred? Or at its best, is it the place where we can learn to make moral decisions, test ourselves physically and mentally, excel, make lifelong friends, influence and inspire others as positive role models, create memories and even be part of a celebration of compelling drama and exhilarating passion?

Let's look at a more optimistic view – this time from Nelson Mandela, the former President of South Africa, anti-apartheid activist and Nobel Peace prize winner of 1993. Mandela says:

> 'Sport has the power to change the world, the power to inspire, the power to unite people in a way that little else can. It speaks to people in a language that they understand. Sport can create hope when there was once only despair. It is an instrument for peace, even more powerful than governments. It breaks down racial barriers. It laughs in the face of all kinds of discrimination. The heroes sport creates are examples of this power. They are valiant, not only on the playing field but also in the community. Spreading hope and inspiration to the world.'

Let's define sport as: an organised, competitive and skilful physical activity requiring commitment and fair play.

TASK 12

Study the pictures below. Can you see and list characteristics of sport?

225

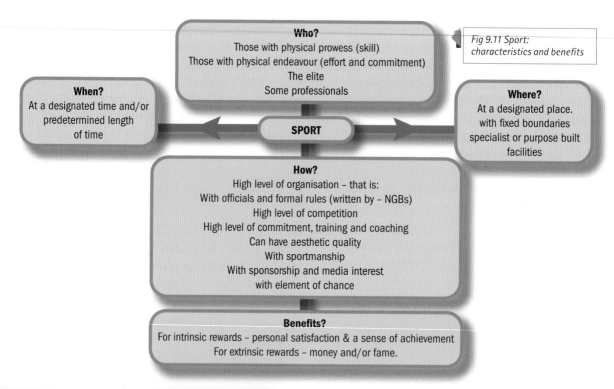

Who?
Those with physical prowess (skill)
Those with physical endeavour (effort and commitment)
The elite
Some professionals

When?
At a designated time and/or predetermined length of time

SPORT

Where?
At a designated place.
with fixed boundaries
specialist or purpose built facilities

How?
High level of organisation – that is:
With officials and formal rules (written by – NGBs)
High level of competition
High level of commitment, training and coaching
Can have aesthetic quality
With sportmanship
With sponsorship and media interest
with element of chance

Benefits?
For intrinsic rewards – personal satisfaction & a sense of achievement
For extrinsic rewards – money and/or fame.

Fig 9.11 Sport: characteristics and benefits

REMEMBER

The attitude of the performers needs to be considered when deciding if a physical activity is being done as physical recreation or sport. After all, an elite performer can sometimes show a playful or recreative attitude (can you think of an example from high level sport?) – just as someone playing for fun can slip into a highly competitive sporting attitude from time to time.

We would all probably agree that the winner of the London Marathon, the competitor in the winter Olympics, and the regular league netball player are all taking part in sport. But what about the person who comes last in the London Marathon whilst dressed as Superman and raising thousands of pounds for charity? And what about aerobics, chess, skipping, body building, fishing or ballroom dancing?

KEY TERM

Aesthetic

Movement that is pleasing to the eye or beautiful to watch.

In terms of characteristics we have already established that sport is organised, competitive, skilful and physical, with commitment and fair play. What else? Well, sport attracts media coverage, sponsorship and professional performers and is organised by national and international governing bodies who sort out the rules and other administrative aspects of their individual sports. Sport is big business nowadays and winning is of huge importance, so the quality of kit and equipment needs to be superlative with up to the minute technology and cutting edge design. Losing by a micro-second can be expensive in high level sport!

To be classified as a sport an activity needs to display certain characteristics

In analysing these activities it might help to consider the following.

- **Tradition** – do we traditionally call the activity a sport in this country?
- **Vigorous physical exertion** – does the activity involve strenuous movement?
- **Competition** – does the activity involve competition against oneself or others?
- **Administration** – does the activity follow National Governing Body rules?

- **Behaviour** – does the performer show commitment, skill and fair play?

The more often that these features fit a particular activity, the more likely it is that the activity could be classified as sport.

TASK 13

In pairs, make a list of activities whose descriptive word or phrase (e.g. jogging) tells us that it is being practised as a recreational pastime rather than as something more serious or competitive. What words or phrases are there for recreational horse riding, swimming, playing tennis, playing football, fitness training? Can you think of some more?

There are certain terms associated with sport that you need to know and understand.

- **Physical prowess** is to do with competence, expertise and proficiency – in other words it is skilfulness.
- **Physical endeavour** is effort, enterprise or trying hard.
- **Sportsmanship** is fair play or observing both written and unwritten rules, whilst showing respect for others and graciousness in both victory and defeat.

And so, a performer showing physical prowess, physical endeavour and sportsmanship is skilful, never gives up and plays fair.

On the other side of the coin are **gamesmanship** and **deviance**. **Gamesmanship** is the use of unconventional but not strictly illegal tactics (i.e. stretching the rules to their limit) in order to gain an unfair advantage. Examples of gamesmanship might be time wasting or 'sledging.' Sportsmanship and gamesmanship have very different effects on sporting situations.

KEY TERM

Sledging

Attempting to undermine opponents (often in cricket) by verbally abusing, taunting, intimidating or antagonising.

Sportsmanship	Gamesmanship
Helps flow and success of event	Disrupts continuity of event
Admired by spectators	Can irritate spectators
Admired by players	Irritates players and causes retaliation
Increases goodwill	Causes bad feeling and friction
Support of officials' decisions strengthens sport as an institution and raises its status.	Undermines officials and undermines sport as an institution thus lowering the status of sport
Gives good example to young people producing positive role models	Gives bad example to young people producing negative role models

Table 1 Effects of sportsmanship and gamesmanship on sporting events.

TASK 14

In groups of three think of as many instances of gamesmanship as you can. How did they make you feel as you saw or experienced them?

Now try to name instances of performers (both your peers and the elite) who are known for their sportsmanship. How did you feel as you saw or experienced sportsmanship?

Deviance is behaviour that is sharply different from generally accepted standards being far more than an accidental foul or deviation from written rules as managed by umpires and referees. Deviance in sport includes deliberate dangerous fouls and extends to violence, drug abuse and other forms of cheating.

Physical endeavour

Effort.

Sportsmanship

Fair play.

Gamesmanship

Stretching the rules to gain an unfair advantage.

Deviance (in sport)

Seriously breaking the rules and norms (of sport).

KEY TERMS

Physical prowess

Skill.

ExamCafé

Relax, refresh, result!

Refresh your memory

Revision checklist for Physical Activity

You should now know and understand about:

▷ Participation in physical activity, including

- physical activity as an umbrella term

- the meaning of exercise, healthy balanced lifestyles, lifetime sport/life long physical activity

- possible benefits of regular participation in physical activity

- factors contributing to increasingly sedentary lifestyles

- recommended amounts of physical activity for health

- possible barriers to participation by young people.

▷ Definitions, characteristics and benefits of physical recreation and outdoor recreation.

▷ Definitions, characteristics and benefits of physical education and outdoor education.

▷ Definitions, characteristics and benefits of sport, including

- meaning of terms physical prowess, physical endeavour, sportsmanship, gamesmanship, deviance.

REVISE AS YOU GO!

1. Explain the idea that physical activity is an umbrella term.
2. What is the key difference between physical activity and physical exercise?
3. What are some characteristics of a healthy balanced lifestyle?
4. Give examples of specific benefits of regular participation in physical activity under the headings: physical, mental, personal and social.
5. Identify three factors that have contributed to increasingly sedentary lifestyles in recent years.
6. Define each of the following: physical recreation, physical education and sport.
7. Explain the meaning of and give an example of both real and perceived risk.
8. What increases when a game is played with a sporting rather than with a recreative attitude?
9. In relation to sport explain the term 'deviance'.
10. Fill in the following question marks with two different key words: Physical ? (a word meaning skill) and Physical ? (a word meaning effort).

Get the result!

Examination question

Discuss possible benefits to young people of a school high quality Physical Education programme. (6 marks)

examiner's tips

- The first thing to do here is to check the command word 'discuss'.
- Now check the key subject focus 'physical education'.
- Now check how many marks are available. (6)

Examiner says:

This candidate has answered about the correct subject – (occasionally they see the word physical and skim read the next word and write about physical **recreation** by mistake!) This is a very brief, answer showing lack of depth and lack of discussion with the command word having been ignored. There is no clear explanation that health and fitness will be **improved** through PE – just a list of words separated by commas. It might be useful to give each key point that you make (and that you hope will gain a mark) its own sentence.

Student answer

PE has many benefits including health, fitness, learning skills, and improving the quality of your life.

Student's improved answer

The benefits of Physical Education are many and varied and extend beyond the purely physical.

They can usefully be categorised into four groups as follows: physical, personal, preparatory and those that can have a positive impact on the quality of your life.

Let's look at each category in turn. Physical benefits might be improved health and fitness or learning sport specific skills such as being able to do a penalty flick in hockey.

Personal benefits might include increased self esteem due to improved performance or the development of leadership qualities as a result of being named team captain.

As captain you would also be encouraging sportsmanship and positive behaviour in your team. PE can prepare young

Examiner says:

Useful introduction which sets the scene concisely without wasting time.

Examiner says:

I'm glad that you didn't stop after this sentence. What you have written is accurate – but at this stage you are still only identifying.

Examiner says:

Good use of example.

Examiner says:

Again, I like the way you have named the key benefit and developed the point with an example – that's what makes your answer a discussion.

people for many things – from a career as a PE teacher to preparing for a lifetime of physical activity due to a positive attitude gained at school. Finally PE has the potential to improve the quality of your life by giving you an experience of excellence – whether personal excellence of aesthetic appreciation of someone else's performance.

All in all an excellent subject!

Examiner says:

Although this might seem to be a flippant conclusion – at least there is one (which you really need in a discussion). Good quality of written communication throughout.

An A grade answer

Sport and culture – sport and physical activity as a reflection of the culture in which it exists

LEARNING OBJECTIVES

At the end of this chapter you should be able to demonstrate knowledge and understanding of:

- Ethnic sports and games that are still played in the UK
- The role of nineteenth century public schools in promoting and organising sports and games
- The relatively recent move from the traditional amateur approach to a more professional approach in sport in the UK
- Characteristics of the American and Australian nations and the nature of sport in each of those countries
- American football and Australian rules football.

INTRODUCTION

Sports and games reflect the culture in which they exist – in other words, people play games that suit them and their environment. In this chapter we will look at how sport and physical activity reflect a community's true nature and personality.

We will start in the UK with some of the unique sports and games that are still played – many of which have been going on for hundreds of years and which continue as important community festivals and celebrations. We also need to know how our sports and games evolved and how sport has become so much more professional in recent years. Then we will look at the USA and Australia to see how sport in each of those countries reflects their national traditions and behaviour, i.e. their culture.

Those of you who opt for Comparative Studies at A2 will develop this socio-cultural work further. You will carry out an in-depth study of themes relating to sport and PE in both the USA and Australia. You will then compare these with the same themes in the UK.

KEY TERMS

Society

A *community* of people bound together by similar traditions, institutions or nationality.

Culture

The traditions, beliefs, customs, practices, sports, pastimes and social behaviour of a particular society or nation of people.

Sport and culture

The link between a particular society or nation and the physical activities that exist within it.

Ethnic identity

Unique behaviour, cultural traits and characteristics of a group often based on tradition and ritual.

Alone or in groups of three, read the following account of the annual Lewes Fire Festival in Sussex. Discuss your impression in small groups.

LEWES FIRE FESTIVAL

Each November 5th the inhabitants of Lewes in Sussex, transform this normally small town into a riot of flame, gunpowder and noise as the five local bonfire societies compete to provide the most explosive pyrotechnic display of the evening.

Spellbound sometimes terrified spectators (many local and many more who have travelled to the display) pack into the narrow streets to see Vikings carrying huge flaming crosses, and cowboys, Indians, Victorian soldiers and samurai warriors carrying burning torches. Sailors pull blazing barrels alongside policemen, judges and priests, while huge drums of bangers and strips of firecrackers explode close to or even into the crowd.

A group of 'Bishops' surrounded by flaming crosses exchange fierce banter with the crowd whom they pelt relentlessly with fireworks. As part of the ritual they call for the burning of Guy Fawkes – a massive effigy, packed with fireworks. The crowd then shout for the Pope to be burned and after lively exchanges with the Bishops, the Pope's effigy is dramatically torched.

The finale is the lighting of a huge contemporary effigy – both Osama Bin Laden and George Bush have been victims in recent years.

The United Kingdom

SURVIVING ETHNIC SPORTS AND GAMES IN THE UK

Do you think that Morris dancers are strange, laugh at the idea of wassailing your apple trees and think that people who turn up for annual pancake races are a bit weird? What about eating hot cross buns on Good Friday, hanging up mistletoe at Christmas, and going to Halloween parties? The British Isles are rich in traditional festivals and customs that are bound up with the changing seasons and the rhythm of country life. Many are of medieval or pagan origin, such as the Furry Dance at Helston in Cornwall. They can be both single sport occasions and multi-sport festivals, such as the Lakeland and Highland Games.

Robert Dover's Cotswold Olympics is a multi-sport occasion which was originally established by permission of James I in 1605. It was an annual event until 1851 when it was disrupted by hooligans. Dover's Olympics were revived in Chipping Campden, Gloucestershire in 1963 and continue today. The original activities ranged from throwing the sledgehammer, sword fighting and horse riding, to shin kicking, dancing, fireworks and picnicking. Today the celebrations include wrestling, Morris dancers, cross-country running, hot air ballooning, marching bands, fireworks and a torchlight procession with dancing in the square at the end of the day.

Traditional festivals have a always suffered criticism and attack for several reasons such as:

- the Reformation (which took power from the Church to the Crown)
- Puritanism, which discouraged folk games and festivals
- the weakening of traditional, rural community life due to nineteenth-century industrialisation
- the First World War – which wiped out a generation and changed people's views about stability and tradition
- the Second World War, followed by a modern age of improved technology
- hooliganism, which caused some festivals to be banned
- concern over danger to participants.

THE HIGHLAND GAMES, SCOTLAND: TOSSING THE CABER

There are over 50 different Highland Games meetings throughout the year, with Royal Braemar being the most famous. Highland games are celebrations of Scottish and Celtic culture and heritage and include bagpipes, kilts, pipes, drums and traditional dancing alongside athletic events. A Highland athletics competition includes the caber toss, stone put, Scottish hammer throw, foot racing, wrestling, weight throw and sheaf toss (in which a bundle of straw is tossed vertically with a pitchfork over a bar).

The Highland Games are grand social occasions as well as being displays of athleticism in keeping with the needs of a hardy lifestyle in remote and sometimes severe conditions.

ROYAL SHROVETIDE FOOTBALL – ASHBOURNE, DERBYSHIRE

This annual mob game has survived since medieval times despite several attempts to abolish it. It starts with the singing of the national anthem and is followed by a battle between the Up'ards and the Down'ards centred on the River Henmore. The game has few rules, any number of players and mill wheels form the goals that are three miles apart. Only rarely is a goal scored, possibly because the ball is filled with cork dust to make it heavy and the game more static. The ball is hardly ever kicked, but mostly 'hugged' by a forward moving scrum.

HAXEY HOOD GAME, LINCOLNSHIRE

"Hoose agen hoose, toon agen toon, if tha meets a man, nok im doon, but doant 'ot im"

This is a rugby-type game, where a leather tube is slowly walked by a large unorganised scrum to one of four local pubs, where it stays until the following year's game.

It takes place on Twelfth Night as according to legend it was on Twelfth Night that the wife of Sir John de Mowbray was riding on horseback across the fields near Haxey when her silk riding hood was caught and blown away by the wind. Thirteen labourers in a nearby field gave gallant chase to the hood. It was finally caught by one who was too shy to hand it back to the lady himself so gave it to another to hand over. Lady Mowbray thanked the man and complimented him that he had acted like a Lord, whereas the shy one was a Fool. Lady Mowbray so enjoyed the act of chivalry and the associated chase that she donated 13 acres of land on condition that the episode be re-enacted each year.

HURLING THE SILVER BALL - ST COLUMB MAJOR, ST COLUMB MINOR AND ST IVES, CORNWALL

Take a silver ball weighing ½ kg, a vast playing area, teams of up to 500 a side, few rules, two goals (but no goal keepers), no referee, shops that barricade their windows for protection and an entire community and you have this ancient Pagan Shrove Tuesday game. It is extremely rough and involves rugby-type tackling, with throwing, rather than kicking of the ball by the two teams of 'Townsmen' and 'Countrymen.' The game starts when the ball is thrown to the crowd at the market square. The 'scrum' continues in the square for about an hour after which the ball is carried towards the goals.

Four hours later, a winner returns to declare victory for Town or Country and everyone ends up in the pub where the ball is dunked into jugs of beer.

CHEESE ROLLING - COOPER'S HILL, GLOUCESTERSHIRE

This annual event takes place on the Spring Bank Holiday and is now a major attraction for spectators, media, and medics who deal with the injuries. Competitors hurl themselves down the steep hill (which is one in two in places), in pursuit of a massive Double Gloucester cheese. The cheese rolls at an estimated 70 miles per hour! There are currently five downhill races and an uphill race on the day. Cooper's Hill is the most famous venue for cheese rolling though there are others in other parts of the country.

TAR BARREL BURNING - OTTERY ST MARY, DEVON

This annual event takes place on 5th November and involves racing through the streets with flaming wooden barrels of burning tar. The event probably began as a pagan ritual to cleanse the streets of evil spirits. Each of Ottery's central pubs sponsors a barrel which is soaked with tar before being lit. Once the flames take hold, the barrels are hoisted onto the runners' backs, and a flaming pub crawl ensues! Barrel carriers take the weight for as long as possible before passing on to the next team member. Similar barrel burning festivals take place elsewhere.

TASK 2

Make a poster! Research any surviving ethnic sport or game in the UK, either mentioned in this chapter – or another that you know of or can find out about. Include the following:

- What is it called?
- What are its origins?
- Where does it take place?
- When and how regularly does it take place?
- Does it have any special festival or cultural features?
- Why do you think that it still exists?
- Add pictures if possible.

Some other surviving sports, games and festivals:

- 'Cradle rocking' in Blidworth, Nottinghamshire
- 'Firing the Poppers' at Penny Stratford, Buckinghamshire
- 'Hobby-horse' festival in Padstow, Cornwall
- 'Dicing for Bibles', in St Ives, Huntingdonshire
- Mob football games at Alnwick, Northumberland; Sedgefield in County Durham and Corfe Castle in Dorset

While reading about these traditions that still occur, you will have noticed that they share some features. For example, several of them take place on Shrove Tuesday or November 5th; you need to be pretty brave to take part in some of them and the pub is often a central feature. For your exam you need to be able to describe the characteristics of surviving ethnic sports and give reasons for their continued existence and popularity. Most of them have some or all of the following features:

The role of nineteenth century public schools in promoting and organising sports and games

Many of you will study the historical development of sport in detail at A2. For now, we need to know and understand some basics. The nineteenth century (1800–1900) was a time of change. During Queen Victoria's reign (1837–1901), Britain shifted from a rural to an urban society and gradually became more civilised.

Public baths were built in the new big cities to counter the devastation of cholera and there was a reduction in working hours plus more free time for the working class. Also, the formation of the RSPCA hastened a ban on cruel baiting and blood sports such as dog fighting. Improved transport

Fig 10.1 Surviving ethnic sports

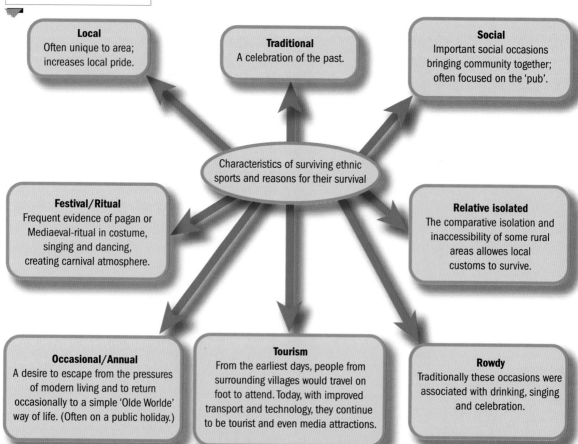

Local
Often unique to area; increases local pride.

Traditional
A celebration of the past.

Social
Important social occasions bringing community together; often focused on the 'pub'.

Characteristics of surviving ethnic sports and reasons for their survival

Festival/Ritual
Frequent evidence of pagan or Mediaeval-ritual in costume, singing and dancing, creating carnival atmosphere.

Relative isolated
The comparative isolation and inaccessibility of some rural areas allowes local customs to survive.

Occasional/Annual
A desire to escape from the pressures of modern living and to return occasionally to a simple 'Olde Worlde' way of life. (Often on a public holiday.)

Tourism
From the earliest days, people from surrounding villages would travel on foot to attend. Today, with improved transport and technology, they continue to be tourist and even media attractions.

Rowdy
Traditionally these occasions were associated with drinking, singing and celebration.

and communications (particularly the railways) meant that distant football teams could play each other for the first time and spectators could travel too. Increased literacy meant that sporting celebrities and heroes were 'born' as fans could now read about successes. Association football became a spectator craze.

Meanwhile large numbers of middle and upper-class boys attended the elite public boarding schools such as Eton, Rugby and Harrow where they were prepared for future leadership roles. These public schools (so called because they were not privately owned but were controlled by a body of trustees) and the young men they produced had a massive impact on the development, promotion and organisation of sports and games.

These schools had a lot going for them. For a start, there was enough money to build specialist facilities and employ a good number of academic staff ('assistant masters') who helped with games

each afternoon. Professional coaches were also employed for some games (e.g. cricket) so standards were high. As many public schools were boarding schools, there was a lot of free time after lessons so boys ended up playing for hours each day which raised standards. Many public schools were built in vast grounds, giving more than enough space for pitches to be levelled, squash courts to be built and general expansion to occur. No wonder boys of the 1880s became obsessed with and so good at team games.

The boys did a lot of the organising themselves. The 'house' games captain would put up the daily team lists and encourage everyone to be involved while headmasters went out of their way to encourage participation as a way of keeping pupils occupied and out of trouble. Gradually, fixtures between schools because more regular. By the end of the nineteenth century public schools had highly organised games programmes which reflected the growing regularity and place of sport in society.

Games-playing at Rugby School in the late 1800s

THE RUGBY BOYS AT FOOTBALL.

KEY TERM

The House system

The system of pastoral care in nineteenth century public boarding schools. Boys lived in boarding houses while at school. These houses became the centre of their social and sporting life. The houses that you might have in your school evolved from this.

The character building benefits of team games became widely accepted both in the schools and in society at large. Participation, it was thought, would give young people qualities such as courage, leadership, endurance, self-reliance and self-control.

REMEMBER

When we looked at the benefits of Physical Education in schools today we mentioned very similar personal values to those developed through games-playing in the public boarding schools of the nineteenth century (see page 223).

On leaving school the young men took their passion for team games to university with them. When they left university they took this passion for team games and their supposed values into adult life. In the nineteenth century (1800–1900), Britain governed a vast empire of sovereign states around the world – and the ex public schoolboys went abroad to manage them. Missionaries, intent on spreading Christianity, joined them too. These late Victorian and Edwardian imperial administrators, educators and disciples went to the tropical rain forests of Africa, the islands of the Pacific, the plains of India and the prairies of Canada.

They were busy at home too! As vicars, industrialists, parents, teachers back in their old schools or simply in the communities in which they lived they spread the word and took their games and the games' associated benefits with them. They wanted to create loyal, brave, truthful Christian gentlemen.

In addition, ex-public schoolboys set up a huge number of National Governing Bodies (NGBs). The Football Association (FA), Rugby Football Union (RFU) and Amateur Athletics Association (AAA) are examples of NGBs which were formed by ex-public schoolboys.

Sports and games were promoted by:

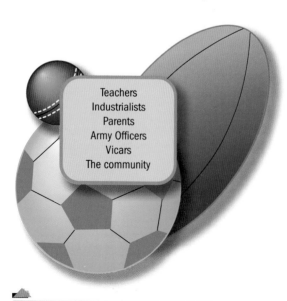

Teachers
Industrialists
Parents
Army Officers
Vicars
The community

Fig 10.2 The promotion of sports and games

TASK 3

Re-read the section on 'the role of nineteenth century Public Schools in promoting and organising sports and games.' Extract key words and phrases and make three revision lists for your file, entitled:

- What helped to promote games?
- How were games organised?
- How did the ex-public schoolboys help to spread team games?

KEY TERMS

Public schools

Elite boarding schools such as Rugby School.

Assistant masters

Junior masters who did not have the responsibility of running a house. They taught an academic subject and were fully involved in the games programme.

Character building

Developing strength of mind and feeling usually as a result of coping with testing and difficult experiences.

Games ethic

A belief in the value of team games for the development of character.

National Governing Bodies

Organisations that look after all aspects of their individual sports, e.g. the Hockey Association (HA).

British Empire

The spread of British forms of government, religion and culture to nations considered to be less advanced or civilised. This included the building of roads, schools and hospitals but usually at a loss of inherent traditions and culture.

From the traditional amateur to a more professional approach to sport

Today, sport is a multi-million pound industry where the word 'amateur' can be used in a slightly derogatory way to describe something that is great fun but rather unsophisticated and unpolished – a bit like amateur dramatics. The word 'amateur' stems from the Latin word *amare* which means 'to love'.

Amateurs take part in sport for the love of it rather than for monetary reward. Successful athletes in Ancient Greece were highly trained and committed, but they needed specialist equipment and food in order to achieve their success. So, although they received no payment, and just a laurel wreath as their prize, they were supported and sponsored by their employers or wealthy individuals. Were they amateurs?

The concept of amateurism really evolved in nineteenth-century England among the privileged upper classes whose sons attended the elite public schools. (see above) At the beginning of the nineteenth century, these schools were rowdy even riotous institutions, where the boys behaved like hooligans and where the teachers had little control outside the classroom. This unruly behaviour actually reflected society as a whole, which was rather uncivilised by twenty-first century standards. We've seen how headmasters used team games to control the boys and to channel excess energy (so that they were too exhausted to cause trouble) and how, over time, games became important in their own right.

Certain wealthy upper and upper-middle class individuals who excelled at games were known as 'gentleman amateurs'. They could afford to spend time away from work playing sport for enjoyment. Working-class men, however, could not afford to miss work to play. So at a time when spectator sports (particularly association

football)were becoming popular, if a working class man was good enough, he might get a chance to play full time for payment thus becoming a working class professional. Sport became his job and for that he was very much looked down on by the 'gentleman amateurs'.

It is important to understand that from the mid–1800s, the key distinction between amateurism and professionalism was social status or class, not payment. Being an amateur was all to do with a set of unwritten rules about how life should be lived as well as how sport should be played. Not until the 1960s was the annual 'gentlemen versus players' cricket match at Lord's abolished. Today, the meaning of the word *professional* has a somewhat broader context and denotes an expert, specialised, skilful or proficient approach or outcome.

In terms of:

- getting people involved in sport (mass participation)
- winning medals (sporting excellence)
- how sport in the UK is organised and administered and
- how the government supports sport, it could be argued that over the last twenty years there has been a shift from a somewhat unreliable, inconsistent, erratic, part-time approach to a more serious, focused and expert approach.

APPLY IT!

In cricket, both 'gentleman amateurs' and working class professionals played in the same team, but they:

- had different titles ('gentleman' v 'players')
- appeared differently in the programme – Bloggs, J. (for a working class player) or J. Bloggs Esq. (for a middle or upper class player)
- ate and travelled separately
- changed separately and dressed differently
- walked on to the field of play from different entrances
- had different roles – professionals were likely to be the hard-working bowlers while the stylish batsmen were always amateur ex-public schoolboys.

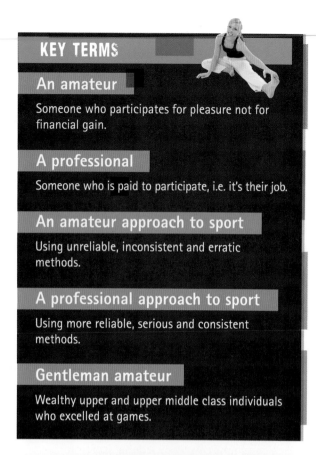

KEY TERMS

An amateur

Someone who participates for pleasure not for financial gain.

A professional

Someone who is paid to participate, i.e. it's their job.

An amateur approach to sport

Using unreliable, inconsistent and erratic methods.

A professional approach to sport

Using more reliable, serious and consistent methods.

Gentleman amateur

Wealthy upper and upper middle class individuals who excelled at games.

REMEMBER

It was class not payment that originally determined status as amateur or professional.

TASK 4

In twos discuss and list possible advantages and disadvantages of netball in the UK being an amateur rather than a professional sport. Consider effects on both the game as a whole and on individual performers.

MASS PARTICIPATION

The government recognises the negative economic impact and social consequences of low levels of participation in physical activity and puts the cost of inactivity at about £2 billion per year. The aim is to have 70% of the population being reasonably active, (that is taking 30 minutes of moderate exercise five times a week) by 2020. Initiatives and structured action plans to increase mass participation are in place and are being constantly updated and renewed (see page 279).

SPORTING EXCELLENCE

We all know that medals don't happen by accident or good fortune. Many different factors must merge in exactly the right quantities and at exactly the right time for even a chance of success on the international sporting stage. Much has been made of the professional approach by management towards winning the Rugby World Cup back in 2003. There were some outstanding and inspirational players and leaders in that squad, whose physical and psychological needs were considered with precision. In addition, lawyers, opticians, image consultants and chefs were significant members of the tour party. Not a single issue was left unconsidered or unaccounted for. And this professional approach paid off.

UK Sport (see page 265) became responsible for all Olympic and Paralympic performance-related sport in this country in April 2006 and aims to lift Team GB to fourth place in the medals table by 2012. Nowadays, much less is being left to possibility, individual prowess, passion and endeavour. There is planning, policy and an increasingly professional approach to sport.

THE ORGANISATION AND ADMINISTRATION OF SPORT IN THE UK

The current and complicated system for organising sport in the UK has evolved over the last 150 years. National Governing Bodies (such as the Amateur Swimming Association – ASA) that were founded more than a hundred years ago have taken a while to progress from the 'old school' methods of enthusiastic and dedicated volunteers. Some would argue that, in spite of progress and efforts by NGBs (see page 276) much needs to be done before the UK can boast a smooth running, proficient and professional system that matches the needs of modern day sport.

There is a system in place for the government to support sport, but how efficient and effective is it? The current Department for Culture, Media and Sport (DCMA) appoints the Minister for Sport and gives an annual grant to key organisational agencies such as UK Sport, Sport England, the Sports Council for Wales, sportscotland and the Sports Council for Northern Ireland. The Department for Education and Employment (DfEE) is responsible for Physical Education in schools.

Traditionally, while government ministers have applauded victory and have even hosted celebratory receptions in Downing Street for successful teams and individuals it hasn't really supported sport in a tangible way – specifically with funding. And certainly not when compared to governments from some other countries such as Australia. Government may have talked the talk, but did they walk the walk! Government policy (which includes initiatives and support) doesn't seem to have had sport as a priority. In fact over the years many politicians have clearly stated that sport and politics don't mix and that sport should be left to its own devices.

More recently, however, some thoughts have changed. Following Great Britain's disappointing performance in the Olympics in Barcelona in 1992 and in Atlanta in 1996, politicians have shown greater interest, involvement and support. Financial aid has been channelled into the pursuit of excellence, particularly from the National Lottery (see page 256) and the status of high-level sport has risen in line with increasingly professional attitudes and approaches. Visionary policy – and the funding to make it work – has

the potential to change the sporting culture of the UK. Will it be in time for 2012? (See page 321)

The United States of America

The USA is the most powerful nation on earth, yet just over 200 years ago it was new, young and vulnerable and occupied just a narrow strip of land on the Atlantic coast of North America.

Beyond the border lay vast areas of unclaimed land, the frontiers of which were gradually pushed westwards in fierce fights against the native Indians who did not want to give up control of their land. During the nineteenth century (1800-1900) millions of immigrants left Europe and arrived on the east coast of the USA attracted by the dream of freedom and fortune in the 'land of opportunity.' For Irish people escaping famine, eastern European Jews fleeing persecution, and countless others, going to America was a chance to make something of their lives. By 1890, half a million immigrants were arriving each year resulting in the country becoming a mixture of many different cultures and religions.

KEY TERM

Hispanic

Descendents of Spanish or Latin-American people.

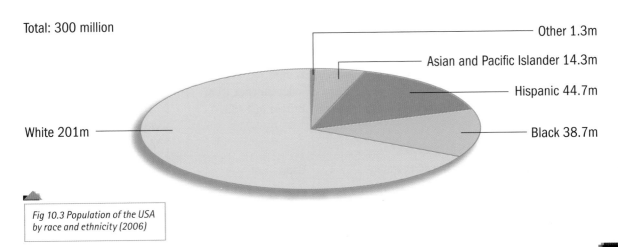

Total: 300 million
Other 1.3m
Asian and Pacific Islander 14.3m
Hispanic 44.7m
White 201m
Black 38.7m

Fig 10.3 Population of the USA by race and ethnicity (2006)

By 1900 the nation's farms and factories were producing more than any other country in the world thus increasing wealth and power. This healthy start, along with the notion of individualism, (where each person is responsible for their own destiny and success), meant that an economic system of individual enterprise evolved. The system is known as *capitalism* and is dominated by individual or shared ownership of business for profit. Capitalism encourages individuals to accumulate wealth and directly influences the nature of sport in the USA which is a gigantic profit orientated business.

The USA has a large population of around 300 million. It is the fourth largest country in the world and stretches from the Atlantic to the Pacific oceans and from Mexico to Canada. It has 50 states including Hawaii (a group of tropical islands in the Pacific Ocean) and Alaska (which is separated from the other states by Canada).

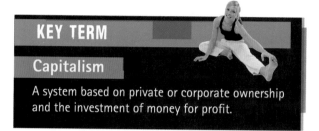

KEY TERM

Capitalism

A system based on private or corporate ownership and the investment of money for profit.

Fig 10.4 Some basic facts about the USA

- Young nation
- George Washington was first president in 1787
- Capitalist
- 300 million people approx.

The nature of sport in the USA

WIN ETHIC

Sport in the USA is a superb reflection of the country's culture. In the late 1800s, European games arrived and were quickly adapted to suit their new environment and rapidly evolving culture. Some games, such as basketball, were invented. This new 'land of opportunity' with its pioneering spirit of enterprise and drive needed games that were high scoring and action packed.

The 'win ethic' dominates sport in the USA. Coming second is not an option.

	UK	USA	Australia
Population	< 61 million	300 million	21 million
Size	250,000 sq km (approx)	9.3 million sq km (3.6 million sq m)	7.8 million sq km (3.0 million sq m)
Colonialism	Britain colonised large parts of the world to build the British Empire.	Fought for and won independence from Britain in 1783	Independence from UK in 1901 – but remained part of Commonwealth with English Queen as Monarch
Economic system	Mixed economy	Capitalism	Prosperous, mixed economy

Table 1 Key comparisons

The outcome is all that matters. The win ethic is attributed to the legendary National Football League (NFL) coach Vince Lombardi who famously asserted that: **'winning isn't everything, it is the only thing.'**

One hundred per cent commitment and sacrifice is needed by everyone. There is evidence of performers being required to perform when injured or even to use performance enhancing drugs to 'win at all costs'.

COMMERCIALISM

- In the USA sport means business! At every level it is driven by commercialism.
- Professional sport dominates in US society reflecting the country's competitive and capitalist nature.
- Both private and corporate business use sport to promote their products and to achieve goodwill.
- Even school sport attracts big sponsorship. In many states, entire towns ritualistically throng to the Friday night ball game with the marching band, pom pom girls and cheerleading squad. Young players become heroes or villains overnight and are either praised or mercilessly criticised in the local newspapers and on TV. The most promising performers compete for athletic scholarships to colleges and universities.
- College players receive top level coaching and support and are under enormous pressure to win in a highly competitive field, which is heavily funded by TV and sponsorship deals.
- The very best college athletes may be 'drafted' into professional sport which receives enormous public interest and is inextricably linked with and dependent upon commercialism.
- TV and advertising not only fund professional sport, but also govern procedures and influence its rules. Exciting bursts of sporting activity are sandwiched between commercial breaks.
- The top professional sports stars are on multi-million dollar playing contracts and can earn even more from advertising and sponsorship deals.

There are both positive and negative outcomes of commercialism in sport.

- **On the positive side,** funding gives athletes a better chance of success and promotes events which otherwise might not happen.

- **On the negative side,** only very few sports, or performers, get super rich and those who do become little more than 'mobile adverts' in an arena where money determines the location, timings and nature of sport. This can lead to the traditional values of sport being lost. But does that matter?

TASK 5

In threes discuss whether modern commercial sport does and should retain the traditional ethics of sportsmanship or have things moved beyond that? Have we returned to gladiatorial combats where anything goes as long as you can get away with it and profit it made?

One should speak to retain traditional ethics, one should speak against and one should manage the discussion, summing up at the end and writing down the key points.

VEHICLE FOR ACHIEVING AMERICAN DREAM

Rich and famous sports stars can be said to have achieved the 'American Dream'. The term 'American dream' refers to the idea that prosperity depends on your own ability and hard work, not on class. It is the dream of success, freedom of equality and of security. It is the chance of going from 'rags to riches.' or from 'zero to hero.' It assumes that anyone can be a success, irrespective of age, gender or ethnic background and sport is a particularly useful vehicle for success. For some, the dream is the opportunity to achieve greater prosperity than they could in their countries of origin; for others it is the opportunity for their children to grow up with an education and become professionals; for others still, it is the chance to be free of discrimination imposed by race, gender or ethnicity. As well as immigrants to the USA, native-born Americans can also be described as 'pursuing the American Dream' or 'living the American Dream'.

American football

ORIGINS, NATURE OF THE GAME, AND VIOLENCE

We refer to the game as 'American Football' or 'gridiron' (from the original pitch markings, widthways and lengthways forming a grid). But in the USA, it is simply football. It is the most popular spectator sport in the USA.

Physical contact is allowed between players who are not in possession of the ball and obstruction of opponents' moves by deliberate body-checking is allowed. The game involves intricate planning with carefully concealed strategic moves and very complicated tactics whereby each player has a specialist task in each play or move. It has been described as both 'mobile chess' and 'a mixture of brute force and science'.

The game developed in the prestigious 'Ivy League' universities such as Yale, Harvard, Princeton and Rutgers which are in the north eastern US. In the early 1800s there were no generally accepted rules to the game – some universities allowed running with the ball while others did not. Play was so rough and wild that the university authorities banned it for a while.

In 1869 the universities of Rutgers and Princeton competed in the first inter-collegiate game. Handling or carrying of the (then) round ball were not allowed and there were 25 players a side. By 1900 the game had developed into a violent, sensational, hazardous conflict with survival and success dependent almost entirely on physical force. Serious injury and even death were not uncommon as players wore very little protective clothing at the time. President Roosevelt intervened to clean up the game!

Characteristics of toughness, endeavour, ferocious courage and physicality which were needed to be successful in the game reflected the spirit of the early settlers to the US. American society was established and later prospered as a result of these characteristics. The 'frontier spirit' of the early pioneers and their determination to stand up to a harsh and sometimes unforgiving environment has shaped aspects of American society today.

Many Americans are known for their strong work ethic with normal holiday entitlement being below that of the UK at between 13–20 days per year.

Gradually handling and carrying of the now oval ball were introduced, along with the forward pass and the 'snap back' to the quarterback. After further adaptations, revisions and modifications American football developed its own rules, tactics and style of play.

APPLY IT!

In the 1910 season, six players were killed which resulted in changes to the rules of the game.

APPLY IT!

Just as for American football in the early 1800s, British football and rugby were also evolving with different public schools playing their own versions of 'mob' games.

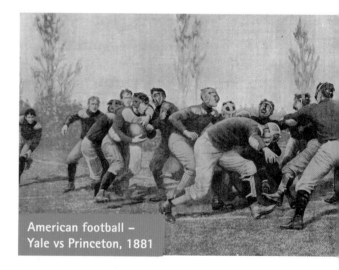

American football – Yale vs Princeton, 1881

AMERICAN FOOTBALL AND COMMERCIALISM

- American football is a multi-billion dollar business and the NFL is a group (or cartel) of companies.

- Teams are either privately owned (e.g. Chicago Bears) or run as public companies (e.g. the Green Bay Packers Foundation).
- Teams are bought or inherited and run as 'franchises.'
- Competition between TV networks for coverage rights inflates the cost of NFL franchises which sometimes relocate hundreds of miles from their traditional fan base just for profit.
- The NFL is made up of two sections: the American football conference and the National football conference
- Each of the two conferences has four divisional sections – north, south, east and west – giving eight groups in total.
- The Super Bowl is the championship game of the NFL. It takes place on 'Super Bowl Sunday' which has become the second-largest food consumption day in the US after Thanksgiving!
- In recent years the Super Bowl has become the showcase for extravagantly expensive adverts with the estimated cost of a 30 second commercial break being $2.6 million. Half time at the Super Bowl is one hour long and many TV networks take advantage of the huge TV audience by scheduling independently produced half-time entertainment.
- In recent years, the Rolling Stones, Joss Stone, Justin Timberlake, Janet Jackson (who suffered a wardrobe malfunction!) and Paul McCartney have performed during the half time show.

- The Super Bowl is much more than a football game.

Year	Cost of franchise
1920	$100
1960	$2 million
1995	$150 million
2007	$600 million

Table 2 The rising cost of owning a franchise (approximations)

APPLY IT!

In the early days of commercialism (1960s) some colleges went dangerously into debt to provide themselves with expensive stadiums. The professionals then agreed not to play on Saturday afternoons so that colleges could have their share of TV coverage.

KEY TERM

Conference
Similar to a league.

USA – The National Football League (NFL, 2007)				
	East	North	South	West
AFC	Buffalo Bills	Baltimore Ravens	Houston Texans	Denver Broncos
	Miami Dolphins	Cincinnati Bengals	Indianapolis Colts	Kansas City Chiefs
	New England Patriots	Cleveland Browns	Jacksonville Jaguars	Oakland Raiders
	New York Jets	Pittsburgh Steelers	Tennessee Titans	San Diego Chargers
	East	North	South	West
NFC	Dallas Cowboys	Chicago Bears	Atlanta Falcons	Arizona Cardinals
	New York Giants	Detroit Lions	Carolina Panthers	St. Louis Rams
	Philadelphia Eagles	Green Bay Packers	New Orleans Saints	San Francisco 49ers
	Washington Redskins	Minnesota Vikings	Tampa Bay Buccaneers	Seattle Seahawks

Table 3 NFL teams 2007

KEY TERMS

Franchise

The business that own runs and has voting rights for a team.

APPLY IT!

The game of American football was redesigned back in the 1960s to suit television and since has had many and regular commercial breaks.

- Young nation
- Sparsely populted: 21 million people
- Colonial influence
- Immigration

Fig 10.5 Some basic facts about Australia

TASK 6

Read this list of pre-requisites that a venue must have in order to be considered to host the Super Bowl. Which of them are to do with commercialism?

- Space for 10 photo trailers and 40 television trucks.
- 600,000 square feet of exhibit space for fan events.
- 50,000 square feet of space for news media.
- Stadium with 65,000 seats or more.
- Large, luxury hotel for teams and NFL.
- Enough 'quality' hotel rooms within a one-hour drive for 35% of the stadium's capacity.
- Average high of 50°F (10°C) in February, unless game to be played in indoor stadium.
- Separate practice facilities for each team.

Australia

Australia is a comparatively young nation and until a few hundred years ago, it was inhabited solely by its indigenous aboriginal peoples. In 1770 the James Cook sailed into Botany Bay and claimed Australia as a colony for Britain.

Australia is massive and it takes 6 hours to fly from Perth to Sydney, i.e. from one side of the country to the other across three time zones. It is sparsely populated with just 21 million people compared to 300 million in the USA and 60 million in Britain. Australia consists of six states and two territories. With the vast majority of the country uninhabitable, the majority live in one of the eight capital cities which are all located close to the coast. Eighty-five per cent of the population live in only just over 3% of the land.

	State	Capital city
States	New South Wales	Sydney
	Queensland	Brisbane
	South Australia	Adelaide
	Tasmania	Hobart
	Victoria	Melbourne
	Western Australia	Perth
Territories	Australian Capital Territory	Canberra
	Northern Territory	Darwin

Table 4 Australia's states, territories and capital cities.

TASK 7

Download a map of Australia for your file. Add states and main cities if they are not already identified.

The Union Jack (Fig. 10.6) is still part of the Australian flag as a symbol of British colonialism. When colonialists arrived over 200 years ago they brought the British way of life, government, education and judicial systems plus sports and games with them (see Fig. 10.7). Most schools have sports afternoons, and many school colours in the English tradition. Australia adopted many English games (unlike the US where there were adaptations and inventions) and a great sporting rivalry between the two countries developed which continues today. Perhaps the passionate desire for victory has been reversed in more recent years with England now fighting for victory against its former outpost.

In 1901 Australia became an independent commonwealth country of the British Empire. Although historically, Australia is steeped in colonial values, we should not underestimate the assimilation of new culture and identity that has taken place.

Captain Cook's arrival in 1770 was followed in 1788 by an influx of British convicts. Throughout the nineteenth century (1800–1900), the population of Australia continued to grow with more convicts and European immigrants transported to the colony, and then the arrival of Chinese seeking their fortunes in the gold rush of the 1850s. After the Second World War (post–1945) the Australian government launched a massive immigration campaign due to the perceived need to 'populate or perish'. Most newcomers were from Britain, Ireland, Greece, Italy, Germany, Yugoslavia and the Netherlands. Britons who emigrated for a better life 'Down Under' via a £10 one-way passage were collectively known as *Ten Pound Poms*.

Since the abolition of the white Australian policy in the early 1970s multiculturalism has been promoted. During the 1970s, 90,000 Indo-Chinese refugees from Vietnam and Cambodia resettled in Australia. The largest groups (of the 23.1% Australians born overseas) are currently from the United Kingdom, New Zealand, Italy, Vietnam and China. Between 2005 and 2006 more than 131,000 people from Asia and Oceania migrated to Australia. For the last 40 years Australia has been committed to a policy of multiculturalism – and more recently has embarked on a policy of reconciliation – aimed at ending the discrimination against the Aboriginal people which started in the colonial period.

APPLY IT!

Unlike America which invented its own sports because it wanted to be different and isolated, Australia was happy to adopt traditional British sports such as cricket and rugby.

Fig 10.6 The Union Jack in the corner of the Australian flag is evidence of the country's colonial roots

Fig 10.7 Stages of Australian immigration

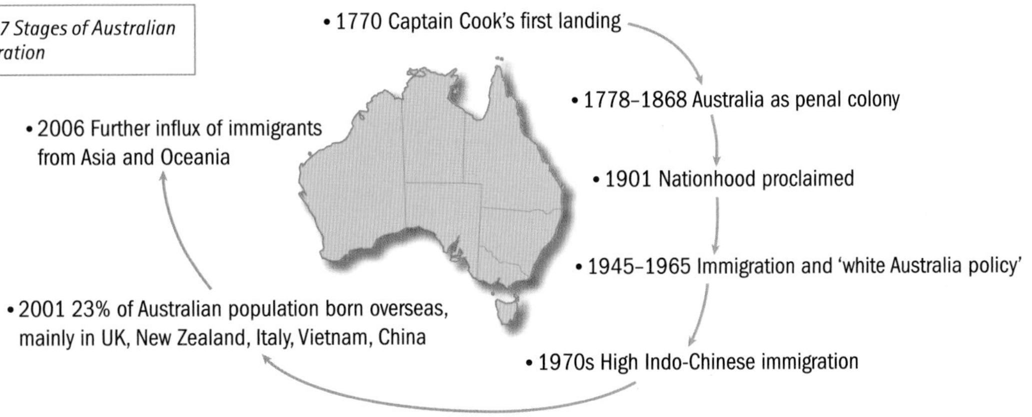

• 1770 Captain Cook's first landing

• 1778–1868 Australia as penal colony

• 1901 Nationhood proclaimed

• 1945–1965 Immigration and 'white Australia policy'

• 1970s High Indo-Chinese immigration

• 2001 23% of Australian population born overseas, mainly in UK, New Zealand, Italy, Vietnam, China

• 2006 Further influx of immigrants from Asia and Oceania

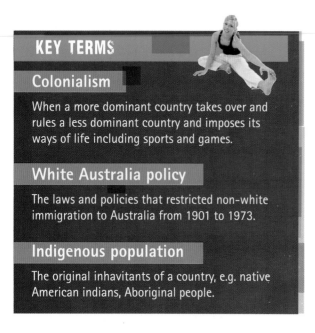

KEY TERMS

Colonialism

When a more dominant country takes over and rules a less dominant country and imposes its ways of life including sports and games.

White Australia policy

The laws and policies that restricted non-white immigration to Australia from 1901 to 1973.

Indigenous population

The original inhavitants of a country, e.g. native American indians, Aboriginal people.

The nature of sport in Australia

SPORT AS A NATIONAL PREOCCUPATION

- Sport is an integral part of Australia and its people and has helped to shape the identity of this relatively young country.
- Sport in Australia is a nationasl passion or even obsession.
- Census data shows that 90% of Australians participate in sport and that sport accounts for 15% of TV time.
- When England beat Australia at the Oval back in September 2005, 12.5% of this country watched. By contrast, when the winning horse and jockey crossed the line in the prestigious Melbourne Cup in 2004 nearly 90% of Australia watched!

- Sporting articles appear regularly on the front page of national newspapers and nearly everyone is either directly involved in or at least interested in sport. Not surprising when you consider that the country gains remarkable sporting success per head of its population.
- The Sydney Olympics of 2000 were an international triumph and Australia enjoys numerous victories in world events with particularly strong teams in cricket, hockey, netball, rugby league, rugby union and also performs well in cycling, rowing and swimming.

WHY IS IT THAT SPORT IS SUCH A HIGH STATUS NATIONAL PREOCCUPATION IN AUSTRALIA?

To find the answers to this we need to look at Australian society and culture.

- **The manliness, strength and 'bush culture'** that shaped Australian society was suited to certain rugged, physically demanding sports.
- **Australia's favourable climate** has an enormous positive impact. Whether participating as a youngster for enjoyment, an adult maintaining a healthy lifestyle, an elite athlete in training, a parent on the sideline or a paying spectator – good weather helps!

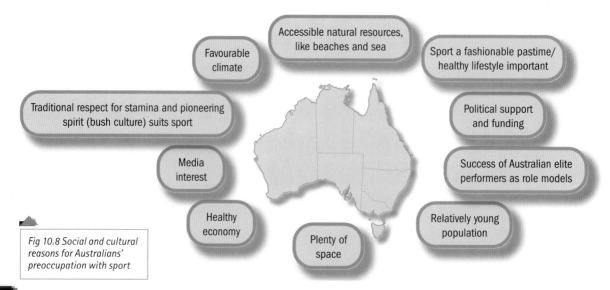

Favourable climate

Accessible natural resources, like beaches and sea

Sport a fashionable pastime/ healthy lifestyle important

Traditional respect for stamina and pioneering spirit (bush culture) suits sport

Political support and funding

Media interest

Success of Australian elite performers as role models

Healthy economy

Plenty of space

Relatively young population

Fig 10.8 Social and cultural reasons for Australians' preoccupation with sport

- **The outdoor life** is the norm in this health conscious society where adequate space and natural resources such as beaches and sea are readily accessible.
- **Political support** for sport is also strong. Governments invest heavily in sport. It is a vote catcher. Political parties, and the nation as a whole, benefit when Australian sport stars succeed on the international stage.
- **A tradition of success** provides role models, raises the profile of the country, proves Australia is a progressive 21st century nation and unites the relatively small and young population with a 'feel good' factor.
- **Sport is fashionable and encouraged.** Just as in the UK, there is a growing obesity problem in Australia.
- **Australia has a healthy economy** with a significant rise in disposable income over the last 25 years resulting in the majority being able to afford the necessary specialist kit and equipment to take part and watch.
- Also **Australia is an egalitarian society** (which promotes equality) where sport was and is for all. Inequalities of opportunity, provision and esteem are less of an issue than in the UK.
- **Sport and PE have high status** in schools and the media supports and profits from coverage. All in all, Australia and sport suit each other very well.

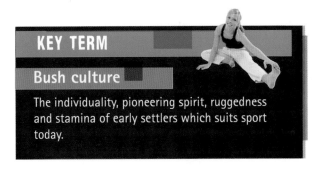

KEY TERM

Bush culture

The individuality, pioneering spirit, ruggedness and stamina of early settlers which suits sport today.

'Australian rules' football

ORIGINS

- This game is also known as 'Aussie Rules' or simply 'footy' (pronounced 'fudy'), and is a game that clearly reflects Australian society and culture.

- Clips from Sky Sports or the odd YouTube video sometimes give the wrong impression and elicit comments such as:

   'There don't seem to be many rules.'
   'It's just a big punch up on a cricket pitch.'
   'It's a bit like rugby with dodgy shorts and sleeveless vests.'

- None of these comments accurately represents the game, however, which is hard and physical but with a solid rule structure and strong ethos of fair play.
- The game is played on large cricket 'ovals' (lots of available space), with nine officials. There are 22 players per side, many of whom often run up to 15 miles during a game.
- Argument continues about the game's exact origins, but whatever the details, the game was the 'idea' of English born Tom Wills and was originally intended as winter training for cricketers.
- Most argue that the game is genuinely Australian and that Wills combined an aboriginal leaping game with what he had seen in the English public schools.
- Others say that it is simply a mixture of Rugby and Gaelic football. As Gaelic football was not codified by the Gaelic Athletic Association (GAA) until 30 years after Wills' Melbourne Rules were established, however, such a strong Irish link seems tenuous. In fact, the rules of 'footy' were established before most other forms of modern football.
- The game is more popular than rugby union, rugby league or association football (soccer) in most states and there has been a 42% increase in participation from 2001 to 2005.
- Although the game has not taken a very firm hold overseas and overseas players are a very

TASK 8

Go to YouTube.com and watch a few clips of Australian Rules football. Would you describe the game as hard, spectacular, unique, exciting and exhilarating? What evidence do you see of commercialism and the impact of the media on the game?

small percentage of players worldwide the game is growing in more than 20 countries.

- It is the fourth most played team sport in Australia after netball, soccer and cricket.
- Whilst making up only 3% of the Australian population, aboriginals account for approximately 16% of the players in the AFL elite competition.

FACTORS SHAPING DEVELOPMENT OF THE GAME

Various factors have shaped the game's development.

- Australians living or travelling abroad have spread the news
- Occasional festival exhibition matches attract interest.
- Many players have also converted from other football codes and sports because of the money and celebrity status that the game attracts.
- As the game is taught and played in Australian schools and has extensive pathway programmes, interest and involvement among young people has grown.
- In more recent years, with the introduction of a truly national competition at the elite level, and the subsequent increased exposure in the electronic and print media, the game has grown in what have previously been considered rugby states (New South Wales and Queensland).
- The game appeals to all and can be played successfully by both sexes and by all body types, from 6'10" ruckmen weighing 16 stone, to 5'6" rovers weighing 9 stone.
- The Super Rules competition for players over 35 years of age, which limits body contact, has grown expediently, as have the participant numbers in junior and senior female competitions.

COMMERCIALISM AND IMPACT OF MEDIA

- Australian rules football is the most highly attended spectator sport in Australia and has blossomed as a result of commercialism.
- Interest in the game is at an all-time high.
- Today it is a multi-million (Australian) dollar business, with a National Competition and an extensive network of local and regional leagues and competitions.

'Australian rules' football

- Similar to American football, it is a good product for media promotion with regular commercial breaks.
- Business enterprise and financial backing have helped the sport which has produced high status stars who earn huge fees from advertising, sponsorships, endorsements and other commercial ventures.

TAKE IT FURTHER

Research the Australian Football League on the internet. How many elite clubs are there? How does it operate? Where are the clubs situated? Is there a geographical spread or pockets of popularity? What do the players earn? How do earnings compare with Premier League Football and rugby union and league in the UK and with American football?

TAKE IT FURTHER

Research Australia's record in the Rugby Union World Cup; in rugby league, cricket and more recently, association football (soccer). What was its position in the Athens (2004) and Sydney (2000) Olympics? What about Beijing (2008)?

Exam Café

Relax, refresh, result!

Refresh your memory

Revision checklist for: Sport and Culture – sport and physical activity as a reflection of the culture in which it exists.

You should now know and understand about:

▷ Ethnic sports and games that are still played in the UK.

▷ The role of nineteenth century Public Schools in promoting and organising sports and games.

▷ The relatively recent move from the traditional amateur approach to a more professional approach to sport in the UK.

▷ Characteristics of the USA as a young, capitalist nation with a relatively large population.

▷ The nature of sport in the USA – as related to the 'win ethic' commercialism and as a vehicle for achieving 'the American Dream.'

▷ American Football – its origins and the nature of the game.

▷ Characteristics of Australia as a young, sparsely populated nation where there is a colonial influence and preoccupation with sport.

▷ Australian rules football – its origins and factors which shaped its development including the media and commercialism.

REVISE AS YOU GO!

1. Name one single sport occasion and one multi-sport festival that could be classed as 'surviving ethnic sports' in the UK.
2. Identify three characteristics of surviving ethnic sports in the UK.
3. List four ways that nineteenth century public schools helped to promote and organise sports and games.
4. Explain the meaning of each of the following terms: amateur, professional, an amateur approach and a professional approach.
5. State the current population of the USA and identify two key characteristics of the country.
6. Explain what is meant by the term 'American Dream' and how this can be achieved through sport.
7. Describe the game of American football and explain its popularity in the USA.
8. State the current population of Australia and identify two key characteristics of the country.
9. Australian rules football is also known by two other names. What are they?
10. Identify factors which have shaped the development of Australian rules football.

Get the result!

Examination question

Explain how public schools helped to promote and organise sports and games in the nineteenth century (1800–1900). (5 marks)

examiner's tips

- As one of your four shorter questions (rather than your long 10-mark question), it is likely to be marked with a traditional 'one point = one mark' mark scheme rather than with a 'levels of response' mark scheme.
- For each relevant explanation you give, you will therefore get one mark.
- You need to try to get at least five different points in your answer.
- Note that the command word is 'explain', meaning that you should develop your ideas, not just give short bullet points.
- Keep in mind that you must be clear about HOW public schools helped to both promote and organise sports and games. Don't just tell the examiner all you know about the public schools – that would be irrelevant or vague.

A 'C' grade answer

Ex-public schoolboys helped to promote sports and games after they left school in various ways. They took them up to university and on leaving university they went into a variety of different influential careers. For example they became vicars or army officers.

Examiner says:

Everything written here is correct. The focus is rather narrow in that it deals just with how public schoolboys spread team games after they left school. A stronger, more balanced answer would have included some aspects of the schools themselves such as the fact that they had regular inter-house and inter-school fixtures or that because they were boarding schools there was a lot of 'free' time for playing and practising games.

An 'A' grade answer

Nineteenth century public schools (along with various changes in society) had a major impact on promoting and organising the sports and games that are still played today.

A lot of it was down to available money. These were quite wealthy schools that could afford special kit and equipment

Examiner says:

effective introductio

such as boats for rowing. They could also prepare and construct purpose-built facilities such as pitches (they usually had a lot of space) and swimming baths. The money also meant that professional cricket coaches could be employed which raised standards of play.

It was the boys themselves who did most of the organising of games. They ran the inter-house and even inter-school teams. They then took this knowledge and experience — along with their games — to university with them.

Contemporary sporting issues

CHAPTER 11: PART I

Contemporary sporting issues impacting upon young people's aspirations and their regular participation in physical activity in the UK

Since the publication of OCR A Level PE specification, UKSI has ceased to exist. It's work is now carried out by the National Institutes of Sport.

LEARNING OBJECTIVES

Parts I, II and III

At the end of all three parts you will be able to demonstrate knowledge and an understanding of:

* Public, private and voluntary funding (including the National Lottery)
* UK Sport; the National Institutes of Sport and home country organisations such as Sport England
* Current government and national governing body initiatives that influence and promote participation in physical activity
* The sports development pyramid and the continuum from mass participation to sporting excellence
* Opportunity, provision and esteem – in the context of mass participation and sporting excellence
* Social and cultural factors impacting on participation by certain groups in the UK such as people with disabilities and young people
* Measures to increase participation and sporting excellence
* The issues of drugs and violence in sport
* Sport, sponsorship and the Media
* The Olympic Games.

Part I

In Part I you will learn about all the points above, except the last three: Drugs and violence; Sport, sponsorship and the Media, and The Olympic Games – these are covered in Parts II and III.

This is the first part of a three-part chapter entitled 'Contemporary sporting issues', which is divided into three parts:

- Part I: Contemporary sporting issues impacting upon young people's aspirations and their regular participation in physical activity in the UK.
- Part II: Drugs, the Media and sponsorship in sport.
- Part III: The Olympic Games.

INTRODUCTION

There is a lot happening in this chapter! We will start by looking at how physical activity is funded in the UK; then at some organisations that influence our two big issues – *mass participation* (taking part) and *sporting excellence* (getting to the top as an elite performer).

We will then consider a number of issues relating to sport. Firstly, the factors affecting mass participation and sporting excellence. This will

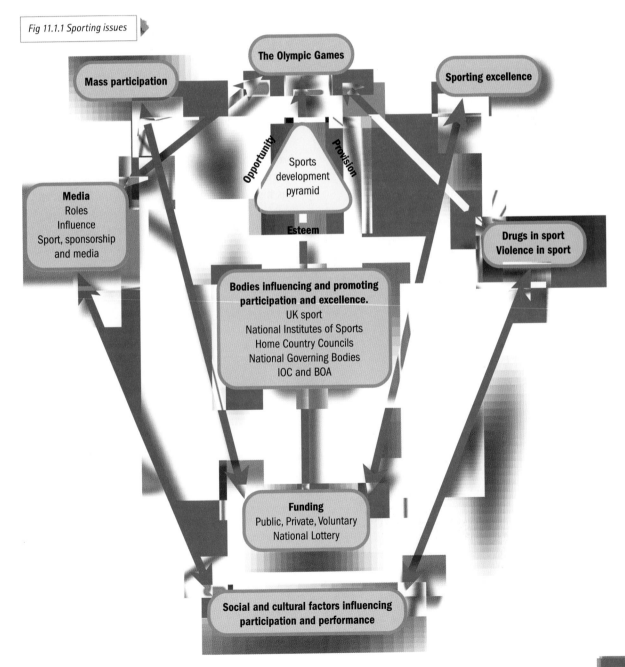

Fig 11.1.1 Sporting issues

The Olympic Games

Mass participation

Sporting excellence

Media
Roles
Influence
Sport, sponsorship and media

Opportunity

Sports development pyramid

Provision

Esteem

**Drugs in sport
Violence in sport**

Bodies influencing and promoting participation and excellence.
UK sport
National Institutes of Sports
Home Country Councils
National Governing Bodies
IOC and BOA

Funding
Public, Private, Voluntary
National Lottery

Social and cultural factors influencing participation and performance

include identifying the opportunity, provision and esteem of certain societal groups such as people with disabilities. What stops or helps these groups taking part and/or winning medals?

Part II will continue with a study of two issues that show sporting deviance: violence (by both performers and spectators), and drug taking by some performers. Sponsorship and the Media will also be examined in terms of positive and negative effects on sport.

Part III will have an analysis of the Modern Olympic Games – including its background, aims and four-yearly format. Two key organisational agencies involved with the Games – the International Olympic Committee (IOC) and the British Olympic Association (BOA) will be reviewed.

You need to be able to explain the increased commercialisation of the Olympic Games since it was hosted by the USA in Los Angeles back in 1984 and describe potential benefits and drawbacks to Britain hosting the 2012 Olympic Games.

Finally we will consider how the Olympic Games can increase the reputation of a country both in the eyes and hearts of the people of the host nation and in the eyes of the rest of the world.

REMEMBER

Deviance in sport means seriously and deliberately breaking sporting rules or customs.

Funding of physical activity

Sport makes money and costs money. Gold medals cost a lot of money! Fig 11.1.2 shows the three key types of funding that you need to be aware of.

British politicians have traditionally looked on sport as a low status activity. In the UK, sport has historically received insufficient government (public) funding, resulting in the need for cash from private and voluntary sources. Increasingly, however, the vote-winning potential of providing quality facilities for all and of achieving international success has led to some changes of political heart. Today, it would be more than a politician's position in the opinion polls was

APPLY IT!

England's failure to qualify for the Euro 2008 football tournament meant a loss of an estimated £2 billion to business.

| Fig 11.1.2 The funding 'pie' |

Public
(funding from government
and local authorities
including National Lottery)

Private
(funding from businesses,
companies and investors
often by way of sponsorship)

Voluntary
(funding from donations or
charities or private clubs)

worth to voice the view that sport was a waste or misuse of government money (even if they secretly thought it!).

'We are...funding...£34 million for a new national sports foundation...(which) ...will bring together public and private finance for new local sports facilities and grassroots participation'.

Gordon Brown (during his Budget speech as Chancellor of the Exchequer in 2006)

KEY TERMS

Public funding

Funding from the government and local authorities including the National Lottery

Private funding

Funding from businesses, companies and investors whose main aim is to make money and who fund sport to improve their status and profit

Voluntary funding

Funding from donations or charities or local clubs that exist for their members

EXAM TIP

Any organisations or initiatives that are named in the specification could be directly examined. If an organisation or initiative is NOT specifically named in the specification it will NOT be directly examined – though relevant knowledge could get you credit in more general questions. An example of this would be mentioning the work of School Sport Coordinators (SSCOs), when answering a question initiatives that promote participation.

EXAM TIP

Note that public funding includes the National Lottery. As the Lottery Sports Fund (among other things) funds the World Class Pathway Programme (see page 260), UK Sport, (see page 264) the National Institutes of Sport (see page 265) and the home country organisations such as Sport England (see page 268), these are all important too!

Funding for sport is available from a wide range of sources, including the National Lottery – see Fig 11.1.3

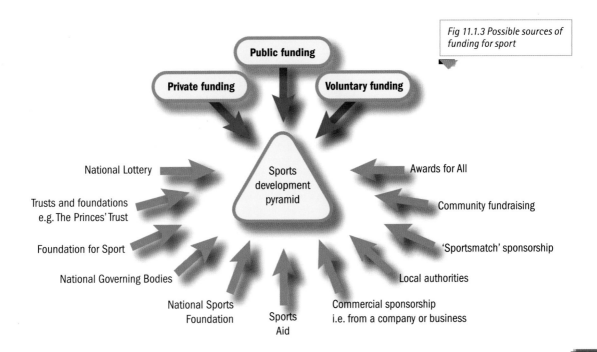

Fig 11.1.3 Possible sources of funding for sport

Public funding

Private funding

Voluntary funding

National Lottery

Trusts and foundations e.g. The Princes' Trust

Foundation for Sport

National Governing Bodies

National Sports Foundation

Sports Aid

Sports development pyramid

Awards for All

Community fundraising

'Sportsmatch' sponsorship

Local authorities

Commercial sponsorship i.e. from a company or business

Public sector			
Central Government		**Local Authorities**	
In	**Out**	**In**	**Out**
From: • Taxes • Gaming duties • National Lottery ticket sales	Cost of: • Local Authorities • Awards and grants e.g. to UK Sport • Sportsmatch sponsorship • Sport for Armed Forces	From: • Government • Council taxes • Grants from central government and lottery • Business/ commercial sources • Charges for facility use	Cost of: • Schools – staff and facilities • Community sport facilities • Grants to local clubs

Private sector	
In	**Out**
From: • Business profit • Ticket sales • Sale of TV rights	Cost of: • Sponsoring of individuals and/or teams • Running and maintaining private sports clubs and facilities • Buying TV rights • Sport Aid grants • National Sports Foundation

Voluntary sector	
In	**Out**
From: • National Lottery grants and awards • Awards for All (lottery grant scheme) • Sportsmatch grants • Local authority grants • National Governing Bodies • Fundraising • Foundation for Sport and the Arts • National Sports Foundation • Commercial sponsorship • Members' subscriptions	Cost of: • Facility building, maintenance and development • Developing performers (e.g. coaching fees) • Running the club

Table 1 Funding that comes in and goes out of the public, private and voluntary sectors

TAKE IT FURTHER

Using the Internet research the following. What do they do? What is their aim? Write up a couple of sentences on each of them for your file:

- National Sports Foundation
- Foundation for Sport and the Arts
- Sportsmatch
- The Prince's Trust
- Awards for All.

You will not get **direct** questions on these in the exam as they are not stated in the specification; however, reading and researching around the subject of sports funding will increase your knowledge and understanding, and provide examples that you can use in discussion-type exam answers.

In the Budget on 22 March 2006, Chancellor Gordon Brown announced additional 2012 performance funding of £200 million, an average of £33.5 million per year. Will this be enough to reach the 'ultimate goal' (laid down by UK Sport) – of achieving fourth place in the 2012 Olympic medal table, and first in the Paralympic medal table?

There are positive and potentially negative features of sports funding in the UK. The following table lists these.

Positive	Negative
National Lottery money available for excellence and mass participation.	Lottery money needs to be evenly distributed.
Some clubs are very wealthy, e.g. Manchester United.	There is not financial equality between clubs.
Since turning professional in 1995, Rugby Union can compete on more even financial terms with Southern hemisphere sides.	When ambition outweighs financial resources, smaller clubs can go bankrupt.
Having won the 2012 Olympic bid the government has put more money into sport.	Limited Government aid (in comparison to some other countries) means that commercialism has a greater role to play in British sport. This can lead to lack of control by clubs over their own management and destiny.
Large sums of money can be made through sporting links with the Media.	National Governing Bodies (NGBs) need to be careful when 'selling' their sport for commercial reasons. They can lose their autonomy.
If a performer fails to qualify for lottery funding there are other sources available (see Fig 11.1.2)	The complexity of funding sources has led to an imbalance of provision for different sporting activities and for individuals on different levels of the sports development pyramid (see Fig 11.1.20).

Table 2

The national lottery

THE DEPARTMENT FOR CULTURE, MEDIA AND SPORT

'We are committed to supporting British Sport at every level and have invested some £3 billion in sport since 1997. Winning the right to host the 2012 Olympic Games and Paralympic Games has given us an exciting opportunity to transform sport in Britain'.
The Department for Culture, Media and Sport

The Department for Culture, Media and Sport (DCMS) is the government department responsible for sport. It decides and organises how lottery grants are distributed through organisations such as UK Sport (see page 264) and the Olympic Lottery Distributor.

REMEMBER

The Department of Culture, Media and Sport (DCMS) is the government department responsible for sport.

Since 1994, the National Lottery has had a huge impact on British sport and is now the primary source of sports funding in the UK. For every pound spent on a Lottery ticket, 28p goes towards 'Good Causes' such as sport. Fewer people buy lottery tickets now than when the lottery was first established, so the amount of lottery money generated through sales has declined. For example, *sportscotland* received £32 million in 1998 and around £18 million in 2006–2007.

The Lottery Sports Fund provides grants of around £200 million annually. These grants go to and are distributed by UK Sport and the four home country sports councils (see p x), to support and encourage both mass participation and sporting excellence.

Before the National Lottery, both up and coming and established elite performers relied on parents and families, part-time work, NGBs, donations from private companies and money from charities to 'buy into' the chance of international sporting success. On the other hand, performers from certain other countries, such as France, were well funded by their governments. It is widely accepted that Britain would never have achieved the number of medals at either the Athens (2004) or Sydney (2000) Olympic Games without the National Lottery.

The National Lottery and Excellence – The World Class Pathway Programme and the World Class Events Programmes are funded by the Lottery Sports Fund.

THE WORLD CLASS PATHWAY PROGRAMME

This was introduced by UK Sport in April 2006. The programme gives three different levels of support to elite Olympic and Paralympic performers:

1. **World Class Podium:** If you are likely to be a finalist or medallist in the next Olympic Games you will be receiving World Class Podium funding now. It is for sports with a real chance of medal success at 'the next' Olympic or Paralympic Games. Senior performance managers, support senior performance coaches and personal coaches work with podium performers.

   Whether or not a sport receives podium funding depends on:
   - results at the last Olympic Games
   - competitive record
   - probable medal capability
   - its ability to consistently produce athletes through the Pathway.

   National Governing Bodies distribute the funding to performers through athlete personal awards.

Athlete Personal Awards (APAs): These are from UK Sport, but given to athletes by their NGB. The money is used for support such as coaching, training camps, competition and sport science. Elite athletes can also apply for a subsistence award towards essential personal living and sporting costs during training and competition.

TASK 1

Discuss the advantages and disadvantages of World Class Podium funding being based on results at the last Olympic Games.

2. **World Class Development**: This is for performers who show performance evidence that they are about six years away from a likely medal – so success at the next but one Olympics. Importantly and unusually, in the years leading up to 2012, performers can qualify for this funding even if medal winning potential is slim, as long as they are likely to be 'competitive,' at the Games.

3. Gifted and motivated performers who have the world class talent, traits and characteristics to seriously compete on the world stage are carefully selected by their NGBs for this level of funding. It is for performers who are a maximum of eight years from a medal.

REMEMBER

In 2007, just over 1,000 athletes were funded through the World Class Pathway programme.

Case study: UK Athletics (UKA)
Membership and receipt of funding from the UKA World Class Programme (at podium, development and talent levels) is conditional upon athletes signing an agreement. This agreement requires World Class standards in all areas of athletes' sporting lives from meeting challenging performance targets to managing themselves professionally e.g. with the Media.

Athletes undergo an end-of-season performance review based on published performance standards that could result in a change in funding status either up or down.

THE WORLD CLASS EVENTS PROGRAMME

This supports the bidding for, and staging of major sporting events in the UK. Currently, UK Sport distributes approximately £3.3 million of lottery funding each year to the world class events programme which boasts the opportunity of bringing sporting, social, cultural and economic benefits to the host nation via major sporting events.

TASK 2

In twos think of one sporting, one social, one cultural and one economic benefit to Britain of hosting a major sporting event such as the rugby, hockey or football world cup finals.

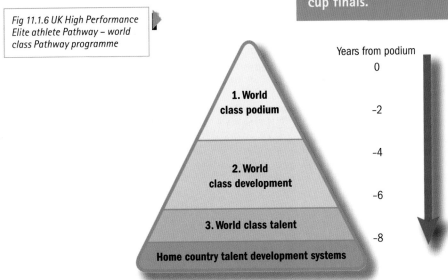

Fig 11.1.6 UK High Performance Elite athlete Pathway – world class Pathway programme

THE NATIONAL LOTTERY AND MASS PARTICIPATION

As part of their work to increase mass participation in sport and physical recreation, home country councils such as Sport England (see page 265) invest in a range of community and national projects. Funding goes towards helping sports clubs, community schools, local government and local NGBs. Over £1 billion of grant aid has been awarded to thousands of sporting projects throughout the UK since the lottery was established. Increasing participation by young people and improving sports provision in schools is a priority along with supporting deprived areas, ethnic minorities, people with disabilities and women, via Sport Action Zones.

Bodies influencing and promoting participation and excellence in physical activity

Sport in the UK is influenced by a wide range of organisational bodies including national and local government, sports councils, National Governing Bodies (NGBs) of sport, special interest groups and local schools and clubs. Fig 11.1.7 is one way of illustrating this. It shows a complicated and inter-connected system that has evolved over many years as both participation and competition have grown.

The UK has a decentralised system of sports administration which means that power is not centrally held but spread out. Grass roots clubs and local associations are self-governing, with central government providing very little in terms of overall sporting policy.

In recent years and particularly since the awarding of the 2012 Olympic Games to Britain there has been a period of organisational change and attempted improvement. Note the following points:

- UK Sport (see page 265) is particularly keen to minimise organisational inefficiency in the system as a whole.

Positive	Negative
Limited outside interference allows sporting associations to build on tradition and to use their initiative to meet needs	A decentralised system can be inefficient with everyone 'doing their own thing' without coordinated focus.
Historically, keen and committed volunteers have run sport in the UK. From small local clubs to NGBs and major associations, unpaid staff have run the system.	With no overall policy, a lack of professional training and very few full-time paid administrators, there has been inconsistency of effectiveness both in, and between organisations. Excessive bureaucracy has also been an issue in the past.

Table 3 Positive and negative consequences of a decentralised sporting system

- NGBs are also making improvements to their management and systems.
- While small private clubs continue to depend on volunteers, the larger and more determined clubs and associations are taking an increasingly businesslike and professional approach.

The structure of sport in the UK, although complex, caters for all levels from grass roots recreational activity to elite sportsmen and women who represent the UK on the world stage.

KEY TERMS

Organisational bodies

Organisations or agencies that run sport.

Decentralised

When parts of a system are self governing or when power is not centrally held.

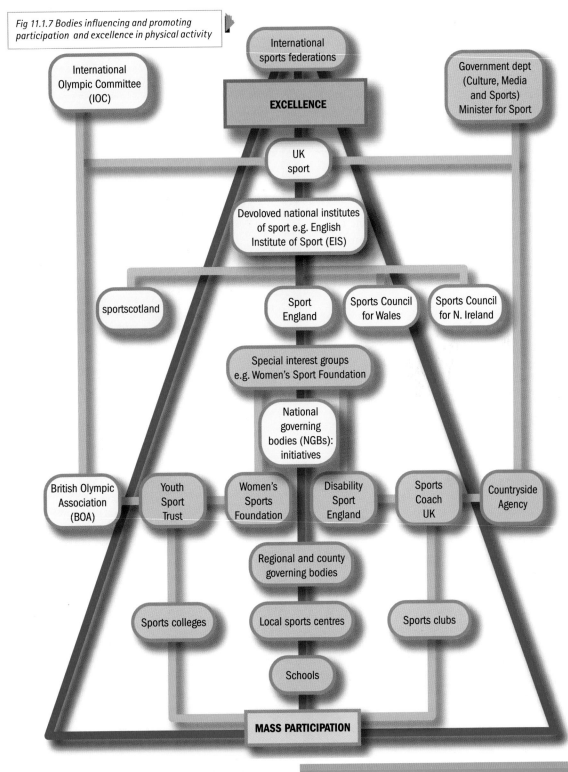

Fig 11.1.7 Bodies influencing and promoting participation and excellence in physical activity

Grass roots clubs

Community clubs that exist for people at the base of the participation pyramid – see page 261.

EXAM TIP

The 'bodies' in the yellow boxes are directly mentioned in the specification and so can be directly examined.

TAKE IT FURTHER

Keep up to date by signing up to receive a free weekly online/email newsletter from UK Sport at www.uksport.gov.uk.

UK Sport

UK Sport wants world class success! It is responsible for developing elite sport in the UK and is funded by the Department for Culture, Media and Sport (DCMS). In 2006-2007, UK Sport received just over £53m from the government.

REMEMBER

The World Class Pathway Programme, which gives financial support on three different levels.

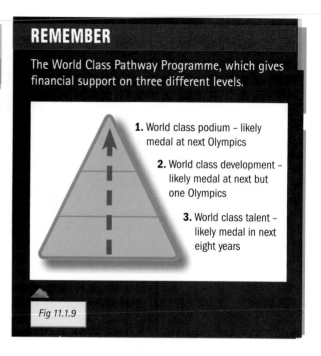

1. World class podium – likely medal at next Olympics

2. World class development – likely medal at next but one Olympics

3. World class talent – likely medal in next eight years

Fig 11.1.9

Fig 11.1.8 Key bodies that influence and promote mass participation and sporting excellence in the UK

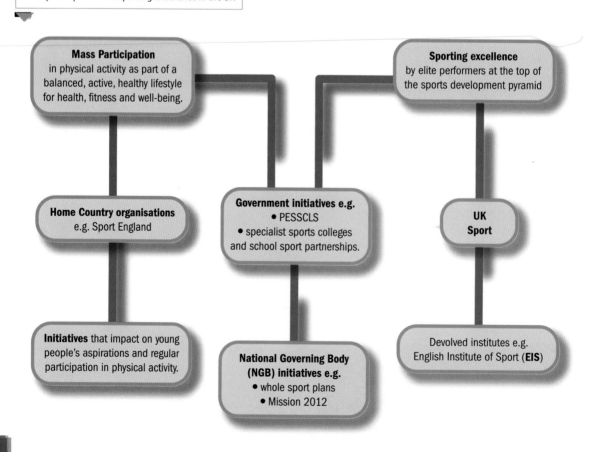

WHAT DOES UK SPORT DO?

It:

- manages and distributes public investment and National Lottery funding through the World Class Pathway Programme
- promotes ethical standards of behaviour through its athlete-centred anti-doping programme called 100% ME – see 'Drugs in sport' in Part II, page 310
- coordinates programmes to attract major sporting events
- manages the UK's international sporting relationships
- helps elite performers develop a 'performance lifestyle'
- runs a World Class Coaching Strategy to support world class coaches
- coordinates other organisations in the UK encouraging administrative efficiency.
- works with the home country sports councils (e.g. The Sports Council for Wales) and other agencies to achieve its goals
- is responsible for the strategic direction of the the National Institutes of Sport e.g. English Institute of Sport (EIS) (see page 267)
- launched Mission 2012 to support, monitor and evaluate the work of the NGBs
- The Talented Athlete Funds Scholarship Scheme (TASS).

KEY TERM

Performance lifestyle

A support service designed for athletes which helps them to create a winning environment. It can include:

- lifestyle support (including time management, budgeting and finance, dealing with the Media, sponsorship and promotion activities and negotiation and conflict management)
- career and employment advice (including: work placements and planning a career after sport)
- guidance on education (e.g. regarding courses, choices and getting a flexible study programme).

TALENTED ATHLETE SCHOLARSHIP SCHEME (TASS)

- TASS is for athletes who want to combine sport and education. It is a government funded programme managed by UK Sport where athletes are nominated by either their NGBs or Higher Education Institution/ university.
- TASS Scholarships are worth up to £3,000 and are for young people up to 24 years old who are studying at least 50 percent of a full time higher level course
- TASS Bursaries are also worth up to £3,000 and are for 16- to 18-year-olds who are in further education or starting out in employment.
- TASS 2012 Scholarships are for sports people with the potential to be a medallist in the 2012 Olympics or Paralympics.

National Institutes of Sport

ENGLISH INSTITUTE OF SPORT

'We have the talented athletes who can be winners on the world stage and we must give them the best services and facilities in the world so they have the best possible chance to succeed'.

Sir Steve Redgrave (five times Olympic gold medal winner)

WHAT ARE THE NATIONAL INSTITUTES OF SPORT?

- A network of satellite centres giving practical support to the UK's top sportsmen and women.
- There are four devolved Home Country Sports Institutes in England, Scotland, Wales and Northern Ireland.

WHY ARE THE INSTITUTES NECESSARY?

Because elite athletes need a huge amount of varied support to help them reach the top of the sports development pyramid.

WHAT DO THE INSTITUTES PROVIDE?

Practical support for athletes including:

- sport science and sports medicine
- medical consultation and medical screening
- physiology
- biomechanics
- nutritional advice
- podiatry (care of feet and ankles)
- performance analysis and planning
- psychology,
- physiotherapy
- strength and conditioning
- career, education and lifestyle advice
- sports massage
- sports vision
- performance lifestyle advice.

The London central services team provides advice and guidance to individual sports and to the network centres, e.g. it provides a coaching programme, scholarship and mentoring opportunities and a website for athletes and coaches.

WHO PAYS FOR THEM?

- The National Lottery has provided about £200 million so far.
- The Government has also helped with some of the running costs.

WHAT DO THEY ACHIEVE?

- Increased British sporting success.
- British sportsmen and women who have the best chance of winning medals at World Championships, Commonwealth Games, Winter and Summer Olympic and Paralympic Games.

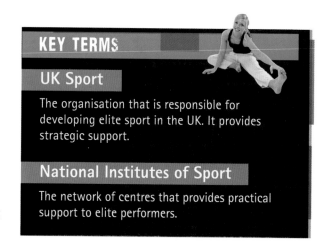

KEY TERMS

UK Sport

The organisation that is responsible for developing elite sport in the UK. It provides strategic support.

National Institutes of Sport

The network of centres that provides practical support to elite performers.

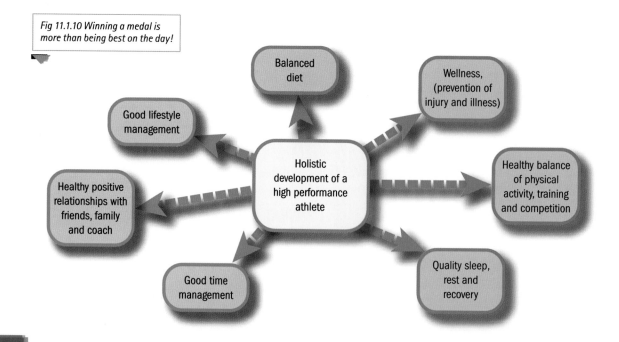

Fig 11.1.10 Winning a medal is more than being best on the day!

Balanced diet

Wellness, (prevention of injury and illness)

Good lifestyle management

Healthy positive relationships with friends, family and coach

Holistic development of a high performance athlete

Healthy balance of physical activity, training and competition

Good time management

Quality sleep, rest and recovery

Devolved institutes

Now, let's have a look at each of the national institutes.

KEY TERM

Devolved

A system that is decentralised with power and autonomy given to and owned by partner bodies.

APPLY IT!

Gateshead International Stadium
In the north-east of England, it specialises in athletics and netball.

THE ENGLISH INSTITUTE OF SPORT (EIS)

The EIS is a *'dynamic, pro-active organisation dedicated to realising the potential of the modern competitor'*. It wants to make the best better!

ENGLISH INSTITUTE OF SPORT

The EIS:

- provides high quality practical support to elite athletes including sport science and medical support
- works closely with NGB performance directors and coaches
- has around 2,000 competitors in the system
- is grant-funded from the lottery via UK Sport
- is not responsible for building, funding or managing the facilities it uses.

THE SPORTS INSTITUTE NORTHERN IRELAND (SINI)

- *'Creates an environment that nurtures and leads high performance*

Sports Institute Northern Ireland

athletes and coaches through the provision of facilities, services and expertise'.*

- provides high quality practical support to elite athletes including sport science and medical support
- is a partnership between the Sports Council for Northern Ireland and the University of Ulster and is based at the University of Ulster, near Belfast.

THE SCOTTISH INSTITUTE OF SPORT (SIS)

- *'prepares elite athletes for the world stage'*
- provides high quality practical support to elite athletes including sport science and medical support
- has a central base in Stirling which is a focus for high performance coach development and learning.

THE WELSH INSTITUTE OF SPORT

- *'provides for the best sports men and women throughout Wales'*
- provides world class facilities, sports science, sport medicine and lifestyle support.

REMEMBER

The key role of an institute is to support elite performers with practical help such as world-class coaching, facilities and medical advice.

TASK 3

In twos discuss: What do elite performers gain from being part of an institute? Make a comprehensive list for your file.

Home country organisations

SPORT ENGLAND

This is the Government agency responsible for community sport in England. It is funded by the government and the National Lottery.

WHAT DOES SPORT ENGLAND WANT?

- Most importantly, it wants to get people active and regular participation to increase by two million by 2012.
- It wants:
  - current non-movers to start exercising
  - current limited-movers to build to 30 minutes three times a week.
  - current regular-movers (30 minutes three times a week) to do more.
- It wants to ensure that young people stay in sport once they leave school.

WHAT DOES SPORT ENGLAND DO?

- It invests in, advises on and promotes community sport for children, young people and adults.
- It works to increase opportunities to take part in community sport and physical recreation – especially in hard-to-reach or priority groups such as people with disabilities.

- It supported the government's target *'that by 2008 at least 85% of school children aged 5-16 spend at least two hours each week on high quality PE and school sport'*, and the government's updated aim (July 2007) for *'the equivalent of an hour of "sport" every school day'* (including two hours within the curriculum and three hours extra-curricular/community participation)
- It promotes volunteering, coaching, leadership and officiating as well as actual performing.
- It works closely with NGBs, regional sporting bodies, coaches, clubs and volunteers – all in order to increase participation.
- Creates and funds initiatives such as **Sporting Champions** – which organises visits by world-class athletes to schools
- Develops school/club links.
- It is keen to use sport to fight obesity.
- It works with partners to ensure that the London 2012 Olympic and Paralympic Games leave a lasting sporting legacy.
- It is responsible for funding elite performers in sports that are non-Olympic, such as squash and netball.

SPORTS COUNCIL FOR NORTHERN IRELAND

Sport Northern Ireland 'Through sport, to contribute to an inclusive, creative, competent, informed and physically active community.'

It aims to:
- to increase participation especially among young people
- to improve performance in sport
- to improve the management of sport and the image of Northern Ireland, using sport.

Sport Northern Ireland (established 31 December 1973) is an executive non-departmental public body sponsored by the Department of Culture, Arts and leisure. It has a community sport programme that aims to:

- increase participation in disadvantaged areas and by people with disabilities
- improve the health and wellbeing of people in disadvantaged communities through participation, coaching and competition
- improve knowledge and skills enabling more people to make a contribution in their local communities and to be involved in sport long term
- show how sport can help to solve social issues such as youth offending, or drug use in the community.

SPORTSCOTLAND

This is the national agency for sport in Scotland whose strategy is called 'Reaching Higher'. In short, *sportscotland* aims to increase participation and improve performances in Scottish sport.

It aims to:

- develop sporting people, organisations and facilities
- create pathways of opportunity for people to take part in sport at any level and at any stage in life
- tackle discrimination and promote equality of opportunity ensuring safe and fair participation and performance.

In short, each of the home country sports councils want people to start getting active and stay being active.

THE SPORTS COUNCIL FOR WALES

sports council wales
cyngor chwaraeon cymru

The Council wants to get more people, more active, more often!

Like other home country sports councils it develops and promotes sport and active lifestyles. It advises the Welsh Assembly Government on sport and is responsible for distributing National Lottery funds to sport in Wales. It wants:

- active young people
- active communities (they encourage adults to be active for 30 minutes a day, and children for 60 minutes a day)
- high level performance and excellence which focuses on the talented performer and surrounds them with support.

EXAM TIP

You don't need to get bogged down with detail about UK Sport, National Institutes of Sport and home country councils such as Sport England or the Sports Council for Northern Ireland. Just be able to show that you know and understand what they do and how they do it.

You will not get a question in the exam on a particular home country sports council, e.g. *sportscotland*. Instead, an exam question is likely to be worded as follows: 'With reference to home country sports councils such as Sport England... (and then continue with the actual question) .... '.

TASK 4

Make a set of revision cards for all of the bodies named in the specification.

EXAM TIP

It can be difficult to stay up to date with some aspects of your socio-cultural studies. For example, initiatives that were 'current' when the text here was published may have been replaced by the time you read it! Don't worry – examiners will be reasonable regarding dates and timings of what is 'current'. Keep your eye on relevant websites to check what is happening and changing, e.g. at www.teachernet.gov (visit hotlinks website)

KEY TERM

Sporting legacy

Positive benefits that remain after an event such as high quality facilities – see section on the Olympic Games in Part III, page 311.

Government initiatives

'Watching sport is a national pastime. Talking about sport is a national obsession. But now we need to make taking part in sport a national characteristic'.

Prime Minister Gordon Brown – 13 July 2007

We need to look at government initiatives that impact upon participation and sporting achievement by young people in state schools. Government initiatives are ideas from Government departments. Government departments involved in sport include the Department for Culture, Media and Sport (DCMS) and the Department for Children, Schools and Families (DCSF).

Government departments can be split, renamed, disbanded or created as a Prime Minister thinks appropriate.

State education is directed centrally by the government, and state schools have to follow the National Curriculum.

THE NATIONAL CURRICULUM

This has been compulsory in schools since 1988 and has four key stages as follows:

- Key stage 1 (5-7 years)
- Key stage 2 (7-11 years)
- Key stage 3 (11-14 years)
- Key stage 4 (14-16 years)

REMEMBER

The specific requirements for each Key Stage are different, though themes throughout are:

- Competence (body and mind skillfulness)
- Performance (applying competencce)
- Creativity (problem solving, techniques and tactics)
- Healthy active lifestyles (physical activity for health)

REMEMBER

Key sporting bodies and organisations such as UK Sport are not told what to do by the government. UK Sport is, however, answerable to the government because of the government funding it receives.

KEY TERMS

Initiative

A scheme, proposal, plan or idea.

Government department

Departments within the government that are led by a Government Minister who is normally a member of the cabinet (the key team supporting the Prime Minister) and who, in turn, is supported by a team of junior Ministers. Government departments are administered by a senior civil servant.

Relatively recent initiatives revolve largely around the PE, School Sport and Clubs Links Strategy (PESSCLS).

THE PE, SCHOOL SPORT AND CLUB LINKS STRATEGY (PESSCLS)

This strategy was launched by the Prime Minister in October 2002 and its key aim is to increase participation in all age groups from 5 to16. It wants more high quality activity for more children more often.

The initial aim was for a minimum of two hours each week of high quality PE and school sport within and beyond the curriculum – for a greater number of young people because:

'high quality PE and school sport produces young people with the skills, understanding, desire and commitment to continue to improve and achieve in a range of PE, sport and health-enhancing physical activities in line with their abilities'.

(Department of Education and Skills)

The PESSCL strategy – different 'strands'

In July 2007 the Prime Minister pledged an extra £100M to the PESSCL strategy:

PESSCL – THE AIMS?

- the equivalent of an hour of 'sport' every school day for every school child (including two hours within the curriculum and three hours extra-curricular/community participation)
- a fitter Britain
- a greater sporting nation.

PESSCL – THE PLANS?

- More competition within (intra) and between (inter) schools.
- More coaches in schools and the community.
- A network of competition managers across the country to work with primary and secondary schools to increase the amount of competitive sport.
- A National School Sports Week where all schools will be encouraged to run sports days and inter-school tournaments.

WHERE WILL THE EXTRA £100 MILLION GO?

- To competition managers who will deliver the programme of inter-school competitive sport.
- To sports coordinators to increase sport opportunities to those in further education.
- To experienced coaches and volunteers to work inside and outside schools to provide the five hours (see 'The aims' overleaf).

EXAM TIP

You can only be asked questions on material that is clearly in the specification. So, you will not get a specific question on the PESSCL strategy. Information on the PESSCL strategy has been included as it is a 'current government initiative' to do with sport and PE. 'Current government initiatives' are in the specification. When in doubt and with the help of your teacher/s, check the specification!

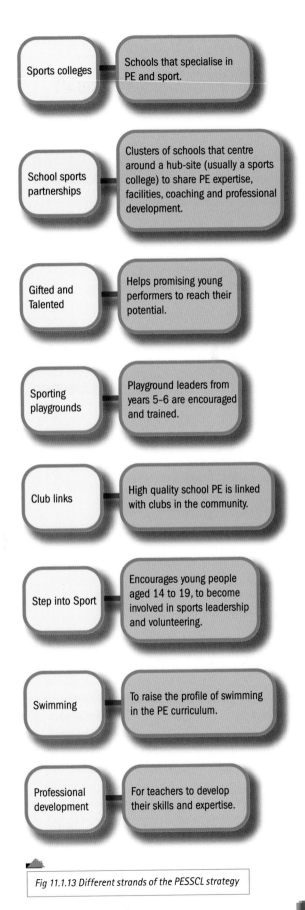

Sports colleges	Schools that specialise in PE and sport.
School sports partnerships	Clusters of schools that centre around a hub-site (usually a sports college) to share PE expertise, facilities, coaching and professional development.
Gifted and Talented	Helps promising young performers to reach their potential.
Sporting playgrounds	Playground leaders from years 5-6 are encouraged and trained.
Club links	High quality school PE is linked with clubs in the community.
Step into Sport	Encourages young people aged 14 to 19, to become involved in sports leadership and volunteering.
Swimming	To raise the profile of swimming in the PE curriculum.
Professional development	For teachers to develop their skills and expertise.

Fig 11.1.13 Different strands of the PESSCL strategy

hours (see 'The aims' above).

Some 'PESSCL' strands in

TAKE IT FURTHER

Start developing a critical evaluation of initiatives and strategies.

- Is your school involved with the PESSCL strategy?
- Do you know someone who is part of the gifted and talented programme or who has 'stepped into sport?'
- What do they think of it?
- What do your PE teachers think of it? Good and/or bad? Interview them and make some notes for your file.

more detail

SPECIALIST SPORTS COLLEGES

The Specialist Schools programme gives state-run (or state-maintained) schools the chance to specialise in areas such as: arts, business and enterprise, engineering, humanities, language, mathematics and computing, music, science and of course, sport.

The mission statement of Specialist Sports Colleges is to:

> '...raise standards of achievement in physical education and Sport For All students across the ability range. To be regional focal points for promoting excellence in physical education and community sport, extending links between families of schools, sports bodies and communities, sharing resources, developing and spreading good practice and helping to provide a structure through which young people can progress perhaps to careers in sport and physical education. Sports Colleges are expected to develop a visible sports ethos throughout the school and within their local community'.

SCHOOL SPORT PARTNERSHIPS (SSPs)

These are clusters or 'families' of schools that work together to develop PE and sport opportunities for young people within their cluster.

A typical partnership consists of:

1. A full-time partnership development manager (PDM) who is usually based in a Sports College. The PDM works with their school sport co-coordinators (SSCos) to write the Partnership Development Plan, manages the partnership and develops sporting links with the wider community.
2. Up to eight SSCos who are each based in a secondary, middle or special school and concentrate on improving school sport opportunities – including out-of-hours school learning, intra- and inter-school competition and club links – across a family or cluster of schools and across the partnership. SSCos work in line with the overall Partnership Development Plan and dovetail their Family Plans into it. They need to coordinate well with their Family of schools and with other Families within their Partnership to ensure that schools feel part of the process and do not feel that they are simply having more work and administration imposed upon them. They are employed by their host schools to carry out the role of an SSCo for up to two days a week.
3. Primary (and special school) link teachers (PLTs) who are based in primary and special schools and whose aim is to improve the quantity and quality of PE and sport in their schools – with the help of their SSCo and PDM.

What are some of the opportunities and challenges about being a PDM?

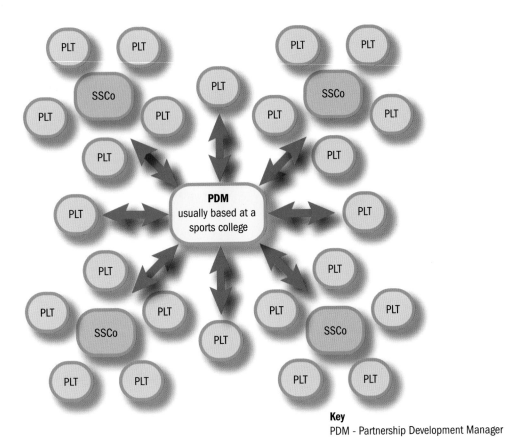

Key
PDM - Partnership Development Manager
SSCo - Shool Sport Co-ordinator
PLT - Primary Link Teacher

Fig 11.1.4 A typical school sport partnership (SSP) model

Opportunities:
- The strengths of each member of the team can be used by the Partnership.
- PDMs and SSCos can work creatively to achieve the Partnership outcomes.

Challenges:
- Keeping all the plates spinning!
- Keeping up with people, time, organisation and finance.
- Working with so many different agencies.
- To accurately monitor the work being done without increasing the work load of primary and secondary teachers.
- To achieve the two hours of high quality PE each week.

who work in a secondary school for three days per week and who work as an SSCo for up to two days per week. This can sometimes cause challenges in relation to workload and time management. There is unlikely to be a conflict of interest between the two parts of the job, but there could be conflict of time.

Here is an extract from the diary of an SSCo:

Monday: Secondary school PE teaching commitments

Tuesday: SSCo work including:

- meeting with PDM;

- training a group of Yr 5-6 playground leaders in one of the cluster schools;

- admin including: work on an 'Awards for All' grant plan; phonecalls re primary schools skipping workshop; sports write-up for local newspaper.

- read up on BADMINTON England level I and leaders courses.

Wednesday: Secondary school PE teaching commitments.

Thursday: Secondary school PE teaching commitments.

Friday: SSCo work including:

- planning meeting for year 7 'curriculum football focus week'.

- meeting with local golf professional to organise sessions for primary schools with the view of children visiting the golf club out of school hours.

- multi-skills club at main cluster school with junior sports leaders as helpers.

- admin including: email PLTs in cluster to inform them of due date for PESSCL survey and offer help/support; write letter of thanks to local theatre for offering their venue for dance festival.

KEY TERMS

Inter-school competitions

Competition between different schools.

Intra-school competitions

Competition between different groups within one school, e.g. between different 'houses' or tutor groups.

Awards for All

A lottery grant scheme for local communities which might go towards: a campaign to promote healthy eating and more exercise; improving a village hall to provide better facilities for all members of the community or a crèche facility for a rural community.

GIFTED AND TALENTED

The main aim of the Gifted and Talented strand of PESSCL is to improve the identification of and support and provision for gifted and talented pupils. Up to 10% of pupils in primary and secondary schools should ultimately be supported by this initiative.

THE GIFTED AND TALENTED STRAND HAS FOUR KEY THEMES

1. Identifying the 'excellence' standard and helping schools to achieve the standards by providing professional development for teachers.
2. Talent Identification by PE teachers in their schools.
3. Provision of a network of Multi-skill Academies to develop the core skills needed in all sports.
4. Support for talented athletes via the Junior Athlete Education (JAE) programme which gives lifestyle management and performance planning to young people and their teachers.

It also offers:

- web-based resource for teachers, coaches and parents see the Youth Sports Trust website
- a national support network for talented young disabled athletes
- NGB-organised national performance camps for elite young athletes
- a national faculty of Gifted and Talented trainers to provide continuing professional development
- a school-based profiling and tracking system.

KITEMARKING FOR SCHOOL PE

Special Kitemarks are awarded to maintained schools within a partnership, and reward delivery of the national PESSCL strategy. The Kitemarks are:

- Activemark (primary and special schools)
- Sportsmark (secondary and special schools)
- Sports Partnership Mark.

Kitemarks are awarded annually through the national school sport survey which all partnership schools complete. Special provision will therefore need to be made for Independent schools who wish to have their student participation rates

Activemark (primary)	Sportsmark (secondary)	Sports partnership mark
If percentage of pupils participating in at least two hours of quality PE and school sport each week is significantly above the national average.	If percentage of pupils participating in at least two hours of quality PE and school sport each week is significantly above the national average.	If at least ninety per cent of pupils across the partnership are doing at least 2 hours high quality PE and school sport each week.
If school holds a sports day	If school holds a sports day	
If school meets or betters the national average for pupils involved in sports leadership and volunteering OR the percentage of pupils participating in sports clubs linked to their school.	If school meets or betters the national average in three or more of the following areas: • percentage of pupils taking part in inter-school competitive sport. • the range of sports offered. • percentage of pupils participating in sports clubs linked to their school, or • the percentage of pupils actively involved in sports leadership or volunteering.	

Table 3

acknowledged by a Kitemark as they are not currently in partnerships.

Table 3 on page 275 shows how schools within a partnership receive the Kitemark award (2007).

OTHER GOVERNMENT INITIATIVES

- 'Sport: Raising the Game' – the 1995 document which resulted (among other things) in specialist sports colleges and the National Institutes of Sport.
- 'A Sporting Future for All' – the 2001 document which set out the government's vision for sport and highlighted the need for cooperation, communication and coordination between schools, local clubs and organisations.
- 'Game Plan' – the 2002 action plan based on 'A Sporting future for All'. Game Plan recognised the importance of physical activity to health and the potential social and economic costs of increasing inactivity in the population. Game Plan stated clearly that government regarded sport and physical activity as potential ways of reducing inequalities of opportunity. The idea was and is, that through sport and physical activity, more people could gain better health and employment, be diverted from antisocial behaviour and be better educated since 'given its popularity and inherent properties sport can contribute to neighbourhood renewal'

(Game Plan 2002).

- The National Sports Foundation – a Government-led initiative to encourage partnerships between private investors and community sports projects in England. The Foundation matches new and additional private investment with Foundation funding, on a pound for pound basis.

TAKE IT FURTHER

Visit www.sportdevelopment.org.uk/ (visit the hotlinks site) and find out more detail about Game Plan.

Governments throughout the world get involved in sport for a variety of reasons, including those here (only some of which are relevant to the UK). To increase:

- a 'feel good' factor among the population
- international goodwill by way of coming together for sport competitions, e.g. the Olympic Games or World Cup competitions
- the health and efficiency of the army
- loyalty and patriotism among the people
- the health and productivity of the workforce.

Also:

- to influence the beliefs of the nation.
- to pass laws, e.g. to do with safety at football stadia
- to make money.

TASK 6

Class discussion.

- Which of the potential reasons for government involvement in sport are applicable to the UK?
- Which other countries might get involved in sport for some of the other identified reasons?

TASK 5

Find out whether your school is in a partnership and/or has a Kitemark. Would your school qualify for a Kitemark if it doesn't currently have one? (see Table 3 on page 275)

National Governing Body (NGB) initiatives

Each sport is controlled by its National Governing Body (NGB), for example BADMINTON England whose goal is to '*develop badminton as a Sport For All and to encourage the best players to progress up through the ranking both at club,*

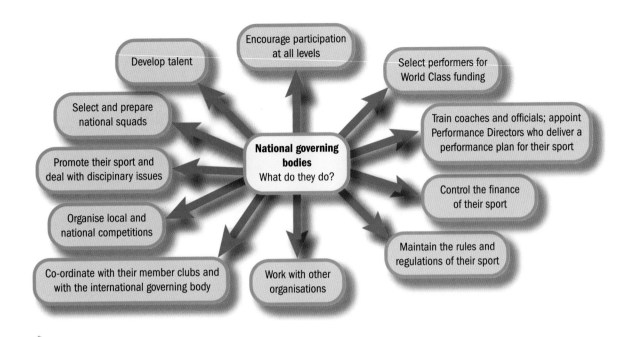

Fig 11.1.15 The work of National Governing Bodies in the UK – which you may be familiar with from GCSE PE

county and International level'. NGBs affiliate to their International Sports Federation (ISF), e.g. the International Badminton Federation (IBF).

You need to know and understand current NGB initiatives that impact upon mass participation and sporting excellence, for example: whole sport plans.

WHOLE SPORT PLANS (WSPs)

These are produced by English NGBs, and One Stop Plans (OSPs) are produced for sports development in Wales, Scotland and Northern Ireland.

STRATEGIES

Plans must include strategies:

- to increase the number of participants, clubs, active members of clubs, qualified coaches and active volunteers
- from grass roots to elite level
- to increase international success
- for the effective running of their organisation.

In other words NGBs must map out their vision and get people to start, stay and succeed in their sport.

TASK 7

In twos research, using the Internet, a couple of NGB websites.

- What initiatives do they have for both mass participation and sporting excellence?

EXAM TIP

You will not get a general exam question on the role/s of NHBs. Examiners are interested in NGB initiatives.

FUNDING

NGBs receive funding from their home country councils as a result of their WSPs. The councils are then able to check NGB 'results' against clearly identified plans and predictions and either continue with or cut funding. The aim of this modernising strategy is for individual sports and sport in general in the UK to benefit and be ready for the Olympics in 2012 and to fit the needs of 21st century sport. It might include the appointment of 'performance directors' and the building of new national centres.

NGBs for professional, media-happy sports such as The Football Association (FA) and the Rugby Football Union (RFU) have a comparatively high level of independence due to their capacity to attract media funding for TV rights.

TASK 8

The National Tennis Centre opened in Roehampton, SW London in 2007. Write a mini article for a tennis magazine praising the benefits and qualities of this venue. Research the Lawn Tennis Association (LTA) website at www.lta.org.uk (visit the hotlinks website) and/or use any of the following phrases in your article:

- high quality sport science support
- state-of-the-art facilities
- greatest opportunities
- maximise potential
- national focus for the sport
- good transport links
- support for elite players
- practice courts for all Grand Slam surfaces including six indoor acrylic, six outdoor acrylic, six clay and four grass courts
- injury prevention and rehabilitation.

TAKE IT FURTHER

Find out as much as you can about 'Mission 2012' – the initiative launched by UK Sport that aims to help NGBs of Olympic sports be aware of how they are progressing against certain key criteria.

TASK 9

In twos discuss: What is done to identify, support and develop the best sports performers in the UK? Think about schools, organisational bodies, government, NGBs etc.

TAKE IT FURTHER

In twos research, using the Internet, the NGB website of a chosen sport.

- Does the NGB provide evidence about meeting targets for improvement?
- If so, what are they doing?
- Gather class evidence and as a group, try to evaluate differences between NGBs.

TASK 10

A group 'workout'! This is for the 10-mark part of a socio-cultural studies question where the command might be 'critically evaluate' or 'discuss' or 'outline adantages and disadvantages of . . .' .

In twos or threes think about the items you have studied in this section ('bodies influencing and promoting participation in physical activity as part of a balanced, active and healthy lifestyle; the promotion of health, fitness and wellbeing and/or sporting excellence').

- How do they impact upon young people's aspirations (potential hopes, desires and goals) and regular participation in physical activity?
- Can you find any evidence that they are: good or bad; working or not working; well received or badly received?

Think about:

- UK Sport
- National Institutes of Sport
- Home country councils e.g. Sport England
- Government initiatives
- National Governing Body (NGB) initiatives.

THE CONTINUUM FROM MASS PARTICIPATION TO SPORTING EXCELLENCE

mass participation   sporting excellence

Fig 11.1.17

Excellence and participation in the UK

You need to understand and be able to explain sports development in terms of the sports development pyramid and the continuum from mass participation to sporting excellence.

EXAM TIP

You could be asked to name and explain each layer of the performance pyramid in the examination. Ensure that you are clear about the two layers beginning with the letter 'P' – candidates often get these two muddled.

A continuum is an imaginary scale or range between two extremes where one point merges into the next. You could stand with classmates and form a human continuum from tall to short people which would have a gradual range and change of heights along the line. We are interested in the line along which mass participation narrows to sporting excellence. Here, as you move right or left along the continuum there will be an increase or decrease in things such as level of skill, commitment and organisation.

MASS PARTICIPATION

At one end of the continuum is mass participation which is an inclusive concept. Where taking part

Fig 11.1.16 The sports development pyramid (formerly called the 'performance pyramid')

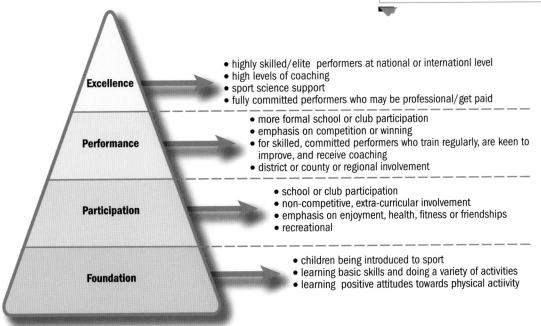

Excellence
- highly skilled/elite performers at national or internationl level
- high levels of coaching
- sport science support
- fully committed performers who may be professional/get paid

Performance
- more formal school or club participation
- emphasis on competition or winning
- for skilled, committed performers who train regularly, are keen to improve, and receive coaching
- district or county or regional involvement

Participation
- school or club participation
- non-competitive, extra-curricular involvement
- emphasis on enjoyment, health, fitness or friendships
- recreational

Foundation
- children being introduced to sport
- learning basic skills and doing a variety of activities
- learning positive attitudes towards physical actiivity

is more important than winning and the physical activity is pursued, among other reasons, for health or fitness or enjoyment. It is associated with lifelong physical activity and lifetime sport that can result in lifelong participation. For these reasons, home country sports councils in the UK have been campaigning for 'Sport For All' for over thirty years.

A benefit of mass participation is that it (theoretically at least) enlarges the pool from which talent can be trawled and supported to 'the top'. Some individuals may strive for personal peak performance here but that is not usually the main intention. Mass Participation supports the idea that everyone should have the chance take part in sport, as regularly as they wish and at whatever level they choose, irrespective of where they live, the school they attend, their ability, age, wealth, gender, race or religion.

REMEMBER

- Lifelong physical activity is enjoyable, health-enhancing movement that is sustained throughout life, e.g. yoga.
- Lifetime sports are activities that can be enjoyed over the course of a lifetime, e.g. table-tennis.
- Lifelong participation is taking part in a chosen lifelong physical activity or a lifetime sport for the duration of one's life – see Chapter 9, page 210.

SPORTING EXCELLENCE

At the other end of the continuum is **sporting excellence**. A dictionary definition of excellence is 'a state of exceptional merit or quality'. It involves elite or professional, highly skilled and highly committed performers taking part at national or international level to win. The back-up team of sport scientists and coaches is equally dedicated and expert. This is a selective or exclusive idea – very few make it to the top. Yet more make it in some countries than others... Why? Because of different levels of opportunity, provision and esteem.

TASK 11

1. Plot your position on the sports development pyramid (page 279) in: swimming, hockey or (any style of) dance.
2. Plot your position on the continuum from mass participation to sporting excellence in both athletics and badminton.
3. Plot your position on the sports development pyramid in your best sporting activity (if not already done in 1 above).

Opportunity, provision and esteem

The term 'access' literally means 'way in' or 'right of entry' and is a useful over-arching or umbrella term under which Opportunity, Provision and Esteem can be considered. As identified, these

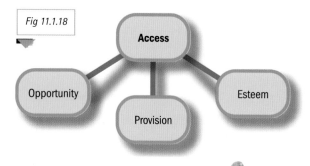

Fig 11.1.18

KEY TERMS

Opportunity

Having the chance to take part and/or get to the top

Provision

Having the conditions or physical tools to take part and/or get to the top

Esteem

Issues to do with confidence, respect, admiration, value and appreciation. The perception that society has of an individual or group affects their likelihood of both taking part and of achieving excellence.

Factors relating to Opportunity, Provision and Esteem that can influence mass participation and sporting excellence.	
Mass participation	**Sporting excellence**
OPPORTUNITY – having the chance to take part and/or get to the top	
Disposable income	Funding and financial support, e.g. National Lottery or sponsorship money.
Ability, skill, health or fitness or playing standard	Skill level and performance lifestyle.
The amount of time available after work and other commitments	Chance to train full time.
Do you actually want to take part? Are suitable and appealing activities available?	Whether individuals choose to make the sacrifices and give the all round commitment needed to get to the top.

PROVISION – having the conditions or physical tools to take part and/or get to the top.	
The presence or absence of suitable equipment and/or facilities	The availability of world class facilities and equipment.
Access – for example for wheelchairs if necessary	The availability of sport science and other 'high tech' support – see Part II, page 279] modern technological products
Availability of suitable transport – privately owned or public transport	Distance from or access to high performance or National Institute centres e.g. the National Tennis Centre in Roehampton, SW London; warm weather training in Cyprus or high altitude training venues for athletes.
Suitable and available clubs or activities or leagues or competitions or courses nearby	Suitable and regular competitions with and against other high level performers.
The right coaching at the right level by suitably qualified staff	The right highly qualified and experienced coaches.
Well-maintained and equipped, private and clean changing and social areas	Performance lifestyle advice and a holistic approach to excellence.

ESTEEM – issues to do with respect, admiration, value and appreciation. The perception that society has of an individual or group affects the chances of their both taking part and of achieving excellence.	
Self-confidence and self belief – which influences self perception.	Self-confidence and self belief which impact on performance.
Respect from others and social acceptance of everyone's 'right' to take part in any chosen activity.	Respect from others – including team mates, opponents and the Media.
Positive or negative perceptions of certain physical activities.	Recent results (good and/or bad) and national and international ranking.
Status in society i.e. if from a disadvantaged group.	Status in the sporting world.

Table 4

three key variables affect both participation and excellence. If you have or haven't got certain things your chances or taking part and/or of winning are increased or decreased.

SOCIAL AND CULTURAL FACTORS

Social and cultural factors impact upon participation and sporting excellence.

Opportunities for mass participation and the achievement of sporting excellence should exist for everyone in the UK – but they don't. Social and socio-cultural factors (things to do with society and culture), have a big impact. By society we mean the people in the communities we live in and by culture we mean the traditions, customs and way of life within those communities.

SOCIETY

Society is *stratified*, which means that it has imaginary layers into which groups fit. This unfair layering or 'stacking' of society is most evident in places with high immigration. The 'dominant group' in society (in the UK this is the white, middle-class male group) is at the top of the stack and has the greatest freedom and opportunity while other groups, such as Asian women, are lower down and enjoy less opportunity.

Not everyone within a group has the same needs and wants. Also, combinations of factors can lead to double deprivation, more under-representation and more under-achievement. For instance, for a black female with a disability, the constraints and restrictions are likely to be multiplied.

DISCRIMINATION

A key factor is *discrimination*. Discrimination is unfair treatment. It occurs when a group is constrained or held back by factors that are not applied to the dominant group. In a stratified or layered society where stacking occurs, minority groups often experience discrimination. This discrimination will then probably exist in physical and activity sport.

'Minority' groups

We need to know and understand factors that impact on the following groups (often referred to as 'target', 'priority', 'minority' or 'focus' groups):

- young people
- the elderly
- people with disabilities
- women
- ethnic minorities.

These are the groups that are most likely to suffer from *discrimination* and *social exclusion*. A high priority will most likely be given to these groups by organisations such as Sport England, who are keen to increase participation and excellence among them.

The constraints that impact on people, which limit their chance of regular participation are illustrated in Figure 11.1.19.

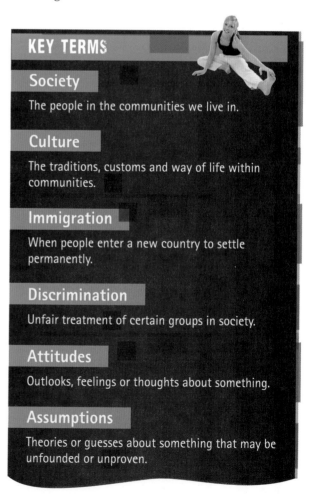

KEY TERMS

Society
The people in the communities we live in.

Culture
The traditions, customs and way of life within communities.

Immigration
When people enter a new country to settle permanently.

Discrimination
Unfair treatment of certain groups in society.

Attitudes
Outlooks, feelings or thoughts about something.

Assumptions
Theories or guesses about something that may be unfounded or unproven.

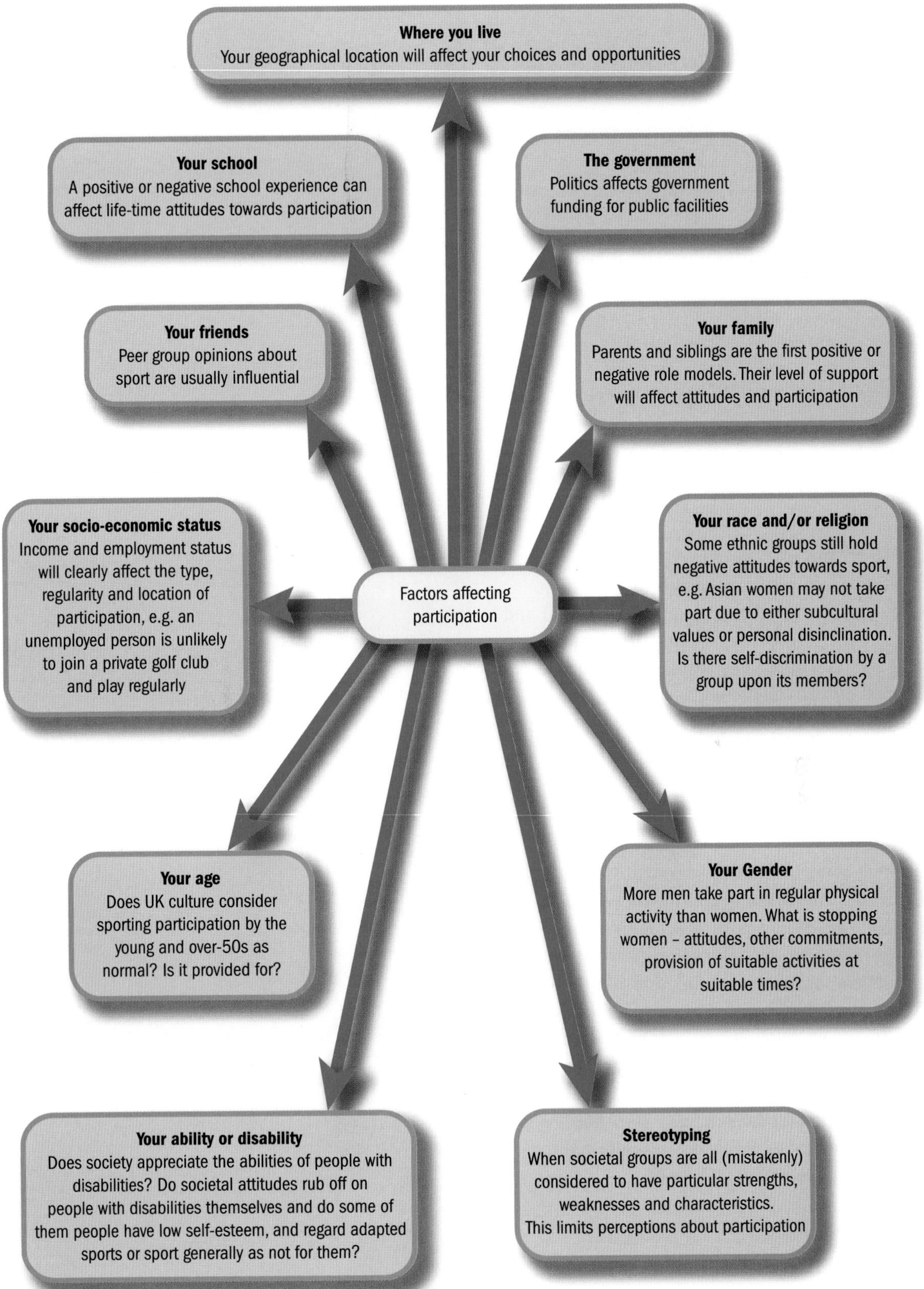

Where you live
Your geographical location will affect your choices and opportunities

Your school
A positive or negative school experience can affect life-time attitudes towards participation

The government
Politics affects government funding for public facilities

Your friends
Peer group opinions about sport are usually influential

Your family
Parents and siblings are the first positive or negative role models. Their level of support will affect attitudes and participation

Your socio-economic status
Income and employment status will clearly affect the type, regularity and location of participation, e.g. an unemployed person is unlikely to join a private golf club and play regularly

Factors affecting participation

Your race and/or religion
Some ethnic groups still hold negative attitudes towards sport, e.g. Asian women may not take part due to either subcultural values or personal disinclination. Is there self-discrimination by a group upon its members?

Your age
Does UK culture consider sporting participation by the young and over-50s as normal? Is it provided for?

Your Gender
More men take part in regular physical activity than women. What is stopping women – attitudes, other commitments, provision of suitable activities at suitable times?

Your ability or disability
Does society appreciate the abilities of people with disabilities? Do societal attitudes rub off on people with disabilities themselves and do some of them people have low self-esteem, and regard adapted sports or sport generally as not for them?

Stereotyping
When societal groups are all (mistakenly) considered to have particular strengths, weaknesses and characteristics. This limits perceptions about participation

Fig 11.1.19 Factors impacting on participation in sport and physical activity

Myths

Untruths, such as the view that males cannot do cartwheels or women cannot park cars.

Stereotyping

Typecasting, labelling or pigeon-holing people. A stereotype is a simplified or standardised image or view held by one person or group about another.

Social exclusion

The negative results of factors such as low income, discrimination, poor housing and health, lack of employable skills, living in an area with a high crime rate etc., all of which can put communities at a disadvantage.

YOUNG PEOPLE

Young people need to take part in physical activity to get the physical, mental, personal and social benefits identified in Chapter 9. Habits and attitudes about physical activity that are formed during childhood have a great impact on behaviour later in life, so it is essential that youngsters develop positive habits.

THE IMPACT OF SOCIAL AND CULTURAL FACTORS

As long ago as 1960 a government statement called the *Wolfenden Report* identified a post-school 'gap' of non-participation, into which many school leavers fell as they progressed from school and childhood to work and adulthood. School-age children need to have a positive experience of PE to ensure their continued participation in physical activity when they leave school. The varied interests of this group need to be provided for, according to their needs and abilities, so that all levels of the performance pyramid are potentially accessible.

POSSIBLE MEASURES TO INCREASE PARTICIPATION AND SPORTING EXCELLENCE

Increasing participation and excellence are ultimately the responsibility of the government,

REMEMBER

Possible barriers to regular participation in physical activity by young people include:

- lack of suitable kit, facilities and friends who take part
- not enough money
- fatigue after school or college
- dislike of: exercise, showing their body and/or sweating
- anxiety about jogging or walking outside, particularly after dark
- dislike of cold, wet, outdoor conditions – see Chapter 9.

UK Sport, the four home country councils and NGBs. Other bodies are also involved, but the OCR specification doesn't require knowledge of them.

REMEMBER

1. Government initiatives and programmes include:
   - The National Curriculum
   - The PESSCLs strategy, including strands such as sportts colleges, Gifted and Talented and club links.
2. UK Sport:
   - Oversees the National Institutes of Sport (formerly UKSI) centres which give full practical support to elite young people as well as performance lifestyle advice
   - introduced the World Class Pathway (funding) Programme in 2006 (Podium, Development and Talent)
   - runs the Talented Athletes Scholarship Scheme (TASS).
3. Home Country councils:
   - want to get young people to stay and (perhaps even to) succeed in physical activity and sport
   - invest in, advise on and promote sport for young people
   - support the PESSCL strategy relating to PE and school sport club links
   - promote volunteering, coaching, leadership, and officiating as well as performing by young people
   - run 'sporting champions' whereby successful sports personalities, e.g. Dame Kelly Holmes,

go into schools to encourage and inspire young people (role-modelling).

4. NGBs
   - Whole Sport Plans
   - Performance directors
   - Mission 2012.

TAKE IT FURTHER

Class discussion:

What else can be done to help young people achieve sporting excellence? Think about features to do with Opportunity, Provision and Esteem.

Should PE in schools change? If so – how?

Make a list for your file.

THE ELDERLY

Back in 1983 the Sports Council had a campaign called 'Sport For All: 50 + All to Play For' which encouraged participation among this age group, by emphasising the following benefits of regular participation:

- **Health benefits** – improved cardiovascular function, strength and flexibility and an increased sense of wellbeing
- **Social benefits** – increased self-confidence, enjoyment and friendships
- **Psychological benefits** – a focus for older people who may feel 'lost' after retirement or redundancy.

THE IMPACT OF SOCIAL AND CULTURAL FACTORS

There has always been a tradition of low or non-involvement in sport and physical activity by elderly people in the UK. Perhaps it is because the Media still portrays the image that sport is for young people. Older people have always had a place as spectators and voluntary administrators, but they must also be encouraged to stay active even when their performance levels go down. The reality is that ageing normally begins to take effect around the age of 30.

As already identified, combined inequalities increase problems and constraints so that elderly women and elderly people from ethnic minority groups, for example, will suffer greater limitations to participation – all linked to opportunity, provision and esteem.

POSSIBLE MEASURES TO INCREASE PARTICIPATION AND SPORTING EXCELLENCE

In order for elderly people to pursue healthy balanced lifestyles characterised by lifelong participation in physical activity and lifetime sports, certain things are needed. Not surprisingly, they need opportunity, provision and esteem: the chance to take part; the 'tools' to take part; a positive attitude. The 'product' must be accessible and attractive.

TASK 12

Using Fig 11.1.20 as a guide draw a spider diagram to show what can be done to increase participation in physical activity by elderly people. Think of factors to do with opportunity, provision and esteem such as offering reduced rates for the elderly.

TASK 13

Research the course and class timetable at your local sports or leisure centre/s. What special provision is there (if any) for elderly clients?

PEOPLE WITH DISABILITIES

'A disability is any restriction or lack of ability (due to an impairment) to perform an activity in the manner or within the range considered normal for a human being'.
World Health Organisation (WHO) 1980

'An impairment is any loss or abnormality of psychological, physiological, or anatomical structure or function.' WHO – 1980

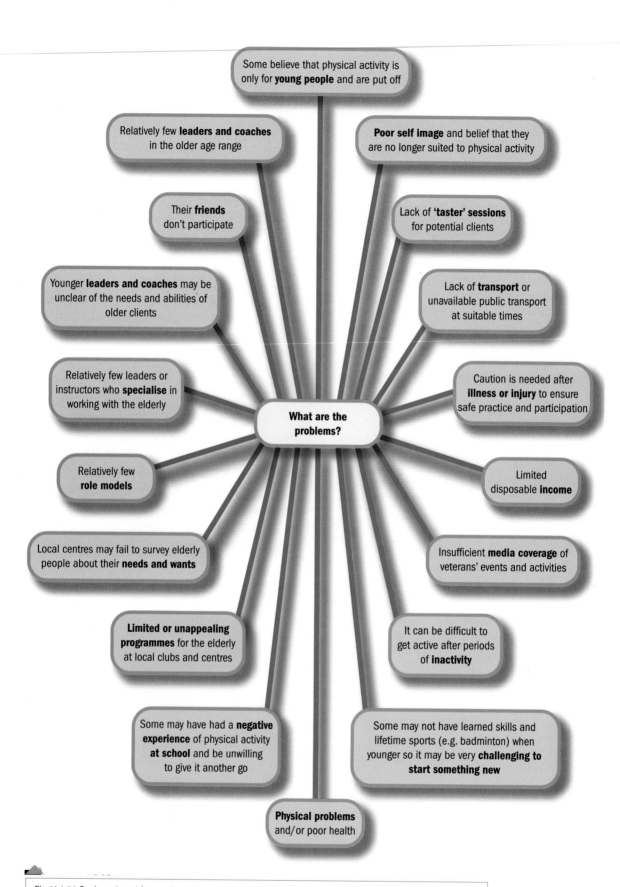

Fig 11.1.20 Socio-cultural factors impacting upon participation and the pursuit of excellence by elderly people

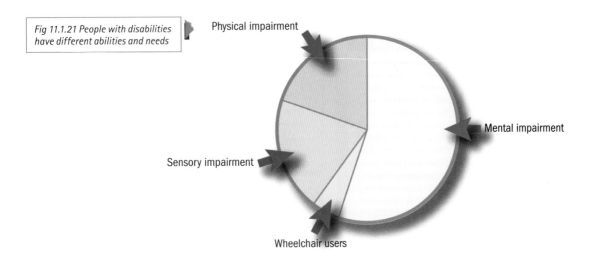

Fig 11.1.21 People with disabilities have different abilities and needs

Physical impairment

Mental impairment

Sensory impairment

Wheelchair users

Six million people in Britain have some form of sensory, physical or mental impairment. Society continues to discriminate against, handicap and impose barriers on people with disabilities. Significantly, as three quarters of adults with a disability rely on state benefits as their main source of income they are also financially disadvantaged, which adds to the problem.

BACKGROUND

Traditionally, disability has been viewed from a medical perspective. People with disabilities have been considered dependent and passive rather than independent and self-governing, probably because of being supported by carers and health professionals. This limited and limiting view has more recently been updated with a social view which recognises that attitudes, assumptions, myths and stereotyping, along with inadequately designed environments had, until relatively recently, placed restrictions on this group of people.

Frank Kew argues (in *Sport, Social Problems and Issues*, 1997) that: '*The key issue for disabled people...is not to mimic the non-disabled in sport, but rather to celebrate difference, acknowledge abilities in modified sports, and to recognise on the basis of those abilities, outstanding sporting achievement*'.

PARALYMPICS

The Paralympics (a parallel set of Olympic events for elite athletes with disabilities), raise awareness of elite disabled sport and focus on sporting achievement rather than disability. Crucially, the Paralympics also create positive role models such as the 400m runner Danny Crates.

With a promising rugby career ahead of him, Danny Crates was in a serious car accident in Australia in 1994, losing his right arm. He has since become the (T46 arm amputee class) 400m World Champion, Paralympic Champion, European Champion, Paralympic World Cup winner.

Danny's affirmations include:

'*Life does not put hurdles in front of you that you cannot handle*'

'*Do not dwell on your mistakes and misfortunes*'

'*Learn from them, move on and become a better and stronger person*'

TAKE IT FURTHER

In disabled sport it is necessary to 'profile' participants to ensure that they are competing against people with similar abilities and that there is a 'level playing field'. In 'profiling', performers are assessed in their a) power, b) range of motion, and c) coordination. After assessment, the disabled performer gets a profile number which can be checked at regional, national and international competitions.

APPLY IT!

Goalball is a 3-a-side game where goals are scored by rolling a large ball (with a bell inside) along the floor (with tactile markings) into a goal. All players wear eyeshades to ensure equality of sight and perception. Goalball is a Paralympic sport. Look at some clips of goalball on: www.youtube.com (visit the hotlinks website).

APPLY IT!

Disability Sport England (the organisational body that promotes sport for people with disabilities) has suggested the following ways of adapting games:

- use larger, smaller, lighter, coloured balls and shorter-handled racquets and sticks
- lower net heights and limit playing areas
- increase team numbers
- give participant-specific play areas to avoid intimidation by more able performers
- use foam equipment to limit bounce heights
- use beanbags and other easy grip equipment
- use callers for direction control, e.g. guttering for bowls.
- use everyday items to help participants, e.g. guttering for bowls.

As a result of the Education Act of 1988 many young people with a disability have been integrated into mainstream schools. There are advantages and disadvantages to both integration and separation in PE.

As with other focus groups our task is to identify the social and cultural factors that impact on participation and excellence and to identify measures that have been or could be taken to improve the situation.

Integration (mixing or assimilating people)		Separation (parting or dividing people)	
Advantages	Disadvantages	Advantages	Disadvantages
• Increases awareness. • A better reflection of society, which increasingly integrates rather than separates.	• Safety issues and possibility of bullying. • It is expensive to get specialist teachers for each school and difficult for one PE teacher to cope with a great diversity of abilities in one class. • It is expensive to adapt and modify sports and to provide specialist facilities	• Specialist teachers focus on specific needs. • Specialist equipment more likely to be available. • All levels of the sports development pyramid more easily accessed.	• Children with disability more likely to see themselves as different. • Could make it harder for integration later in life. • Presumes that all disabilities are the same. • Reduces opportunities for children with disability to mix with able-bodied children when, in many cases the disability is irrelevant.

Table 5

TASK 14

Using Fig 11.1.19 as a guide, and by re-reading this section on disability sport, make a spider diagram or list, to show the factors impacting on the achievement of both mass participation and sporting excellence for people with disabilities.

Think of factors to do with opportunity, provision and esteem.

LOOKING FORWARD

What about possible measures to increase participation and sporting excellence? What can be done or is already being done to get more involvement and medals?

- Promote positive images of sportsmen and women with disability.
- Smash myths and reduce ignorance.
- Increase awareness of sports facilities and organisations which cater for people with disabilities.
- Provide good facilities locally, and world class facilities for elite performers.
- Provide specialist training for specialist coaches – ultimately increasing the number of coaches with disabilities.
- Increase links between organisations involved with disability sport.
- Ensure equality of access to facilities (which legally must conform to minimum access requirements). The following should be considered: toilet and changing facilities, ramps, lifts, wide car-parking bays, hand rails on stair flights, lever taps on wash basins, automatic doors, non-slip floors, signs in Braille, signs in a colour appropriate for partially-sighted, accessible bar counters, placement of lift control buttons and of vending machines.
- Raise awareness of specialist sports centres, for example the Ludwig Guttman Sports Centres at Stoke Mandeville.

- Continue to raise awareness of the abilities of performers with disabilities through the Paralympic and Commonwealth Games.
- Continue to use modern technological products to improve specialist equipment for disability sport.
- With unemployment among disabled people very high, and those in employment earning, on average, just 80% of the salaries of able-bodied people, sports organisations must: continue to invest – perhaps disproportionately – in provision for people with disabilities; ensure that reduced fees at sports clubs and centres continue.
- Increase funding for potential Paralympians through the World Class Performance Pathway, and positively discriminate towards athletes with disability in terms of their placement on the Pathway.

WOMEN: STEREOTYPING

There are obvious differences between men and women, just as there are between some women and other women. Consequently not all sports are for all women. The issue here is that gender stereotypes need to be broken. Also, girls and women need the freedom to choose, and equal opportunities and provision to both participate and to excel. Figure 11.1.22 illustrates the various factors influencing participation and achievement of excellence by females in sport.

MYTH-BUSTING

An American professional baseball player once declared: 'Women were not created by God to be physical. God created women to be feminine'. Over time, gender roles emerge in societies, which become the socially accepted ways for each sex to behave – stereotypical models for masculinity and femininity. These stereotypes can lead to myths. A myth finally overcome by women in the late nineteenth century was that cycling would ruin their chances of having children.

Gender roles take a while to develop, and longer to change. They still suggest dominant characteristics such as creativity and sensitivity for females and aggression, determination and confidence for males. This has a profound effect

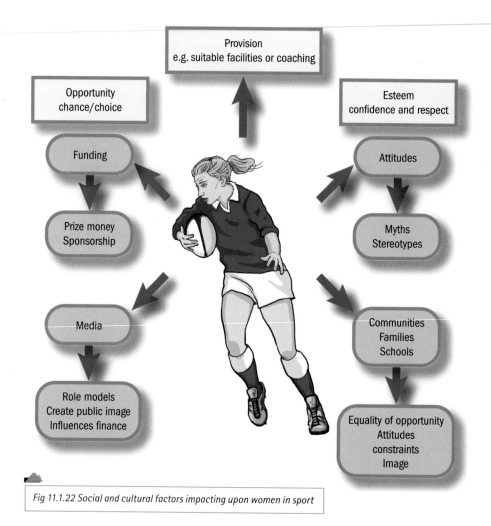

Fig 11.1.22 Social and cultural factors impacting upon women in sport

on how children are socialised – i.e. how they learn to behave and fit into their environment – and on how a society views their participation in sport. It also gives some women a problem, in that competitive sport usually needs the attributes more normally associated with masculinity.

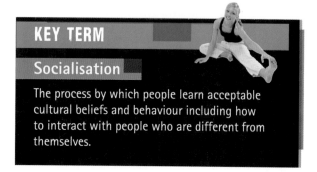

KEY TERM

Socialisation

The process by which people learn acceptable cultural beliefs and behaviour including how to interact with people who are different from themselves.

A society might support women's participation in gymnastics and dance, which highlight

traditionally perceived female characteristics, but oppose their participation in traditionally male activities such as rugby or boxing, for example. Males and females alike often disapprove of the image of successful female body-builders who are highly committed to rigorous training programmes and who reach the top of their sport.

MEDIA COVERAGE/REPRESENTATION

Women are still under-represented in all areas of the Media. This has been the case since the first publication of the sporting paper *Bell's Life* in 1822. The Media creates a public image of sport generally and of individual sports in particular. It creates role models and influences finance. The issue is about quality as well as quantity of coverage.

SPECTATORS AND THE MEDIA

The sporting audience is predominantly male. And generally, men seem to prefer the power, speed and dynamism often associated with traditional male sports, rather than the aesthetic and technical brilliance of some women's sports or women performers. With some notable exceptions, the majority of presenters, as well as editors and sports journalists are still also male. Even with various female presenters now in the limelight, sports reporting is still a male driven and dominated industry whose individual newspapers and channels are cautious about 'rocking the boat'.

The Media creates superstars who become role models who influence participation, but unless minorities receive air time in the first place, this opportunity is lost. Similarly, sports with large audiences attract media attention, advertising and sponsorship, which all generate income and increase opportunities for excellence and interest by the masses. Sports with small audiences are consequently at a disadvantage.

APPLY IT!

In 2007 the Wimbledon Tennis Championships gave women and men equal prize money for the first time, thus falling line with other Grand Slam tennis tournaments. Do you agree or disagree with this move? State clear reasons for your views.

APPLY IT!

In 2006, Tiger Woods (golf) earned over $11 million (£5½ million) while Roger Federer (tennis) earned $8 million (£4 million).

In the same year, the world number one female tennis player, Justine Henin earned over $4 million (£2 million) while Loren Ochoa (who topped the Ladies Professional Golf Association (LPGA) Tour) earned $2.5 (£1 ¼ million).

Please comment on these stats considering the influence of sponsorship, the Media and the relative popularity of professional tennis and professional golf.

In many sports, women receive less prize money for doing the same job as men. Is this discrimination? If female sport receives less sponsorship than male sport then opportunities for development are clearly unequal and restricted.

It is interesting to consider whether families, school sports clubs and communities discriminate. Do parents offer the same amount of support to their female as to their male children? Do schools work to make the image of girls' PE upbeat, attractive and positive, or in some schools are girls still put off by asexual kit and awful showers? Do communities offer the same opportunities for girls as for boys? If not, why not – could it be something to do with the disproportionate number of dads rather than mums who are involved with community sport? Why is that?

Other constraints to women's participation might be lack of time and disposable income, access in terms of transport, inappropriate role models in terms of coaches and leaders as well as appropriate/convenient session times at local centres.

EXAM TIP

When you are thinking of measures to increase participation and excellence (i.e. thinking of solutions to a problem) start by thinking of the problem and then solve it! For example, think of the problem that there are not being enough specialist coaches for people with disabilities. Then solve the problem by saying 'train more specialist coaches'. Easy!

ETHNIC MINORITY GROUPS

Britain is a multi-cultural and multi-racial society. The population of non-white groups in Britain rose from less than 1% in 1951 to approximately 8% in 2001. 70% of the non-white population lives in Greater London, the West Midlands, West Yorkshire and Greater Manchester. Over 60% of the non-white population is under the age of 30, compared with 43% in the population as a whole. And only 5% are

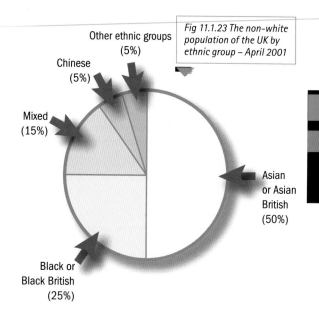

Other ethnic groups (5%)

Chinese (5%)

Mixed (15%)

Black or Black British (25%)

Asian or Asian British (50%)

Fig 11.1.23 The non-white population of the UK by ethnic group – April 2001

over 60, compared with over 20% of the general population. This all affects sporting aptitudes, needs, opportunity and provision.

KEY TERM

Positive discrimination

Favouritism or special treatment for the focus group in order to give them a chance.

RACIAL DISCRIMINATION

Racial discrimination, or racism, stems from prejudice (intolerance and narrow-mindedness), linked with the power of one racial group over another. Although

Perception	Reality
The participation of black people in sport is often considered as a non-existent issue because of their comparative over-representation.	In fact, black participation in sport is limited by stereotyping which channels people into certain sports or certain positions within sports teams.
Over-representation of black athletes in some national sports team seems to indicate equality of opportunity.	Black athletes become what Cashmore (1982) referred to as sporting 'gladiators' for white society and are, in fact, a result of institutional racism. Channelling towards sport might channel *away* from other equally valuable experiences and opportunities such as education and qualifications.
Black sportspeople are encouraged into competitive and professional sport to make a living, and to achieve an avenue for upward social mobility.	Ethnic minorities need equally to be encouraged into recreative mass participation.
Successful black athletes become positive role models.	Hundreds of young black people find that sporting success is very rare.
Ethnic groups are still under- represented in coaching, managerial and organisational team roles – perhaps due to discrimination or to lack of educational opportunity and aspiration.	Positive discrimination might be a workable short-term strategy.
Ethnic groups are still under- represented in terms of participation.	Group leaders who may encourage others to take part should be trained. Information about provision needs to be readily available.
The majority of ethnic communities use inner city, public facilities.	These inner city public facilities need to be improved still further in order to raise participation. Sport development officers from ethnic minorities should be appointed. Single-sex provision must also be improved in order to attract Asian women to centres.

Table 6

illegal, discrimination still exists on the grounds of colour, language and cultural differences. In 1993 the Professional Football Association (PFA) started a campaign (with the Commission for Racial Equality) to 'Kick Racism out of Football'. It is now called 'Kick It Out' – see www.kickitout.org (visit the hotlinks website)..

Performers from ethnic minorities are highly visible on the track, football pitch and cricket field and so many people think there is no problem. However, the following table shows that some common perceptions are untrue.

Possible measures to increase participation and sporting excellence

Here are some possible ways to increase perticipation and excellence by ethnic minority groups:

- raise awareness of racial inequality in sport
- improve skill levels in, and positive attitudes towards sport by black and ethnic minorities, by the using role models
- increase the number of black and ethnic minority decision makers and organisers in sport
- challenge stereotypical thinking perhaps through race-awareness training
- provide for different cultural groups to pursue their own cultural activities, for example the game kabbadi.

APPLY IT!

Kabaddi is a 4000 year old team sport originally from the Indian sub-continent. The name *kabaddi* (which is often chanted during a game) comes from a Hindi word meaning 'holding of breath' which is actually a crucial part of the game. In 2002 in the South Asian community of Peel in Canada there was an episode of racial tension between the community and the police. It was caused by a misunderstanding. In an attempt to re-establish racial harmony in the community the police department started their own Kabaddi team, becoming the first competitive non-South Asian team in the world. It had a great positive impact on the community.

EXAM TIP

If you really know and understand the impact of your three key terms: Opportunity, Provision and Esteem, and can apply them to young people, the elderly, people with disabilities, women and ethnic minority groups, you will be able to have a good go at most exam questions that are asked on this section.

TAKE IT FURTHER

Check out the rules of Kabaddi (try Wikipedia) and look at a game on: www.youtube.com (visit the hotlinks website)

ExamCafé

Relax, refresh, result!

Refresh your memory

Revision checklist

You should now know and understand about all the points below.

▷ Public, private and voluntary funding (including the National Lottery).

▷ UK Sport; the devolved National Institutes of Sport and home country organisations such as Sport England.

▷ Current government and national governing body (NGB) initiatives that influence and promote participation in physical activity.

▷ The sports development pyramid and the continuum from mass participation to sporting excellence.

▷ Opportunity, provision and esteem – in the context of mass participation and sporting excellence.

▷ Social and cultural factors impacting on participation by certain groups in the UK such as people with disabilities and young people.

▷ Measures to increase participation and sporting excellence in the UK.

REVISE AS YOU GO!

1. Explain each of the following three key terms for funding: Public, Private and Voluntary.
2. What does EIS stand for?
3. What do National Institutes such as the EIS do to help increase sporting excellence?
4. Name a home country sports council.
5. What are THREE key aims of a home country sports council?
6. State some current government initiatives that promote participation in physical activity for young people.
7. Name the four levels of the sports development pyramid.
8. Describe each level of the sports development pyramid.
9. With reference to participation in sport, explain the three key terms: Opportunity, Provision and Esteem.
10. Name three groups in society (other than elderly people) who may be under-represented in sport and physical activity.

Drugs, the media, sponsorship and violence in sport

LEARNING OBJECTIVES

In Part II of this chapter you will learn about:

- the reasons for and the consequences of the use of drugs in sport
- possible solutions to the use of drugs in sport
- the impact on performance in sport of modern technological products
- the roles and the impact of the media on sport
- the relationship between sport, sponsorship and the media
- possible causes and solutions to violence in sport.

INTRODUCTION

The oath sworn on behalf of all Olympic athletes includes:

> '*In the name of all competitors, I promise that we shall take part in these Olympic Games... without doping and without drugs in the true spirit of sportsmanship.*'

It seems that not all Olympic performers keep their promises. Recent Olympic Games and other major sporting competitions have surprised few people with their drug scandals. At the Athens Olympics of 2004, 23 athletes – the most ever in an Olympic Games – were found to have taken a banned substance. There exists a covert, systematised and multi-million pound drugs industry whose sole purpose is to enable some sportsmen and women to illegally enhance their performance. In some events the difference between first and tenth place is just hundredths of a second and millions of pounds. The lure of success is great and the penalties for cheating are comparatively small. Is it any wonder that some competitors are tempted to break the rules?

The reasons and consequences of the use of drugs in sport

The use of drugs in sport is a very expensive, serious and dangerous game of cat and mouse. As testing systems and random testing intensify, and known drugs become more easily detectable, new drugs become available, and improved 'masking' drugs help users to avoid detection. Naïve performers and corrupt or inefficient testing laboratories leave the careers and personal lives of some innocent performers in tatters, while guilty competitors go free.

The radical 'counter-culture' suggestion to 'level the playing field' and legalise and carefully monitor the use of performance enhancing drugs would surely not solve the problem. The richest countries would remain ahead of the game, athletes would become victims in a power struggle and their lives would continue to be put at risk. Meanwhile, young people would receive the wrong messages about drug abuse and the traditional, true spirit of sport would disappear for good.

THE MANCHESTER COLLEGE
COLLEGE LIBRARIES
ASHTON OLD ROAD
MANCHESTER
M11 2WH

KEY TERM

Counter Culture suggestion

An idea or way of behaving that is consciously and deliberately very different from the cultural values of the larger society that it is part of.

Fig 11.2.1 The use of drugs and sport

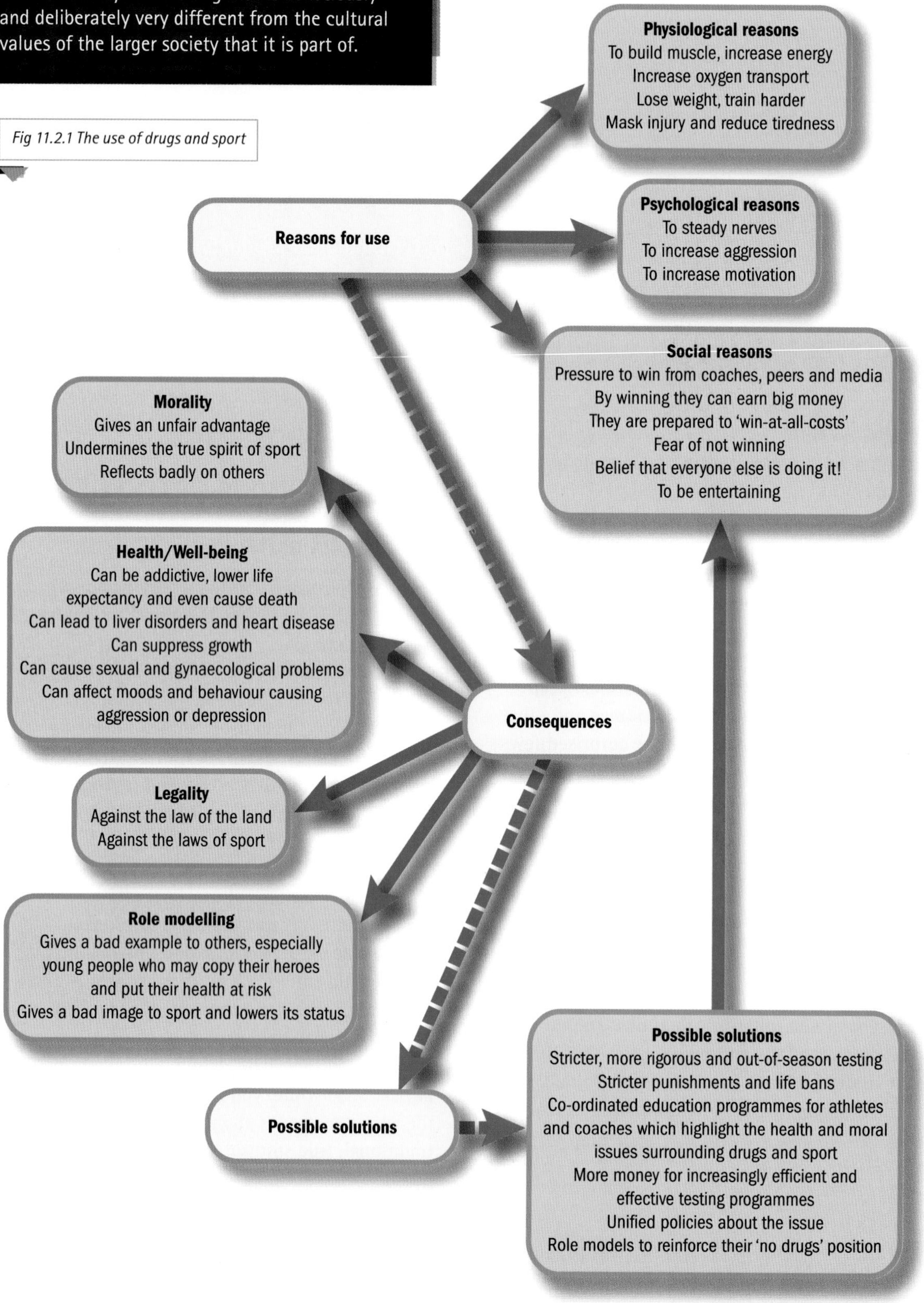

Our task is to analyse why some performers are tempted to take drugs, to identify reasons why they should avoid temptation and to suggest ways of solving the existing problem.

Reasons for use

Physiological reasons
To build muscle, increase energy
Increase oxygen transport
Lose weight, train harder
Mask injury and reduce tiredness

Psychological reasons
To steady nerves
To increase aggression
To increase motivation

Social reasons
Pressure to win from coaches, peers and media
By winning they can earn big money
They are prepared to 'win-at-all-costs'
Fear of not winning
Belief that everyone else is doing it!
To be entertaining

Morality
Gives an unfair advantage
Undermines the true spirit of sport
Reflects badly on others

Health/Well-being
Can be addictive, lower life
expectancy and even cause death
Can lead to liver disorders and heart disease
Can suppress growth
Can cause sexual and gynaecological problems
Can affect moods and behaviour causing
aggression or depression

Consequences

Legality
Against the law of the land
Against the laws of sport

Role modelling
Gives a bad example to others, especially
young people who may copy their heroes
and put their health at risk
Gives a bad image to sport and lowers its status

Possible solutions

Possible solutions
Stricter, more rigorous and out-of-season testing
Stricter punishments and life bans
Co-ordinated education programmes for athletes
and coaches which highlight the health and moral
issues surrounding drugs and sport
More money for increasingly efficient and
effective testing programmes
Unified policies about the issue
Role models to reinforce their 'no drugs' position

EXAM TIP

If a question asks for solutions to the problem of drugs in sport, make sure you don't list all the different types of drugs and explain what they are used for – this is not needed and will not gain you marks.

REMEMBER

Answer the exact question that has been set.

The Sporting Times, 19 September 2008

THE BIG DEBATE

The time has come to legalise drugs in sport.

15th Sept. 2008

Dear Sir

The goal of 'cleaning up' sport in impossible! The idea that is can be done is self-deluding nonsense! Just accept it – modern high-level sport is miles away from the original Olympic and amateur ideal and rich countries are investing millions into developing athlete-robots. We have two choices: either to try to turn back the clock (which won't work) or to rethink what sport is and start a new 21st century Super Olympics. Make drugs legal and available and you immediately solve the problem of cheating – and add to the enthralling spectacle of great human performance! The fight against drugs in sport has failed – so let's be honest and welcome them!

Yours truly
Frank Smith, Yorkshire.

If we live in a civilised society – we must behave in a civilised way! Once we allow drugs into sport we might as well re-start Roman gladiatorial combats – how about paying to watch athletes fighting lions at Wembley?

17 September 2008

Dear Sir

Athletes aren't just super-rich sprinters and over-paid footballers. They are keen, local athletes winning their age group triathlons; students trying to get into university basketball squads and youngsters desperate to make U16 county swimming teams.

If we legalise drugs it will force everyone to take them and it will no longer be possible to compete seriously without them. Have we no respect for humanity? It would be a catastrophe in a civilised society. Drugs maim, mutilate and kill – just like war. The war against drugs in sport must continue.

Yours,
Sam Dunlop, Bournemouth.

TAKE IT FURTHER

Have a class debate on the pros and cons of legalising drug use in sport, with two students speaking for the motion, two speaking against the motion and a voting 'house' (the rest of the class), who may ask questions when the debate is opened up by the 'chair'. Formulate your thoughts and arguments based on your own knowledge, views, reading and research. Consideration of the following should help:

Possible arguments for allowing drugs in sport	Arguments against drugs in sport
The rules against drugs are based on old–fashioned amateur values that are irrelevant in modern professional sport. Allow freedom of choice and let those who want to do it, do it!	The majority would lose freedom of choice as they would have to take drugs to succeed. The sporting world would be plunged back to the days of institutional doping – as carried out by countries such as East Germany over 30 years ago.
It would level the playing field. Cheats are always ahead of testers and legalising drugs would allow everyone to compete legally.	It would be a disaster for athletes who may become addicted and whose life expectancy could be lowered. Many retired elite performers in their 40s or 50s have died from a variety of complaints linked to abuse of anabolic steroids, growth hormones and/or blood–boosting agents just a few years after leaving top–level sport.
It would be a more entertaining spectacle for spectators.	Spectators enjoy skill and finesse as well as raw power. Health of athletes should not be sacrificed for public pleasure.
Current rules are random and unfair e.g. cyclists could have heart surgery which would increase circulation and improve performance.	Younger athletes and children are not able to make fully rational and informed decisions. Children would be selected on both talent and their willingness to take drugs.
Many accusations of doping fail to succeed in court. Also, in some case, testing has been faulty which can destroy athletes' careers and private lives.	Poorer nations are disadvantaged due to less advanced medical and pharmaceutical industries. Athletes from poorer nations would no longer be able to compete on talent alone.
If legalised, drugs could be medically monitored which would be safer than the current situation.	Reform is preferable to surrender. Keep improving research, testing methods and funding into testing. Increase punishments to automatic life bans.
Have a 'Drugs Olympics' and a 'Clean Olympics'	A 'Drugs Olympics' and a 'Clean Olympics', would soon lead to drug cheats in the 'Clean Olympics'.

Table 1

An example of a performer found guilty of a doping offence – Marion Jones

constantly improving. Certain British universities now offer BSc and other courses in sports technology.

By the 1990s performance in the javelin had improved so much that track runners were in danger of being speared by throwers at the other end of the stadium. Javelins were, therefore, redesigned to be harder to throw. Now throws are shorter and a special conversion table is used, which allows current results to be compared with those of the past.

We are interested here in the links between human performance and product design, and the impact of technology on sporting equipment, footwear and clothing.

KEY IMPACTS

The key impacts are:

- increased safety, and
- increased comfort, both of which might lead to...
- improved performance.

EXAM TIP

Depending on the exact question set, you may be able to make relevant mention of the following in an answer about drugs in sport:

100% ME – the programme that promotes drug free competitive sport throughout the UK by providing high quality information on anti-doping and by promoting positive attitudes and values in sport.

The World anti-Doping Agency (WADA) – the organisation that promotes, coordinates, and monitors the fight against doping in sports at international level.

APPLY IT!

Before the Mexico Olympics of 1968 sprint timings were calculated using a stopwatch which recorded to the nearest tenth of a second. This quickly became too vague in an event dealing with tiny fractions of a second.

The impact of modern technological products

What could be further from modern technology than a 100m race? Surely it just needs eight fast runners, a track and a tape? Not so. The influence of science is found throughout modern sport including the 100m. Materials technologists are constantly working on better footwear and clothing. Even the track itself will have been specially designed to maximise performance. Timing equipment and replay techniques to check and make decisions about 'photo-finishes' are also

TASK 1

In twos, find out a) the winning times in the Women's 100m and Men's 100m events at the Beijing Olympic Games of 2008 and b) the winning times in these events when the Games were held in London in 1948. What are the reasons for improved performance over the last 50 years or so? List as many reasons as possible – including the impact of specific modern technological products.

Safety: • Gum shields • Rugby scrum caps • Cricket head gear • Padded equipment for hockey goal keepers and rugby players.	Technology: • High tech super bikes • Bobsleigh and F1 car manufacture • Gym equipment e.g. treadmills and rowing machines • Ball feeding machines for tennis and cricket • Items that become part of popular culture e.g. skateboards • Arenas with retractable roofs	Materials: • Carbon fibre and titanium for various items of equipment e.g. poles for pole vault, golf clubs, racquets. • Large-headed clubs and racquets • Astroturf, rubberised, bouncy tracks that give fast times and sprung floors in indoor venues • Soft landing areas
Officiating: • Electronic timing equipment that measures fractions of seconds. • Sports 'watches' for performers.	Shoes: • Boots with bladed studs • Track shoes that dampen muscle vibration and are said to boost performance	Clothing: • Lycra body suits and hooded swift suits for track athletes • Hydrodynamic swimming caps • Full body suits for swimming • Socks with an anti-microbial finish to help prevent the fungus that causes athletes foot
Motion analysis: • Motion analysis e.g. of golf swing or discus throw which can be computer analysed.	Comfort: • New fabrics that draw sweat away from the body, insulate, cool or breathe as needed	Science/Medicine: • Improved physiotherapy and sports medicine techniques including ultrasound, ice baths etc. • Nasal strips, e.g. for athletes • Improved/advanced surgery including artificial ligaments and joint replacements • Lycra for compression bandages.

Table 2 Examples of modern technological products

REMEMBER

The key impacts of modern technological products are to do with: safety, comfort and improved performance.

The roles and the impact of the media on sport

'*Spectator sport and the media have fused together. The one is inconceivable without the other.*'

Sport in Britain 1945–2000
– Holt and Mason

MEDIA I – ITS ROLES

Sport is a central feature of TV and radio, of newspapers and magazines, of the Internet, books, films and videos. Sport-related TV programmes range from live coverage, recorded highlights and quiz shows, to educative documentaries, the latest news and reality shows. Newspaper articles feature pre-event predictions and post-event analysis, news on the size and behaviour of the crowd, the state of the facilities and behind the scenes stories about the celebrity sport stars.

There are also numerous specialist sports magazines, which not only give information on skill development, but also feature personalities and events and adverts. An ever-increasing number of biographical and autobiographical books is also being published, sometimes it seems, only days after a major sporting events has finished – and always in time for Christmas!

Improvements in recording and editing technology, camera angles and interactive features have all increased the potential of TV to fulfil media roles. The four roles of the media that you need to know and understand are as follows:

- inform
- educate
- entertain
- advertise.

In any particular media feature, programme or report, one role might dominate, or elements of each might exist.

INFORM

To inform is to tell, notify or let someone know about something. The media lets us know about sport. We get live coverage, factual information and analysis; rules, reports, replays and results; scrutiny of teams and performers' behaviour; highlights and comments. Developments in school PE and sport are also occasionally reported. We are informed via newspapers, magazines, TV, the radio and the Internet. The media preview upcoming events, comment on likely outcomes and then debrief on what has happened when they are over.

EDUCATE

To educate is to teach. Documentaries and programmes such as 'Trans World Sport' teach us about global sport. Also, the public can be educated about sport skills, coaching techniques, contemporary sporting issues (such as the issue of doping in sport), and developments in school and community sport. Ethics of fair play can also be reinforced through the comments and behaviour of role models either on TV or via 'master class' websites.

ENTERTAIN

To entertain is to interest, occupy or amuse. The media certainly use sport to interest and amuse the public. It can be argued that sport has had to change in order to be more entertaining for the media – but more of that later. Sport is central to the increasingly popular home-entertainment industry, with huge screens and 'in-home' cinemas abounding. Many sports and teams have seriously committed fan bases; sports stars' private lives attract great interest in, for example, 'Hello' magazine, and viewers watch televised sport for its drama, skill and intensity. Which TV screen were you glued to when you saw Jonny Wilkinson's drop goal in the 2003 Rugby World Cup final?

Back in July 1990, when the potential audience for any programme was 52.8 million, 25,210,000 viewers (the biggest audience for any single event in British TV history) watched the World Cup semi-final between England and West Germany. Nearly half of the nation shared in the intense emotion of an international soccer penalty shoot-out.

Has the media created a nation of armchair spectators? Are more people now obese because they are leading sedentary lifestyles, watching rather than taking part in sport and physical activity? (See pae 215.)

TASK 2

As a class, find examples of programmes or articles, the primary roles of which are to either inform, educate, entertain or to advertise. Research from the following sources:

- tabloid newspapers (e.g. Mirror, Sun, Mail or Express)
- compact/broadsheet newspapers (e.g. Times, Telegraph, Independent or Guardian)
- specialist sports magazine/s (e.g. Ace Tennis)
- BBC sports-related coverage (in the Radio Times)
- Sky and ITV sports-related coverage
- Radio 5 sports coverage

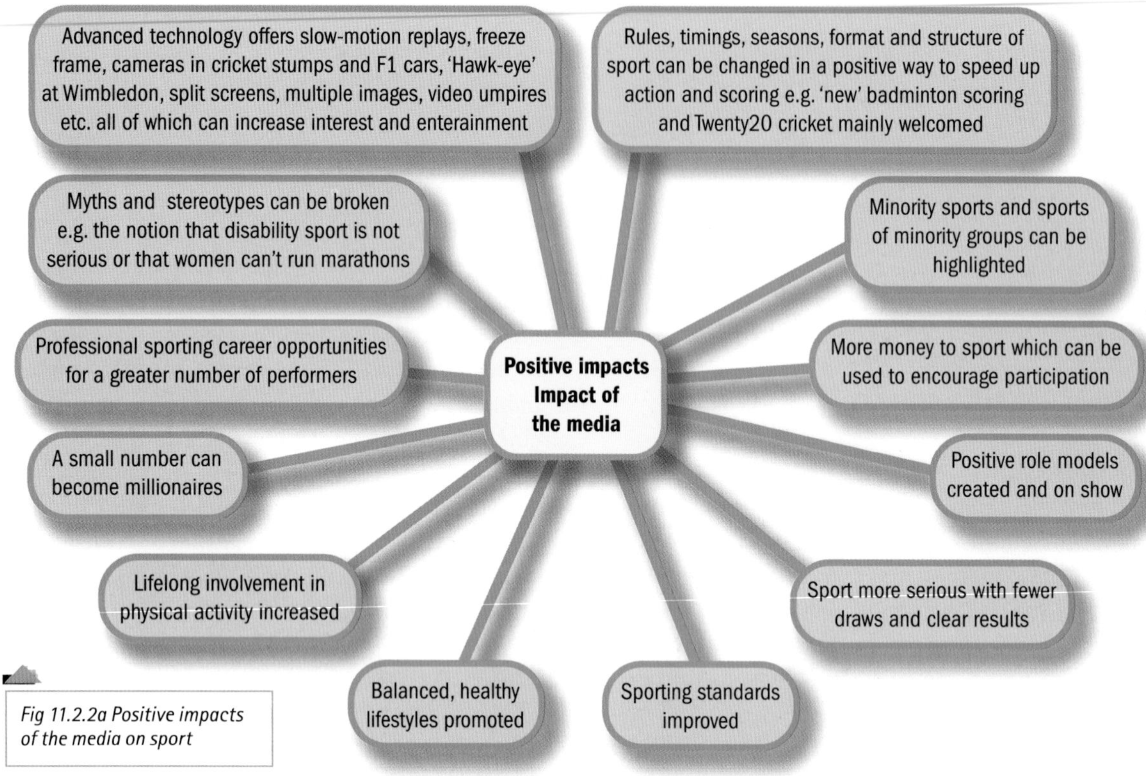

Advanced technology offers slow-motion replays, freeze frame, cameras in cricket stumps and F1 cars, 'Hawk-eye' at Wimbledon, split screens, multiple images, video umpires etc. all of which can increase interest and enterainment

Rules, timings, seasons, format and structure of sport can be changed in a positive way to speed up action and scoring e.g. 'new' badminton scoring and Twenty20 cricket mainly welcomed

Myths and stereotypes can be broken e.g. the notion that disability sport is not serious or that women can't run marathons

Minority sports and sports of minority groups can be highlighted

Positive impacts Impact of the media

Professional sporting career opportunities for a greater number of performers

More money to sport which can be used to encourage participation

A small number can become millionaires

Positive role models created and on show

Lifelong involvement in physical activity increased

Sport more serious with fewer draws and clear results

Balanced, healthy lifestyles promoted

Sporting standards improved

Fig 11.2.2a Positive impacts of the media on sport

The public can have their views dictated by the media

Only very few get high financial rewards

Increased 'win-at-all-costs' ethic/loss of enjoyment factor

Minority sports get minimal coverage and remain disadvantage etc.

Loss of privacy

Audiences may suffer from sporting overload and boredom

Reduced participation – more armchair spectators and fewer playing participants

Media focus on trivial, sensational or negative features such as private lives or bad behaviour of stars, with negative role models on show

Some performers may be forced to perform more frequently than is sensible or safe

Negative impacts of the media on sport

National prejudices can be encouraged, by bigoted and sensational headlines

Rules, timings, seasons, format and structure can be changed in a negative way. The media can end up controlling sport/s e.g. regular breaks in play for advertising

Certain events become unavailable unless you have certain channels or 'pay to view'

Myths and stereotypes can be reinforced if coverage is poorly managed or disproportionately in favour of one sport. Unless people see the outstanding skill, speed and excitement of elite netball, many will continue to think of it as a slow, limited and over-structured school game

As the stakes get higher and the result becomes more important, there is increased pressure on everyone involved. This can increase problems such as corruption, violence and drug abuse

Bright lights/intrusive cameras could put performers off

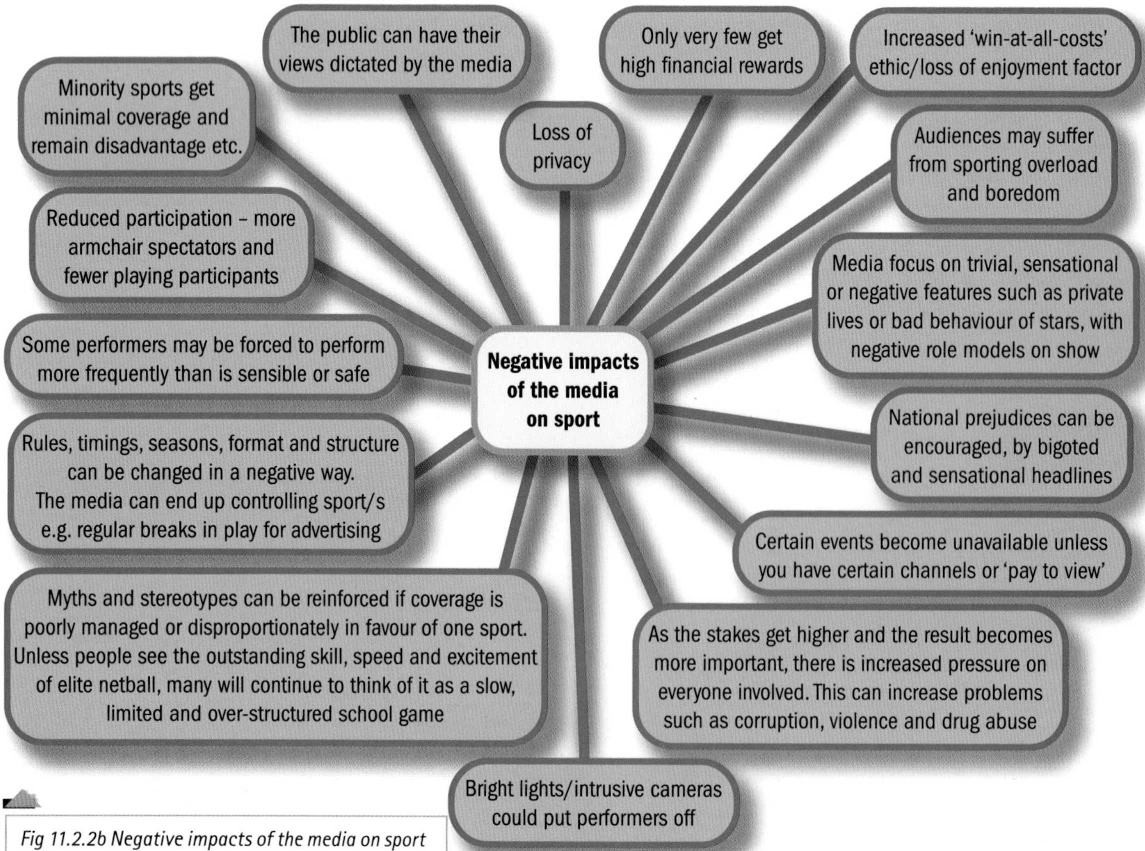

Fig 11.2.2b Negative impacts of the media on sport

ADVERTISE

To advertise is to promote or publicise. Sport is used either directly to advertise products (from sports goods to crisps, beer, cars and mobile phones), or indirectly through sponsorship. Companies sponsor individuals, teams, leagues and events to heighten corporate awareness. Preview programmes also promote events. In contrast to the BBC, independent TV has always had to sell advertising in order to pay for itself – see Part III, page **317** – Commercialisation of the Olympic Games)

MEDIA II – ITS IMPACT

BACKGROUND

To have an impact is to have an influence or an effect on something. The media certainly have an impact on sport. In the early 1950s, less than one in ten British households owned a TV. Twenty years later, only one in ten did not. Many homes now have two or three or more TVs, located in different rooms, along with personal computers whose Internet access enables 24/7 connection to the outside world of sport. TV companies once paid relatively small amounts to sports bodies to buy entertainment and information for their audiences – now they pay millions.

The media, especially TV, has had a profound effect on modern day sport. High level professional sport is now a media commodity driven by market forces. It is a big earner that, in some ways, has had to bow to its master.

APPLY IT!

The men's marathon in the Los Angeles Olympics of 1984 was scheduled at the hottest part of the day. Similarly cricket, rugby and football matches sometimes go ahead when pitches are flooded or snow-covered, just to meet media demands and/or avoid losing income. What about third and fourth round play-off games in big tournaments? What is their main role?

The relationship between sport, sponsorship and the media

INTER-RELATIONSHIP

A pyramid, or triangular shape can be used to demonstrate a solid, interrelated, mutually-dependent relationship. Modern sport has been referred to as a 'golden triangle' (Hargreaves, 1986) or pact between professional sport, advertisers (sponsorship) and the media. Whether this is a match made in heaven or an unholy alliance is debatable. Either way, there is no doubt that sport and the media (and therefore sponsorship, which depends on the media) are inextricably linked. With TV being the most powerful aspect of the media.

APPLY IT!

Class discussion:

- Has sport benefited from its mutually dependent relationship with the media?
- Has the media saved sport from economic disaster when it was becoming more expensive and had fewer people paying at the gate?
- How can sport retain its true traditional nature and values while benefiting from the money offered by commercialism?
- Should it even try to?
- Has the price been too high?
- Has money corrupted sport?
- Has sport been manipulated for the sake of sponsors, advertisers and passive armchair spectators?

APPLY IT!

It has been suggested that:

- In tennis there are widespread allegations of corruption. Players will allegedly lose matches in order to move on to higher paid tournaments, or share the first two sets and play a legitimate third set to fill a particular TV time slot. Another accusation is that umpires are directed by tournament organisers to treat big name players well to ensure their continued involvement.
- In boxing, ranking lists are manipulated to stage 'world' title fights.

SOME BACKGROUND

In the 1950s, the Government, the BBC and ITV identified and agreed on ten sporting events that should 'belong' to everyone and not be given exclusive coverage by any one TV organisation. They wanted exclusive coverage to be avoided. The listed events were: the Olympics (Summer and Winter), the World Cup, the Commonwealth Games, the FA cup final, Wimbledon, Test Match cricket, the Derby, the Grand National and the Boat Race.

At first there was little competition between ITV and BBC and the viewer was not threatened. The threat came with the rise of satellite TV 30 years later.

BSkyB

British Satellite Broadcasting began in 1988, and used sport to attract a mass audience. The Broadcasting Act of 1990 declared that all rights to broadcast sport could be sold to the highest bidder and in November 1990 British Satellite Broadcasting merged with Sky to create BSkyB. Exclusivity now forced fans to sign up to the entire channel. BSkyB paid £304 million for a five-year deal with the top clubs, which then broke away from the Football League and formed the Premiership. BSkyB had turned soccer, historically the game of 'the people', into 'big business'.

CRICKET AND FOOTBALL

Channel 4 paid £50 million for the rights to televise cricket Test Matches from 1999–2002 and ITV had to pay £44 million in 1992 for a four-year deal for exclusive live coverage and recorded highlights of league football, forcing it to drop coverage of other sports. By 1997, when two-thirds of Football League clubs were losing money, Premier League clubs were massing around £8 million a year from broadcasting and sponsorship rights. Relegation is now a serious business involving loss of media revenue and reduced demand for merchandising.

In summer 2002, the BBC and BSkyB stepped in when ITV Digital's short-lived coverage of League football ended in disaster. ITV Digital collapsed owing nearly £200 million to football clubs, many of whom faced economic ruin having contracted expensive players on the promise of their slice of the multi-million pound financial cake. This not only illustrates the mutually dependent relationship between sport and the media, but also the firm control and profound effect that television can have over one particular sport.

SPONSORSHIP

Let's re-cap on some work that you possibly covered in GCSE PE. Sponsorship has been called 'the most visible relationship between sport and business in the modern world' (*Only a Game,* Mason), with company names and logos appearing on shirtfronts, hoardings, and playing areas. We regularly see top performers purposefully turning drinks, equipment and kit bags towards conveniently positioned cameras in order to maximise their sponsors' media coverage. There would be none of this if people weren't going to see it or know about it.

ADVANTAGES AND DISADVANTAGES

Sponsorship has advantages and disadvantages to both performers and sponsors.

Formula 1 car on the race track

– The Performer –	
Advantages of sponsorship	**Disadvantages of sponsorship**
Full time training possible because sponsor meets expenses.	Performers can become reliant on a particular sponsor.
Financial security after retirement can be provided.	Sponsorship can be limited or withdrawn – which doesn't provide security.
Full concentration on sport possible.	Some sponsorship gives bad image to sport eg alcohol.
	Performers, teams and events can be manipulated or exploited to suit the sponsor.
	Generous sponsorship only available to the few.
– The Sponsor –	
Advantages of sponsorship	**Disadvantages of sponsorship**
Healthy, positive image forged.	If performer behaves badly it can reflect on the sponsor.
Tax bill reduced.	It is an uncertain investment – sporting success not guaranteed.
Excellent advertising can be gained which generates income	If event/s disrupted, media exposure is lost.
Hospitality at big sporting events.	
Goodwill increased.	

Table 3 Advantages and disadvantages of sport sponsorship to both sponsor and performer.

EXAM TIP

You will <u>not</u> find the following types of questions on your exam paper:

- 'What is sport sponsorship?'
- 'What are the advantages of sponsorship to performers or to sponsors?'

It is useful, however, to be aware of the basic features of sponsorship, as you may be able to use them when answering a question on the relationship between sport, sponsorship and the media.

APPLY IT!

Features of sponsorship:

- Sponsorship is the provision of funds or other support to individuals, teams, events and organisations in order to get favourable publicity and a commercial return.
- Sponsorship agencies bring sponsors and sports bodies together to organise events or programmes.
- Agents promote particular competitors for each other's mutual financial benefit.
- Athletes endorse, or give their backing to products by displaying the company name on their clothing or equipment while performing.
- Performers also use their celebrity status to advertise products away from the sport.
- Companies invest in perimeter advertising around, and on pitches.

TAKE IT FURTHER

Look in some newspapers or on the Internet. Which companies are currently sponsoring big sports or big sporting events? Can you find out how much they are spending? They must think it is worth it! Try to find out about: Sunday league cricket; the Oxford and Cambridge boat race; golf; ice hockey; motor racing and equestrianism, as well as the more straightforward top level Rugby League, Rugby Union and Association Football.

COMMERCIAL PRESSURE

Top-level sport is now inextricably linked with big business. Though the aim of both sport and business is to win, the drive to win at any price undermines the true ethic of sport whose traditional values of enjoyment, participation, fair play and a fair chance may not survive a wholesale business take-over. Modern commercial sport earns millions for the very best performers in the most media-exposed sports, yet other participants are exploited in the interests of profit. One concern is that the need to win for money might lead to corruption and the temptation to cheat.

FOOTBALL VS NETBALL

There is also the problem that sponsorship is uneven across sports, with high-profile sports attracting generous sponsorship and low-profile sports next to nothing. A vicious circle ensues: if low-profile sports such as volleyball, or those sports (such as netball) pursued by minority groups, fail to attract media attention, then they also fail to attract sponsorship; if they don't get sponsorship they can't market themselves, improve or compete on even terms with those that do!

Some performers may be driven to trivial and sensational articles and pictures that have nothing to do with their skilfulness or commitment, just to attract the sponsorship they need. International and National Governing Bodies of sport strive to retain autonomy and to safeguard their sports against their profit-orientated colleagues.

With careful management, the unique qualities and potential of sport can hopefully be retained, and the media's roles of advertising, informing, educating and entertaining us with and about sport will have a positive influence on sport, sports performers and the viewing public.

Violence in sport

HISTORY – AN OVERVIEW

AGGRESSION

Controlled aggression is a fundamental part of many sports. Sometimes, however, this spills over into an uncontrolled situation where legs and fists fly and where serious physical injury is caused. Notably, when similar violence occurs on the streets, rather than in the name of sport, it is a crime.

This is not a new phenomenon. The occasional 'mob-football games' of pre-industrial days, some of which (you may recall) survive today, were once characterised by severe violence and brutality – see Chapter 10, pages 233–36, 'surviving ethnic sports'.

CONTROL

After 1850, however, helped by the civilised ethics that emerged from the English public schools, games became linked with fair play and sportsmanship. Games were not to be taken too seriously in these schools – see Chapter 10, pages 236–38, taking part was more important than winning, and honesty was the only policy. Even though physical determination and courage were applauded, they always had to go hand in hand with gentlemanly behaviour, courteous attitudes and respect for the opposition. The late Victorian public schoolboy and his descendants, played games to the letter of the law, but also to their spirit or underlying unwritten principles of good manners.

TODAY

Times have changed, and these middle class amateur attitudes have been largely squeezed out of modern sport. The stakes are high, the outcome imperative, the pressure intense, and the sporting stadium like a cauldron. Gamesmanship, or the stretching of rules to the absolute limit in order to gain an advantage, is commonplace.

REMEMBER

Sportsmanship = fair play

Gamesmanship = stretching the rules to gain an unfair advantage

Deviance (in sport) = seriously breaking the rules and norms (of sport)

Here we are concerned with the social causes of violence in sport by both players and spectators.

VIOLENCE BY PARTICIPANTS

This can be categorised and explained in terms of:

- **Cheating** – it is a blatant infringement of agreed sporting codes and a disregard of the true values of sport as an experience
- **Health** – it causes injury and physical damage, which can be life-threatening
- **Legality** – physical violence is against the law of the land and is increasingly being punished with legal action when it occurs in sport

- **Role-modelling** – elite sports performers have a responsibility to be role models, especially to young people.

VIOLENCE BY SPECTATORS

'Peace, Peace is what I seek and public calm; Endless extinction of unhappy hates.'

Matthew Arnold, quoted by Mr Justice Popplewell in his interim report on football in 1985, after the Heysel Stadium disaster.

BACKGROUND

Aggressive and rebellious behaviour at sporting events is not new. As Holt argues 'hooliganism exemplifies to perfection the difficulty of disentangling what is new from what is old in social history' (Holt in *Sport and The British*).

The problem was around in pre-industrial days and throughout the Victorian period, when the constant fighting of the Irish immigrant Hooligan family added a new word to the language of the 1890s. Hooliganism forcefully raised its head as a major social problem again in the 1960s in connection with the collective, aggressive behaviour of predominantly white, urban, unskilled teenage males at football matches.

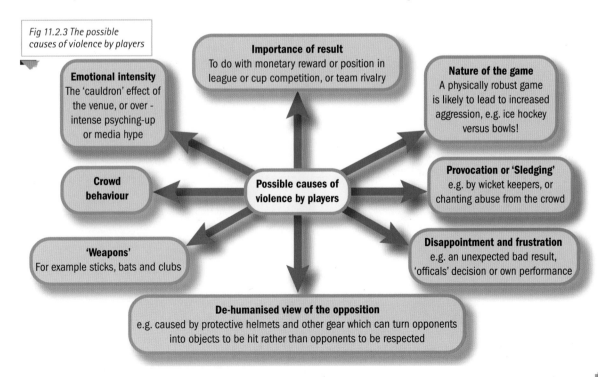

Fig 11.2.3 The possible causes of violence by players

Importance of result
To do with monetary reward or position in league or cup competition, or team rivalry

Emotional intensity
The 'cauldron' effect of the venue, or over-intense psyching-up or media hype

Nature of the game
A physically robust game is likely to lead to increased aggression, e.g. ice hockey versus bowls!

Crowd behaviour

Possible causes of violence by players

Provocation or 'Sledging'
e.g. by wicket keepers, or chanting abuse from the crowd

'Weapons'
For example sticks, bats and clubs

Disappointment and frustration
e.g. an unexpected bad result, 'officals' decision or own performance

De-humanised view of the opposition
e.g. caused by protective helmets and other gear which can turn opponents into objects to be hit rather than opponents to be respected

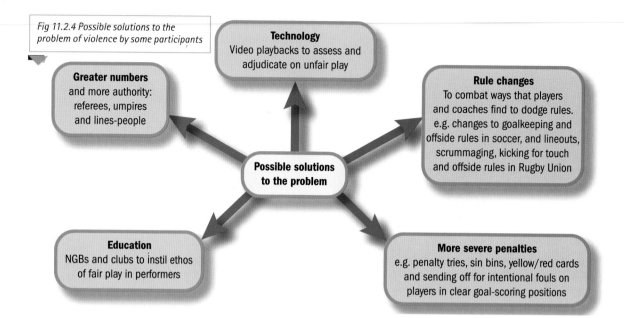

Fig 11.2.4 Possible solutions to the problem of violence by some participants

Technology
Video playbacks to assess and adjudicate on unfair play

Greater numbers
and more authority: referees, umpires and lines-people

Rule changes
To combat ways that players and coaches find to dodge rules. e.g. changes to goalkeeping and offside rules in soccer, and lineouts, scrummaging, kicking for touch and offside rules in Rugby Union

Possible solutions to the problem

Education
NGBs and clubs to instil ethos of fair play in performers

More severe penalties
e.g. penalty tries, sin bins, yellow/red cards and sending off for intentional fouls on players in clear goal-scoring positions

POSSIBLE CAUSES

There has been much research and debate about the nature and reasons for football hooliganism. Some say that the phenomenon arose due to exaggerated and sensational reporting of incidents by the press, which included headlines such as 'Smash the Thugs!' which instilled anger and resentment in the alleged 'thugs', who willingly rose to the challenge. Others say that a chauvinistic and primitive desire to assert maleness is at the heart of the issue. Groups dress the same in order to be easily identified, but wear different boots or socks or differently tied scarves to identify their rank in the group.

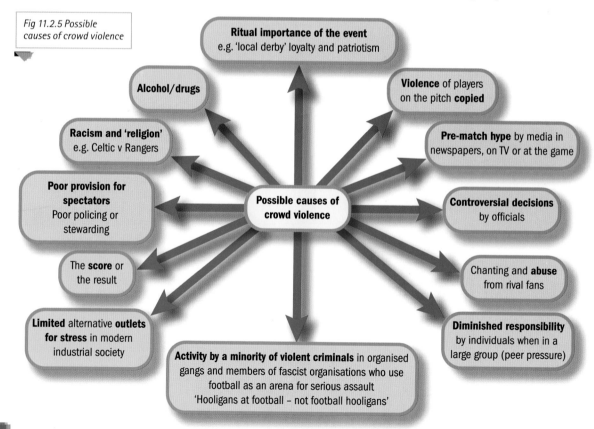

Fig 11.2.5 Possible causes of crowd violence

Ritual importance of the event
e.g. 'local derby' loyalty and patriotism

Alcohol/drugs

Violence of players on the pitch **copied**

Racism and 'religion'
e.g. Celtic v Rangers

Pre-match hype by media in newspapers, on TV or at the game

Poor provision for spectators
Poor policing or stewarding

Possible causes of crowd violence

Controversial decisions
by officials

The **score** or the result

Chanting and **abuse** from rival fans

Limited alternative **outlets for stress** in modern industrial society

Diminished responsibility
by individuals when in a large group (peer pressure)

Activity by a minority of violent criminals in organised gangs and members of fascist organisations who use football as an arena for serious assault
'Hooligans at football – not football hooligans'

Despite criminal incidents of beatings and stabbings, it has been argued that the chanting, charges and threatening behaviour are just symbolic rituals and that injury or worse is a result of panic rushes to escape attack, rather than as a result of attack itself.

HEYSEL – 1985

This was certainly the case in the Heysel stadium disaster of 1985 when 39 spectators, including 31 Juventus fans were crushed or trampled to death when trying to escape a charge by Liverpool supporters. More than 250 others were injured when violence erupted between rival fans – all in front of a huge European TV audience. The Italian Prime Minister, Bettino Craxi, said Britain was 'a country submerged in disgrace by the criminal actions of violent and irresponsible groups'. Britain was banned from European football for five years.

HILLSBOROUGH – 1989

Another major football tragedy, which had nothing to do with hooliganism, occurred at Hillsborough in Sheffield in 1989, when Liverpool were playing Nottingham Forest in the FA Cup semi-final. Hundreds of Liverpool fans were channelled into an already crowded section of the ground, resulting in a catastrophic crush at the front, which caused 95 deaths. The then Prime Minister, Margaret Thatcher, immediately instructed a thorough investigation. The resulting

Taylor report identified overcrowding and poor facilities as central to the problem.

POSSIBLE SOLUTIONS

Much has since been done to make venues safer, and to prevent and control violence by spectators at football matches, such as the removal of perimeter fencing, and the conversion of terraces, to create all-seater stadiums.

AN ENDURING PROBLEM?

Is violence in sport by players and spectators still an issue?

NGBs continue to successfully eradicate violence from their games, and push the need for elite performers to be role models to youngsters. What about football hooliganism? The number of arrests and the need for police presence have both declined in recent years.

Also, as football becomes more 'Americanised,' user-friendly and glamorous, with family enclosures, cheerleaders, mascots and music, some young male fans are beginning to 'vote with their feet' and find fun elsewhere. In addition, high ticket prices, the loss of terracing, and some oppressive management and stewarding have started to keep certain groups away.

The negative image that football in the UK so recently had, seems to be changing.

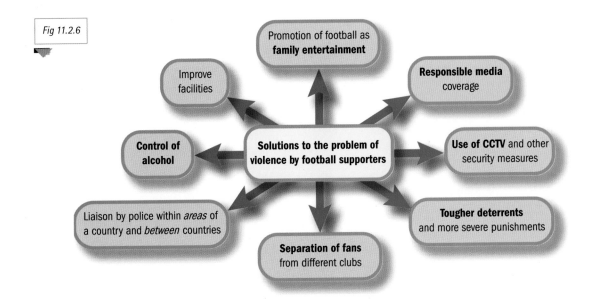

Fig 11.2.6

Promotion of football as **family entertainment**

Improve facilities

Responsible media coverage

Control of alcohol

Solutions to the problem of violence by football supporters

Use of CCTV and other security measures

Liaison by police within *areas* of a country and *between* countries

Separation of fans from different clubs

Tougher deterrents and more severe punishments

ExamCafé
Relax, refresh, result!

Refresh your memory

Revision checklist

You should now know and understand about:

▷ The reasons for, and the consequences of, the use of drugs in sport.

▷ Possible solutions to the use of drugs in sport.

▷ The impact on performance in sport of modern technological products.

▷ The roles and the impact of the media on sport.

▷ The relationship between sport, sponsorship and the media.

▷ Possible causes and solutions to violence in sport.

REVISE AS YOU GO!

1. Identify three reasons why performers may be tempted to take performance enhancing drugs.
2. Identify three consequences of the use of drugs in sport.
3. Identify three possible solutions to the problem of the use of drugs in sport.
4. What are the three key impacts of modern technological products on sport?
5. Give some examples of modern technological products that impact of performance in sport.
6. Identify the four key roles of the media.
7. State two positive and two possible negative impacts of the media on sport.
8. What is meant by the term 'golden triangle'?
9. Identify three possible causes of violence by players in sport.
10. Identify three possible solutions to the problem of violence by spectators at a sporting event.

In 1994, Juan Antonio Samaranch, then president of the International Olympic Committee (IOC), visited Much Wenlock and laid a wreath at Brookes' grave saying:

> *'I came to pay homage and tribute to Dr Brookes, who really was the founder of the modern Olympic Games.'*

The Wenlock Olympian Games are still held in July each year, attracting athletes from all over the UK.

TAKE IT FURTHER

Visit the website www.wenlock-olympian-society. org.uk. (visit the hotlinks website). Make a poster or prepare a 10-slide-maximum PowerPoint presentation on the Much Wenlock Olympic Games. Include information on: Dr Penny Brookes; his first games; the work of the Much Wenlock Olympian society; links between the Much Wenlock and modern Olympic Games; the Much Wenlock games today.

EXAM TIP

Be clear about the vision of De Coubertin and the principles, aims and philosophy of the modern Olympic movement.

EXAM TIP

You will not be asked direct closed questions on the Ancient Olympic Games, Robert Dover's Cotswold Games or on the Much Wenlock Olympian Games. You could, however, be asked a question that tests your knowledge and understanding of the background to the modern Olympics and the vision of De Coubertin in which you could include some of this information.

Principles, aims and philosophy of the modern olympic movement

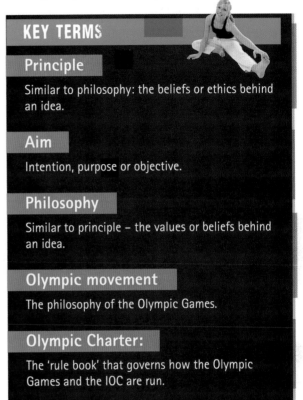

KEY TERMS

Principle

Similar to philosophy: the beliefs or ethics behind an idea.

Aim

Intention, purpose or objective.

Philosophy

Similar to principle – the values or beliefs behind an idea.

Olympic movement

The philosophy of the Olympic Games.

Olympic Charter:

The 'rule book' that governs how the Olympic Games and the IOC are run.

THE OLYMPIC CHARTER

The International Olympic Committee (IOC) states that the fundamental principles of the Olympic Games are:

> *'To contribute to building a peaceful and better world by educating youth through sport practiced without discrimination of any kind and in the Olympic spirit, which requires mutual understanding with a spirit of friendship, solidarity and fair play.'*

The British Olympic Association (BOA) adds:

> *'The modern Olympic Movement was designed to link sport with culture and education. The founders wanted to promote the practice of sport and the joy found in effort. The Olympics would help to build a better world by bringing together people from around the globe to compete to the*

best of their abilities in the spirit of fair play and friendship. These core values are still at the heart of the Olympic Games today.'

We can learn more from the Olympic Creed which states: 'The most important thing in the Olympic Games is not to win but to take part, just as the most important thing in life is not the triumph but the struggle. The essential thing is not to have conquered but to have fought well.'

AIMS

Baron Pierre de Coubertin himself explained:

'Why did I restore the Olympic Games? To ennoble and strengthen sports, to ensure their independence and duration, and thus to enable them better to fulfil the educational role incumbent upon them in the modern world. For the glorification of the individual athlete, whose muscular activity is necessary for the community, and whose prowess is necessary for the maintenance of the general spirit of competition.'

TASK 2

Rewrite the words of De Coubertin, above, into more modern English. Find out what the word 'prowess' means.

REMEMBER

The Olympic Movement has always tried and continues to try to bring people of different countries together to compete in a friendly environment under the banner of sport.

THE PHILOSOPHY OF THE OLYMPIC GAMES

Known as Olympism, the philosophy promotes:

- balance between body, mind and will
- effort – for the joy it can bring
- role-modelling to educate and inspire others
- tolerance, generosity, unity, friendship, non-discrimination, and respect for others.

TAKE IT FURTHER

The official Olympic Motto is a Latin phrase *'Citius, Altius, Fortius'*, meaning 'Swifter, Higher, Stronger'.

The Olympic symbol of five interlocking rings represents the coming together of the world's five continents with the white background of the Olympic flag symbolising peace throughout the festival.

BACKGROUND

You already know that in developing his vision, De Coubertin adopted the ethics and values of the nineteenth century English public schools which were summed up in the Latin saying, *mens sana in corpore sano* – a sound mind in a healthy body. Until relatively recently, the modern Games were strictly for amateurs who took part for the love of their sport and to test themselves against well respected opponents.

AMATEURISM

Originally, to be an amateur meant more than not being paid to take part. Then, amateurs also had to be 'gentlemen' by birth. Taking part was much more important than winning, because society expected gentlemen to be good all-rounders rather than expert specialists. Thus, the modern Olympics were exclusively for the middle- and upper classes. And after all, it was only these gentlemen who could afford the time and money to participate.

'FAIR PLAY'

As well as class there was the concept of 'fair play'. Practicing or training was considered almost as bad as cheating as it meant that you valued winning more than simply taking part, and professionals were thought to have an unfair advantage over those who participated as a hobby.

Professionalism, win-at-all-costs, prize money and cheating were unheard of in the early days.

APPLY IT!

Two British cyclists Edward Battell and Frank Keeping worked at the British Embassy in Athens in the 1890s. They caused uproar when they entered the cycling events at the Games of 1896. Their fellow competitors complained that as Battell and Keeping were employed they could not be classed as 'gentlemen'.

THE OATH

The Olympic Oath is taken by one athlete and one judge from the host nation at the opening ceremonies of each Games.

The athlete holds a corner of the Olympic Flag while reciting the oath:

> 'In the name of all the competitors I promise that we shall take part in these Olympic Games, respecting and abiding by the rules which govern them, committing ourselves to a sport without doping and without drugs, in the true spirit of sportsmanship, for the glory of sport and the honour of our teams.'

The judge, also from the host nation, also holds a corner of the flag and says:

> 'In the name of all the judges and officials, I promise that we shall officiate in these Olympic Games with complete impartiality, respecting and abiding by the rules which govern them in the true spirit of sportsmanship.'

TASK 3

Re-read the above section. Make a clear list or spider diagram on the principles, aims and philosophy (including background, amateurism 'fair play' and the oath) of the modern Olympic movement and add it to the notes in your file.

SUMMER AND WINTER FORMAT

The Olympic Games has summer and winter events. Both the summer and winter Games are each held every four years. Until 1922 they were both held in the same year. Since then, however, they have been separated, two years apart.

- Great Britain is one of only five countries – along with Australia, France, Greece and Switzerland – to have competed at every summer Olympic Games since 1896.
- With France and Switzerland, Great Britain is one of only three countries to have taken part in every winter Olympic Games since 1924.
- London hosted the summer Olympic Games in 1908 and 1948.
- After 2012, Great Britain and Greece will each have hosted the Olympic Games three times.

REMEMBER

There is either a summer or a winter Olympic Games every two years, e.g. winter 2006 in Turin, Italy; summer 2008 in Beijing, China; winter 2010 in Vancouver, Canada; summer 2012 in London, England.

The International Olympic Committee (IOC)

The IOC was founded in Paris on June 23, 1894 and is now based in Lausanne. Switzerland.

FUNCTION

- It is an international, non-governmental, non-profit organisation and receives no public money.
- It is funded by profits from marketing and TV broadcasting rights.
- Members of the IOC include athletes, administrators, lawyers and journalists.
- Members are ambassadors of the IOC representing it in their countries. They are not delegates representing their countries at the IOC.

- The main responsibility of the IOC is to supervise the organisation of the summer and winter Games.
- It tries to ensure that commercialisation of the Games is well managed and controlled and that events are not exploited to the detriment of the Olympic Games.
- It makes decisions about future Olympic Games.
- It makes decisions on any changes to the Olympic Charter.
- It works in areas such as sport science and sports medicine; women in sport; Olympic education; 'Sport for All' and environmental issues affecting sport.
- It supports and supervises the running of each Olympic Games by National Olympic Committees (NOCs) such as the BOA.
- It owns all rights to the Olympic symbols, flag, motto, anthem and Olympic Games.

APPLY IT!

An example of the environmental issues work done by the IOC, and its negotiations with Beijing Olympic Committee in trying to ensure clean air for the Summer Games of 2008.

REMEMBER

The IOC is the organisation responsible for the Olympic Games.

The British Olympic Association (BOA)

The BOA is the National Olympic Committee (NOC) for Britain and is part of the IOC. It is the pivot around which Team GB revolves before and during the Olympic Games. The BOA is not funded or controlled by government, has no political interests and is completely dependent on commercial sponsorship and fundraising income.

For more information on the BOA, see the list in the Exam Café CD that accompanies this book.

REMEMBER

The BOA is the organisation responsible for the UK's participation in the Olympic Games.

TAKE IT FURTHER

In addition, the BOA runs or is involved with various programmes for Team GB athletes including:

- The Olympic Medal Institute: a specialist support centre giving sports specific medical advice for Team GB athletes recovering from serious injury.
- The Olympic Training Centre in Austria which provides world class training and preparation for Team GB athletes, coaches and support staff.
- The Olympic and Paralympic Employment Network which helps athletes with their out of sport career plans and strategies.
- Performance Lifestyle with UK Sport and the UKSI.
- The Olympic Passport Scheme that gives elite athletes a 'passport' to free or reduced cost access to local and national sports centres, the Olympic medical institute and Olympic Training Centre.
- The Athlete Medical Scheme for ill and injured athletes who have already seen their NGB nominated doctor and who need further help and advice.
- Planning for Success workshops with goal-setting and time management advice from ex-Olympians.
- Networking for Olympians and ex-Olympians who are available for after-dinner and motivational speaking engagements via BritishOlympians.com
- Links with a hotel and resort in Cyprus (the BOA's official warm weather training facility in Europe), which was used as a holding camp for Team GB before Athens 2004.
- The British Olympic Foundation is the charitable arm of the BOA and helps to raise the profile and understanding of the Olympic principles and ideals through a wide range of initiatives. Its website includes a 'Chill Zone' with competitions, interviews, information about events, sport and athlete information, and some really funky downloads.

Commercialisation of the olympics

The Los Angeles (California, USA) Summer Games of 1984 were the first to be seriously associated with commercialism. They were a crucial turning point in the marketing and sponsorship of the Olympic Games which are now a giant commercial spectacle.

AMATEURISM

Amateurism started to cause serious problems for athletes from some countries from around the 1960s. While athletes from the USA were well funded through the University scholarship system, and athletes from former Communist bloc countries such as the Soviet Union were heavily State funded, British athletes were starting to struggle. In order to compete on the world stage they needed to commit more time and effort to training which by now was an acceptable

aim. When athletes were tempted with offers of financial support it was increasingly difficult to decline.

All sorts of scandals and problems arose. Early in the 20th century, for example, a Canadian athlete, Tom Longboat, lost his amateur status and was barred from the Olympics after someone bought him a pair of shoes!

COMMERCIALISATION

Eventually, the IOC accepted commercialism. With previous host cities such as Montreal in Canada (1976) losing millions and almost going bankrupt under the strain of hosting the Games, Peter Uberroth was appointed to make the 1984 Games both possible and practical for the city of LA and for the IOC.

This big shift towards commercialisation happened at a time when TV was building a huge global audience which not only made the Games

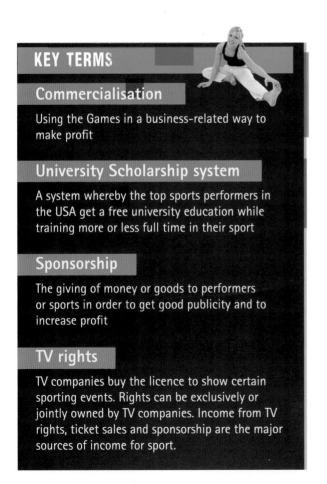

KEY TERMS

Commercialisation

Using the Games in a business-related way to make profit

University Scholarship system

A system whereby the top sports performers in the USA get a free university education while training more or less full time in their sport

Sponsorship

The giving of money or goods to performers or sports in order to get good publicity and to increase profit

TV rights

TV companies buy the licence to show certain sporting events. Rights can be exclusively or jointly owned by TV companies. Income from TV rights, ticket sales and sponsorship are the major sources of income for sport.

Peter Uberroth brought high impact commercialism to the Olympic Games

attractive to sponsors but also gave nations, political groups and individuals a prominent stage or 'shop window' on which to make their point. (For more on the 'shop window' effect – see pages 326–27.)

Uberroth charged huge sums for TV and radio rights, persuaded private companies to build the major facilities and invited sponsors to invest.

Since the LA Games, multinational companies wanting to get financially involved might become:

- official sponsors,
- official suppliers, or
- official licensees,

. . . and so become appointed companies.

'TOP' PROGRAMME

Appointed companies then became part of The Olympic Partner (TOP) Programme which is managed by the IOC. In return for their investment, TOP companies can use Olympic logos on their products and get exclusive worldwide marketing opportunities. TOP companies also get the first choice of advertising slots on TV and are allowed to showcase their products at the Games.

APPLY IT!

Past and present TOP companies include: Visa, Coca-Cola, IBM, McDonald's, Kodak, Panasonic, Lenovo, Omega, Samsung, General Electric, UPS and Swatch.

No wonder companies are keen to be associated with the Olympics! But it isn't necessarily all good news. In spite of the financial problems of the 1980s having been solved by allowing professional athletes and sponsorship, the huge number of athletes, media and spectators now involved makes the safe and smooth running of each Olympic Games a huge challenge for host cities.

APPLY IT!

- In Sydney 2000 there were over 16,000 journalists and media staff and an estimated 3.8 billion TV viewers.
- In Athens 2004 there were over 20,000 journalists and media staff and more than 44,000 hours of TV coverage to a potential global audience of four billion people in more than 160 countries.

TASK 4

Class discussion: Read the comments below and have a class discussion/debate on the following:

Has the Olympic ideal been ruined by commercialism and sponsorship? Is commercialisation of the Games good, bad, inevitable, irrelevant?

- One café inside the Olympic complex had to remove a bacon and egg roll from its menu because it was too similar to an Egg McMuffin – property of official sponsor, McDonald's.

  Lynda, Christchurch

- Yes, the Atlanta Olympics (1996) were commercial, but at least they were paid for without any local tax increases!

  Claire, Dorset

- Apparently the organisers of the Olympics have recruited teams of 'brand police' to check whether people in the Olympic complex are wearing clothing advertising non-sponsors' brands. Offenders face expulsion from the complex.

  David, Newcastle

- Why the fuss? The Olympics have long since lost their credibility as a 'sporting' event. The inclusion of ballroom dancing was the final nail in the coffin. What next? Ballet, tap, darts, pool, charades, or my particular strength – sleeping?

Dan, Cheltenham.

- **Fact of life – IOC want money – sponsorship provides money. End of story. When drug use is rife within sport I don't think there are many ideals left to live up to!**

Vicky, Truro

- The Olympics have always been about entertainment, not some 'higher ideal'. If people want to see spectacular events and a big show then it has to be paid for. Who better than advertisers? At least you can choose not to buy what they advertise.

Danny, Godalming

- **The Olympic Games has become like any other sporting event – big business! Move on!**

Anna, Bristol

- The junk food and drink sponsors of the Games are taking the mick! Who will sponsor the Games next time? A cigarette company? An alcohol company? Or perhaps, as a novelty, an organisation that vigorously supports health and fitness ahead of profit?

Ken, North Wales

- I find it amazing that companies that sell disgusting fast foods and fizzy drinks – items linked to obesity – should be allowed to sponsor any sporting event let alone the Olympic Games.

Katherine, Crookham Village

TAKE IT FURTHER

1. Read the following abridged Times Online article by Michael Payne, March 11 2005 which argues that commercialism saved the Olympic Games.
2. What is the key point of each of Payne's paragraphs?
3. Try to make an evaluative comment or critical judgement on each of his key points.

'For Beijing 2008, at a cost of $40 billion (approx £20 billion) the Chinese Government will have transformed the nation's capital. The new stadium will be the most visible sign of a huge capital investment programme in China's sporting, transportation and economic infrastructure. No expense will be spared.

More journalists will visit China during the 17 days of the Olympics than visited the country in the previous 100 years. By the time the 2008 Games are officially declared open, companies supporting China's Olympic effort will have invested millions in the event and many more billions globally in advertising and promotional campaigns connected to the Olympics.

Over the last 25 years, the Olympic Games has undergone a dramatic reversal of fortune, one of the greatest turnarounds of all time, a story of how a nearly bankrupt organisation, effectively written off by most commentators, quietly developed a strategy to use broadcast rights and sponsorship of the Olympic image to create a unique corporate marketing platform – and secure the future of one of the world's iconic institutions.

The IOC has come to manage the Olympic Games like a franchise, with the IOC as the franchisor, and the local organising committees as the franchisees, tightly controlling all commercial aspects of the Games and the Olympic visual identity. Along the way, the IOC adopted many of the principles and disciplines of corporate brand management to protect and enhance the Olympic image. This strategy has not only revived the financial health of the Olympic Movement, but has also proved to cities the value of bidding for the world's greatest event.

The Olympic story tracks the overall evolution of the sports marketing industry, which has seen phenomenal growth over the last 20 years, from a cottage industry into a multi-billion dollar global success – making, and breaking media empires, launching, and re-invigorating global brands and changing perceptions of whole nations.

Twenty five years ago it was a very different story. Back then cities had to be cajoled into hosting the Games. Far from being a national showcase and money-spinner, the Games were regarded as a financial millstone, with most of the cost being borne by the host city. With no secure source of funding, the IOC relied on hand outs.

Shortly before the Moscow Olympics in 1980, the Olympic Movement was staring into the financial abyss. The IOC was on the verge of collapse with less than $200,000 (approx £100,000) in cash and only $2 million (approx £1 million) in assets. What revenue potential that did exist, came from US broadcasting rights. But with the boycott of the Moscow Games underway, the US Department of Commerce had placed an embargo on any payments by the broadcaster NBC to the Moscow organisers. President Carter subsequently extended this embargo to the IOC.

What had gone wrong? How could the greatest sporting event in the world fail to attract sufficient funding? The answer lay within. In an era of rampant commercialism, the Olympics was hopelessly ill-equipped to survive. Locked in a mythical halcyon age of amateurism, the Games was anachronistic, and out of step. Yet, by the time of the 2000 Sydney Games and the 2002 Salt Lake City Winter Games the Olympic brand had regained its exalted position as the most prized event in the sporting and cultural calendar.

Financial support flooded in. Salt Lake City generated $850 million (approx £425 million) in sponsorship, with single sponsors paying up to $70 million (approx £35 million) – far more than the total amount generated at the Winter Olympics at Lake Placid in 1980 from 200 corporations. The 2004 Games was broadcast to a global audience of 4 billion people – making it the largest media event in the world. Nine of the most famous cities in the world originally announced their ambition to host the 2012 Games – Istanbul, Havana, Leipzig, London, Madrid, Moscow, New York, Paris, and Rio de Janeiro.

The Olympic Movement is now a hugely successful enterprise. It has succeeded by negotiating an honourable alliance with business.

REMEMBER

- The Olympics have become big business – mainly because of TV.
- The LA Games of 1984 were the first to be highly commercialised.
- Amateurism had been causing problems, with athletes from some countries such as the USA having an advantage by being able to train full time.
- Commercialism has turned the Olympics into an event for full-time athletes only.
- The IOC agreed that commercialism was necessary.
- IOC decisions are increasingly dictated by funding and finance.
- In the past, the IOC has faced charges of corruption such has accepting bribes from potential host cities.
- Through massive TV revenues, the IOC has become a major commercial enterprise, operating like a multinational corporation.
- Companies use the Games to raise their profile and to make profit – the Games are a marketing person's dream as they reach a global audience.
- Each Olympic Games becomes more expensive as nations compete to host them.
- The IOC requires host cities to have increasingly elaborate and expensive new stadiums, housing, offices etc.
- Official sponsors become part of the TOP Programme.
- Gold medals become a way for athletes and sponsors to make money.
- The mass media uses sport to sell to advertisers.
- Sporting success is a means of selling products.

REMEMBER

Acronyms:

NGB – National Governing Body
NOC – National Olympic Committee
IOC – International Olympic Committee
BOA – British Olympic Association
TOP – The Olympic Partner Programme

London 2012

Where were you on July 6th 2005 when it was declared that Britain had won the right to host the 2012 Games? Do you remember seeing the TV coverage of the moment when IOC president, Jacques Rogge, opened the result envelope and announced that the Games of the 30th Olympiad were: 'awarded to the city of London'?

London won a two-way tussle with Paris by 54 votes to 50 at the IOC meeting in Singapore, after bids from Moscow, New York and Madrid were eliminated.

Immediately, several opportunities and implications for sport and society in the UK arose. The Games will run from 29 August – 9 September 2012 but if carefully managed, the benefits will last much longer.

BENEFITS TO SPORT

More money must be invested in sport at every level in order for Britain to successfully host the Games and to compete at them realistically. Money for UK Sport and UKSI centres will directly benefit athletes. Funding is also needed to build world class sports and administrative facilities. Throughout Britain, other facilities will also be built or improved for training camps, many of which will be left as a legacy after the Games. Also, several temporary sporting venues constructed in London are to be relocated elsewhere in the UK after the Games.

TASK 5

Re-read this section on commercialisation and the Olympic Games, and have a small group discussion on: What makes the Olympic Games one of the most effective international marketing platforms in the world?

Sport will also benefit from a higher profile, especially among young people excited by the first Games in the UK since 1948 – which was the first Games after the Second World War had ended. Everyone should also be inspired by Team GB success, especially if the home nation achieves its aim of fourth place in the medals table!

	Gold	Silver	Bronze	Total
USA	35	39	29	103
China	32	17	14	63
Russia	27	27	37	91
Australia	17	16	16	49
Japan	16	9	12	37
Germany	14	16	18	48
France	11	9	13	33
Italy	10	11	12	33
Korea	9	12	9	30
GB	9	9	12	30

Table 1 Medals table for Athens 2004

	Gold	Silver	Bronze	Total
USA	40	24	33	97
Russia	32	28	28	88
China	28	16	15	59
Australia	16	25	17	58
Germany	13	17	26	56
France	13	14	11	38
Italy	13	8	13	34
Netherlands	12	9	4	25
Cuba	11	11	7	29
GB	11	10	7	28

Table 2 Medals table for Sydney 2000

TASK 6

Research a medals table for the Beijing Summer Olympic Games of 2008. (try www.olympic.org.) (visit the hotlinks website) Does it look as though Team GB is heading for 4th place in 2012?

The organisation and administration of sport in the UK is being overhauled and modernised in readiness for the Games – see page 321. This organisational 'shake up' with improved communication, co-operation and efficiency among and between various bodies will benefit sport directly.

BENEFITS TO BRITAIN AS WHOLE

- The Olympics provides a great opportunity to improve physical and mental well-being by getting more people to participate regularly in sport and physical recreation. It is a golden opportunity for boosting the numbers of young people who are regularly involved, and is a way of promoting healthy lifestyles – a key government aim.
- Media coverage – including special features on children's TV and campaigns and competitions in schools – will generate interest among young people, and Olympic programmes and campaigns run by sporting bodies should also help. Before, during and after the Games, role models will motivate and inspire.
- The UK is likely to experience a 'feel-good factor' and excitement, resulting both from the carnival atmosphere and its intended success on the podium.

COMMITMENTS

One of the key reasons that Britain won the bid for 2012 was due to the promised improvements to transport and communications systems in and around London. Competitors, officials and visitors will need to move to and around the Games safely and efficiently and their experiences on the roads, railways, rivers, canals and Underground during the Games could make or break their visit, and their judgment of the Games and of London. This is a big challenge.

The Olympic Park will be served by ten rail lines, with a train arriving on average every 15 seconds. Permanent improvements to the transport system in and surrounding the capital would be a very popular legacy as the current daily travel experience of Londoners and commuters is patchy.

TAKE IT FURTHER

Go to www.london2012.com (visit the hotlinks website). and look at the Transport Plan for the Games. The plan includes work to treble capacity at Stratford Regional Station; to extend the Docklands Light Railway, and to build a high speed rail link – the Javelin shuttle service.

IMPACT AND IMPLICATIONS

Tourism will be huge throughout the summer of 2012 and the money that tourism brings will boost the economy.

The Paralympic Games (for elite athletes with disabilities) which run alongside the Olympics should enhance general attitudes towards equality regarding 'disability sport' in particular.

There will also be an opportunity to improve National Health Service (NHS) service provision, particularly of high quality sports medicine services, not only in London, but in the areas with regional training camps.

EXAM TIP

In the exam you will not be asked questions about the Paralympic Games.

BENEFITS TO LOCAL AREA

- The Games will help the local economy; companies should be attracted to London, with the opportunities that the Olympics will create. This will create employment before, during and (hopefully) after the Summer of 2012.

- By working together on local projects associated with the Games, social integration in the area should also be increased and local people will have a chance to gain or develop their employable skills, leaving a legacy of higher skilled jobs for better-skilled people. At the 2000 Games in Sydney, Australia customer service training for 50,000 staff, helped to develop world class standards which continued after the Games. Even though many jobs will be temporary for 2012, sociologists suggest that the experience could improve attitudes and behaviour and reduce crime due to an increased sense of belonging.

- The Olympic site in the deprived area of Stratford in London's East End is being renewed and restored in readiness for the Games. The Olympic Village will stay, creating 3,500 residential housing units.

APPLY IT!

It has been estimated that the Games will generate:

- approx 35,500 person years of employment in construction, in the years leading up to the Games
- approx. 15,000 person years of construction employment after the Games due to planned 'legacy' work
- 30,000 jobs during the Games – mostly temporary
- approx. 7,000 jobs showcasing London: including jobs in retail, hotels and restaurants, transport and entertainment
- 70,000 jobs for volunteers.

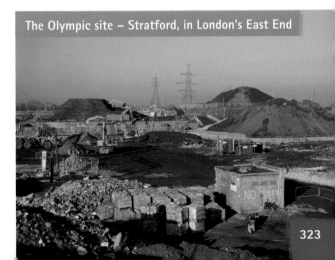

The Olympic site – Stratford, in London's East End

Potential benefits of hosting the Olypic games

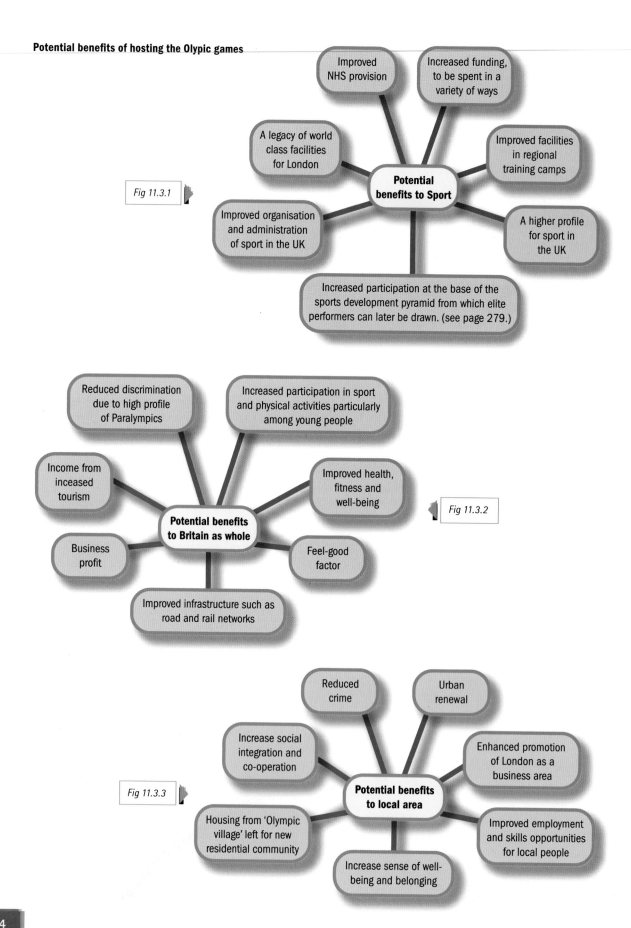

Fig 11.3.1

Potential benefits to Sport

- Improved NHS provision
- Increased funding, to be spent in a variety of ways
- A legacy of world class facilities for London
- Improved facilities in regional training camps
- Improved organisation and administration of sport in the UK
- A higher profile for sport in the UK
- Increased participation at the base of the sports development pyramid from which elite performers can later be drawn. (see page 279.)

Fig 11.3.2

Potential benefits to Britain as whole

- Reduced discrimination due to high profile of Paralympics
- Increased participation in sport and physical activities particularly among young people
- Income from inceased tourism
- Improved health, fitness and well-being
- Business profit
- Feel-good factor
- Improved infrastructure such as road and rail networks

Fig 11.3.3

Potential benefits to local area

- Reduced crime
- Urban renewal
- Increase social integration and co-operation
- Enhanced promotion of London as a business area
- Housing from 'Olympic village' left for new residential community
- Improved employment and skills opportunities for local people
- Increase sense of well-being and belonging

TASK 7

Why not sign up as a volunteer for the London 2012 Games? Up to 70,000 volunteers are needed to ensure success. The recruitment of volunteers starts in 2010, but you can register your interest by visiting the London 2012 website www.london2012.com (see the hotlinks website). You will meet new people, learn new skills and have a great experience while taking part in a piece of history!

TASK 8

Argue the point in twos. Player A states a potential drawback of hosting the Games from the above list and Player B argues against that point, e.g. Player A states that 'house prices will rise' and Player B might respond that 'current homeowners will therefore benefit.' In round 2, Player B goes first with a disadvantage which is rejected with a sound argument by Player A. Continue taking it in turns to go first.

DRAWBACKS

Critics of hosting the Games in London make these observations:

- Soaring costs and potential legacy of debt as was experienced by Montreal in 1976.
- Rising Council tax bills for local people.
- Lack of long term job opportunities.
- Increased housing and rental prices which discriminates against local people.
- A focus on elitism rather than participation.
- Too much focus on London with regional areas such as Cornwall and the Lake District experiencing limited, if any, direct benefits.
- An emphasis on Nationalism which could result in discrimination.

The olympic games and nation building

SHOWCASING

The Olympic Games is a perfect 'stage' for nation building – that is, showcasing or promoting a country. For both the host nation and successful competitors from around the world, the Olympic Games is a vehicle for gaining publicity, improving a country's image and increasing national pride. This is the 'shop window' effect whereby politicians use sport to promote their country and their political system worldwide.

EXAM TIP

During the lead-up to 2012, keep an open mind; re-visit ideas you have already thought of – including the benefits and drawbacks of the Games – and add and amend them to suit the evolving situation.

KEY TERM

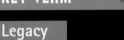

Legacy

What remains after an event. The Olympic legacy will hopefully include world class sporting facilities, improved road, rail and communication networks and increased participation in physical activity.

The Olympic podium is the perfect stage for putting a country in the 'shop window'.

KEY TERM

'Shop window' effect

When sporting success equates with political success, and positive role models promote the country's status.

It could be argued that when the Games were in cities such as Sydney or Athens they were just spectacular sporting festivals. In Tokyo (1964) and Seoul (1988) however, political implications dominated. In this context, how do you think Beijing 2008 came accross?

CHINA

China is a one-party Communist state where sport is controlled, funded and encouraged by the government in order to increase political prestige and morale among the workforce. The Communist Party was eager to stage a successful Summer Olympics in Beijing in 2008 and the Chinese public were delighted to be the host nation. Some say that China saw the event as a 'coming-out party' to highlight its economic rise, and emergence as a world power. International opinion was divided between:

- those who thought the Games could help to reform the world's largest authoritarian state and force the Communist Party in China to change and 'open up' society still further, and
- those who thought that the Games would validate or legitimise the Communist regime.

KEY TERM

Communism

A centralised political system that opposes capitalism and democracy.

HUMAN RIGHTS

Some argued that sending teams to Beijing endorsed China's poor record on Human Rights and that the 'free world' should not repeat what allegedly happened in 1936, when by participating in the (Nazi) Germany Olympics, Hitler's anti-Semitic rule was endorsed.

TASK 9

In threes discuss this question, and make a list of your ideas for your file.

In what ways did the Beijing Summer Olympic Games of 2008 showcase China to the rest of the world?

POLITICS

It is now almost universally accepted that sport and politics are linked. As eastern European countries showed in the 1970s and 80s, sport can be used for internal and external political motives, and with both functional and dysfunctional outcomes.

KEY TERMS

Centralised system

A system where political and administrative power is held centrally with no regional or local government control.

Elitism

To be exclusive or to select the best and to forget the rest.

In Communist Russia from the 1950s, the entire population was tested, and talented children were selected and given the best facilities: coaching, diet and even drugs to ensure international success and perceived political superiority. Athletes were given token jobs in the army or industry, so that they could devote themselves full time to sport. The government centrally controlled all of this. In reality, the minority were funded at the expense of 'equality for all'.

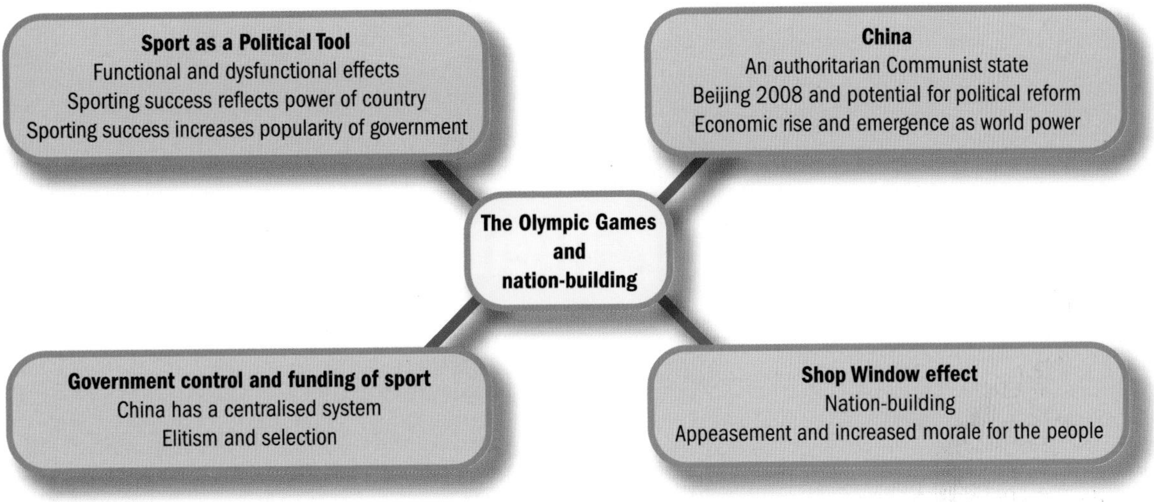

Sport as a Political Tool
Functional and dysfunctional effects
Sporting success reflects power of country
Sporting success increases popularity of government

China
An authoritarian Communist state
Beijing 2008 and potential for political reform
Economic rise and emergence as world power

The Olympic Games and nation-building

Government control and funding of sport
China has a centralised system
Elitism and selection

Shop Window effect
Nation-building
Appeasement and increased morale for the people

Fig 11.3.4

For about as long as the modern Olympic Games have existed, (and against their philosophy) they have been a political as well as a sporting stage.

- Berlin 1936 – Hitler and Jesse Owens
- Helsinki 1952 – the beginning of the Cold War
- Mexico City 1968 – the Black Power salute
- Munich 1972 – 11 Israeli athletes killed
- Moscow 1980 – boycotts due to the Soviet invasion of Afghanistan
- Los Angeles 1984 – boycott by the Soviet Union in return
- Seoul 1988 – public demonstrations leading up to the Games helped to bring down an authoritarian regime and bring about democracy.

KEY TERMS

Functional effects

Helpful or useful results or conclusions

Dysfunctional effects

Unhelpful results or conclusions caused by failure to act in a normally acceptable way

Appeasement

To pacify, or to provide a feel good factor

TAKE IT FURTHER

Do some mini research into Jesse Owens and the 1936 Olympics; the meaning of the Black Power salute in 1968, and what actually happened in Munich in 1972.

EXAM TIP

You will only get direct examination questions on the Olympic Games as a vehicle for nation building in China.

ExamCafé
Relax, refresh, result!

Refresh your memory

By now you should know and understand about:

▷ The vision of Baron Pierre de Coubertin in establishing the Modern Olympic Games in 1896.

▷ The principles, aims and philosophy of the Olympic Games.

▷ The British Olympic Association and the International Olympic Committee – two bodies that are central to Olympic organisation and administration.

▷ Commercialisation of the Games after 1984.

▷ London 2012 – opportunities and implications for UK sport and society.

▷ The Olympics as a vehicle for nation building, when sport is used as a political tool, e.g. in China.

REVISE AS YOU GO!

1. What was De Coubertin's vision is establishing the Modern Olympic Games?
2. What were the original aims of the modern Olympic movement?
3. Explain the summer and winter format of the Games.
4. State two roles of the International Olympic Committee (IOC)
5. State two roles of the British Olympic Association (BOA)
6. Where were the Olympic Games in 1984?
7. In terms of funding and finance, what were the 1984 Games famous for?
8. State some likely benefits of hosting the Summer Olympic Games in London in 2012.
9. Try to think of a couple of potential drawbacks of hosting the Games in London in 2012
10. Explain each of the following terms: shop window effect; nation building.

Get the result!

- There will only be ONE socio-cultural studies question on your exam paper and it will have five parts.
- The first four parts will be out of four, five or six marks.
- The last/fifth part will be out of 10 marks and will require more depth and detail.
- The last/fifth part should give you an opportunity to show what you have read around the subject or discussed outside of the main constraints of the specification.
- Here you can give evidence of your ability to think and make judgements.
- Write with a fluent style using linking words such as 'because', 'however', 'on the other hand', 'it could be argued', etc. This will add quality to your written communication.
- Have a look at the subject area being examined.

Examination question

Explain how the Olympic Games can be a vehicle for nation building. (10 marks)

examiner's tips

- First have a look at the command word in the question which, in the following question. is 'explain'. This requires far more than identify, list, state or outline.
- This is not the most popular area of the specification and some students find it quite tricky – possibly because of some of the language involved (see below).
- This 10-mark question is examining the following from of the specification: 'Explain how the Olympic Games is a vehicle for nation building', e.g. China; the 'Shop Window' effect; government control and funding of sport; sport as a political tool. Stick to that in your answer!
- It is an excellent idea to be as familiar with the specification as possible – then you will have the best chance of knowing exactly what is being examined in each part-question. So read through the specification from time to time. Your teachers have probably given you a copy for your file or you can get it from the internet at www.ocr.org.
- To answer this part-question at the very highest level you should be confident with at least some of the following terms:
  - Communism
  - authoritarian one-party state/s
  - Nation building
  - a centralised political system
  - shop-window effect.

Student answer

The Olympic Games is a vehicle for nation building as countries that win medals get shown on the TV and people will think that the country is good. When China won gold medals at the Beijing Olympics it made Communism look good and so the popularity of the government was increased. The people of China felt happy that the Olympics was in their country too.

Student's improved answer

Since 1896 when the Olympic Games were revived in Athens by Baron Pierre de Coubertin they have been a stage on which countries could promote themselves.

That is the meaning of nation building — to improve a country's image in the eyes of the rest of the world and also in the eyes of the population of that country. People are appeased or made happy by their country's success in either hosting or competing in an Olympic Games. This was certainly the case when the Summer '08 Olympics were in Beijing and is also likely to happen when the Summer Olympics are held in London in 2012.

China is an authoritarian one-party communist state. By hosting the Olympics in 2008 millions of eyes throughout the world were on that country. People's view of China and indeed of communism itself were influenced by what they saw in a way that could never have happened just be reading a paper.

What happened is called the 'shop window' effect where China was keen that its sporting success should be linked to political success. They wanted to showcase their regime.

Examiner says:

It's great that you clearly knew which part of the specification was being examined. Good use of the Beijing example.

Your answer needs more depth and detail. It feels as though you didn't really know enough information – perhaps because you hadn't revised this section carefully enough.

Planning would have helped and might have given you more to say.

3 out of 10 marks.

Examiner says:

I would have liked this key term to have been explained.

Can you think of a better word than 'good'. Maybe 'efficient' or 'of high quality'?

Use of the more technical term 'appeasement' would have improved this sentence.

Examiner says:

Great introduction. Clear, concise and correct.

Examiner says:

Excellent – clear and accurate definitions

Examiner says:

Sound use of contemporary example.

Examiner says:

Much better! You have very good subject knowledge and understanding with high quality language. I am also impressed with the accurate technical language that you use in context such as: appeasement; authoritarian one-part communist state; shop window effect.

Examiner says:

In the middle I would have liked you to go into just a little more detail about China having been a very 'closed' country which opened up as a result of the Olympic microscope. I would also have liked to have seen a short conclusion to draw your answer together.

Well done! 8 out of 10 marks.

Interestingly, because the Olympics attracts vast global audiences it also has the chance of diminishing the reputation of a country if, for example, athletes from a particular nation are all caught for drug offences.

Acquiring, developing and evaluating practical skills in physical education

CHAPTER 12:

Performance

LEARNING OBJECTIVES

At the end of this chapter you should be able to:

- Understand which practical activities you can choose to be assessed in
- Understand which roles you can be assessed in
- Understand how you will be assessed in each of these roles
- Understand the terms 'standardisation' and 'moderation'
- Appreciate how you can improve your performances
- Appreciate how you can improve your coaching/leading
- Appreciate how you can improve your officiating.

INTRODUCTION

Advanced level PE has as its central aim the linking of theory to practical and practical to theory. This means that we use practical activities to help us gain knowledge, understanding and appreciation of theoretical concepts whilst also applying those concepts to our practical activities to help us to improve their performance. Advanced level PE recognises that students should be able to capitalise on their practical talents by being assessed in practical activities with the marks gained contributing to their examination grade.

In this chapter we will explore the opportunities that you have within AS PE to be assessed in practical activities and in different roles as well as ways in which you can improve the marks you can achieve.

Participation and assessment in your activities at AS also prepares you for your A2 practical work when you will apply your skills in a more open situation.

You will find useful information in this chapter, but to improve your practical performance there is no substitute for actual practice which can be performed both in and outside your centre.

Acquiring, developing and evaluating practical skills in physical education (coursework)

MODULE CONTENT

You will be assessed in:

1. Performing two chosen activities from two different activity profiles and evaluating and planning for the improvement of performance.

   OR

2. Performing one chosen activity and coaching/ leading one chosen activity from two different activity profiles together with evaluating and planning for the improvement of performance.

   OR

3. Performing one chosen activity and officiating one chosen activity in two different activities, together with evaluating and planning for the improvement of performance.

In performing, coaching/leading and officiating you will be assessed out of 30 marks (per activity) giving 60 marks in total whilst your evaluating and planning for improvement response is assessed out of 20 marks which enables you to score a maximum of 80 marks in this coursework unit.

CHOICE OF ACTIVITIES

The activities are grouped together by profile into eleven categories. You must choose two activities, each from a different category. For example, you could choose judo and basketball but not hockey and basketball.

The activities in Table 1 are just some of those that appear in the specification, but there are other activities which your centre may allow you to take part in and be assessed on. You can find a list of these activities on the OCR website.

Activity category	Activity
Athletic activities	Track and field athletics
Combat activities	Judo
Dance activities	Contemporary dance
Invasion game activities	Association football, basketball, field hockey, Gaelic football, hurling, netball, rugby league, rugby union
Net/wall game activities	Badminton, squash, tennis, volleyball
Striking/fielding game activities	Cricket
Target games activities	Golf
Gymnastic activities	Gymnastics, trampolining
Outdoor and adventurous activities	Mountain walking, canoeing, skiing, sailing
Swimming activities	Competitive swimming
Exercising safely and effectively	Circuit training

Table 1

EXAM TIP

Remember that you will have to select one of these activities to be assessed in when you do your A2 PE course.

ASSESSMENT

Your teacher(s) will assess you throughout your practical activity course. This means that the assessment will be more accurate rather than having just one assessment session towards the end of the course when you may have an 'off' day. This will also ensure that if you are injured your teacher(s) will have some marks on which to base your assessment. The final assessed marks have to be sent to the exam board by 31 March.

You will probably be videoed doing your practical activity. This is to provide OCR with evidence of your performance.

The teachers in your centre will consult with each other to check that activities assessed by different teachers or coaches in your centre are all at the same standard. Standardisation is particularly important for many activities which cannot be done in your centre and are sometimes taught by coaches who are based at clubs. In cases such as these, the PE teacher responsible for A level will liaise with the coach to ensure that they are aware of what you need to do in your activity. This teacher will assess you with the help and advice of the coach.

At some point between Easter and Whitsun some students in your centre will be chosen to perform their practical activities alongside students from other centres in your area. This moderation may be at one of these centres. A moderator from the exam board will look at all the students' performances to check that they have been assessed correctly and that marks awarded by the different centres are all at the same level. The moderator knows the correct levels and standards of performance which have been set nationally by OCR.

If you are selected by the moderator to perform at the moderation you have to attend as this is part of your AS examination. If you fail to attend you may be considered as being absent from the examination of this coursework unit.

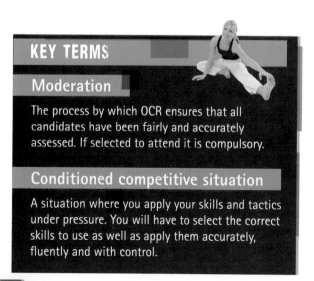

KEY TERMS

Moderation

The process by which OCR ensures that all candidates have been fairly and accurately assessed. If selected to attend it is compulsory.

Conditioned competitive situation

A situation where you apply your skills and tactics under pressure. You will have to select the correct skills to use as well as apply them accurately, fluently and with control.

EXAM TIP

If you are selected to attend moderation make sure that you can perform at the standard you were assessed at. You should ensure that you can perform well in terms of skills and fitness.

1. Performing an activity

You have to be assessed in performing at least one practical activity although you can choose to be assessed performing two practical activities.

CONTENT OF THE PRACTICAL ACTIVITIES

The specification indicates that the focus of your activities will be on 'acquired and developed skills'. This means that you will have to work specifically on the techniques and skills of your activities. These skills, however, will not be performed in isolation but in a situation where you are put under some pressure either from opponents or having to apply them to circumstances relevant to that particular activity. These are called *conditioned competitive situations*.

Conditioned competitive situations allow you to show that you are able to:

- select and perform the correct skill for a particular situation, e.g. choose the correct stroke when batting in cricket
- repeat skills consistently, e.g. get the skill right each time you perform it
- adapt skills where and when required, e.g. adjust your pass in netball to avoid the opponent marking you intercepting it
- show some tactical awareness
- perform all the above when under pressure
- demonstrate physical and mental fitness
- apply the relevant rules, regulations and code of practice of the activity.

The conditioned competitive situations also allow you to show how well you have learned your skills and how well they stand up to the pressure of these situations. It is important to realise that the pressure of competition is not the same for all activities and that the conditioned competitive situations will differ according to the activity category. For example, in gymnastics, in the conditioned competitive situation, students have to perform vaults and agility sequences. The 'competition' is to get your vaults and agilities as close as possible to the perfect model, and to make them flow and look aesthetically pleasing when linked together.

In invasion games the competition will be from opponents in a small sided game, whilst in outdoor adventurous activities it will be a situation where you have to combine your skills in an amended version of the 'normal' situation. For example, in mountain walking you will complete a two-day, 14-hour walk which covers 36 km.

Examples of conditioned competitive situations for each category are shown on page 336.

These conditioned competitive situations will allow you to practise your skills whilst also permitting you to develop your strategies and tactics. Strategies and tactics are more obvious

Activity category	Conditioned competitive situation
Athletic activities (sprinting)	sprint starts, sprint action, finishes
Combat activities (judo)	contests limited in terms of techniques permitted, size of mat area and time allowed
Dance activities (contemporary dance)	choreograph and perform three solo dance routines each lasting 1 minute and containing leaps, balances and rolls
Invasion games (association football (soccer)/hockey)	half pitch game of 5 attackers and 3 or 4 defenders with a goalkeeper
Striking/fielding games (cricket)	feeder to a batter who has to play one of 3 shots and score runs off them. Fielders will try to run batsman out
Net/wall games	shot rallies, shot accuracy, short games
Target games (golf)	series of targets of different distances and sizes to test club selection and accuracy of shot
Gymnastics activities (trampolining)	a ten-contact sequence to include a jump, a twist, a drop and a somersault
Outdoor adventurous activities (mountain walking)	two-day journey with 14 hours of walking in appropriate terrain
Swimming activities (competitive swimming)	racing starts, stroke technique in short race, racing finish
Exercise activities (circuit training)	The design and implementation of two training programmes from: • body weight exercises • free weights and resistance machines • cardiovasclar equipment

Table 2

One of the conditioned competitive situations for gymnasts is to perform the perfect vault

and applicable in some activities than others. For instance, in invasion games you will need to develop an awareness of such things as support for teammates, width in attack and depth in defence. In other activities, for example, outdoor adventurous, they will take the form of awareness of safety aspects, group work and appropriate codes, for example, the Country Code. In gymnastics your strategy may be to include only movements that you can perform really well and place them in the order that allows your sequence to flow.

The conditioned competitive situation for mountain walking is a two-day, 14-hour, 36km walk.

TASK 1

Find out what the conditioned competitive situations are for your assessed performances.

You need to focus on building up the range of your skills as well as their quality and consistency. You will remember from your studies of skill acquisition that skills are perfected through practice and receiving feedback on the results of your practice. It is therefore important for you to get as much practice as possible with the appropriate people to advise you, these will be your teachers and coaches.

TASK 2

a) Read a coaching manual for your activity which identifies the skills necessary for that activity.
b) Prepare a list of the skills you need to be successful in that activity and compare the skills you have to this list.

WHAT ARE THE ASSESSMENT CRITERIA?

There are several areas that your teacher will be looking at in your performance:

- how good your range of skills is and the accuracy, control and fluency with which you perform them
- if you have advanced skills and can use them when appropriate with accuracy, control and fluency
- your understanding of tactics and strategies, shown by your application of them
- your overall standard of performance.
- your levels of physical and mental fitness
- your knowledge and understanding of the rules/ regulations and conventions of your activity and your ability to apply them when you perform.

Your teacher will use these criteria to put you into one of five bands (0–6, 7–12, 13–18, 19–24, 25–30) before they finally decide the exact mark you will be given out of 30.

Your teacher will carry out this assessment over a period of time, but might have one last assessment session to finalise your mark. It may be that in this session they decide where to place you in a band and confirm your actual mark.

WHAT WILL I BE REQUIRED TO DO FOR MY ASSESSMENT?

How you will be assessed and what the focus of the assessment will be has been identified for each practical activity in OCR's *Teacher Support: Coursework Guidance* booklet. Conditioned competitive situations are used to determine how you will be assessed and we identified some examples earlier. The list below identifies the focus of assessment for a sample range of activities.

Activity	Assessments
Track and field athletics	two events from two of the following areas: track, jumps, throws
Contemporary dance	leaps, balances step patterns, turns and travelling
Football	passing and receiving, control, shooting, heading, tackling, intercepting, closing down, beating an opponent. in attack or defence
Golf	club selection and distance; stroke action and target accuracy
Gymnastics	vaults and an agility sequence
Trampolining	a ten-contact sequence containing a jump, a twist, a drop and a somersault

Mountain walking	use of maps and their symbols, navigation, planning the route, calculation of distance, organisation of equipment, application of safety principles, obtaining bearings
Competitive swimming	two strokes from: front crawl, back stroke, breast stroke, butterfly

Table 3

More detail, including the focus for other activities can be found in *Teacher Support – Coursework Guidance* on the OCR website, which can be accessed through www.heinemann.co.uk/hotlinks.

TASK 3

Access the OCR website and identify the assessment focus for your assessed performances.

Focus of assessment for track and field athletics is two events from track, throwing and jumping events.

The focus of assessment for competitive swimming is on any two strokes, e.g. the back stroke

HOW CAN I IMPROVE MY PRACTICAL ACTIVITY PERFORMANCES?

You should now be aware of how and when you will be assessed as well as the focus for your assessment. This understanding will help you plan how you should use your time to improve your performances in your practical activities and thereby increase the marks you are awarded.

You should try to get someone to video one of your performances so that you can analyse it yourself, probably with the help of your teacher or coach. This analysis should identify the good aspects of your performance together with the weaknesses. It should cover skills, tactics and fitness. This will enable you to structure an action plan to improve your performance.

PHYSICAL FITNESS

This is an important aspect in any practical activity and will be a key part of your preparation for both your performance activities. Different activities have different fitness requirements and through your training and by talking to your teacher/coach you should be able to identify which of the four main fitness components below are important in your activity.

- Strength
- Speed
- Stamina
- Suppleness.

You will be able to use your knowledge from your anatomy and physiology studies to help you appreciate how you can work on your fitness. You will be able to use fitness tests to measure your fitness and any improvement.

If you can increase your levels of fitness in the relevant components then you will undoubtedly improve the standard of your performance and therefore your marks.

TASK 5

a) For each of your activities consult your teacher/coach and the relevant manuals to establish the important physical fitness components.
b) Build ways of improving your fitness into your own action plan.

TASK 4

a) Get your teacher or coach to analyse your performance.
b) Create an action plan to improve your performance concentrating on skills, tactics/ choreography,/compositional ideas and fitness.
c) Find the websites of the governing/ organising bodies of your performance activities to see what coaching manuals and materials are available to help in developing your action plan..
d) Check in your centre's library to see if these manuals are available.

MENTAL FITNESS

You should make sure that you know the appropriate tactics and strategies, particularly in a team game and can remember them. From your theoretical knowledge of phases of learning you will know that if you practice your skills so that you are in the autonomous phase of learning then it allows you to focus your attention on other information such as tactics and strategies. You should also try to become accustomed to the competitive situation so that you are not affected by it so that your performance deteriorates. Remember also that reaction time is improved by practise so you can work on improving this.

APPLY IT!

Use your knowledge of arousal and learning theories to ensure that you can perform at your best.

IMPROVING THE QUALITY AND RANGE OF YOUR SKILLS

If you look at expert performers they will undoubtedly have a wide range of skills which they can perform with accuracy, control and fluency. They achieve this range and a high level of performance by practising and spending a great deal of time developing and perfecting their skills. You should work on improving the quality and range of your basic and advanced skills.

Your knowledge of acquiring movement skills will help you to plan the focus and structure of your practices. First, you should consult the coaching manuals to identify both the basic and advanced skills that are required for your activity and the appropriate practices to develop them. Your teachers and coaches are also valuable sources of information. They will also identify the coaching points you will need to concentrate on in each of the skills.

You should be aware that in some activities the basic skills will require you to be proficient in a variety of ways, e.g. kicking/passing with both feet or playing forehand and backhand shots.

It is essential that you have and remember this information as you will also need it for your evaluating and planning for the improvement of performance response. Valuable additional and specific information can be found in coaching books which are normally published by the governing or organising body. You should consult these for ideas and information on improving your performance.

EXAM TIP

Know the skills necessary for your activity, their coaching points and the progressive practices to develop them.

REMEMBER

When you have researched the skills necessary for your activity together with the coaching points and the practices needed to develop these skills, remember that you will need this knowledge when you do your evaluation and planning for improvement response.

TASK 6

a) Consult your teacher/coach and the relevant coaching manuals to identify the basic and advanced skills that you will need to be proficient for each of your assessed activities.

b) Make detailed notes on the coaching points and progressive practices to develop each of these skills.

DEVELOPING YOUR SKILLS

You should start your learning by practising each skill in its simplest form. The practice situation should allow you to concentrate on the coaching points and getting the skill right. Once you have mastered this simple skill you should make the practice a little more difficult and bring in further coaching points. As the skill practices get more difficult they should also get more 'open', bringing in more decision making and opposition.

An example of this is the short serve in badminton, where you could go through the following progressive practices.

1. Practise the shot concentrating on the coaching points relating to the phases: preparation (stance/body position, feet and hand position), execution (transfer of weight, contact with shuttle, follow-through), recovery (balance and return to be ready for the return shot), result (was the shot good both in terms of performance and success?), overall efficiency (general nature of the shot, fluency, closeness to technical model).
2. Increase the need for accuracy and precision – aiming to get shuttle into a target within the service area. Impose restrictions on how high above the net the shuttle may pass.
3. Practise the shot initially with an opponent just threatening the serve.
4. Practise the serve with an opponent who can attack the serve.
5. A practice which mixes short and long serves and is competitive with points for a successful serve and points for the receiver if they are able to return it.

It is important that you receive, listen to and act upon feedback

Progressive practices will help you not only to improve your basic skills but also to learn advanced skills. Eventually, your practice situation will become very similar to the conditioned competitive situations in which you will be assessed.

ANALYSING SKILLS

For each activity profile the *Teacher Support: Coursework Guidance* booklet identifies the phases into which the skills will be analysed for assessment purposes. These analytical phases may also help you to improve your skills and extend your range of skills.

Some examples of these phases are identified in the table below.

TASK 7

Select a skill from your performance activity and describe in detail the progressive practices you would use to develop this skill.

FEEDBACK FROM YOUR TEACHERS AND COACHES

A critical part of the practice of skills is feedback and it is important that you receive this from your teacher and coach, listen to and act upon it. This will improve the quality and rate of your learning.

Activity	Phases
Track and field athletics – track events	Posture, leg action, arm action, head carriage, overall efficiency
Track and field athletics – jumping events	Approach, take off, flight, landing, overall efficiency

(Cont.)

Track and field athletics – throwing events	initial stance, grip and preparation, travel and trunk position, throwing action, release, overall efficiency
Games	Preparation, execution, recovery, result, overall efficiency
Gymnastics	Vaults; shape and aesthetic quality, flight on the box, flight off the box, repulsion and landing, overall efficiency
Competitive swimming	Arm action, leg action, body position, breathing, overall efficiency

Table 4

TASK 8

Access the OCR website and identify the phases into which the skills for each of your assessed activities will be analysed.

STRUCTURING AND IMPLEMENTING YOUR PRACTICES

Once you have identified these phases it will allow you to structure your initial practice when you are attempting to perfect the basic skill and get it to match the model you will find in the coaching manuals.

Your skill practices can be done in a variety of ways but it is unlikely that there will be enough time in your lessons for you to perfect your skills. You must therefore look for additional opportunities to practise. Within your centre there will be clubs and teams which will offer valuable opportunities to improve your skills. Other opportunities may be found by joining a local club where you will receive coaching and performing experience. It is important that you

and your teacher talk to the coaches to make them aware of exactly what you have to do in your practical activity and how you will be assessed.

Joining a local club is particularly important if you do not have the opportunity in your centre to perform your activity 'competitively'. This could be a small sided game in hockey or an expedition in mountain walking. This experience, under the guidance of a teacher or coach, is important in developing your awareness and understanding of strategies tactics.

TASK 9

Identify the basic tactics/compositional ideas which are used in your performance activities.

EXAM TIP

Make sure that you join a club for your performance activities in order that you can practise and improve. You will need this time and practice in addition to any that you get as part of your course if you are to get good marks in your coursework.

2. Coaching/leading an activity

The specification indicates that the focus of the assessment of your coaching/leading is on a range of applied and acquired skills, abilities and qualities. These skills will be assessed while you lead safe, purposeful and enjoyable activities. A suitable arena for these activities could be with primary school children in Top Sport or Dragon Sport activities or with other similar groups.

You may, within your centre, undertake the British Sports Trust Community Sports Leader's Award and successfully completing this award may allow you to develop many of the skills on which your assessment will be based. Alternatively you could undertake a level two governing/organising body coaching/leading award.

As with your performance you will need to practise your coaching/leading if you are to improve and will also need someone to observe you and give you feedback on your performances. There may be opportunities for practice created by your centre but you may have to seek opportunities with local clubs or with your local sports development officer.

In order to produce evidence for your assessment you will have to keep a log which contains the following detailed information:

- a record of your coaching/leading activities over a three-month period
- a scheme of work for ten hours of coaching in which the participants and activities show progression
- evaluations of your sessions
- a video record of you coaching/leading for at least forty minutes
- health and safety issues relating to the activity and your sessions together with risk assessments undertaken
- details of your first aid qualification
- child protection procedures relevant to the activity
- the health and fitness benefits of the activity for both participants and coaches/leaders
- If you have undertaken and successfully completed either the Community Sports Leader's Award or a Governing/Organising Body Level two coaching qualification then you can include this in your log. (You don't have to have done either of these.)

Start your coaching, leading or officiating log early

TASK 10

Access the OCR website – *Teachers' Support: Coursework Guidance*, and look at the assessment criteria descriptors.

The focus of your assessments will be on your:

- ability to apply your coaching/leading skills in delivering sessions
- organisational and planning skills
- use of a range of coaching/leading strategies
- overall performance in coaching/leading
- awareness of health and safety
- implementation of risk assessments
- awareness of child protection
- awareness of the fitness and health benefits of the activity
- organisational skills in planning and delivering sessions
- knowledge of the rules/regulations of the activity
- evaluative skills.

Your teacher will use these assessment criteria to put you into one of five bands (0–6, 7–12, 13–18, 19–24, 25–30) before they finally decide the exact mark you will be given. Your teacher will assess you over a period of time but might watch you do

EXAM TIP

You will need to complete this log as you do your coaching particularly in keeping the record of your coaching sessions and their evaluations. You should not leave it to the end, near the final date for the submission of assessments, before you put your log together.

a final coaching/leading session to finalise your mark out of 30.

TASK 11

Ask your teacher/coach or local sports development officer for details of British Sports Trust Community Sports Leaders Award or level two coaching awards in the activities you are interested in.

HOW CAN I IMPROVE MY COACHING/ LEADING?

You should now be aware of how and when you will be assessed as well as the focus for your assessment. This understanding will help you plan how you should use your time to practise and improve your coaching/leading and thereby improve the marks you are awarded.

You should observe and evaluate the sessions you are taught as part of your A level Physical Education course and any additional coaching/ leading courses you may undertake. This will allow you to see how other coaches operate and pick up ideas, preferably the ones that work and that you enjoy! Any practices that other coaches use and you don't enjoy you can decide not to use them or determine how you would change them to make them better so that you could use them.

It may be helpful if you organise the skills you have to develop into groups, these being:

- Planning/organisation
- Delivery
- Evaluative
- Technical knowledge.

PLANNING AND ORGANISATION

Planning and organisational skills mainly concern things that you will do before your sessions. They usually ensure that your sessions have a good chance of being safe, enjoyable and successful. Knowing that you have planned and organised your sessions gives you confidence and allows you to concentrate on actually delivering the

session and on the participants. Planning properly enables the sessions to run smoothly and although the participants might not be aware of all the time you have spent planning they will appreciate being involved in a purposeful, safe and enjoyable session.

KEY TERM

Scheme of work

A plan of your ten coaching sessions which will include what your aims for the participants are, how you are going to achieve those aims and how you are going to evaluate whether or not you have achieved those aims. The detailed plans of the sessions will also be included together with their evaluations.

TASK 12

Find out about Child Protection procedures from organisations such as Sports Coach UK, the governing body of the activity you are focusing on, local sports development officer, national sports council , N.S.P.C.C. You will need to show, in your log, that you have a knowledge and understanding of Child Protection.

SCHEME OF WORK

Remember that for your assessment you will have to produce a scheme of work for ten hours of coaching/leading. A scheme of work is a general, overall plan which will identify what you hope to achieve, the skills you intend to get participants to learn etc. It will also outline what you plan to do in each of the sessions. A scheme of work has to be flexible as in some of your sessions things might not go according to plan, the participants might find the skills you are introducing easier or harder than you thought and you may have to spend more or less time on them than you had planned. However the scheme of work is important as it outlines what you plan to do, the practices you will use, the facilities and equipment you will use etc.

Your planning and organisation should include:

- **Facilities** – suitability, availability, booking, cost, safety, accessibility, rules of usage
- **Equipment** – availability, suitability, quality, quantity, storage, access, maintenance, distribution in sessions
- **Participants** – numbers, age, gender, ability, experience
- **Health and safety** – risk assessments, first aid availability, emergency procedures
- **Child protection procedures**. How you are going to put them into practice
- **Objectives** – long term, short term
- **Scheme of work** – length, aims, objectives, individual session plans.

REMEMBER

The following well-known sayings:

- Failure to plan is planning to fail.
- The 6P principle – Proper preparation prevents pathetically poor performance.

EXAM TIP

You need to ensure that you produce a detailed plan for each of your sessions.

RISK ASSESSMENT

This is an important part of your role and your planning. It involves you identifying possible hazards, which is any thing or situation that can cause harm if not controlled and then evaluating the risk. The risk is the possible consequence if nothing is done to control the hazard.

TASK 13

Carry out a risk assessment for a coaching session and complete the appropriate forms.

KEY TERMS

Risk assessment

A risk assessment is a careful, systematic examination of things that in your coaching/leading or officiating could harm people so that you can judge whether risks are suitably controlled or whether more should be done to control them.

Hazard

Any thing or any situation that can cause harm, if uncontrolled.

Risk

The chance that somebody will be harmed by the hazard.

DELIVERY

When you deliver your sessions you will need to have prepared a detailed plan to follow. You will probably be given a session plan outline by your teachers or, if you undertake one of the courses mentioned previously by your tutor. The sort of information you will need on your session plans will be:

- number of participants, age, gender, experience, ability
- equipment required
- length of session
- objectives of session
- warm-up activities and their organisation
- activities with their coaching points, detailed progressive practices and organisation.
- cool down.

When focusing on your delivery you should think about:

- your appearance which should be clean, neat, tidy and set an example
- your 'presence' and personality
- giving clear simple instructions
- giving good clear, correct demonstrations
- how you are going to control the group, e.g. with a whistle

Your appearance should be smart

them to do. You will then watch them practising and identify the good things they do, which you will praise them for. If they get something wrong you will have to identify their mistakes and give them remedial drills or exercises.

Another major focus for your evaluative skills will be your evaluation of your own performance. Again you will identify what you did well, what was not so good and how you need to change things so that you do better next time. It is important that you do this post-session evaluation as soon as possible after your session so that things are fresh in your mind. Your teacher, coach or fellow students may also evaluate your session and give you feedback. Once you have received your feedback both from yourself and others who have observed the session, you will need to decide how you are going to apply this feedback to future sessions.

- encouraging, motivating and praising participants
- being enthusiastic and positive
- variation in the tone of your voice
- building a positive relationship with the participants.
- treating all participants equally and fairly
- including all participants
- timekeeping – ensuring that you keep to your planned timings.

KEY TERMS

Evaluation

Looking at a performance and identifying what is good about it and what its weaknesses are.

Strength

Part of the skill/performance that is good and is carried out correctly and efficiently.

Weakness

Part of the skill/performance that is incorrect or carried out poorly or inefficiently.

REMEMBER

Remember that when delivering your sessions that you should follow the plan you have devised. However, a good coach is adaptable and you may need to adjust your plan if things do not go quite as you had intended.

EVALUATION

During and after your session you will need to apply your evaluative skills. These skills enable you to decide what is good about a performance and what is weak and needs to be improved. In your session you will have demonstrated and explained to the participants what it is you want

TECHNICAL KNOWLEDGE

Another area of skills that you need to concentrate on is your technical knowledge of the activity you coach/lead. You will need to know the correct technical models for the skills of the activity, the phases they break down into, the coaching points together with the progressive practices to develop them. You can learn these from the sessions you take part in as part of your A level Physical Education course or you can find them in the coaching manuals which most governing bodies produce. It also improves your credibility with the participants if you can demonstrate the skills that you are coaching so you will need to practise these skills to ensure that you can demonstrate them correctly.

TASK 14

Consult your teacher/coach and the relevant coaching manuals to identify the skills which you will need to know the coaching points for and be able to give good demonstrations of.

EXAM TIP

Watching other coaches/leaders is also a good way of improving your own coaching/leading. You can observe how they approach situations and see the practices they use for different skills. You can then use the good parts of these sessions in your own coaching and make sure that you do not make the mistakes that you see them make!

TACTICS/COMPOSITIONAL IDEAS

You will have to have some knowledge of the tactics and strategies or compositional ideas that are applied in you activity. These will be covered in coaching manuals. You can develop an appreciation and understanding of these by observing the performance and coaching of your activity.

TASK 15

Identify the basic tactics and strategies/compositional ideas which are used in your activity and explain how you would coach them.

3. Officiating an activity

The specification indicates that the focus of your assessment is on a range of applied and acquired skills, abilities and qualities. These skills will be assessed while you officiate safe, purposeful and enjoyable activities. Suitable opportunities for such activities would be primary school sports, local junior sports, inter-form sports or youth groups.

You may within your centre undertake a Governing Body officiating award and successfully completing this course will allow you to develop many of the skills on which your assessment will be based.

You will need to practise your officiating if you are to improve and you will need someone to observe you to give you feedback on what you have done well and areas where you need to improve. Whilst there may be opportunities for practice in your centre you may have to seek opportunities for practice in your local clubs or through your local sports development officer.

You will need to keep a log which contains evidence for your assessment. The log needs the following detailed information:

- a record of your officiating over a three month period
- four evaluations by qualified assessors of sessions officiated
- risk assessments undertaken
- a 40-minute video record of you officiating
- information relating to Health and Safety issues of your activity
- information relating to child protection procedures in the activity
- the fitness and health benefits both from participating and officiating in the activity.

You should complete your log as you officiate rather than leaving it until your final assessment. It is far easier to put together information relating to your officiating sessions as you do them than to wait until your log is due to be assessed by your teacher.

EXAM TIP

Put your evidence log together as you do your officiating sessions rather than leaving it to the submission date. Make sure it has all the detail required.

TASK 16

Find out about the risk assessment and child protection procedures in your activity.

The focus of your assessment will be on your:

- ability to apply your officiating skills in sessions.
- organisational and planning skills
- use of a range of officiating strategies
- overall performance in officiating
- awareness of health and safety
- implementation of risk assessments
- awareness of child protection
- knowledge of the rules and regulations/ conventions of the activity
- evaluative skills
- awareness of the fitness and health benefits of the activity.

Your teacher will use these assessment criteria to put you into one of five bands (0–6, 7–12, 13–18, 19–24, 25–30) before they finally decide the exact mark you will be given. Your teacher will assess you over a period of time but might watch you do a final officiating session to finalise your mark out of 30.

TASK 17

Ask your teacher/coach or local sports development officer for details of governing body level two officiating awards in the activities you are interested in.

HOW CAN I IMPROVE MY OFFICIATING SKILLS?

You should now be aware of how and when you will be assessed as well as the focus of your assessment. This understanding will help you plan how you should use your time to practise and improve your officiating and therefore increase the marks you get in your assessment.

As well as practising your skills and strategies yourself by officiating it is useful to observe and evaluate others officiating. You can pick up ideas on how to deal with situations, different approaches to interacting with participants etc. Sometimes when you are observing others you also find out approaches and ways you should not use!

It is useful if you identify the skills you need to develop and organise them into groups, these being:

- Planning and organisation
- Officiating
- Evaluative
- Technical knowledge.

PLANNING AND ORGANISATION

You need to do your planning and organising prior to your officiating sessions in order that you will be able to officiate successfully. In your planning and organising for your officiating you need to create habits. You should develop routines that you go through prior to officiating. The areas you are looking at are as follows:

- ensuring that you know the type of participants you will be officiating, i.e. age, gender, ability
- ensuring that you are aware of the nature of the competition and any rules, regulations specific to that competition
- being aware of the venue and how long it will take you to get there
- timings: what time the session starts and the time you will need beforehand to carry out your health and safety checks, risk assessments and any child protection issues
- equipment: checks on your own officiating equipment, e.g. watch, whistle, flags, notebook,

pen etc. together with any personal clothing that you will need

- fitness: maintaining your own physical and mental fitness with appropriate training.

A lot of the areas above will be the same for each session that you officiate but you must still go through the process to ensure that you are prepared for each session.

You will need to ensure that you able to carry out a risk assessment for your activity and complete the appropriate forms.

TASK 18

Carry out a risk assessment for a session you are officiating in your activity and complete the appropriate documentation.

When you actually officiate the time you have spent planning and organising will pay dividends. You will have ensured that you arrive with ample time to carry out your health and safety and child protection checks where appropriate. Most officials will also take the opportunity

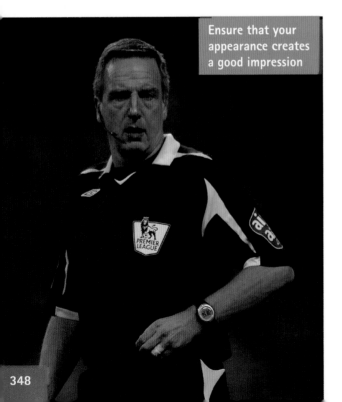

Ensure that your appearance creates a good impression

to introduce themselves to and talk to the participants before the session and this takes time.

If the session you are officiating in involves children then you will need to ensure that all child protection procedures are applied.

If you are officiating in an activity which also involves other officials then you will obviously have to meet them and discuss your strategies. You also need to ensure that you have ample time to change into any special clothing that is required and that your appearance creates a good impression with the participants.

OFFICIATING

Once the session starts you will need to ensure that in your officiating you are:

- decisive – you make considered decisions and communicate those decisions to the participants
- you are fair to all participants in your application of the rules
- control – you are firm in your decisions and communicate with the participants
- communication – you ensure that your decisions are understood by the participants. They should understand how you will convey your decisions i.e. whistle, flags, signals etc.
- positioning – you should, if the activity requires it, ensure that you are able to keep up with play and position yourself so that you are able to make good decisions
- team work – in activities where you work with other officials you should ensure that you communicate with them and listen to their opinions.

EVALUATIVE SKILLS

Once you have officiated your session you should evaluate your performance. You will identify what you did well, what was not so good and how you need to change things so that you do better next time. It is important that you do this post-session evaluation as soon as possible after your session so that things are fresh in your mind. Your teacher, assessor or fellow students may also evaluate your session and give you feedback. It is also important to realise in your evaluation and other people's evaluations that very few officials or indeed performers and coaches/leaders get everything right all the time. What you are doing in your evaluation is identifying areas where you can improve and make yourself a better official as well as praising yourself for the things you did well. In your evaluation you should cover your preparation and planning for the session, your officiating skills and strategies, your knowledge of the rules and regulations and your fitness.

When you have received evaluative feedback both from yourself and others you should decide on how you are going to use this feedback to improve your performance.

EXAM TIP

Get an up-to-date copy of your activity's rules and regulations from the governing body.

TECHNICAL KNOWLEDGE

The fourth category of skills you need to look is your technical knowledge and your fitness. It is essential that an official in any activity has a good, up-to-date knowledge of the rules,

regulations and conventions of that activity. Most governing bodies publish their rules and regulations and you should ensure that you know the current rules and how to apply them. In activities which require you to be physically fit it is obviously essential that you ensure that you reach a required fitness level and maintain it. Some organisations actually carry out fitness tests on their officials! It does not do your credibility any good if you are unable to keep up with play or last the whole period of the activity.

Watching other officials, particularly experienced ones, is a good way to improve your own officiating. You can observe how they apply the rules, communicate with participants and position themselves to see whether they do it differently to you. Remember, however, that we all have different personalities and other people's approaches to officiating may not necessarily work for you.

TASK 19

Watch a video of your activity and evaluate the official's performance.

Exam Café

Relax, refresh, result!

Refresh your memory

You should now be able to:

▷ understand which practical activities you can choose to be assessed in

▷ understand which roles you can be assessed in.

▷ understand how you will be assessed in each of these roles.

▷ understand the terms 'standardisation' and 'moderation'

▷ appreciate how you can improve your performances.

▷ appreciate how you can improve your coaching/leading.

▷ appreciate how you can improve your officiating.

REVISE AS YOU GO!

Test your knowledge and understanding

1. Which activity category do your two activities come from?
2. What are the conditioned competitive situations for your performance activities?
3. Name the basic skills which are important in your two activities.
4. Name two advanced skills which you are able to perform in your activities.
5. Identify the phases into which skills in your activities are analysed.
6. Describe one set of progressive practices for a skill in your activities.
7. Describe the basic strategies and tactics/choreographical and compositional ideas used in your activities and describe your role in them.
8. What should you be looking for in the evaluation of your performance/coaching/leading/officiating?
9. What is a risk assessment in coaching/leading or officiating?
10. What is the Child Protection policy in your coaching/leading or officiating activity?
11. When do your assessments have to be completed?

CHAPTER 13:

Evaluation and planning for the improvement of performance

LEARNING OBJECTIVES

At the end of this chapter you should be able to:

- Understand the structure and contents of the evaluating and planning for the improvement of performance response
- Practise your response
- Successfully complete your response
- Understand how you will be assessed.

INTRODUCTION

Closely linked to your practical activity assessment is the evaluating and planning for improvement response in which you are required to identify the strengths and weaknesses of a performance in one of your chosen activities.

Based on this evaluation you will produce an action plan designed to improve this performance. Additionally you will have to discuss the opportunities there are locally and nationally both to participate and progress in the activity as well as the benefits in terms of health and fitness of participating in the activity. Your evaluating and planning for improvement helps prepare you for the Evaluation and Appreciation of Performance element of your A2 assessment.

What do I have to do in my evaluation and planning for the improvement of performance?

You will choose one of the activities in which you are being assessed for performance and on which you wish to focus for this aspect of your assessment. You will then:

- watch a fellow student performing the activity
- evaluate the performance, identifying the strengths and weaknesses
- select a major weakness and create an action plan to rectify/improve it
- discuss the opportunities locally and nationally for participation and improvement in the activity.
- discuss the health and fitness benefits of the activity.

HOW DO I DO THIS?

You will do this by talking to your teacher.

EVALUATION

When you evaluate you identify what is:

- good about the performance – the strengths
- poor about the performance – the weaknesses.

You will focus on the following areas:

- skills
- tactics/compositional ideas
- fitness.

To help you do this you may want to refer to the phases that are used to analyse the activity and its skills (see Chapters 4 and 5).

ACTION PLANNING

Initially, you have to select one of the major weaknesses identified in your evaluation to be the focus of your action plan. Having selected the focus, your action plan should have the following:

- a clear realistic goal – a major weakness you have identified
- a timescale
- a method for achieving the goal – detailed coaching points and progressive practices.

You now have a clear structure or plan of what it is that you have to do. This can be identified as follows:

- accurately describe the major strengths of the performance
- accurately describe the major weaknesses of the performance
- construct a viable action plan to remedy a major weakness which has:
  - detailed coaching points
  - detailed progressive practices
  - a timescale for the plan.

TASK 1

Write out your checklist for your evaluating and planning for the improvement of performance oral response. It should have the three points identified above. You should use this checklist when you start to practise your observation and oral response.

In addition to your evaluation of the performance you will also have to discuss the opportunities to participate in this activity, both in your area and nationally. You also need to talk about opportunities to improve your performance standard and the level at which you participate. You will obviously need to undertake some research to establish what these opportunities are. Finally you will also need to discuss what the health and fitness benefits are to people who participate in this activity.

REMEMBER

The structure of your full response should be as follows:

- accurately describe the major strengths of the performance.
- accurately describe the major weaknesses of the performance.
- construct a viable action plan to remedy a major weakness which has:
  - detailed coaching points
  - detailed progressive practices
  - a timescale for the plan
- discuss the opportunities locally And nationally to participate in the activity
- discuss the opportunities for you to progress in the activity.
- discuss the health and fitness benefits of participating in the activity.

HOW CAN I IMPROVE MY EVALUATION AND APPRECIATION OF PERFORMANCE?

Like your practical performance, this aspect of your assessment is a skill and to improve it you need to practise it and receive feedback. Like other skills, it can be broken down into parts for you to practise.

ANALYTICAL PHASES

You need to know the movement phases that are used to analyse the activity. This will help you analyse the skills. These can be found in the OCR's *Teacher Support: Coursework Guidance.*

TASK 2

If you have not already done so, access the coursework guidance booklet and identify the movement phases for the activity on which you will focus for your Evaluation and Planning for the improvement of Performance.

COACHING POINTS

You should know the coaching points for the major skills of your activity. You should make a note of these when your teacher covers them in

REMEMBER

If you were assessed performing in this activity refer to your notes and remind yourself of the phases used to analyse your activity.

your sessions or refer to coaching manuals to find them. You need to compare these coaching points to the performance you observe.

EXAM TIP

Make sure that you know the coaching points of all the major skills in your activity.

REMEMBER

If you were assessed performing in this activity refer to your notes to remind yourself of the coaching points of the skills.

IDENTIFICATION OF STRENGTHS

You should start by splitting the activity into the analytical movement phases and identifying strengths in each of these phases. It is suggested that you focus on the following three aspects.

1. **Skills**

   These skills will be being performed under pressure. It is important that you are aware of the 'technical' models to which you are comparing the performance you are observing. As previously suggested, these 'technical' models can be found in the relevant governing or organising body coaching manuals. Knowledge of how the skill should be performed enables you to judge how good it is and to justify your evaluation by identifying why it is good. You will also use this knowledge when you are identifying weaknesses and constructing your action plan.

2. **Tactics and strategies/compositional ideas**

   As performers gain a greater grasp of the skills within the activity, they are able to devote more attention to the tactics and strategies

involved. They show an increased perceptual awareness accompanied by an increased capacity for decision-making. The majority of these increased capacities will be devoted to the performer attempting to influence the outcome of the activity through their use of tactics and strategies/compositional ideas. Sometimes this may be shown through better teamwork or better compositional ideas.

You will need to have a good understanding of the major tactics and strategies/compositional ideas used in the activity to be able to evaluate the performer you are observing. This understanding will be gained from your own involvement in the activity but should be further improved by reading the appropriate coaching manuals and talking to coaches. You will be comparing the performer you are looking at to what you know they should be doing. This will enable you to identify what they are doing correctly. If they are part of a team, you will probably want to comment on the team's effective use of strategies as well as the individual's contribution.

3. **Fitness**

   You should apply your knowledge of fitness to your evaluation. This should enable you to identify accurately the components of physical fitness appropriate to the performance you are evaluating as well as the skill related fitness components. You should evaluate the fitness of the performer you are observing under the following headings as appropriate:

   a. Physical fitness
   - Strength/power
   - Stamina
   - Suppleness/flexibility
   - Speed

   b. Skill-related fitness
   - Agility
   - Coordination
   - Balance
   - Timing

EXAM TIP

Know the tactics/compositional ideas of your activity.

TASK 3

Refer to a coaching manual for your activity and find out about tactics and strategies/compositional ideas.

A skill being performed under pressure

You will be focusing on the aspects of fitness you know are important in the activity to assess whether or not the performer you are observing has good levels in these areas.

Some of the areas suggested above will be more relevant in some activities than others and you need to adapt them to suit the activity you are observing. There may be other fitness aspects which are appropriate to your activity and these should be included.

Not only will you comment on the fitness aspects for which the performer has good levels, but also on his or her application of them to their performance.

IDENTIFICATION OF WEAKNESSES

You should start again, by splitting the activity into the analytical movement phases and identifying the weaknesses in each of these phases.

This aspect will follow the same path as the identification of strengths. You are identifying major weaknesses and those for which you can construct a viable action plan. You do not want to be too negative by identifying every small weakness, particularly those that do not significantly affect the performance. You should be able to place the weaknesses you have identified in a rank order in terms of their importance and when you would correct them.

The areas to focus on should be the same as those looked at when identifying strengths: skills, tactics and strategies/compositional ideas and fitness.

1. Skills
    You will need to focus on the skills in which, when under pressure, the performer either performs poorly or chooses not to use at all. You will be able to identify those performed poorly by comparing them to the correct technical models and the coaching points as well as the level of success. When under pressure, some performers will be very inconsistent in some aspects of their skill production. This means they will be successful on one occasion and unsuccessful the next time. When under pressure, do they choose not to perform advanced skills indicating they are unsure or lack confidence in them?

2. Tactics and strategies/compositional ideas
    These will vary a great deal from activity to activity. They will focus on attempting to outwit the opposition or the environment and in team activities they will also include teamwork. Again, you will be comparing what your performer does against what you know to be good tactics and strategies/compositional ideas. This will enable you to identify where he or she is going wrong. This may be focused on the individual you are observing or the team in general.

3. Fitness
    Using the areas of fitness you have determined are important for the activity, you will identify those areas in which, in your opinion, the performer has weaknesses or in which you consider he or she could perform better by having increased levels of fitness.

It should have become apparent to you by now that in identifying strengths and weaknesses you are using the same information to determine both aspects. You should, however, ensure that you identify the strengths before the weaknesses, as it is easy to overlook them!

KEY TERM

Action plan

Contains a clear realistic goal, a timescale and a detailed method of how you are going to achieve the goal.

CONSTRUCTING A VIABLE ACTION PLAN TO IMPROVE A MAJOR WEAKNESS

This is where you will select one of the major weaknesses you have identified and create a plan to remedy it, thereby improving the performance as a whole. You should already know which weakness needs to be corrected first from your rank order.

You will remember that your action plan had to include the following aspects:

- clear, achievable, realistic goals
- timescale
- method for achieving the goals – detailed coaching points and practices.

These must appear in your action plan.

CLEAR, REALISTIC GOALS

These will be to remedy the major fault you have identified and thereby improve the performance. All you have to do is select one of the major faults you have identified. You should, in addition, identify a specific goal, e.g. to achieve a specific level on the multi-stage fitness test rather than simply to improve stamina.

When choosing the fault you should ensure you are able to suggest ways in which it can be remedied, i.e. to construct an action plan. Sometimes it is easier to focus on weaknesses within a skill or fitness area, as these are easier for creating action plans than tactics/compositional ideas.

EXAM TIP

Ensure that you identify a clear, realistic goal in your action plan.

TIMESCALE

You need to identify how long your action plan is designed to take, how frequent the practices or training will be and so on. Different action plans will have different timescales. Those designed to develop aspects of fitness will usually be over a longer period than those to develop skills.

You should give an indication of the overall length of the action plan, i.e. the number of weeks or months – together with the length of the sessions and their frequency (for example, number of times a week).

METHOD FOR ACHIEVING THE GOALS

Here you will describe the practices and drills you will suggest that the performer does to remedy the weakness. This should be done in detail, identifying the coaching points for the skills you wish to be improved as well as each of the practices you will use. Remember that the practices you identify should show progression, going from simple to complex and closed to open. You should, however, be realistic, starting

Make sure that you identify a timescale in your action plan

the practices at a level that is appropriate to the performer you are observing. Remember that you will probably take the performer back to the cognitive stage of learning.

KEY TERM

Progressive practice

A practice that starts with a skill in its simplest, closed situation and goes through a series of stages to practice the same skill in its natural, open situation.

If in your evaluation of the performance you decide that the performer's fitness is a major weakness, you should demonstrate your knowledge by identifying exactly the aspects of fitness you are going to focus on, together with their relevance and application in the activity.

You should include the detailed programme, exercises etc., together with progressions that you would put in your plan to improve these fitness aspects. You should also detail how you would test the performer to see if they have achieved these goals.

OPPORTUNITIES TO PARTICIPATE AND PROGRESS IN THE ACTIVITY

In addition to this evaluation and action planning you must also discuss the opportunities for participation and improving performance both locally and nationally. This will mean that you will have to do some research both in your own local area and in your country. As you are involved in the activity you will probably have some information about opportunities locally but could find out more by talking to your teachers and coaches, as well as approaching your local sports development officer. You should focus on finding out how many clubs/teams there are in the area and what facilities they have. You should also find out how easy it is to access these opportunities for different groups of people. When looking at the national picture, the governing/organising body website may provide information and guidance. Additionally, the National Sports Council of your country may be able to give you information.

When discussing opportunities to progress in the activity you may talk about:

- Local standards in terms of competition, facilities, coaching.
- Access to higher levels in the activity in terms of travel, finance and time.
- The performance pyramid.

HEALTH AND FITNESS BENEFITS OF PARTICIPATING IN THE ACTIVITY

The assessment criteria also require you to discuss the health and fitness benefits which participants get from taking part in the activity. In your AS Physical Education course you will have talked about a balanced, active and healthy lifestyle and you are being asked to say what contribution taking part in this activity makes to this. You will be able to relate some of the knowledge you have gained from the Anatomy and Physiology part of your course to this part of your response – you could focus on evaluating your activity in relation to its short and long term effects on the various body systems, e.g. skeletal, cardiovascular, respiratory.

You should also talk about the social and emotional benefits gained from participating in the activity. Your own experiences will help you in this aspect but you should think about aspects of you Acquiring Movement Skills part of your

Opportunities to participate

course as well as talking to your teachers/coaches. You may also find information in coaching manuals.

PRACTISING YOUR EVALUATION AND PLANNING FOR IMPROVEMENT

You should practise your evaluation and planning for the improvement of performance as many times as you can. As with any skill, you should break it down to its simplest form, practise this, then move on to practise the next stage until you have mastered the complete skill. At each stage you should add that stage on to those you have already mastered.

REMEMBER

Remember to practise your evaluation and planning response using the progressive part practice method you studied in your acquiring movement skills.

The following stages would be appropriate for you to practise:

- identifying the strengths in each of the movement phases

You may make notes as you observe the performance

- identifying the weaknesses in each of the movement phases
- identifying a major weakness, and creating a viable action plan to remedy it and improve the performance – to include detailed coaching points, progressive practices, and a timescale.

It may be that you can practise by looking at a video of the activity you are focusing on and you can record your response on tape so that you can listen to it and evaluate it yourself.

When you have mastered these aspects you should add on:

- opportunities for participation and progression
- health and fitness benefits.

WHAT WILL HAPPEN WHEN I AM ASSESSED?

Your teacher will ask you to watch one of your fellow students performing the activity. They will ask you to focus on particular aspects of the performance or a particular performer. They will select the aspects on which they wish you to focus. After you have watched the performance for some time, they will ask you to comment on it. You can make notes as you watch the performance to help you with your response. You cannot use any prepared notes. When you have started your response, you may well be able to look at the performance again to refresh your memory as well as referring to your notes.

When you have observed the performance, the teacher will say something like:

'You have just observed Sophie's performance. Describe the strengths and weaknesses of the performance and create an action plan to improve a major weakness of the performance. You should also talk about the opportunities to take part and progress in this activity as well as its health and fitness benefits.'

The teacher will expect you to go through the stages you have already identified (as follows).

1. Identify the strengths of the performance.
2. Identify the weaknesses of the performance.

3. Select the major weakness.
4. Create a viable action plan on which you:
   a. have clear, realistic, achievable goals
   b. identify a timescale
   c. identify the detailed coaching points you will use
   d. identify the detailed practices you will use.
5. Discuss the opportunities for participation and progression locally and nationally.
6. Discuss the health and fitness benefits of participating in the activity.

If you get stuck or miss out a stage, the teacher will probably ask questions to help direct you. These questions should be those that will guide you to think about a particular stage or area rather than needing a specific answer.

Examples of these questions could include the following.

- What were the good elements of the performance you have just seen?

- What are the causes of the faults/weaknesses?
- If you were Sophie's coach, what would you do in order to improve one of the major weaknesses which you have identified?
- What practices would you use to improve that skill?
- Describe the opportunities for you to participate in this activity both locally and nationally.
- Describe the opportunities for you to progress in this activity.
- What are the health and fitness benefits you get from participating in this activity?

Remember, this is your opportunity to tell your teacher how much you know and understand by applying it to the performance you observe. Ideally, once your teacher has asked you the starting question you should be able to keep talking about what you have seen and know until they want you to stop!

REMEMBER

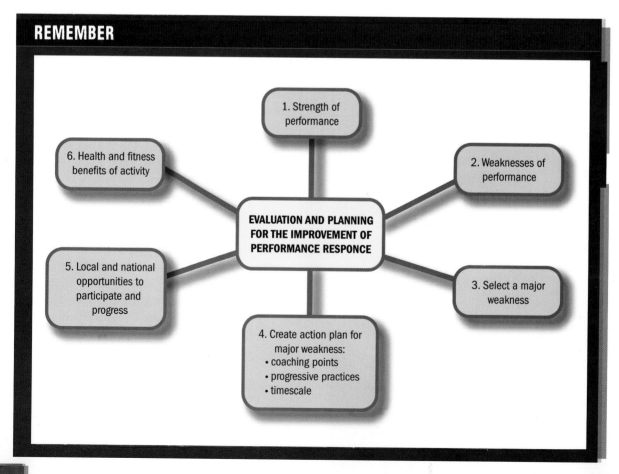

THE ASSESSMENT CRITERIA

Your teacher will be using the following criteria to assess you:

- accuracy of the description of the major strengths of the skills, tactics/compositional ideas
- accuracy of the description of the major weaknesses of the skills, tactics/compositional ideas
- accuracy of prioritising the areas of the performance which need improvement
- creating a viable action plan which has detailed coaching points and detailed progressive practices
- accuracy of the description of opportunities locally and nationally for participation and progression in the activity
- accuracy of the description of the health and fitness benefits of the activity.

They will use these criteria to firstly put you into one of four bands, 0-5, 6-10, 11-15, 16-20. They will then give you a mark from within this band.

TASK 4

Look at a video/DVD performance of your activity and do your oral evaluation and planning for improvement response, then record it on tape or video/DVD. Play back your response and mark it.

Exam**Café**
Relax, refresh, result!

Refresh your memory

You should now be able to:

▷ Understand the structure and contents of the evaluating and planning for the improvement of performance response.

▷ Practise your response.

▷ Successfully complete your response.

▷ Understand how you will be assessed.

REVISE AS YOU GO!

Test your knowledge and understanding

1. Name the activity you have selected on which to do your evaluation and planning for the improvement of performance oral response.
2. Identify the movement phases that are used to assess your activity.
3. Identify the coaching points for the skills in your activity.
4. Identify progressive practices for each of the important skills in your activity.
5. What are the important aspects of health and fitness in your activity.
6. Describe the major tactics/compositional ideas in your activity.
7. Write out the six components you will cover when you do your evaluation and planning for the improvement of performance.
8. What are the opportunities locally and nationally for participation in your activities?
9. What are the opportunities for you to progress in your activities?

Index

Page numbers in **bold** type refer to key terms.

A

abduction 12
acceleration **51**
acquiring, developing and evaluating
  practical skills 322
  coursework 333–4
  performing an activity 334–41
action plan **355**
activity, coaching/leading 341–3
  delivery 344–5
  evaluation 345
  improving 343
  planning and organisation 343
  risk assessment **344**
  tactics/compositional ideas 346
  technical knowledge 345
activity, officiating 346–7
  evaluative skills 348–9
  improving skills 347
  planning and organisation 347–8
  practical officiating 348
  technical knowledge 349
activity, performing (for course
  assessment) 334
  analysing skills 340–1
  assessment 336–7
  content 334–6
  developing skills 339–40
  feedback from teachers and
    coaches 340
  improving performance 338
  improving quality and range 339
  mental fitness 339
  physical fitness 338
  practice, structuring and
    implementing 341
  requirements 337
adduction 12
adductor longus 15
adductor magnus 15
administration 226
adrenalin 75
advertising, impact on sport 303
aerobic **60**
aerobic exercise 32
aerobic system 60
aesthetic 226

agonist muscles **16**
aiming 137
air pollution 88
altitude training 115
altitude, effects on respiration
  114–16
alveoli 101, 102
amateur approach to sports **240**
amateurism and the Olympic Games
  314, 317
amateurs **240**
'American Dream' 243
American Football
  commercialism 244–6
  origins and nature 244
anaerobic **60**
anaerobic exercise 32
anatomical position **11**
angina 94
angular motion **47**, 47–48
ankle joint 14, 15
  muscles 26
antagonist muscles **16**
antagonistic muscle action **16**
anterior 11
anticipation 167
aorta 62
aortic valve 62
appeasement **327**
appendicular skeleton 3
appreciation of natural environment
  219
arousal 167, 183–5, **184**
  catastrophe theory 187–8
  drive theory 185–6
  inverted U theory 186–7
arteries 81, 82
arterioles 81, 82, 83
arteriosclerosis 93
articular cartilage 5, **7**
assistant masters 238
association/linking strategy 161
associationalist theory 194
associative phase of skill learning
  143–4
assumptions **282**
asthma 118–19

atherosclerosis 93, 94
atria of the heart 61, 62
attention 198
attention field **187**
attitudes **282**
Australian Rules Football 249–50
  commercialism and media impact
    250
  factors affecting development 250
Australian sport and culture 246–7
  sport as high status 248–9
  sport as national preoccupation
    248
autonomic nervous system (ANS)
  72–3
autonomous phase of skill learning
  144
AV node 63, 64
Awards for All **274**
axial skeleton 3

B

ball and socket joints 10
ballistic skills **132**
baroreceptors 73, 75, **86**, 113, 114
behaviour 227
biceps brachii 15, 18
biceps femoris 15, 25
bicuspid valve 62
bi-lateral transfer 204
biomechanics 47
  centre of mass **52**
  force **50**
  motion 47–9
  Newton's laws of motion 50–1
blood
  carbon dioxide transport 87
  circulation 61–4
  oxygen transport 87
  viscosity **89**
blood pooling 83
blood pressure 89
  changes during exercise 91
  changes during physical activity
    90–1
  hypertension 92–3
  long-term changes 92

measurement 90
mechanism 89
post-exercise recovery 91–2
resistance 90
risk for coronary heart disease (CHD) 95
blood vessels 80
circulatory networks 80–6
effect of warm-up and cool-down 88–9
structure 82–3
bodies influencing and promoting participation in sport 262
devolved institutes 267–9
mass participation and excellence 263, 264
National Institutes of Sports 265–6
positive and negative aspects of decentralised systems 262
UK Sport 264–5
bone marrow 5, 7
bone spurs 38
bones 2–7
disorders 36–7
types 5–7
bradycardia 64
British Empire 238
British Olympic Association (BOA) 316
bronchoconstriction 119
bronchii 101
bronchioles 101
bronchodilators 119
BSkyB 304
Bundle of His 63, 64
bursa 8
bush culture 249

C

caffeine 119
calcaneus 3
calcium 5
capillaries 81, 82, 83
capitalism 242
capsule (of joints) 7
carbaminohaemoglobin 87, 109–10
carbon dioxide
external respiration 106–7
internal respiration 108
transport 87
transport 109–10
carbonic acid 87
cardiac control centre (CCC) 72–3

hormonal control 74
intrinsic control 74
neural control 73–4
cardiac cycle 64–5
cardiac impulse 63–4
cardiac output (Q) 67, 83, 84
distribution at rest and during exercise 85
response to exercise 70–1
cardiac rate (HR) 66, 83, 84
response to exercise 69–70
cardiovascular system
response of heart to physical activity 59–75
response of vascular system to physical activity 80–97
carpals 3
catastrophe theory of arousal 187–8
centralised system 326
centre of mass 52
character building 238
CHD (coronary heart disease) 93
reducing risk 94–6
risk factors 95
Cheese Rolling (Gloucestershire) 235
chemoreceptors 73, 75, **86**, 113, 114
China and the Olympic Games 326
human rights 326
choice reaction time 165–6
cholesterol 95
chunking 160, 162
circulatory networks 80–1
circumduction of joints 13
clavicle 3
closed loop control
level two control 173–4
level three control 174–6
closed skills 126
coccyx 3
cognitive arousal 184
cognitive phase of skill learning 142
cognitive theory of learning 195–6
collagen 5
colonialism 248
commercialisation 317
commercialism 243
American Football 244–6
Australian Rules Football 250
Olympic Games 317–20
communism 326
comparison aspect of perception 160
competition 226
complex skills 128
concentration 187

concentration/selective attention 167
concentric contraction 28, **29**
concurrent feedback 177
conditioned competitive situation 334
condyloid joints 10
conference **245**
connectionist theory 194
continuity continuum 126–7
continuous skills 127
continuum **124**
cool-down 34–5, **35**, 89
core stability **16**
coronary arteries 63
coronary veins 63
corticosteroids 119
counter culture suggestion **296**
coursework
assessment 333–4
choice of activities 333
module content 333
cue detection 167
cue utilisation **187**
culture **232**

D

decentralised **262**
decision making 157
deltoid 15, 19
deoxygenated 60
Department for Culture, Media and Sport 260
deviance 228
devolved **267**
devolved institutes
English Institute of Sport (EIS) 267
Scottish Institute of Sport (SIS) 267
Sport England 268
Sports Council for Northern Ireland 268
Sports Council for Wales 269
SportScotland 269
Welsh Institute of Sport (SIS) 267
diaphragm 102, 103
diaphysis 5, **7**
diastole 64, 65
diastolic blood pressure 89
during exercise 91
difficulty continuum 128
direct force **54**
direction of behaviour 184
disabled participants in sport 285–7

Paralympics 287–8
discrete skills 126
discrimination 282
display 157
distributed practice 149
dominant response 185
dorsiflexion 14
drive reduction 177, 189
drive theory of arousal 185–6
drugs in sport 295
   arguments against drugs 298
   arguments for allowing drugs 298
   reasons and consequences 295–9
dynamic flexibility 136
dynamic strength 135
dysfunctional effects 327

E

eccentric contraction 28, **29**
eccentric force **55**
effector mechanism 157
effectors 156, 157
elbow joint 8, 14, 15
   muscles 18
elderly people and sport 285
elitism **326**
encoded **159**
end–distolic volume (EDV) 66
end–systolic volume (ESV) 66
enduring skills 134
English Institute of Sport (EIS) 267
enjoyment strategy 162
environmental influence continuum
   126
enzyme **89**
epiphysis 5, **7**
equilibrium 157
erector spinae 21
ergenic **114**
esteem 217, 280, 281
ethnic identity 232
ethnic minority groups and sport
   291–2
   racial discrimination 292–3
evaluation **345**
excellence and participation in UK
   continuum 279
   increasing 293
   mass participation 279–80
   sporting excellence 280
executive motor programme (EMP)
   171
exercise 213
exercise induced asthma (EIA) 119

experience 166
expiration 103
explosive strength 136
extant flexibility 136
extension 11
   horizontal 12
external feedback **174**
external intercostal muscles 104
external oblique 15, 104
external respiration 100, 106–7
   during exercise 110
externally paced 127
extrinsic feedback 156, 158, 176
extrinsic motivation 184
extroverts 187

F

fainting 86
fair play and the Olympic Games
   314–15
fast glycolytic fibres 32, 33
fast oxidative glycolytic fibres 32, 33
fast twitch muscle fibre **32**
feedback 115–16, 156, **157**, 158,
   176–8
femur 3, 8
fibula 3
fine skills 125
finger dexterity 137
fixed practice 149–50
flexion 11
   dorsiflexion 14
   horizontal 12
   lateral 13
   plantar 14
force **50**
   direct force **54**
   eccentric force **55**
franchise 245, **246**
frequency of breathing (f) 105, 106
functional effects **327**
funding of physical activity 256–9
   National Lottery 260–2
   positive and negative aspects 259

G

games ethic **238**
gamesmanship 227, **228**
gaseous exchange 102, 105–8
   changes under exercise 108–12
gastrocnemius 15, 26
general motion 47, 49
generalised movement **178**
genetically determined skills 134

gentleman amateur **240**
Gestalt **196**
Gifted and Talented programme 275
gliding joints 10
gluteus maximus 15, 23
gluteus medius 15, 24
gluteus minimus 24
goal setting **178**
Government initiatives in sport
   promotion and participation 270
   National Curriculum 270
   other initiatives 276
   PE, School Sport and Club Links
      Strategy (PESSCLS) 270–6
grass roots clubs **263**
gravity assistance in blood
   circulation 83
grooved **172**
gross body co-ordination 136
gross body equilibrium 136
gross motor abilities 135–6
gross skills 125
growth plate (of bone) 5, **7**, 37

H

haemoglobin 87, 108–9
hamstrings 15, 25
Haxey Hood Game (Lincolnshire) 234
hazard **344**
healthy balanced lifestyle 210, **213**
heart 61–4
   cardiac cycle 64–5
   cardiac impulse 63–4
   cardiac output (Q) 67
   chambers 62
   healthy lifestyle 71–2
   rate (HR) 66
   rate regulation during exercise 75
   rate regulation during physical
      activity 72–5
   resting values 66–7
   vessels 62–3
heart attack 94
Heysel Stadium disaster (1985) 309
Hick's Law **165**
hierarchical **172**
high organisation skills 129
Highland Games (Scotland) 234
Hillsborough Stadium disaster (1989)
   309
hinge joints 10
hip joint 14, 15
   muscles 23–4
Hispanic 241

horizontal extension 12
horizontal flexion 12
House system **237**
human rights and sport 326
humerus 3, 8
Hurling the Silver Ball (Cornwall) 235
hypertension 92–3, 95
hypertrophy **64**
hypervigilance **187**

I

identical elements theory **205**
iliopsoas 15, 23
imagery strategy 162
immigration **282**
improving physical fitness 167
indigenous population **248**
inertia **51**
inferior **11**
inferior vena cava 62, 63
information processing 154
   improving retention and retrieval
      161–2
   memory and its role in developing
      skills 159–61
   modelling learning and
      performance skills 154–8
   psychological refractory period
      (PRP) 167–8
   reaction time 162–7
   serial and parallel processing 158–9
infraspinatus 15, 20
inhibition **189**
innate skills 134
insertion **16**
insight 196
insight learning **196**
inspiration 103
Inspiratory Muscle Training (IMT)
   116, 119–21
instructing performance skills 145
   manual guidance 147
   mechanical guidance 147
   verbal guidance 146
   visual guidance 145–6
intangible rewards **191**
intensity of behaviour 184
internal intercostal muscles 104
internal oblique 15
internal respiration 100, 108
   during exercise 110
internally paced 127
International Olympic Committee
   315–316

inter-school competitions **274**
intervening variables 195, **196**
intra-school competitions **274**
intrinsic feedback 156, 158, 176
intrinsic motivation 184
introverts 187
intuitive learning 196
inverted U theory of arousal 186–7
isometric contraction 28, **29**
isotonic contraction 29
issues in sport 255–6
   see also drugs in sport
   assumptions **282**
   attitudes **282**
   bodies influencing and promoting
      participation 262–6
   disabled participants 285–7
   discrimination **282**
   elderly people 285
   ethnic minority groups 291–3
   excellence and participation in
      UK 279–80
   funding of physical activity 256–9
   Government initiatives 270–6
   immigration **282**
   media, impact of 300–3
   minority groups 282
   modern technology 299–300
   National Governing Body (NGB)
      initiatives 276–7
   opportunity, provision and esteem
      280–2
   social and cultural factors 282,
      284, 285, 286
   society **282**
   sponsorship 303–6
   violence 306–9
   women, stereotyping of 289–91
   young people 284

J

joint capsule **7**
joint cavity **8**
joint stability **40**
joints 2, 6, 7–11
   disorders 38–40
   movements 9–14
   stability 40
   synovial 7–11

K

kinaesthesis 132, **143**, **174**
kinaesthetics 157
kitemarking of school PE 275–6

knee joint 8, 14, 15
   arthritic 38
   ligaments 39–40
   muscles 25
knowledge of performance (KP) 177
knowledge of results (KR) 177

L

lactate threshold **117**
larynx 101
lateral **11**
lateral flexion 13
latissimus dorsi 15, 19
learning performance skills 142–3
   associative phase 143–4
   autonomous phase 144
   cognitive phase 142
learning skills in physical activity
   application of catastrophe theory
      189
   arousal and motivation 183–5
   catastrophe theory of arousal
      187–8
   critical evaluation of inverted
      U and catastrophe theories
      189–90
   critical evaluation of motivation
      strategies 190–1
   drive theory of arousal 185–6
   inverted U theory of arousal 186–
      7
learning theories
   Bandura's model 197–8
   cognitive theory of learning 195–
      6
   limiting effects of negative
      transfer 205–6
   observational learning 197
   operant conditioning 194–5
   reinforcement 198–9
   varied practice 206
legacy **325**
life-long physical activity 212, **213**
lifetime sport 212, **213**
ligaments 3, 7, 8
line of gravity **54**
linear motion 47, 47–8
living high and training low (LHTL)
   116
London 2012 Olympic Games 321
   benefits to Britain 322, 324
   benefits to local area 323, 324
   benefits to sport 321–2, 324
   commitments 322–3

drawbacks 325
long-term memory (LTM) 159, 161
low organisation skills 129
lungs 101
    air pressure 103
    lobes 102

M

manual dexterity 137
manual guidance for instructing
    skills 147
mass participation in sports 240,
    255, 279–80
    factors affecting 283
    National Lottery funding of sport
        262
massed practice 148–9
meaningfulness strategy 162
mechanical guidance for instructing
    skills 147
media, roles and impact on sport
    300–1
    advertising 303
    BSkyB 304
    educating 301
    entertaining 301
    informing 301
    positive and negative impacts 302
    sponsorship 303
    television 303
medial 11
medulla oblongata 75, 113, 114
memory 157, 159
    multi-store model 159–61
memory items 178, 179
memory trace 173
meniscus 8
mental benefits of physical activity
    213
mental fitness 339
mental practice 151
mental rehearsal 166, 196
metacarpals 3
metatarsals 3
minority groups 282
minute ventilation (VE) 105, 106
modelling learning and performance
    skills 154–5
    Welford's model 155
    Whiting's model 155–8
moderation 334
modern technology and sport
    299–300
motion 47–9

motivation 167, 183–5, **184**, 198
    critical evaluation of strategies
        190–1
motor control 171
    programmes 171–8
    schema theory 178–9
motor nerves **73**
motor programme (MP) **157, 171**
motor reproduction 198
motor skills 124, 142
    acquiring abilities 138–9
    classification 125
    classification of abilities 134–8
    continuity continuum 126–7
    difficulty continuum 128
    environmental influence
        continuum 126
    organisational continuum 129
    pacing continuum 127
    phases/stages 142–5
    practising 130–4
    providing guidance 145–8
movement analysis of physical
    activity 29–32
movement schema 203
movement time **163**
movements effectors 173
multi-limb co-ordination 137
multi-store model of memory 159–61
muscular system 15–29
    actions 16
    impact of physical activity 35–40
    muscle contraction 28–9
    muscle fibres 32–5
    muscle health 40
    muscle pump 83
    muscle tone **40**
musculo-skeletal system 1
myoglobin **108**
myths **284**

N

nasal cavity 101
nation building and the Olympic
    Games
    China 326
    politics 326–7
    showcasing 325–6
National Curriculum and sport 270
National Governing Bodies **238,**
    276–7
    Whole Sport Plans (WSPs) 277–8
National Institutes of Sports 265–6,
    266

functions 266
funding 266
National Lottery funding of sport
    Department for Culture, Media
        and Sport 260
    mass participation 262
    World Class Events programme
        261
    World Class Pathway programme
        260–1
    World Class Talent programme
        261
natural athletes 137
natural environment
    appreciation of 219
    respect for 220
negative feedback 176
negative reinforcement 199
negative transfer 204
    limiting effects 205–6
Newton's laws of motion 50–1
NFL (National Football League, USA)
    245

O

obesity 95
OBLA (onset of blood lactate
    accumulation) **89**
observational learning 197
    Bandura's model 197–8
Olympic Charter 313–314
Olympic Games 311–12
    aims 314
    amateurism 314
    Athens 2004 medals table 322
    British Olympic Association (BOA)
        316
    commercialism 317–20
    De Coubertin's vision 312–13
    fair play 314–15
    International Olympic Committee
        315–316
    London 2012 games 321–5
    nation building 325–7
    oath 315
    philosophy 314
    principles and aims 313–315
    summer and winter format 315
    Sydney 2000 medals table 322
    TOP programme 318
open loop control **173**
    level one control 173
open skills 126
operant conditioning 194–5

practical application 195
opportunity **217**, **280**, **281**
opportunity, provision and esteem
    280–2
optimising transfer **205**
optimum point of arousal 186
oral cavity 101
organisation strategy 161–2
organisational bodies 262
organisational continuum 129
origin (of muscles) **16**
osteoarthritis 38, 38–9
osteoporosis 36, 36–7
outdoor education 223–4
    constraints to widespread
        participation 224–5
outdoor recreation **219**
    appreciation of natural
        environment 219
    respect for natural environment
        220
    sense of adventure and risk 220
over-arousal 187
overlearned **172**
overlearning **150**
oxygen
    external respiration 106–7
    internal respiration 108
oxygen–haemoglobin dissociation
    curve 108
oxygen debt **69**
oxygen transport 87, 108–9
    smoking, impact on 88
oxygenated **60**
oxyhaemoglobin 87, 108–9

P

pacing continuum 127
pad of fat (in a joint) 8
parallel processing 159
Paralympics 287–8
parietal pleura 102
part practice 130–2
partial pressure (PP) 106, 109–10
partnership development manager
    (PDM) 272, 273
patella 3, 8
PE, School Sport and Club Links
    Strategy (PESSCLS) 270–1
    aims 271
    fund allocation 271–2
    Gifted and Talented 275
    kitemarking school PE 275–6
    plans 271

school sport partnerships (SSPs)
    272–4
    specialist sport colleges 272
pectoralis major 15, 19
pelvis 3
perception **157**, 157, **196**
perceptual trace 173
performance improvement 351
    achieving goals 355–6
    action planning 352
    analytical phase 352
    assessment 357–8
    assessment criteria 359
    coaching points 352–3
    constructing an action plan 355
    evaluation 351
    health and fitness benefits 356–7
    identifying clear, realistic goals
        355
    identifying strengths 353–4
    identifying weaknesses 354–5
    participation 356
    practising evaluation 357
    timescale 355
performance lifestyle **265**
personal benefits of physical activity
    214
personality, affect on arousal 187
pH level **86**
phalanges 3
pharynx 101
physical activity 210, **213**
    barriers to participation 216–17
    benefits 213–15
    factors contributing to sedentary
        lifestyles 215
    funding 256–9
    participation 210–12
    recommendations 215–16
physical benefits of physical activity
    213
physical education (PE) 220
    aspects 221
    benefits 222
    definition 220–1
physical endeavour 227, **228**
physical exercise **213**
physical fitness 338
physical proficiency abilities 135
physical prowess 227, **228**
physical recreation 217–19, **219**
    characteristics and benefits 218
pivot joints 10
planes of movement **9**

plantar flexion 14
pleura cavity 102
pocket valve 82, 83
politics and sport 326–7
pool of experience 203
positive discrimination **292**
positive feedback 176
positive reinforcement strategy 162,
    198
positive transfer **132**, 203
posterior **11**
posture 40
practice 166
practice methods 142
    distributed practice 149
    fixed practice 149–50
    massed practice 148–9
    mental practice 151
    phases/stages 142–5
    varied practice 150
practising skills 130
    part practice 130–2
    progressive part practice 132–3
    whole practice 132
    whole-part-whole method 133–4
precapillary sphincter 82
primary link teachers (PLTs) 272
private funding **257**, 258
proactive transfer 204
professional approach to sports
    240
professionals **240**
progressive part practice 132–3
progressive practice **356**
pronation 13
pronator teres 15, 17
proprioception **157**, 174
proprioreceptors 73, 75, 113, 114
provision **217**, **280**, **281**
psychological arousal 184
psychological refractory period (PRP)
    167–8
psychomotor abilities **137**
public funding **257**, 258
public schools **238**
pulmonary **62**
pulmonary artery 62, 63
pulmonary capillaries 101
pulmonary circulation 80, 81
pulmonary valve 62
pulmonary veins 62, 63
pulmonary ventilation 100
punishment 199
Purkinje fibres 64

Q

quadriceps 15, 25

R

racial discrimination and sport
292–3
radio-ulnar joint 14, 15
muscles 17
radius 3
rate control 137
reaction time 137, 162–3, **163**
choice reaction time 165–6
factors affecting 163–4
single channel hypothesis 164–5
recall schema 179
receptors **73**
recognition aspect of perception 159
recognition schema 179
rectus abdominis 15, 21, 104
rectus femoris 15, 25
rehearsal/practice strategy 161
reinforcement **175**, 198
negative 199
positive 198
punishment 199
Thorndike's Laws 199
reminiscence **196**
respect for natural environment 220
respiratory control centre (RCC) 112
at rest 112
during exercise 112
nervous control 112
respiratory pump 83
respiratory system 100–1
active lifestyle 117
adaptations to physical activity
116–17
effects of altitude 114–16
exercising 104–5
resting 103–4
structure 101–3
respiratory volumes 105
response orientation 137
response programming 155
response selection 155
response time **163**
improving 166–7
retention 198
retention and retrieval of
information, improving 161–2
retroactive transfer 204
ribs 3
risk 344

risk assessment **344**
rotation of joints 12–13
rotator cuff **21**
Royal Shrovetide Football
(Derbyshire) 234

S

sacrum 3
scalenes 104
scapula 3
schema 150, **178**
schema theory 178–9
scheme of work 343–4
school sport co-ordinators (SSCos)
272, 274
school sport partnerships (SSPs)
272–4
Scottish Institute of Sport (SIS) 267
sedentary **36**, **93**
sedentary lifestyles, factors
contributing to 215
selective attention **143**, **159**, **187**
self paced 127
semimembranosus 15, 25
semitendinosus 15, 25
sense of adventure and risk 220
sensory information 157
sensory memory (SM) 159
sensory nerves **73**
septum 62
sequential **172**
serial processing 158
serial skills 126, **131**
shop window effect **326**
short-term memory (STM) 159, 160
short-term sensory stores 159
shoulder joint 8, 14, 15
muscles 19–20
showcasing 325–6
simple skills 128
simplicity strategy 161
single channel hypothesis 164–5
sino-atrial (SA) node 63, 64
skeletal muscle 2
skeletal system, impact of physical
activity 35–40
skeleton 2, 2–7
skill drill 150
sledging **227**
slow twitch muscle fibre **32**, 33
smoking, impact on oxygen
transport 88
smooth muscle **82**, 83
social and cultural factors 282

impact 284, 285, 286
social benefits of physical activity
214
social exclusion 284
socialisation 290
society **232**, 282
soleus 15, 26
somatic arousal 184
spectators of sports, violence by 307
speed of movement 137
sphygmomanometer 90
spine 14, 15
muscles 21–2
sponsorship **317**
sponsorship, media and sport
advantages and disadvantages
305–6
BSkyB 304
commercial pressures 306, 317–20
cricket and football 304
football vs netball 306
inter-relationship 303
sport 225–8
characteristics and benefits 226
sport and culture **232**
Australia 246–50
from amateur to professional 239
mass participation 240
organisation and administration
in UK 240–1
sporting excellence 240
UK 233–6
USA 241–2
sport colleges 272
Sport England 268
sporting excellence 240, 255, 280
sporting legacy **269**
Sports Council for Northern Ireland
268
Sports Council for Wales 269
sports development pyramid 257,
279
sports equipment, effect of modern
technology 299–300
Sports Institute Northern Ireland
(SINI) 267
SportScotland 269
sportsmanship **227**
S–R learning bond **189**, 198
stability 53, **54**
stable skills 134
stamina 136
Starling's Law 74, **75**, 83
static strength 135

stereotyping 284
sternum 3
stimulus **155**
stimulus identification 155
stimulus–response compatibility 167
strength **345**
stroke volume (SV) **66**, 83, 84
   response to exercise 68
sub maximal **67**
subscapularis 20
Super Bowl 245
superior **11**
superior vena cava 62, 63
supination 13
supinator 17
support skills 135
sympathetic nervous system 73,
   86–7
synovial fluid **7**
synovial joints 7–11
   movements 9–11
   types 9
systemic circulation 81
systole 64, 65
systolic blood pressure 89
   during exercise 91

T

tangible rewards **191**
Tar Barrel Burning (Devon) 235
tarsals 3
task analysis 129, **130**
television, impact on sport 303
   BSkyB 304
   TV rights **317**
tendons 3
tennis serve 131
teres major 15, 20
teres minor 20
terminal feedback 177
thermoreceptors 113, 114
thoracic cavity volume 103
thoracic wall 102
Thorndike's Laws 199
threshold of arousal 186
tibia 3, 8
tibialis anterior 15, 26
tidal volume (TV) 105, 106
TOP programme 318
trachea 101, 102
tradition 226
transfer **178**, **196**
transfer of learning 203–5

trapezius 15, 20
triceps brachii 15, 18
tricuspid valve 62
triggers of asthma attacks 119
triglycerides 95
trunk strength 136
TV rights **317**

U

UK Sport 264–5, **266**
UK sport and culture 233
   Cheese Rolling (Gloucestershire)
     235
   Haxey Hood Game (Lincolnshire)
     234
   Highland Games (Scotland) 234
   Hurling the Silver Ball (Cornwall)
     235
   nineteenth century schools, role
     of 236–8
   organisation and administration
     240–1
   reasons for surviving ethnic
     sports 236
   Royal Shrovetide Football
     (Derbyshire) 234
   Tar Barrel Burning (Devon) 235
ulna 3
under-arousal 186
underlying skills 135
underpin skills 135
uniqueness strategy 162
university scholarship system 317
US sport and culture 241–2
   'American Dream' 243
   American Football 244–6
   commercialism 243
   win ethic 242–3

V

varied practice 150, 206
vascular system *see* blood vessels
vasoconstrict **82**
vasodilate **82**
vasomotor control centre (VCC) 86
   sympathetic nervous system 86–7
vastus intermedius 15, 25
vastus lateralis 15, 25
vastus medialis 15, 25
veins 81, 82, 83
venoconstrict **82**
venodilate **82**
venous return 68, **75**, 83

ventricles of the heart 61, 62
ventricular contractility **68**
venules 81, 82, 83
verbal guidance for instructing skills
   146
vertebral column 3
vigorous physical exertion 226
violence in sport
   aggression 306
   causes 308–9
   control 306
   enduring problem 309
   Heysel Stadium (1985) 309
   Hillsborough (1989) 309
   participants 307
   solutions 309
   spectators 307
visceral pleura 102
visual guidance for instructing skills
   145–6
VO_2 max **117**
voluntary funding **257**, 258

W

warm-up 34–5, **35**, 88–9, 167
weakness **345**
Welford's model 155
Welsh Institute of Sport (SIS) 267
White Australian policy **248**
Whiting's model 155–8
whole practice 132, 132
Whole Sport Plans (WSPs) 277
   funding 277–8
   strategies 277
win ethic 242–3
women and sport, stereotyping of
   289
   media coverage/representation
     290
   myth-busting 289–90
   spectators 291
World Class Events programme 261
World Class Pathway programme
   260–1
World Class Talent programme 261
wrist joint 14, 15
   extensors 15, 17
   flexors 15, 17

Y

young people and sport 284